Composition

For Beatrice and Celia

An Hachette UK Company
www.hachette.co.uk

First published in the UK in 2023
by Ilex, an imprint of
Octopus Publishing Group
Carmelite House
50 Victoria Embankment
London, EC4Y 0DZ
www.octopusbooks.co.uk

Commissioned by Rachel Silverlight

Publisher: Alison Starling
Commissioning Editor: Ellie Corbett
Managing Editor: Rachel Silverlight
Editorial Assistant: Jeannie Stanley
Art Director: Ben Gardiner
Design: Chris Robinson
Picture Research: Giulia Hetherington
and Jennifer Veall
Assistant Production Manager: Emily Noto

ISBN 978-1-78157-861-2

A CIP catalogue record for this book
is available from the British Library

Printed and bound in Singapore

10 9 8 7 6 5 4 3 2 1

Uncover
the ideas
behind great
works of
modern art

Composition

Michael Archer

ilex

Contents

Introduction

During the late 1930s and 1940s, the American painter Ad Reinhardt devoted considerable energy to drawing cartoons. In this work, which appeared in many publications, he repeatedly used a two-frame visual joke. In the first frame, a laughing gallery-goer is pointing derisively at an abstract composition and saying, 'Ha ha. What does this represent?' In the second frame, the painting has come to life. It now has legs, an arm and a nose, and some of the composition's lines have resolved themselves into the profile of an angry face. The startled visitor reels back as the painting, in turn, jabs a finger back at him, demanding, 'What do you represent?'[1] Reinhardt's point is that a work of art has an autonomous existence. It is not there merely to serve as a visual stamp of approval on some fact or other, but what it can do is offer a viewer the means by which to apprehend the truth and validity of their own experience. In Book 1 of the Latin epic poem *Aeneid* by Virgil, Aeneas stands in Dido's palace before a fresco depicting the Trojan War and weeps. He sees in the depiction his friend Hector, his former king Priam and so many others that there are 'tears in the nature of things, hearts touched by human transience'.[2] The question 'What does this mean?', when addressed to a work of art, is an unproductive one. It would be better to ask a question based on what we are concerned with, such as 'How does what I am seeing here allow me to give shape to my experience of the world?'

There are many books on composition in art. To name only a few, there are wide surveys such as Charles Bouleau's *The Painter's Secret Geometry* (1963) and Rudolf Arnheim's *The Power of the Center* (1982), as well as more focused studies including Erwin Panofsky's work on the emergence of perspective in the fifteenth century in *Perspective as Symbolic Form* (1927), Heinrich Wölfflin's analysis of the shift in compositional priorities from the sixteenth-century Renaissance to the seventeenth-century Baroque in *Principles of Art History* (1915), and Michael Baxandall's *Patterns of Intention* (1985), with his exploration of eighteenth-century vision through apparent errors of perspective in Jean-Baptiste-Siméon Chardin's *A Lady Taking Tea* (1735). In a closely related field, we have works such as Rudolf Wittkower's *Architectural Principles in the Age of Humanism* (1949), in which he discusses the subject through ideas of harmony, proportion and scale that were pervasive in the Renaissance. These all build upon earlier foundational works, such as Leon Battista Alberti's *Della pittura (On Painting*; 1435*)* , and Giorgio Vasari's *Lives of the Artists* (1550). Before all of these, there is the first-century CE Roman scholar Pliny the Elder's *Natural History, Book XXXV*, which is devoted to the major artists of Classical Greece.

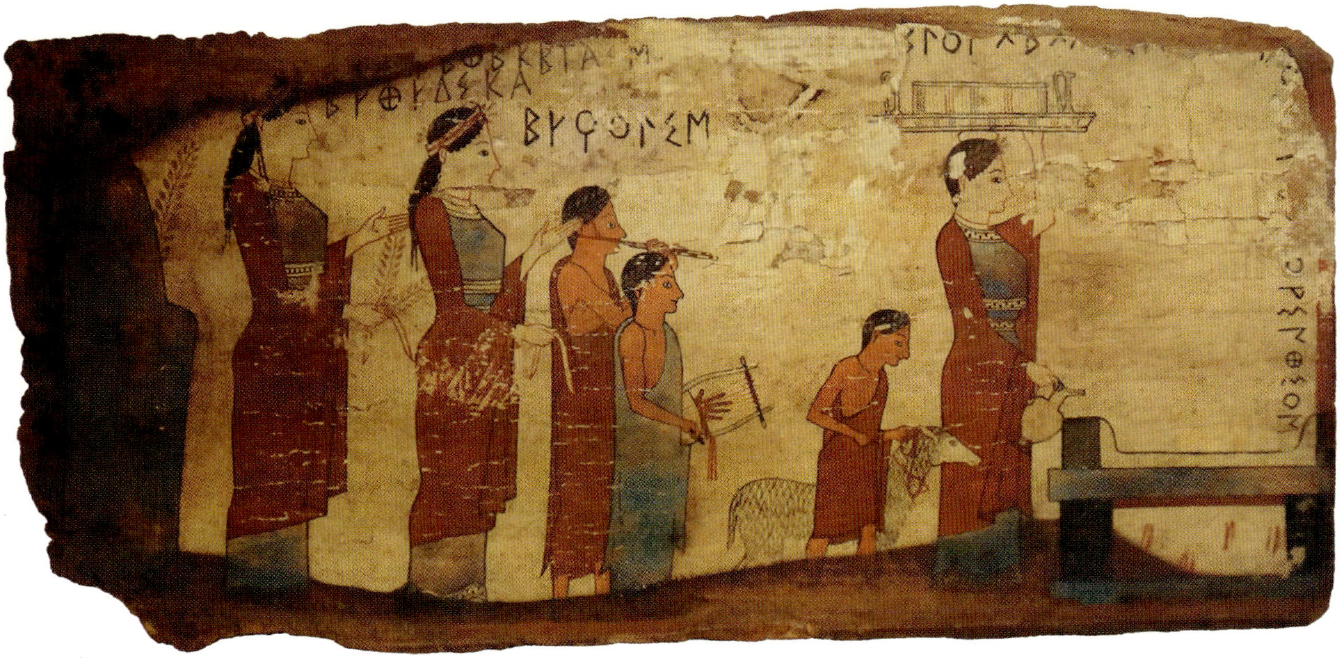

ABOVE: Unknown, votive panel from the Pitsa Cave, Greece, 540–530 BCE.

The one point notable in these mentioned studies is that the main emphasis is placed upon structure, the spatial organization and disposition of forms within the frame of the work, which is itself geometrically divided up. In his preface to Bouleau's study, the sculptor Jacques Villon called the framework of a work of art 'its most secret and its deepest poetry'.[3] Awareness of this structure, through giving attention to the composition of a work, can provide us with a way to think about the possible significance we might ascribe to what we are seeing.

Writing in the early twentieth century, the Viennese art historian Alois Riegl introduced the concept of Kunstwollen (artistic volition) in his study of late Roman art. While artistic volition, a will to find form for ideas and feelings, motivates artists of all periods, the manner in which it finds expression changes as the world changes. Riegl explained that the central means by which such volition finds its expression in the art of Classical Greece is rhythm. He identified various ways in which rhythm might be achieved: through contrast – for example, in the body pose with an opposing raised hip and dropped shoulder that we know as contrapposto – through sequential repetition of similar phenomena, and by use of symmetry and proportion.[4] But for us to be able to apprehend such rhythm, each element must be distinct and separate from its neighbour. They can be side by side, or one above the other, but not in front of or behind another element. In other words, they must be composed 'in the plane' without any representation of depth. We can see this in the decorations on vases and bowls surviving from the period, as well as in the rare examples of painting, such as the Pitsa Panels. The differing heights of the six figures, all seen in profile, describe a curve running from upper left, dipping towards the centre, and rising again towards the right. At the same time, they are linked across the composition by the various items they each hold – corn, flute, lyre, pitcher, and so on – that slightly overlap with their neighbour.

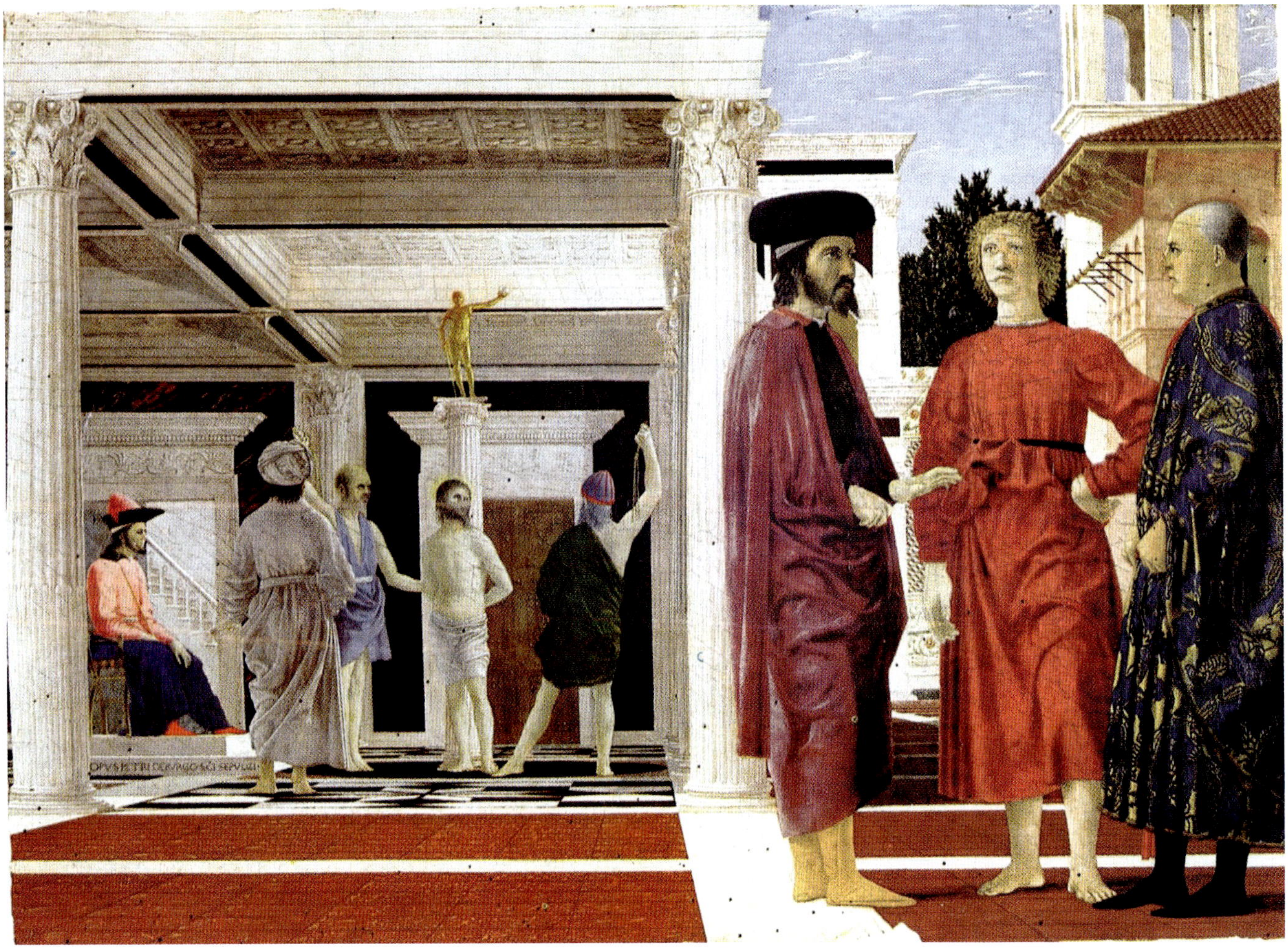

ABOVE: Piero della Francesca, *The Flagellation of Christ*, *c*.1468–70. Oil and tempera on panel, 82×59 cm ($32\frac{1}{4} \times 23\frac{1}{4}$ in).

However, it is not sufficient merely to distribute elements. There needs to be some structuring principle over and above these elements that enables the manner of their distribution to be revealed as more than random. One of the primary factors in the analysis of composition is the question of the frame. If we are to perceive order, it is necessary to be able to recognize the limits within which the various elements under consideration have been arranged. As Bouleau noted, a frieze is already a frame.[5] Even though it is open at either side and could in theory have an endless horizontal extension, it has an upper and lower boundary, and it is this framing that enables us to apprehend the rhythm in the frieze's composition.

In contrast to such planar composition, the developing use of perspective in the Renaissance art of the West saw the predominance of Euclidean space (with three dimensions) as the arena within which painting occurred. A point established on the canvas, towards which all lines drawn from the edges converge, provides the observer with the sense of a coherent and comprehensible space. The physical surface of the canvas sets a forward limit – it is the place in the painting closest to the viewer. Reaching back from there and into the canvas is the place in the painting where lines converge, known as the vanishing point, beyond which nothing further is visible. As Panofsky stressed, the space depicted in this way is a rational space.[6] It is coherent and orderly. Objects closer to the viewer will appear larger, and those at a distance will appear smaller, just as they would in the real world. In this way the painting can depict not just its ostensible subject – a person, a cow, a boat – but, as importantly, the world within which that subject exists.

Alberti's major theoretical advance was to be the first one in the Renaissance to propose the area of vision as a pyramid, with the eye as the apex and the lines from the eye to the four corners of the panel as the outer edges of the pyramid, mirroring the perspectival space inscribed on the canvas. This was a development from earlier ideas of the field of vision being a cone. The change enabled the clarification of one-point perspective along with the depiction of objects always being in proportion, with their decrease in size thus indicating distance from the front plane of the picture. This perspective appears in the work of Piero della Francesca, who Vasari said was 'regarded as a great master of the problems of regular bodies, both arithmetical and geometrical'.[7] Piero's care can be seen, for example, in *The Flagellation of Christ*, where the interior of Pilate's palace and the piazza in which it sits are rendered with such precision that it is possible to reconstruct an accurate plan and elevation of the depicted building, and the paved floor, from the painting's dimensions and details. The trio of bystanders in the foreground of the composition to the right are up against the picture plane, while Pilate, Christ and those involved in his punishment are proportionately smaller in the background to the left. The exact centre of the panel falls in the crook of the scourger's bent right arm, while the vanishing point is in the space immediately below it. Piero's use of light adds to the complexity of the composition. In the external space, it falls on the three large figures and the other buildings in the square from the left. Within Pilate's house, however, Christ is lit from the right, and while the rest of the space is largely in shadow, the ceiling directly above his head is radiantly bright.

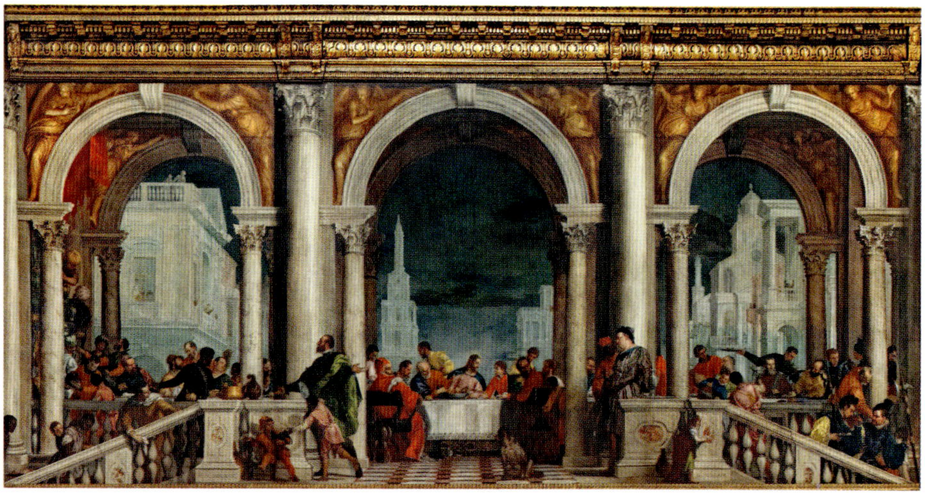

ABOVE: Paolo Veronese, *The Feast in the House of Levi*, 1573. Oil on canvas, 5.5 × 13 m (18 × 42 ft).

Reliance on perspective persisted from its codification in the mid-fifteenth century through to the middle of the nineteenth century, with its basic architecture leaving room for considerable compositional variety. In Paolo Veronese's *The Feast in the House of Levi*, for example, painted a century after Piero's *Flagellation*, the vast scale of the composition alone – the canvas is 5.5 × 13 metres (18 × 42 ft) – almost precludes reliance on a single vanishing point. Instead, the figure groupings set within the three arches of the house's imposing architecture each have their own organizational coherence. The central, Last Supper-like group is flat, parallel to the picture plane and corresponding to the house's facade, which runs the width of the canvas, while those to either side have a circular interrelation between figures. The diagonals set by the staircase rails, and which partition the canvas's surface, meet at the composition's central point above Christ's head. However, there is no single vanishing point; the buildings visible beyond the colonnade lead the eye to a point below Christ's feet, while the floor's tiling suggests a point behind his torso. Bouleau comments on this adoption of a vanishing 'area':

> *Veronese's world is not closed – on the contrary it is vast, airy and luminous; but it never makes a hole in the wall; and this astonishing result is due to his multiple perspective – to his way of, so to speak, breaking up perspective and rendering it inoffensive.*[8]

Almost a century later again, an internalized understanding of perspective leads the viewer of Diego Velázquez's *Las Meninas* to recognize that the composition's organizing principle lies beyond its frame altogether. Low in the centre of the canvas stands the infanta Margarita. She is surrounded by two maids (*las meninas*), two attendees with dwarfism and two courtiers. The left side of the painting is filled with the back of a large canvas, around the edge of which Velázquez peers towards the subjects of the painting on which he is working, who are evidently positioned in the spot from which we are looking at the maids. Those subjects, King Philip IV and Queen Mariana, are reflected in the mirror on the far wall of the hall. While Philip and Mariana are not themselves in the painting, whatever kind of work we take it to be – a portrait of the infanta, a self-portrait of the artist, a group portrait of royalty and courtiers – all of these options are made possible only through the power and patronage of the king.

Our task in addressing the topic of composition today is less to revisit and redo earlier investigations than to consider the impact the convulsive and far-reaching changes of the modern period has on our understanding of what the term might mean. How has the matter of composition been affected by mass industrialization and technological advance? What has it made possible and, in turn, what impositions has it placed upon artists? Equally, how have the force of these broader changes, opportunities and challenges been revealed in and through the structure of modern and contemporary works of art?

In questions of judgement, Pliny made much of competition between artists. Is it Protogenes or Apelles who can mark the most delicate outline? Is it Zeuxis or Parrhasius who can produce the most compelling illusion? That it is Apelles and Parrhasius who are deemed to have triumphed in these contests is less important than the aspects of composition in question, which remain central to the practice and analysis of painting. Alberti saw painting as comprised of three elements: circumscription, composition and reception of light. Circumscription must be delicate, because too apparent a line will 'not indicate a margin of a plane but a neat cleavage'.[9] Composition brings together the various planes of a figure in proper relation to one another, and the third aspect allows the addition of light and shadow to fully model its form. This analysis is as helpful when

RIGHT: Diego Velázquez, *Las Meninas*, 1656. Oil on canvas, 320.5 × 281.5 cm (126 × 111 in).

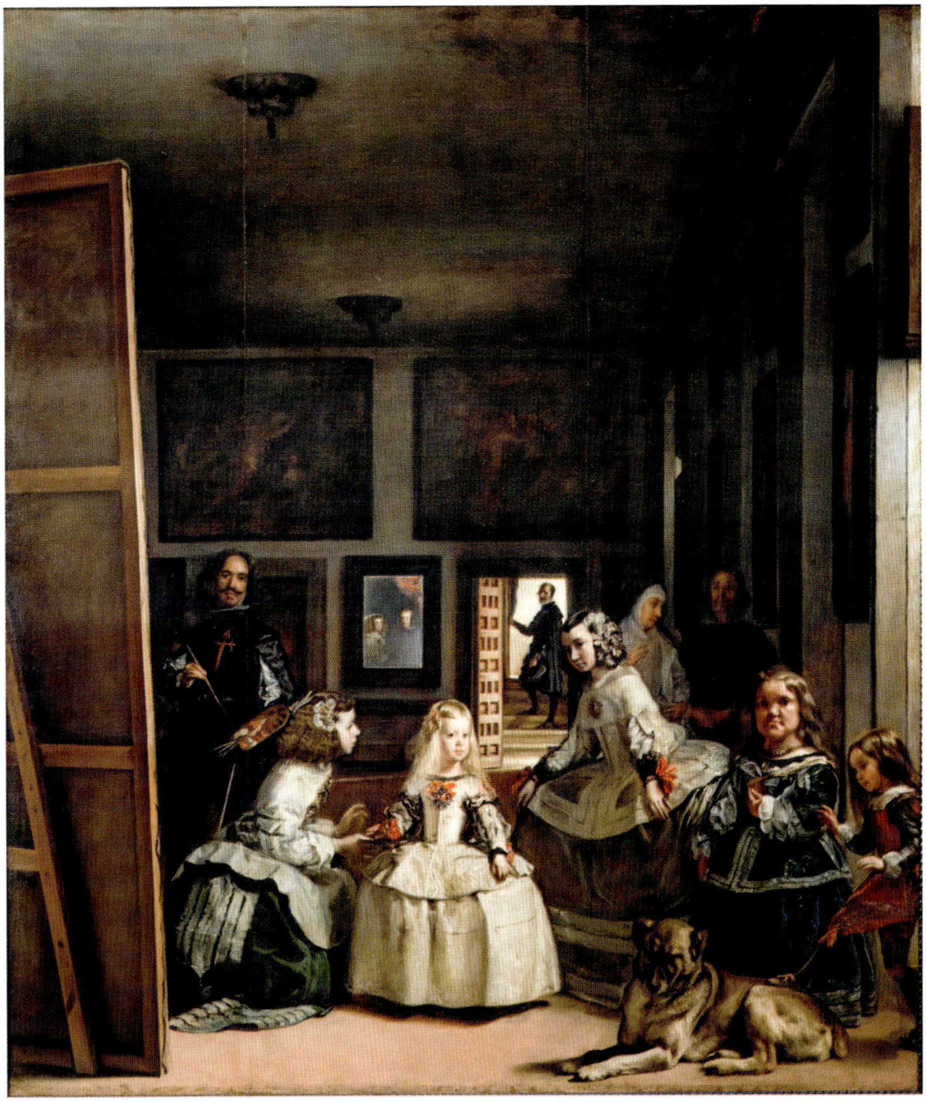

looking at a painting by, for example, the French post-impressionist artist Paul Cézanne, as it is one by the Italian Renaissance painter Masaccio.

'Composition', wrote Alberti, 'is that rule of painting by which the parts of things seen fit together in the painting.'[10] However, far from amassing those parts into a monument to skill and artifice, it was more important that the artist's ambition should be to create a convincing sense of a populated world in which events happen and ideas circulate:

> *The greatest work of the painter is not a colossus, but an* istoria *[narrative painting].* Istoria *gives greater renown to the intellect than any colossus. Bodies are part of the* istoria, *members are parts of the bodies, planes part of the members.*[11]

The ground was already being laid for the hierarchy of painting styles that would become embedded in academic teaching of the following centuries. Of highest importance would be history painting – the representation of historical events, and of religious and mythological themes – below in rank would be portraits, and lower still, genre painting of domestic scenes and other mundane topics. Of these, only history paintings were deemed capable of representing the best of human virtues and ideals.

Those painting styles did not cease to have relevance after the middle of the nineteenth century, albeit that sense of a hierarchy did lose its purchase. What, then, is new? Pliny, writing in the first century CE, mentioned monochrome painting, the beauty of a panel that is entirely white except for the most delicate line, the use of chance – a sponge thrown at a panel – as a means to produce the most realistic effect, the significance of illusion, and the problem of representing spatial depth on a flat surface.[12] He also noted that the compositional innovation of the self-portrait was made by a woman, Iaia of Cyzicus, and that, despite her talent, it was not her work but that of men which filled the galleries.[13] So many issues that we have considered so important in art of the modern period were already of concern two thousand years ago. So, again, what is new?

The American poet and writer Gertrude Stein would answer the question with characteristic succinctness in her lecture, 'Composition as Explanation':

> *The only thing that is different from one time to another is what is seen and what is seen depends upon how everybody is doing everything.*[14]

This book is an examination of that one different thing identified by Stein. It explores how what is seen is less a simple matter of what we find in front of our eyes than of how changing circumstances enable certain things to become visible to us and, in turn, of how that visibility affects the perception of what is possible in the composing of an artwork. Above all else, a key factor for visual art since the mid-nineteenth century has been the development of new ways of picturing the world. In the first, analogue phase, the invention of photography and then film, the appearance of mass printing, and the possibility of adopting hitherto inaccessible viewpoints served radically to unsettle the accepted compositional norms. How might the considered structuring of a scene in the quiet of the studio do due justice to the view from the Eiffel Tower or a Chicago skyscraper, or how might it adequately capture the fleeting and ever-changing sight caught from the window of a steam train, motor car or, shortly thereafter, from the cockpit of an aeroplane? These developments were bound up with and a part of sociopolitical shifts and a growing globalism in commerce and conflict, all of which has affected how we can think about composition.

Subsequent to that analogue phase through the second half of the nineteenth century and the first half of the twentieth, which included radio, telephone and television as well as those technologies already mentioned, there came a digital phase witnessing a vast increase in our capacity to take, store, retrieve and manipulate imagery and other information. There has also been a concomitant expansion of the forms through which art manifests itself. Not only painting and sculpture, but photography, video, installation, performance and much else, too. How can the matter of composition figure in our consideration of such diversity of form? To attempt a treatment of this entire field would be cumbersome, diffuse and require a too-severe editing of pertinent material. For this reason, this book concentrates primarily on the question of the frame, of what is organized within its confines, of how its placement in front of the eye can bring order to what would otherwise appear to be random happenstance, and of how its limits are challenged, expanded and even dissolved. For the most part the frame bounds a flat area – a canvas, a photograph, a monitor screen – but over the period of time covered in this book, it has come to be seen in other ways. Instead of defining the limits of an individual artwork, it can be understood as the rules and procedures of the museum or gallery in which it is shown, or the structuring confines of a market or of the social or political system that supports or hinders its production and display.

The book is divided into four sections. In the main, subjects in the book as a whole are viewed chronologically. In some instances, however, it seemed that a more coherent narrative could be developed by keeping the focus on a particular compositional approach across time. This is the case in the treatment of collage in Chapter II, and some of the different strands of abstraction in the Chapter III. The book's beginning in the middle of the nineteenth century is at a point at which we can find in both word and action the recognition of a need to break with tradition. Paris in 1863 saw the publication of poet and critic Charles Baudelaire's essay 'The Painter of Modern Life', in which he first articulated a theory of modernity, that experience of an ever-changing industrialized urban environment that must now find its expression in art.[15] In that same year, a group of those whose works were rejected by the jury of the official Paris Salon, including Gustave Courbet, Édouard Manet and Cézanne, mounted their own exhibition, the first Salon des Refusés. Secessionist groups in Germany and Austria soon followed, signalling a widespread refusal to be bound by the rules and expectations of the academy. Those rules, imposing adherence to a hierarchy of styles, and assuming without question the desirability of naturalistic representation, were increasingly unable to accommodate the expressive demands of the modern experience. Scientific research in all areas, not least the human body itself – how it worked, physiologically and psychologically – had an impact. Experiments into the physiology of vision influence the approach to painting, just as enquiry into the workings of the mind brings the importance of the world of the imagination increasingly to the fore.

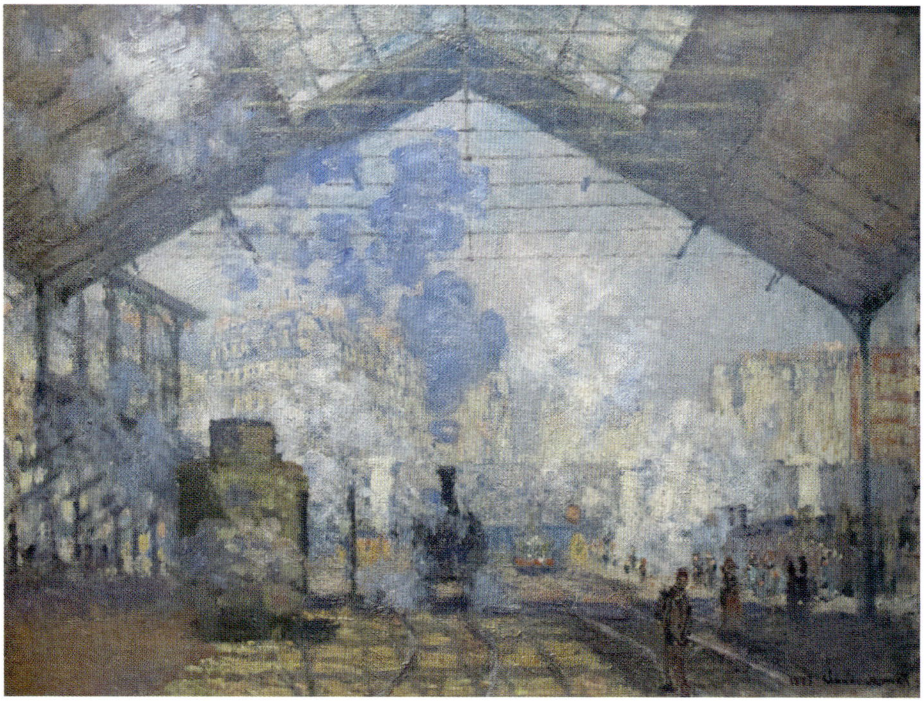

LEFT: Claude Monet, *La Gare Saint-Lazare*, 1877 (see pages 32–3).

Chapter II considers aspects of works largely made in the first half of the twentieth century. Faced with an everyday reality physically and psychically scarred by the savage impact of the First World War, there was an exploration of the subconscious mind as a freely active creative resource. A rational order that precipitated slaughter was met with composition built through chance and random procedures. The New Woman – an urban inhabitant newly at liberty to find employment, live with a degree of relative independence, and to vote – was actively present as a producer of art in a field with a population that was overwhelmingly male, and that had standards of judgement and educational structures controlled by men. Efforts to free the creative impulse saw the promotion of situations in which expectations of normal, 'civilized' behaviour were deemed not to hold sway. A necessary naiveté of approach due to lack of formal art education was one such. Chief among them, however, was an attachment to the idea of non-Western cultures as 'primitive', and thus precisely the places in which to search for more honest, direct and forceful artistic forms. The colonialist mindset that undervalued non-Western art while appropriating it for its own ends was a persistent shaping force in modern art.

What is seen is less a simple matter of what we find in front of our eyes than of how changing circumstances enable certain things to become visible to us.

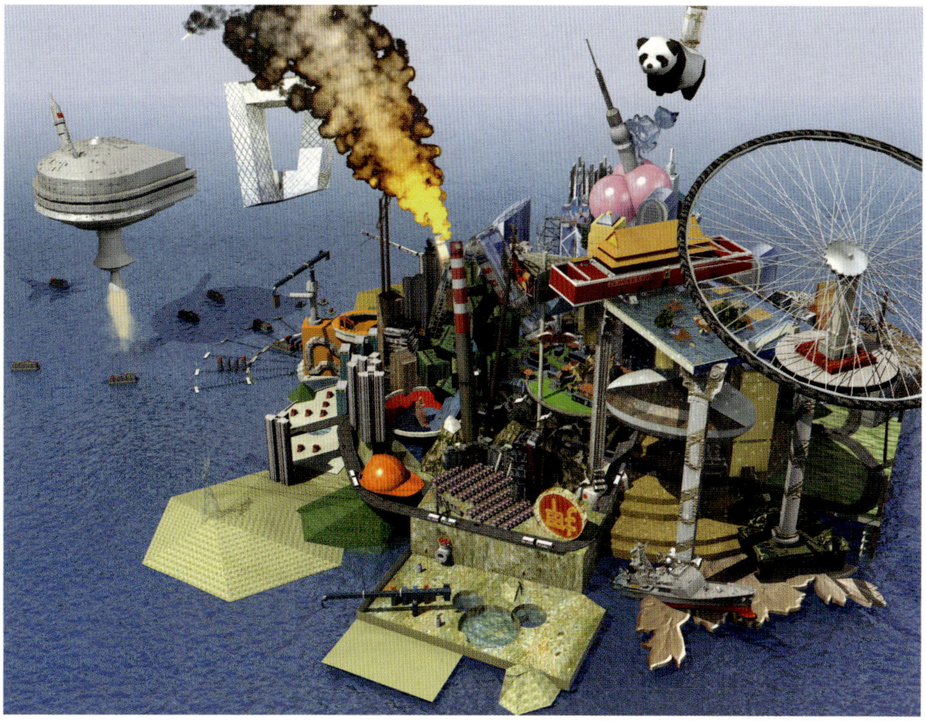

RIGHT: Cao Fei, *RMB City: A Second Life City Planning*, 2007 (see pages 142–3).

The third chapter concentrates on abstraction or non-representation, one of the major features in the art of the last century. Appearing in its first decade, it too was a part of the effort to give shape to imagined alternatives to the pervasive frenzy of the modern experience. Some who moved towards abstraction were influenced by ideas such as those of theosophy, which pointed to contemporary scientific and technological research in support of a belief in a spirit world. With the advent of abstraction, the perspectival rendering of three-dimensional space that had been familiar for so long begins lose its grip. Writing on abstract painting in the 1950s, the American critic Clement Greenberg summarized the history of art since the Renaissance, the advent of abstraction in the modern era and the disappearance of illusionistic space in a few brief sentences:

> *From Giotto to Courbet, the painter's first task had been to hollow out an illusion of three-dimensional space on a flat surface. One looked through this surface as through a proscenium into a stage. Modernism has rendered this stage shallower and shallower until now its backdrop has become the same as its curtain, which has now become all that the painter has left to work on … This spatial illusion or rather the sense of it, is what we may miss even more than we do the images that used to fill it.*[16]

Greenberg's narrative is compelling, not least because it is so simple. But we must be wary. Explanations that follow straight lines are seductive: after A, there is B, C follows, and so on until we arrive at where we are, or where we think we are. The danger, always, is to allow the apparent inexorability of the single path to let other routes be ignored and for things that don't seem to fit be thought of as subsidiary to the main story rather than factors that significantly expand the field under discussion. This is certainly true in the case of artists from newly independent countries of the former European empires, whose approaches constitute major contributions to our sense of the potential in abstraction.

The fourth and final chapter moves from the period following the Second World War into the twenty-first century. In the 1960s, art historian Leo Steinberg wrote about the advent of a new kind of picture surface. Up until then, the plane of the canvas had performed the familiar triple function: it was a window onto the space behind it, a mirror reflecting the space in front of it, and a physical surface upon and across which pigment could be distributed and arranged. As we might expect, Steinberg's example of a painting in which all three of these roles are clearly evident in equal measure is Velázquez's *Las Meninas* (see pages 10–11).[17] While it was possible for an individual artwork to concentrate on one or other of these three functions, more or less to the exclusion of the other two, no painting from the Renaissance through to abstract expressionism had superseded the need for them altogether.

This new kind of surface identified by Steinberg went beyond the primacy of focus accorded to the flat plane of the canvas seen in works by Piet Mondrian (see pages 112–13) and other examples of abstraction. Steinberg called it the 'flatbed plane', likening it to the hard surface upon which a wide variety of material from disparate sources can be brought together and arranged as part of the printing process. The appearance of the 'flatbed', wrote Steinberg, marks 'a change within painting that changed the relationship between artist and image, image and viewer'.[18] Steinberg's essay is called 'Other Criteria', an indication that the yardsticks by which art had hitherto been made and assessed were ceasing to maintain their authority. He described this new kind of work as postmodern, in recognition of the fact that the precepts that had guided the innovations in art from Baudelaire's first definitions of modernity up to abstract expressionism were now exhausted. One key aspect of Steinberg's term, flatbed plane, is that it acknowledges the intrusion into the 'refined' realm of fine art of a process as unrefined as commercial printing. Lawrence Alloway, a key figure in British pop art, commented favourably on this intrusion in a 1958 essay:

> *Our definition of culture is being stretched beyond the fine art limits imposed on it by Renaissance theory, and refers now, increasingly, to the whole complex of human activities. Within this definition, rejection of the mass produced arts is not, as critics think, a defence of culture but an attack on it. The new role for the academic is keeper of the flame; the new role for the fine arts is to be one of the possible forms of communication in an expanding framework that also includes the mass arts.*[19]

In its use of the objects and images of ordinary life – Roy Lichtenstein's comic books, Andy Warhol's soup cans and Brillo boxes, James Rosenquist's tinned spaghetti and other advertising imagery – and its adoption of the commercial processes by which this material was produced, pop art presented a profound challenge to established critical ideas. However, this was only a part of the change we encountered in the latter part of the twentieth century, at that transition from what was the modern into what is the contemporary period (this period being a relative and ever-moving position). In this moment, we can identify two problems. First, how to think of painting in the new, postmodern context, and second, how to rethink the idea of what might constitute a frame adequate to the presentation of any new composition. Conceptual artist Joseph Kosuth addressed the first problem in his 1969 essay 'Art After Philosophy':

> *Being an artist now means to question the nature of art. If one is questioning the nature of painting, one cannot be questioning the nature of art. If an artist accepts painting (or sculpture) he is accepting the tradition that goes with it. That's because the word art is general and the word painting is specific. Painting is a kind of art. If you make paintings you are already accepting (not questioning) the nature of art. One is then accepting the nature of art to be the European tradition of a painting-sculpture dichotomy.*[20]

There will always be painting, but in a field that is now enlarged to include film, photography, video, performance and much else, it can no longer claim to be the activity which, in and of itself, defines and guarantees what art is. By extension, the relationship of terms in our enquiry must also change. Up until this point, it has been possible to ask the question: how has this work of art been composed? Now, the question has become: how is the work of art constituted through this composition? French philosopher Jean-François Lyotard discussed postmodernism as a crisis of legitimation.[21] By what criteria might we decide upon the value and legitimacy of a work, especially when, as Australian art historian and critic Terry Smith has observed, it is no longer possible to identify a centre to the art world in the way once provided by Paris and subsequently New York:

> *Unlike the great art styles of the nineteenth and twentieth centuries, these changes from modern to contemporary art were not a monopolising phenomenon that spread outwards from a predominant centre. Rather, they occurred at different times and in distinctive ways in each cultural region and in each art-producing locality.*[22]

This culturally diverse and geographically dispersed expansion of the art world, with its associated systems of production, distribution, marketing and display, makes it all the more necessary to consider each work as its own specific instance of that changed set of relationships between artist and image, and image and viewer.

CHAPTER I: A NEW VISION

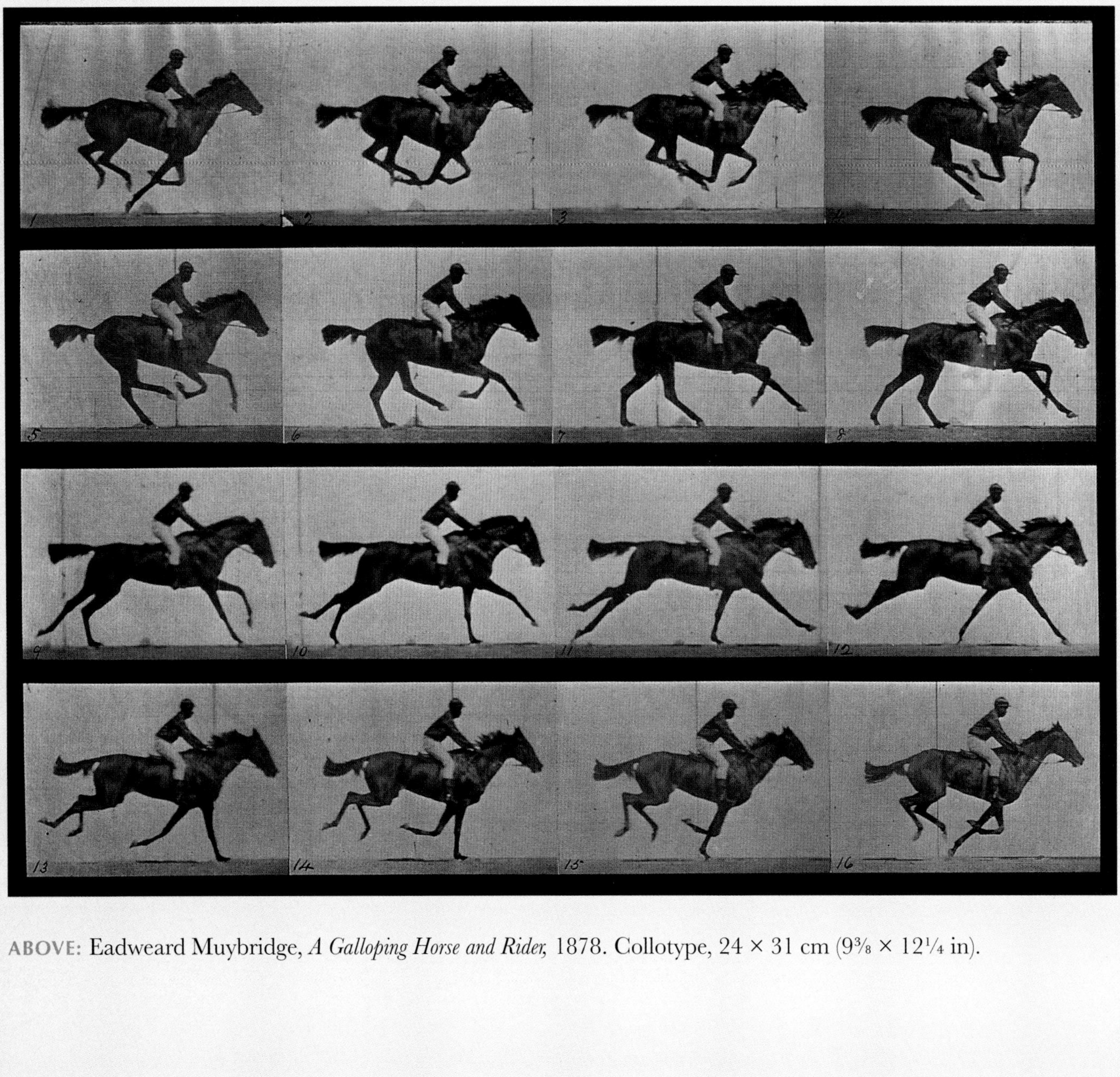

ABOVE: Eadweard Muybridge, *A Galloping Horse and Rider,* 1878. Collotype, 24 × 31 cm (9⅜ × 12¼ in).

THE ADVENT OF MOVEMENT

The late 1870s saw the photographer Eadweard Muybridge experimenting with ways to capture bodies in motion. His patron, Leland Stanford, requested an accurate picture of his racehorse Occident when galloping. The development of a camera with a fast exposure time meant that Muybridge could set up a series of twelve cameras alongside the racetrack at Stanford's ranch in Palo Alto, California. As the horse ran past, it broke wires connected to an electrical circuit, thus sequentially triggering the shutters. Prior to this time, artists had invariably represented a galloping horse by showing its forelegs extended in front and its rear legs straight out behind. Muybridge's sequence of photographs allowed us to see that the horse's legs actually moved in a quite different way.

The immediate benefit of Muybridge's studies, which he continued into the 1880s, was that we could now understand in detail the interrelated articulation of the horse's four limbs and recognize the inaccuracy of previous depictions. What this understanding also introduced was the deeper realization that there were things taking place in our field of vision and before our eyes that the human body's physiological limitations left us unable to see. Once we had this knowledge, we could no longer treat the eye as a passive receiver, the retina as a screen onto which all that stands in the world before it simply falls and makes itself available to the conscious mind. The physiology of the body had to be accepted as an active agent in the context of what is seen. Each one of Muybridge's frames showed how things were at that instant, but by the time of the next frame, the situation had altered. The limitations in what is possible for the eye to perceive, of course, are also what allows the possibility of film. The inability to distinguish between rapidly changing still images, what the French film director Jean-Luc Godard called 'the truth, twenty-four times a second', means that, for us, they must blur into the illusion of continuous movement.[1]

The German cultural critic Walter Benjamin saw the camera's superior capability to capture the briefest of moments as opening the way into what he called the 'optical unconscious'. The idea that such a thing exists led to, for example, the experimention with subliminal advertising in the years after the Second World War. The fact that we cannot see something does not mean that it is not there, nor, in many instances, can it hide our knowledge that it is there. The challenge for artists now was to find a way of working that could reconcile what is visible with what is known.

THE BURIAL OF ROMANTICISM

The French realist painter Gustave Courbet began painting *A Burial at Ornans* in 1849, the year following the revolution in France that removed King Louis Philippe and instigated the Second Republic. When it was shown at the Paris Salon of 1850, the composition, which Courbet described as 'my beginning and my statement of principles',[1] elicited some strong negative responses. To some, it was 'a disgraceful picture', an 'ignoble and impious caricature' full of 'ugly people' showing that 'it must be nauseating to be buried at Ornans'.[2] To other, more sympathetic viewers it represented the 'burial of Romanticism'.[3] In order to make sense of those comments and to understand the challenging nature of *Burial at Ornans*, it is helpful to make comparisons with two earlier artistic responses to revolution.

In Courbet's case, the revolution is the painting.

There had been two revolutions in France in the sixty years prior to 1848; in 1789 and 1830. In each case, the image of the event in the popular imagination is shaped by an iconic painting: in the first instance, Jacques-Louis David's *The Death of Marat*, and in the second, Eugène Delacroix's *Liberty Leading the People*. David's 1793 painting shows the radical journalist Jean-Paul Marat just after he has been murdered in his bath. Marat bathed frequently as a way to alleviate the discomfort caused by a chronic skin complaint, but in David's depiction his skin is without blemish, his body is physically robust, and his well-toned right arm hangs down in a manner strongly reminiscent of the figure of Jesus in Michelangelo's *Pietà* in St Peter's, Rome. Marat did drape his bath in green fabric, as we see in David's painting, and he was indeed murdered by Charlotte Corday, whose signed note of introduction is held in his lifeless hand. Yet, as much as it purports to record an event, David's composition is fundamentally the representation of an idea.

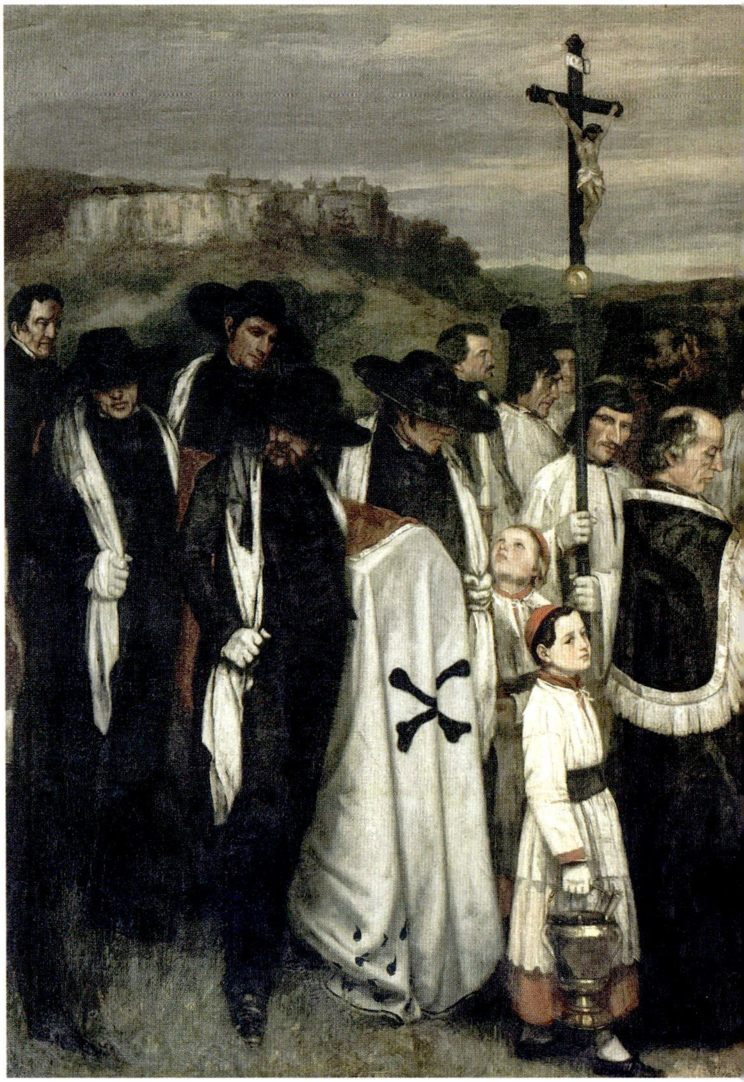

The central figure in Delacroix's 1830 painting is a bare-breasted woman leading a crowd over a barricade upon which lie the bodies of fallen comrades. She is an emblematic figure representing the spirit of freedom shared by all those she leads; she is Marianne, the symbol of Republican France.

Regardless of their distinct styles – David's neoclassical restraint and Delacroix's romantic intensity – in both of these paintings we understand that the depicted scene has been composed and arranged with considerable imaginative licence to better represent more broadly the revolution and its ideals. By contrast, in Courbet's case, the revolution *is* the painting.

BELOW: Gustave Courbet, *A Burial at Ornans*, 1849–50. Oil on canvas, 315 × 668 cm (124 × 263 in).

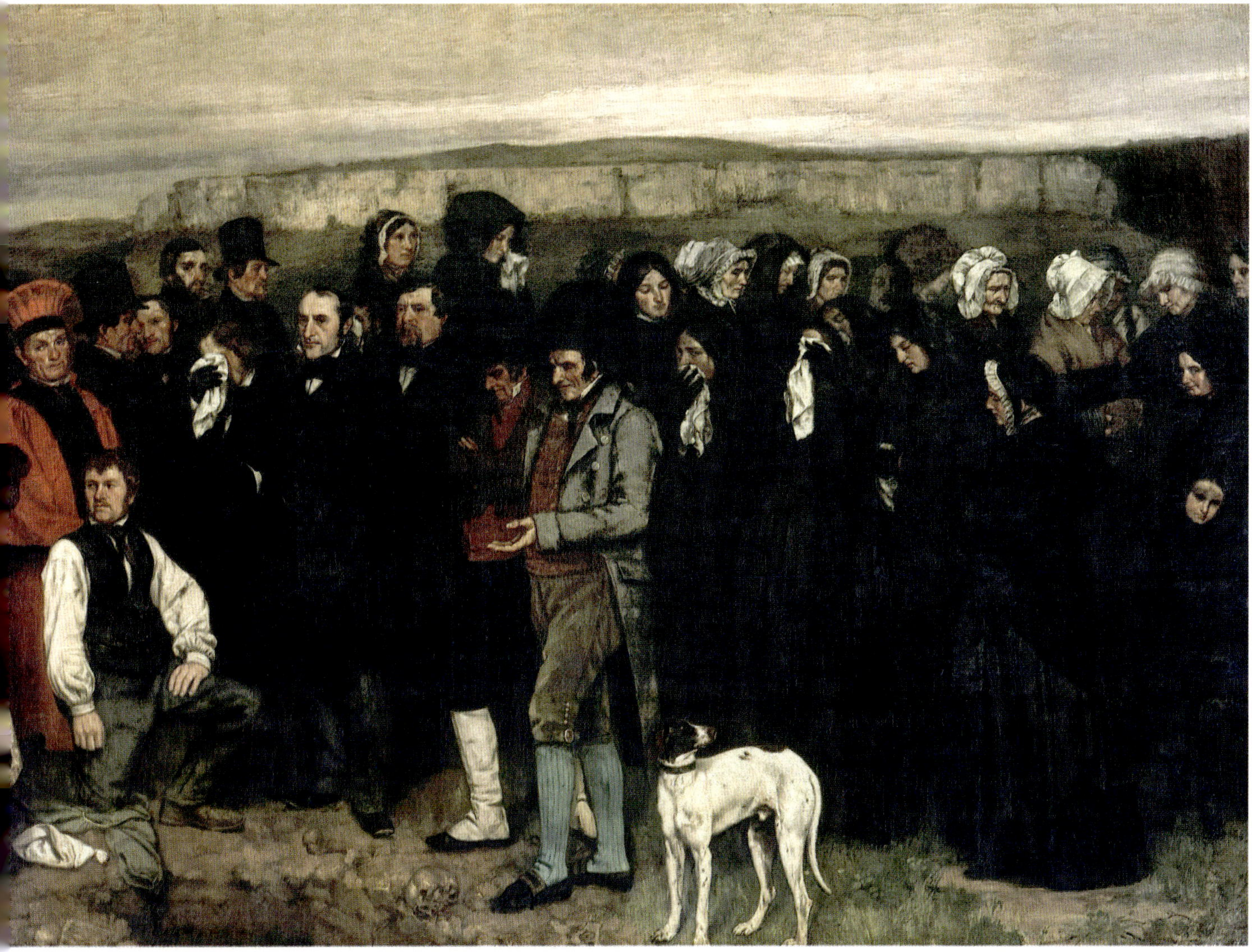

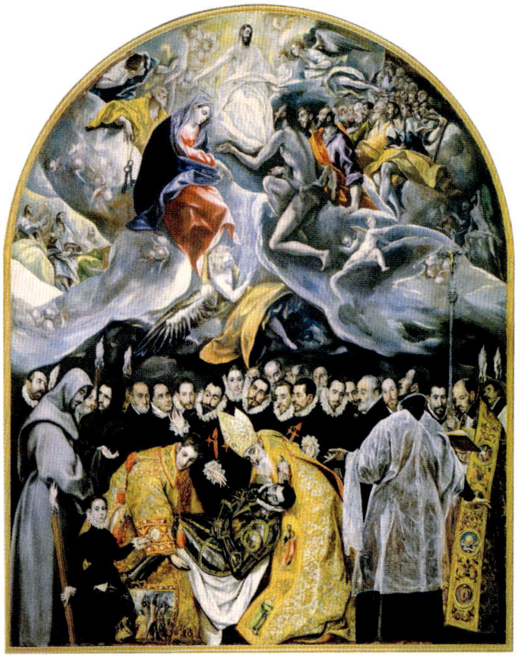

ABOVE AND BELOW: El Greco, *The Burial of the Count of Orgaz*, 1586. Oil on canvas, 480 × 360 cm (189 × 142 in).

A REVOLUTIONARY BURIAL

A conventional arrangement for presenting the subject of a painting would organize the groups to the left and right of the canvas as both lesser than and supportive of the composition's main central figure. We can see this in the Greek-born Spanish painter El Greco's *The Burial of the Count of Orgaz*. In El Greco's painting, the count is the central figure at the bottom, with two senior clerics bending to inter him. Other, lesser attendees at the ceremony stand to either side of the central trio, the count's respectful courtiers stand in a line behind and, in the clouds at the top, God, Saint Peter and a host of others are waiting to welcome the count into heaven. The composition encompasses both a highly stylized and hierarchically ordered terrestrial realm, and a fully imagined heavenly kingdom.

Courbet's composition differs radically from this approach, rejecting in the organization of the canvas the kind of reliance on social, economic and spiritual hierarchies that we can see in El Greco's picture. In one respect, however, his composition is conventionally structured, with the canvas divided into three distinct but interrelated areas: the pallbearers and clergy to the left, the women mourners to the right, and the local dignitaries, male mourners and the grave itself in the centre.

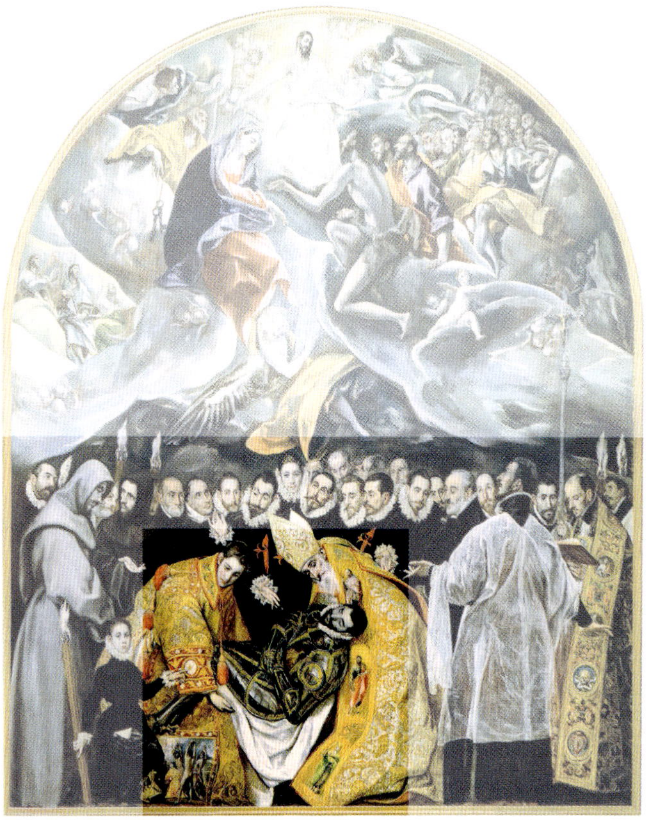

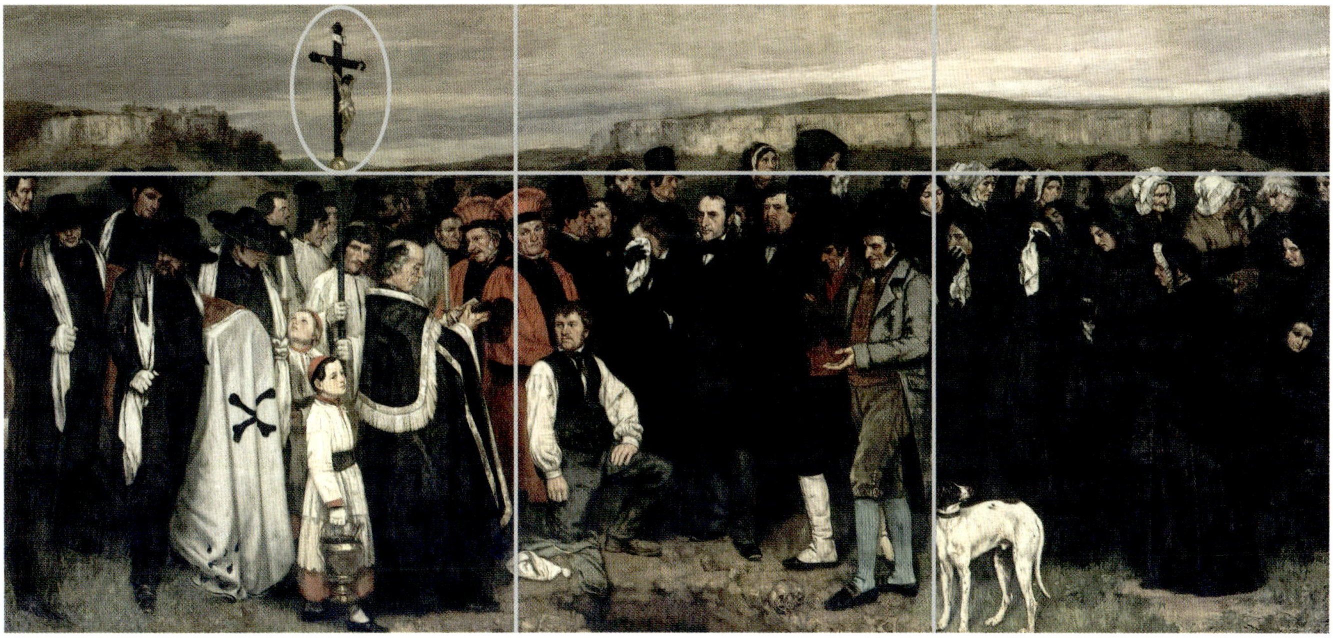

The person being buried in Ornans is, in fact, not seen at all; only the grave in which the deceased person has been laid and around which the mourners are gathered is visible at the bottom centre of the picture.

The characters present in Courbet's painting all carry equal weight, forming a frieze across the entire width of the canvas. As they are standing on even ground, their heads are all at the same height. None of them is painted with greater respect or more attention to detail than any other. Only Jesus, in the form of the crucifix held aloft by one of the clergy, rises above the mourners. Unlike El Greco's creation of the imagination, floating in the heavens, he is as physically present at the graveside as the congregation. The painting is large – 3.1 × 6.7 metres (10 × 22 ft) – dimensions that would hitherto have been associated with the treatment of grand themes and noble sentiment. What Courbet depicts is the scene at an actual burial, that of his great-uncle, and the figures shown, far from being there as representatives of timeless attributes, are real, identifiable people.

A Burial at Ornans epitomizes the search for a realism in art appropriate to a time of scientific and historical investigation into the world, the physical and psychological characteristics of the people who inhabit it, and the rapidly changing circumstances under which they live their lives. The revolution was by the people and for the people. Courbet's composition realizes and embodies the truth of this. It features the people and it presents them as worthy of attention and respect.

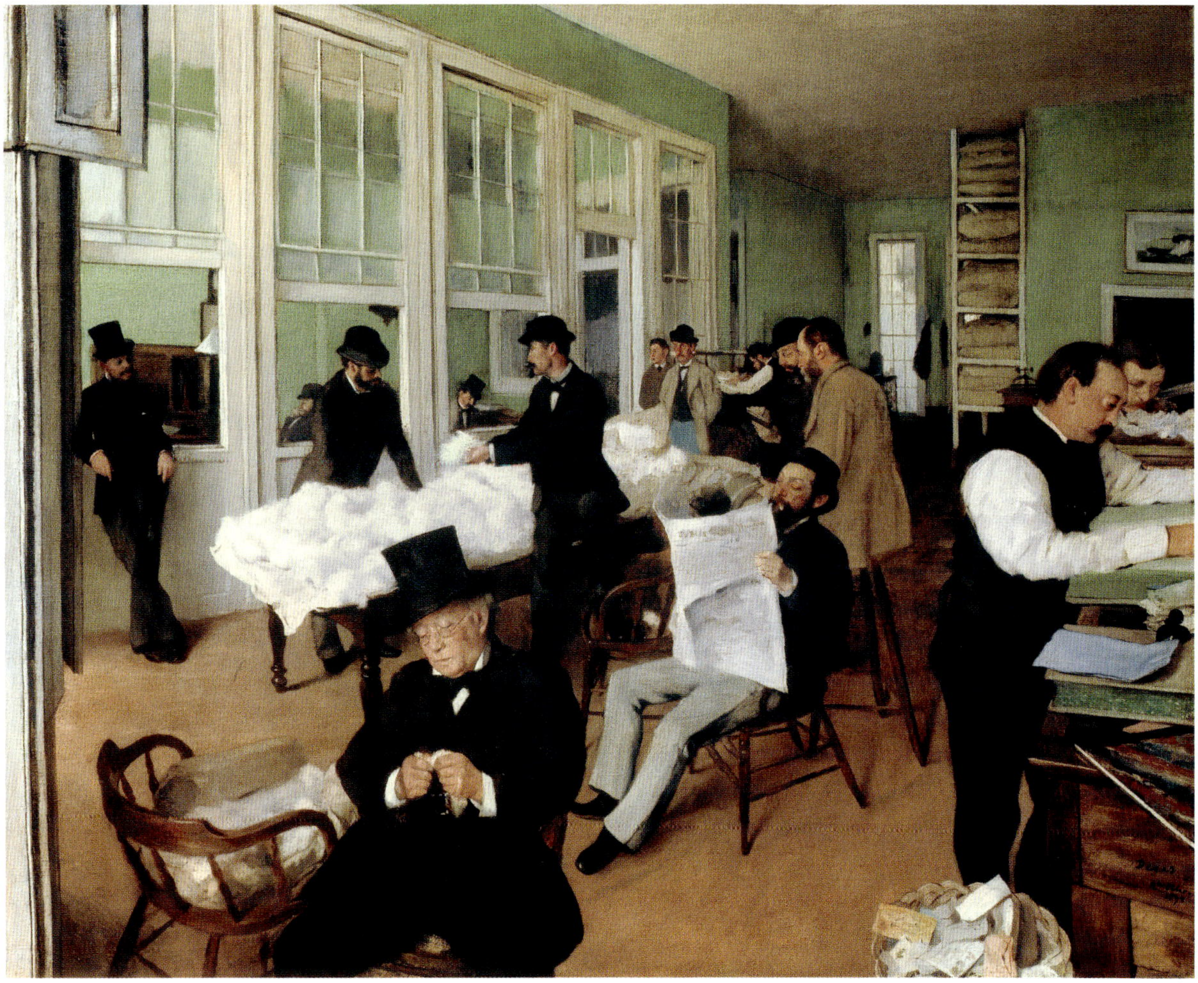

ABOVE AND BELOW: Edgar Degas, *The Cotton Exchange, New Orleans*, 1873. Oil on canvas, 73 cm × 92 cm ($28^{3}/_{4}$ × $36^{1}/_{4}$ in).

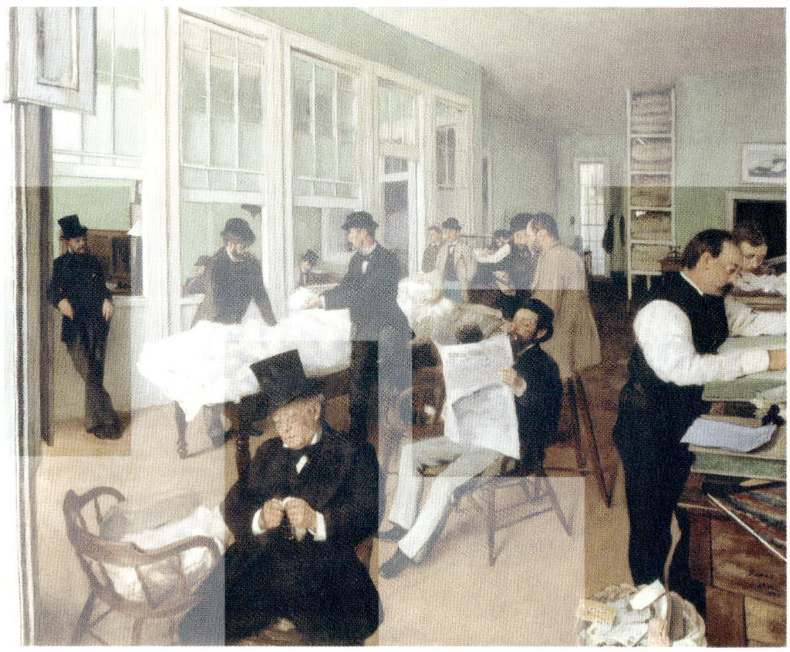

THE IMPACT OF THE CAMERA

In *The Painter of Modern Life*, the 1863 study on the painter and illustrator Constantin Guys, French art critic Charles Baudelaire first uses the term 'modernity' to describe the condition of contemporary existence. Fifteen years before this, at the time Gustave Courbet was painting *A Burial at Ornans,* Karl Marx and Friedrich Engels had already remarked in their 'Communist Manifesto' how 'all fixed, fast-frozen relations ... are swept away', how 'all new-formed ones become antiquated before they can ossify', and that 'all that is solid melts into air'.[1] Baudelaire saw the need for artists to recognize the centrality of this experience of transitoriness in their approach to art making, and the need for us to find it embodied in the art of the period:

> *By 'modernity' I mean the ephemeral, the fugitive, the contingent, the half of art whose other half is the eternal and the immutable.*[2]

In an environment that saw incessant, swift change, capturing the circumstances that pertained at a given moment was at least as important as distilling many such moments in order to arrive at a more lasting truth. The new technology of the camera was of paramount importance, and its impact on composition was immense. Painting took time; figures, objects, background and setting all needed to be arranged, and that arrangement then modelled in paint on canvas. The comparison with photography was stark. In its early days, certainly, exposure times were long, but by the middle of the nineteenth century exposure was already reduced from several minutes to a matter of seconds. Development of relatively portable equipment also made it possible to move outside the studio to photograph landscapes and urban environments, where scenes were not arranged, not least because they were beyond the immediate control of the artist. Photographs taken outside the formalized set up of a studio show how the world happened to be at the moment it was taken.

The Cotton Exchange, New Orleans by French impressionist Edgar Degas evidences the strong influence of photography in its composition. The room is full of calm activity. There are a dozen or so figures present, and a sense of collective enterprise is implicit in the fact that each person is engaged in their own necessary task as part of the larger business of the exchange. The figure in the left foreground, Degas's uncle and head of the exchange, has his back to everything else that is going on while he checks a sample of cotton. In the far right foreground, next to an over-full waste basket, a man stands at a high desk working on a ledger. His shirt sleeve is the same bright white as the new cotton being graded on the large central table. Both of these figures are 'incomplete': the uncle's legs are cropped by the bottom edge, and the clerk's hands by the right-hand edge of the canvas. In a similar way, a door frame running the length of the left-hand edge limits the visible space of the room. It is as if a snapshot has been taken. What is captured by the lens is recorded, and what falls outside its frame is not visible.

Two other people among the room's occupants are striking. In the centre of the picture a man sits reading the newspaper. He provides a major focus for the composition, and yet he is absent from the activity in the room. His mind is elsewhere, absorbed in whatever article he is reading. The second person is to the left, leaning casually against the screen wall, watching all that's going on around him but otherwise he remains uninvolved. He exemplifies the character of the *flâneur*, identified by Baudelaire in 'The Painter of Modern Life' as the dispassionate observer of urban existence:

> *For the perfect flâneur, for the passionate spectator, it is an immense joy to set up house in the heart of the multitude, amid the ebb and flow of movement, in the midst of the fugitive and the infinite. To be away from home and yet to feel oneself everywhere at home; to see the world, to be at the centre of the world, and yet to remain hidden from the world.*[3]

The Cotton Exchange strongly indicates the influence of photography, but it is also the case that through this composition we understand a wider truth. Before the invention of photography, painting was accepted as the chief means of representing the world. From the moment of the invention of the new medium, this could no longer remain the case. Whatever painting was, and whatever it could accomplish, the activity would henceforth need to find its place in a greatly altered cultural landscape. Baudelaire acknowledged that studying the old masters might still be of help to anyone learning how to paint, but this in itself would be insufficient when faced with the task of 'understanding the special nature of present-day beauty':

> *The draperies of a Rubens or Veronese will in no way teach you how to depict moiré antique, satin à la reine or any other fabric of modern manufacture, which we see supported and hung over crinoline or starched muslin petticoat.*[4]

As a result of what photography revealed to us about the world, we could not help but to begin to see that world differently. And because it was a different world, it placed new requirements and limits upon those who sought to represent it. The modern world demanded an equally modern painting free from outdated academic formulae. Like Baudelaire's *flâneur*, our observations could no longer be made from a detached, distant viewpoint, but must necessarily occur from a more intimate, involved position. As much as we are the viewer standing in front of this painting, we are also the figure standing to one side within the scene itself, observing all that goes on around us.

THE NEW VISUAL ORDER

For his short film *The Girl Chewing Gum* (1976), the British artist John Smith set up his camera on a street corner in Dalston, east London. The action of the film simply consists of the comings and goings of the people and traffic using the street. What changes our view of these otherwise unforseeable movements, however, is Smith's voice on the soundtrack, issuing directions as if he were orchestrating events and everyone we see has been patiently waiting off-screen for their cue to appear.

The eponymous gum-chewing girl, only fleetingly present, is just one among the many characters who enter and leave. At one point, the camera tilts upwards to show a clock on top of a nearby building, but this is apparently achieved by Smith asking everything on the set to 'go down'. There is then a slightly erratic zoom in on the clock, which, once again, follows the direction given to it to make a series of jerky steps towards the camera. Later, the camera pans right to reveal a queue of people waiting outside a cinema, a move ostensibly achieved after the instruction to shift the entire set to the left has been issued. Gradually, the director's voice takes on the guise of omnipotence, adding back story to those we see and imputing motive to their actions. Near the end of the film, Smith tells us that he is not, in fact, speaking from the scene, but is actually recording his voice from the edge of a field 15 miles away. The film then cuts to that location and does a 360-degree pan around the empty field while we continue to hear the sound of the street in Dalston.

Walter Benjamin wrote in his 1935 essay 'The Work of Art in the Age of its Technological Reproducibility' that the 'equipment-free aspect of reality' we witness when watching the cinema screen is in truth 'the height of artifice'.[5] Considerable resources are required to deliver the image we see, but none of this is visible to us as we watch. What we see instead is a 'vision of immediate reality', which appears, almost magically, as a 'blue flower in the land of technology'. In *The Girl Chewing Gum*, Smith humorously uncovers the artifice, demonstrating the transformative function of the frame in imposing order and compositional sense upon what is in every other way a haphazard scene. And on this question of the frame, composer John Cage recounted a meeting with the painter Willem de Kooning:

> *I was with de Kooning once in a restaurant and he said, 'If I put a frame around these bread crumbs, that isn't art'. And what I'm saying is that it is. He was saying that it wasn't because he connects art with his activity – he connects with himself as an artist whereas I would want art to slip out of us into the world in which we live.*[6]

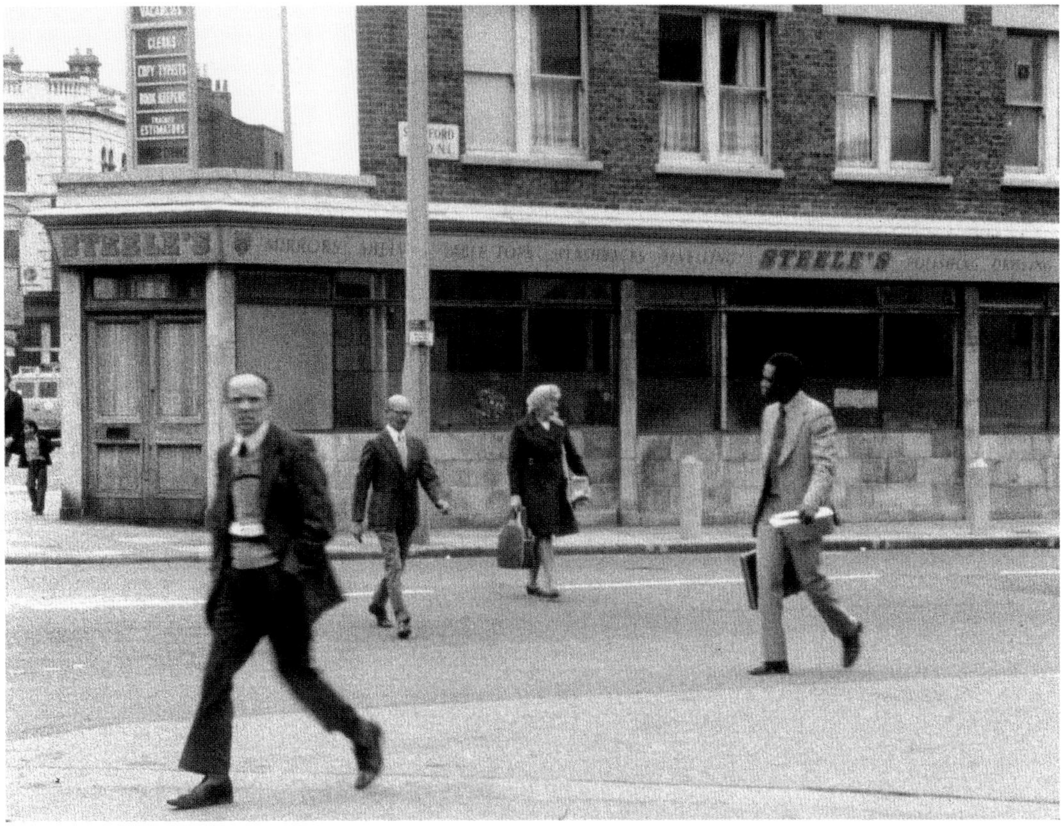

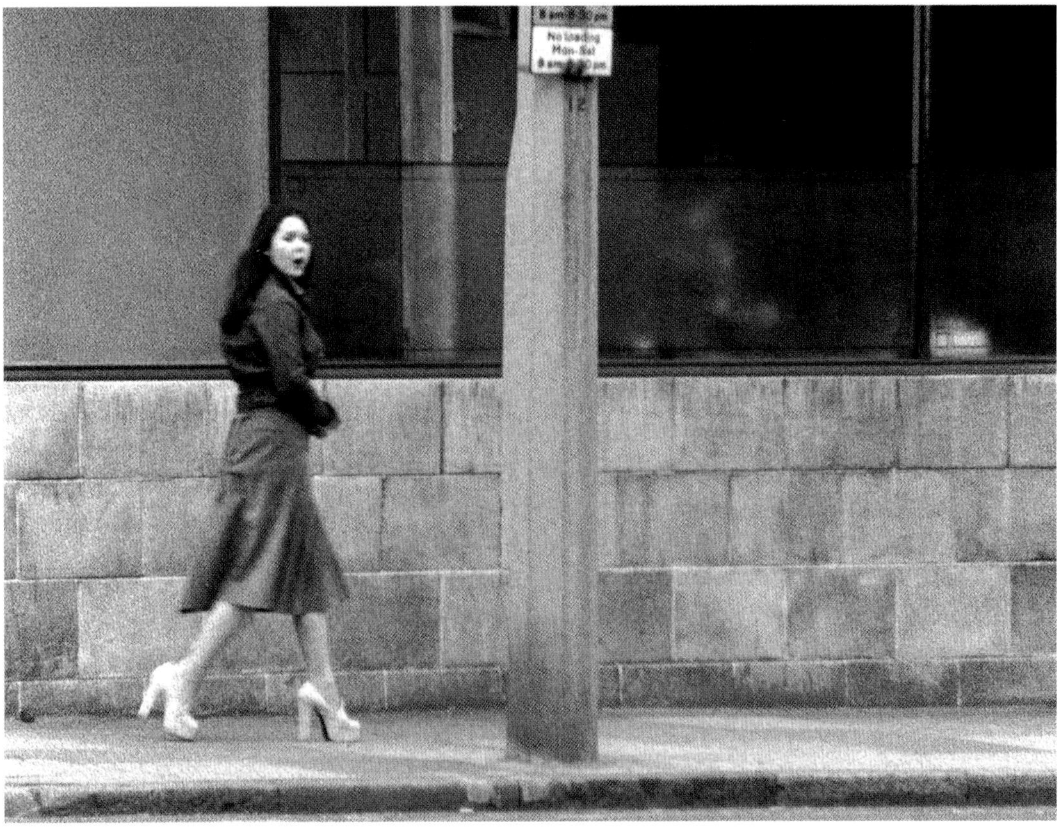

ABOVE TOP AND BOTTOM: John Smith, *The Girl Chewing Gum*, 1976. 16mm film, 12 min.

ATTENTION

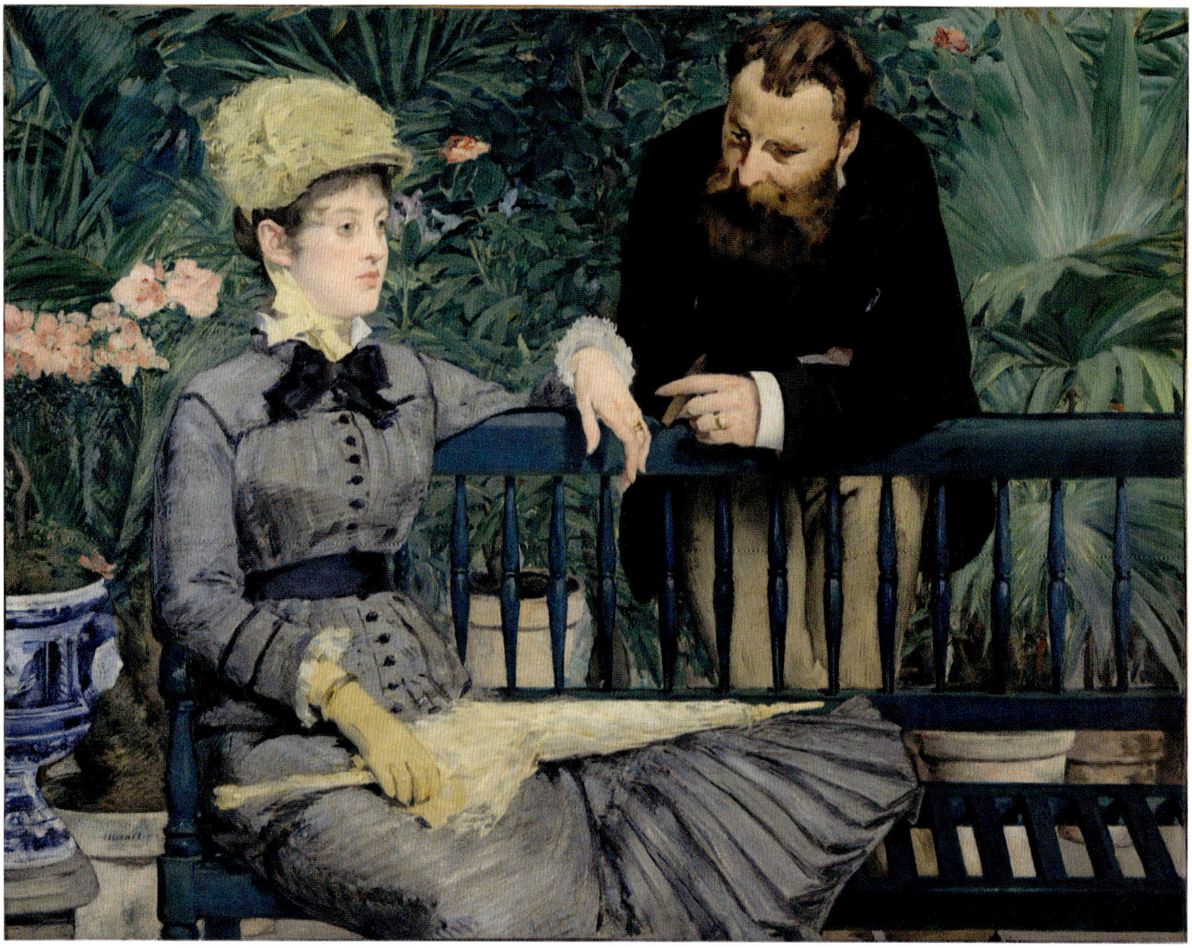

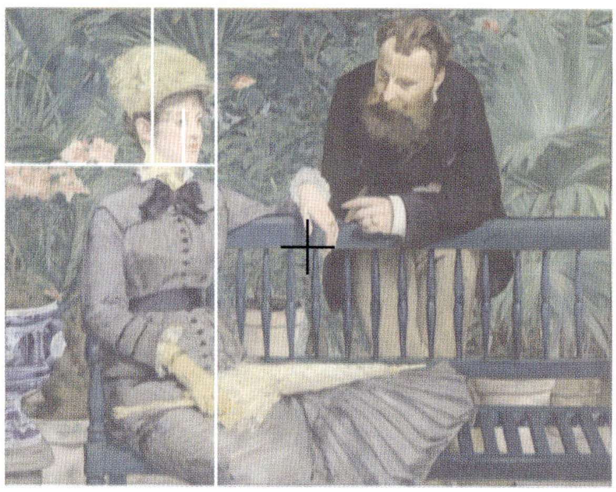

ABOVE AND RIGHT : Édouard Manet, *In the Conservatory*, 1878–9. Oil on canvas, 115 × 150 cm (45¼ × 59 in).

Since the development of perspective in the fifteenth century, we have come to accept, almost to assume, that a painting offers us a view into a space that extends back from the picture surface. There may be much in that space but we are free to stand for as long as we like, and to direct our gaze towards whichever detail we choose, in the certain knowledge that the rest will wait patiently for our attention in due course. The depicted world is complete, and all of it is always available to us, the viewers.

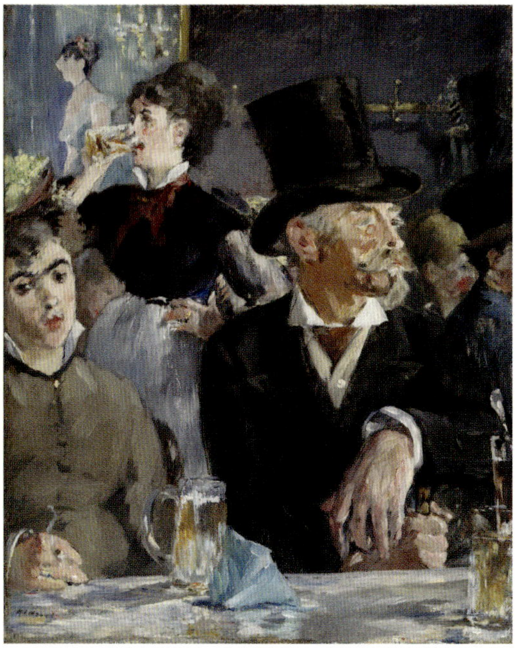

ABOVE: Édouard Manet, *The Café-Concert*, *c.*1879. Oil on canvas, 47.3 × 39.1 cm (18⅝ × 15⅜ in).

Until the nineteenth century, the task of producing a representation of the world was always and inevitably a human one. It had to be drawn or painted or modelled. But the invention of photography, together with concurrent psychological and physiological investigation into the capabilities and limitations of the body, began to quickly disturb any certainties that might hitherto have existed, not least our acceptance of the completeness of the depicted world. How can the artist approach the task of representing a scene once we learn that the functioning of our visual apparatus and the mental activity by means of which we process what passes before our eyes greatly affects our awareness of what we see? Put simply, if we pay attention to one thing within our field of vision, we are necessarily not focusing on something else, and how a picture is put together must reflect our implicit understanding of that inescapable fact.

At first glance, *In the Conservatory*, by the French modernist painter Édouard Manet, has an orthodox compositional structure. Indeed, when it was first shown in Paris at the 1879 Salon, the critic Jules-Antoine Castagnary wondered if Manet had decided to begin 'making concessions to the public'.[1] Castagnary's surprise is understandable if we compare *In the Conservatory* to another of Manet's works, *The Café-Concert*, which was painted the same year. This painting shows a crowded scene at the Cabaret de Reichshoffen on the Boulevard Rochechouart. None of the figures are rendered in precise detail. The face of the man occupying much of the right half of the canvas, in particular, is described in a series of apparently quick, suggestive brushstrokes. The white dabs on his left upper eyelid, around that eye, curving below his right eye and on the end of his nose are picked up by his shirt cuff, the tips of his wing collar, and in the hand and collar of the woman behind. Likewise, the pale yellow of his right cheek resonates with the flowers on the hat of the seated woman at the left side of the canvas, the gold of the beer in the glasses, the brass fittings along the rear wall, the mirror frame, the chandelier reflected in it, and, in the upper centre of the canvas, two suggestive but irresolvable patches above and below the brim of the man's hat. All of this contrasts with and is set against and around large dark areas, particularly those of the man's jacket and hat, the piled-up hair of the standing woman and the bodice of her dress.

One striking feature of the painting is the disparate focus of attention among its characters. The man looks off to his left and, while it is conceivable that he is concentrating on the performance, the position of the singer – deduced from her reflection in the mirror – make this uncertain. His companion has downcast eyes and appears to be preoccupied with her own thoughts rather than with anything taking place in the room around her, and the drinking woman looks elsewhere again, her stance and demeanour indicating that she, too, is neither concerned with the entertainment nor with any conversation being carried on nearby.

The issue of attention and its alternatives – distraction, inattention, oversight – is of particular significance in the case of *In the Conservatory*. In contrast to *The Café-Concert*, the woman in the foreground of *In the Conservatory* is precisely finished, and both her clothes and her face are clearly defined. She is Madame Guillemet, proprietor of a fashionable Paris dress shop, who sits on a bench over the back of which her from behind. The composition has a series of strong horizontals, given by the bench and a number of softer diagonals suggested by the lush leaves of the foliage, the flowers and the pleats of Madame Guillemet's outspread skirt. The front and rear bars of the bench seat, along with the lower and upper bars of its back, establish the horizontals. Above them we can trace another line along the top of the man's forearm as it rests on the seat back, past his index finger, across the woman's shoulders and under the pink blossoms at the left of the picture. Between this line and the upper bar of the bench, the left arms of the husband and wife describe a gentle serpentine meander between the front and rear of the bench, holding the two areas of what is already a quite shallow picture space together. Madame Guillemet's gloved right hand is in her lap, holding her parasol while her ungloved left hand is relaxed and hangs over the seat back. The centre point of the canvas is immediately below her left thumb.

The compositional structure of *In the Conservatory*, combined with the detailed painting of Madame Guillemet's face and outfit, could thus lead to us seeing the painting as quite conventional. Yet there are features that disturb and call into question such a judgement. The front of the bench seat is discontinuous; the line of the right-hand unoccupied section does not match up with the left-hand part that is visible under where the woman sits. And when we look at this part on the left we see it straight on, as if we the viewer were perhaps seated and at the same level as her. At the right of the canvas, however, the bench seat appears as if we were standing and looking down on it.

Despite their physical proximity, the relationship between husband and wife remains ambiguous. She looks out beyond the right-hand edge of the canvas, though her demeanour suggests that she is preoccupied, not with something in the room that lies just outside the picture frame, but with her own musings. Her clearly defined features and her sharp, sensitively assembled, fashionable dress make her a real physical presence in the space, and yet she is also somehow absent. Her husband leans next to her in an easy manner, but his eyes are indistinct and one cannot be certain where he directs his gaze. His more coarsely painted fingers that loosely hold a cigar mimic the shape of the foliage next to him, and his trousered legs echo the plant pots behind the bench. Likewise, Madame Guillemet's ear picks up the form of the flowers to either side of her head, and their pink harmonizes with the yellow of her hat, bow, gloves and parasol, as well as the blue of the elaborate pot beside her. Both figures thus merge with their environment rather than unequivocally separating themselves from it.

How do we look at this painting, and where do we understand ourselves to be situated in relation to it? What it depicts takes place within the frame and outside it, within the room and elsewhere, in the surroundings of the two figures and as part of their inner lives. Whatever we choose to focus on causes other aspects to slip away into incoherence. It is not only that we cannot be sure about where the attention of the man and woman is directed. *In the Conservatory* reveals to us two things. First, that to pay attention is to engage in an active process involving an interplay between the external world and internal psycho-physiological processes. Second, that in paying attention to one thing we are necessarily allowing much else that lies within our visual field to go unremarked. As art historian Jonathan Crary has written in his study of this painting,

> *Manet is the first modern artist to understand what would become crucial in the late work of Cézanne: the ways that an optical attentiveness can dissolve and disorganize the world, thus requiring a fundamental reconstruction of it by the artist.*[2]

How do we look at this painting, and where do we understand ourselves to be situated in relation to it?

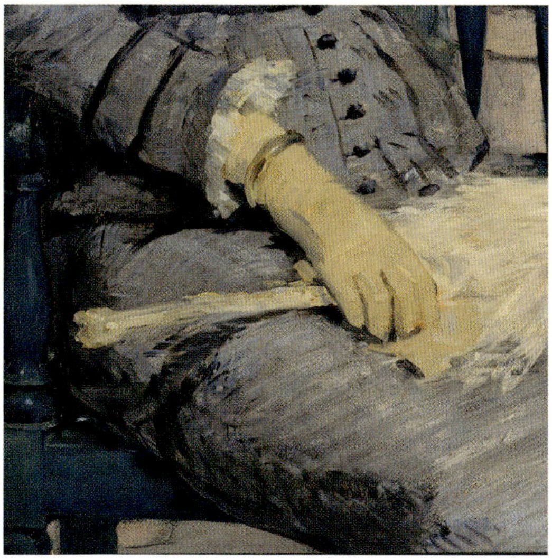
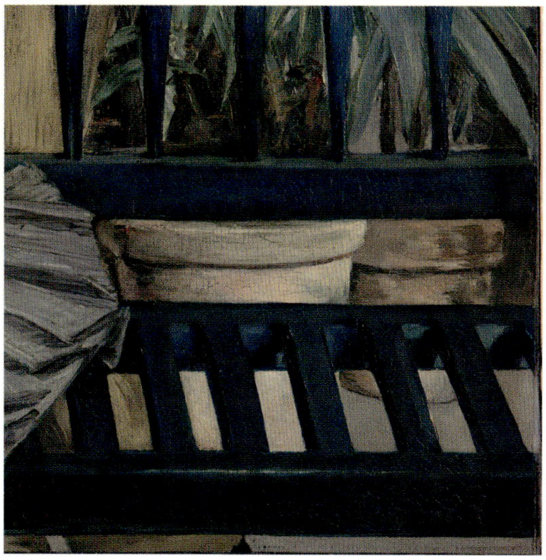

Note the discontinuity between the different parts of the bench where visible.

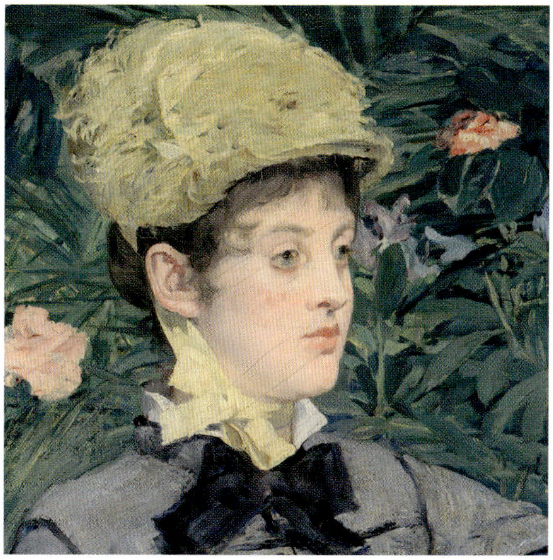
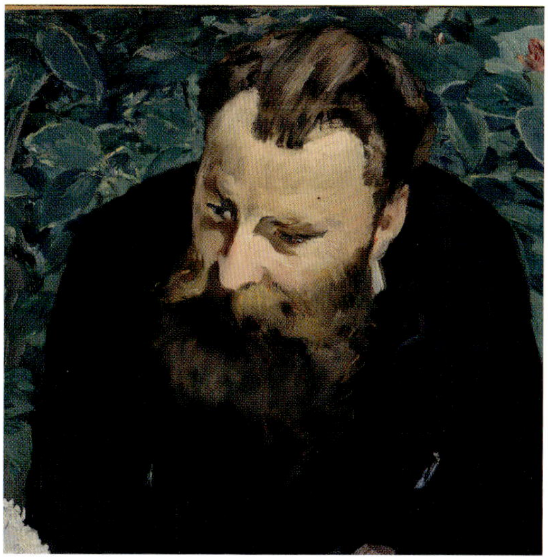

The varied treatment of the gazes and faces of husband and wife emphasize the ambiguity in the relationship.

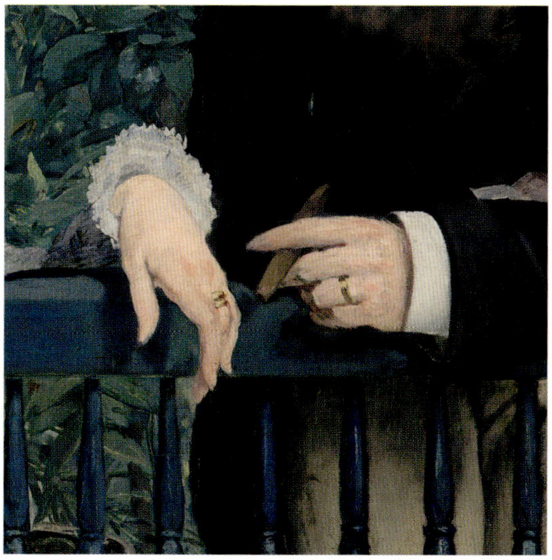
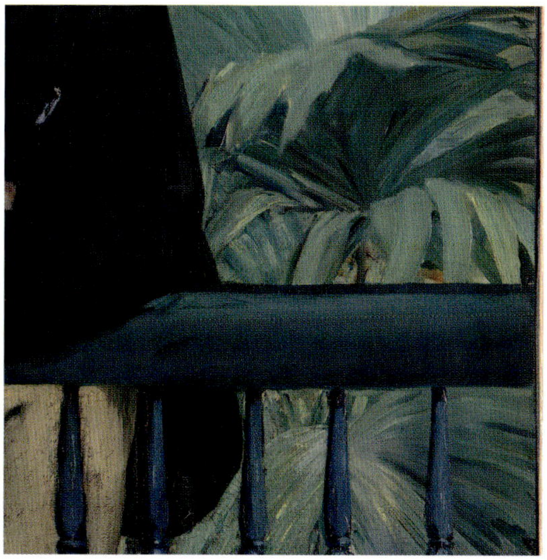

The shapes of the man's fingers are echoed in the foliage behind him.

THE THIRD DIMENSION

Writing on the mechanical arts in 1865, art critic John Ruskin saw the steam locomotive as an invention that could not have been inspired by any of the nine Muses of classical mythology. It was something utterly new, and its appearance could only have been motivated by a 'Tenth muse'.

The development of rail transport inevitably brought with it the demand for an appropriate architecture. Buildings specifically designed to house both these new trains and those who travelled in them were needed. The railway station was, as the art historian Linda Nochlin noted, the 'most modern of all entities'.[1] It was a new gateway into and out of the city, a place of perpetual movement and constant change that epitomized the character and spirit of modern life as described by Karl Marx and Charles Baudelaire. In physical terms, it was a large space with a light, uninterrupted expanse that had only recently been made possible through the innovation of iron and glass construction.

In 1876–7, the French impressionst artist Claude Monet painted around (the exact number is not known) ten views of the Gare Saint-Lazare in Paris, at least four of which show the view from more or less the same position inside the station. In painting *en plein air* (in the open) in this way, he was not attempting to construct a definitive emotional response to the advent of train travel in the reflective quiet of the studio, but making a series of efforts to capture the immediate visual sensations experienced in an ever-changing situation.

In the painting from the series now in the Musée d'Orsay, iron pillars to the left and right of the picture support a pitched roof that spans an open space. The pillars together with the horizontal tie rods provide a frame within the painting that echoes the edges of the canvas itself. Dense puffs of blue smoke rise from the funnel of the arriving train in the centre of the composition while more delicate billows of white steam coming from the trains to either side drift across the tracks and up towards the glazed train shed roof. Light enters from above as well as through the open end where trains enter and leave the station, filling the steamy space with what Nochlin calls 'vaporous iridescence'.[3] Like Paris's arcades, with glass-paned coverings that allowed

I cannot express the amazed awe, the crushed humility, with which I sometimes watch a locomotive take its breath at a railway station, and think what work there is in its bars and wheels, and what manner of men they must be who dig brown iron-stone out of the ground, and forge it into THAT!

– John Ruskin, *The Cestus of Aglaia*, 1860–70[2]

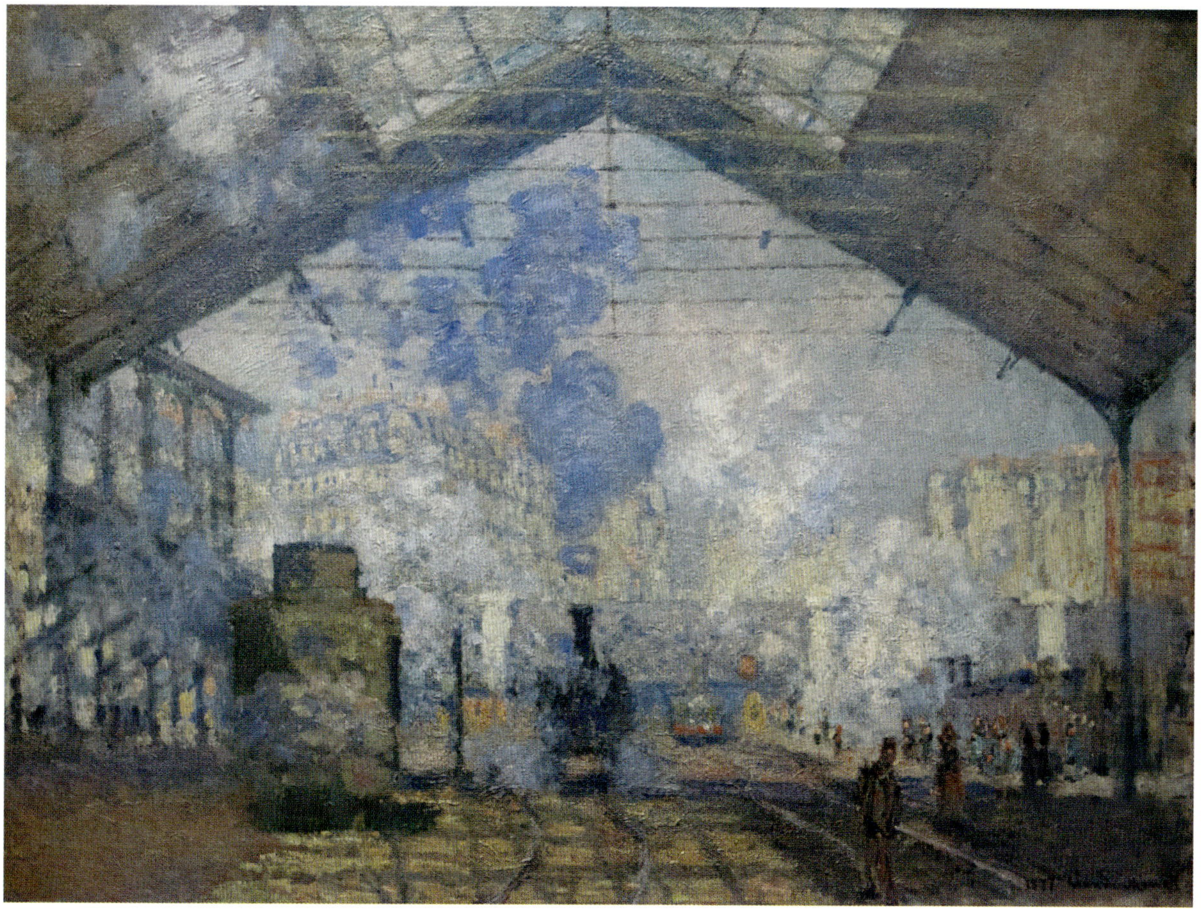

ABOVE: Claude Monet, *La Gare Saint-Lazare*, 1877. Oil on canvas, 75 × 105 cm (29½ × 41 in).

shopping in comfort even under the most inclement conditions outside, the station presents an interior urban landscape, a place with its own weather.

While the station's architecture is held within the rigid lines, the steam and smoke clouds are shifting and imprecise. Monet was familiar with Turner's 1844 *Rain, Steam and Speed – The Great Western Railway*, in which the solid onrushing train and the bridge over which it is travelling is blurred by a summer squall. Like the hazy outlines of boats, masts and buildings of Le Havre seen in *Impression, Sunrise* – the Monet painting that gave its name to the impressionist movement – the locomotives and waiting passengers at the Gare Saint-Lazare are rendered indistinct by the steam and smoke billowing from the engines. The swirling movement and endlessly changing shape of these clouds require new means to capture such diffuse presence. These elements were quite unamenable to the conventional way of modelling – by using light and shadow to describe solid form – so the smoke and steam are figured in dabs, swirls and smears of paint spread across the picture surface. In this we see Monet's attempt to resolve the tension between, on the one hand, the task of representing the three-dimensional scene before him and, on the other, the awareness that what is being undertaken is the production of a two-dimensional construction in paint. Instead of viewing activity in the station taking place in an illusionistic space receding back from the surface of the canvas, we see the endless unfixability of the scene at the Gare Saint-Lazare figured in the paint spread upon that surface.

CAPTURING THE TRANSIENT

After the Gare Saint-Lazare series, Monet would continue to paint multiple canvases on a single subject, notably haystacks, the facade of Rouen cathedral and rows of poplars. The Dutch essayist Willem Byvanck recorded Monet, who remarked to him that the individual paintings 'acquire their full value only by comparison [with the others] and in the succession of the full series',[4] and the art historian and curator Charles Stuckey has gone so far as to say that, 'Monet's dedication to making works in series and presenting these works as ensembles was his most important, influential, and abiding legacy to modern art.'[5]

In part, the decision to paint *en plein air*, the interest in capturing the transient details of a scene, and the relinquishing of traditional compositional techniques can be seen as a response to the technical innovations

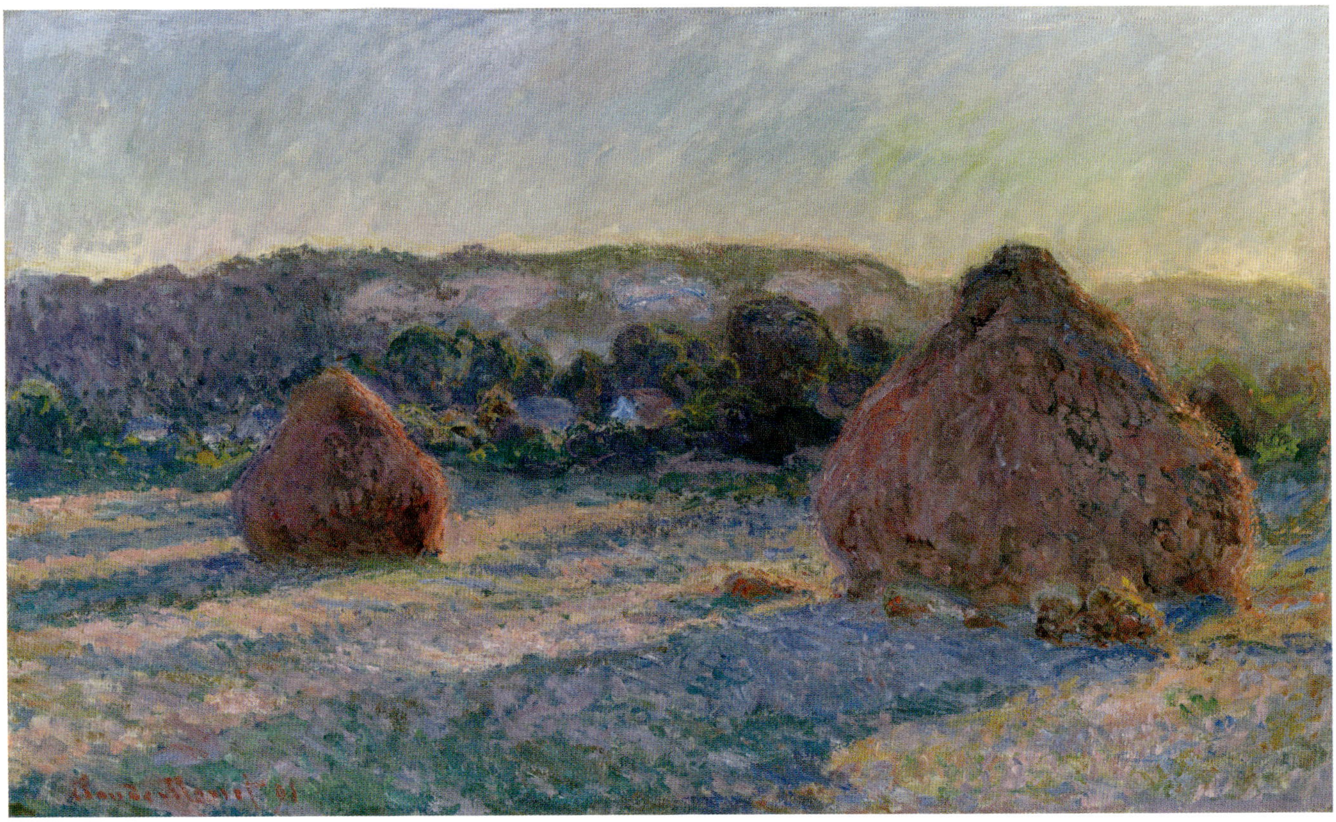

ABOVE: Claude Monet, *Stacks of Wheat (End of Summer)*, 1891. Oil on canvas, 60 × 100.5 cm (23⅝ × 39⅝ in).

that were unavoidably and irrevocably altering the patterns of nineteenth-century life. In addition to these factors, the expansion and acceleration of global trade brought cultural artefacts from many different cultures to the West, enabling artists to view and contemplate them. Beginning with the Great Exhibition in London in 1851, paintings, prints, textiles, costumes, furniture, ceramics and other items from the British colonies and other parts of the world were displayed, along with evidence of their associated lifestyles, in a succession of international exhibitions throughout the latter half of the century. This easy access to new craft techniques and to alternative approaches to pattern and image-making would offer further ways to avoid the strictures of the academy.

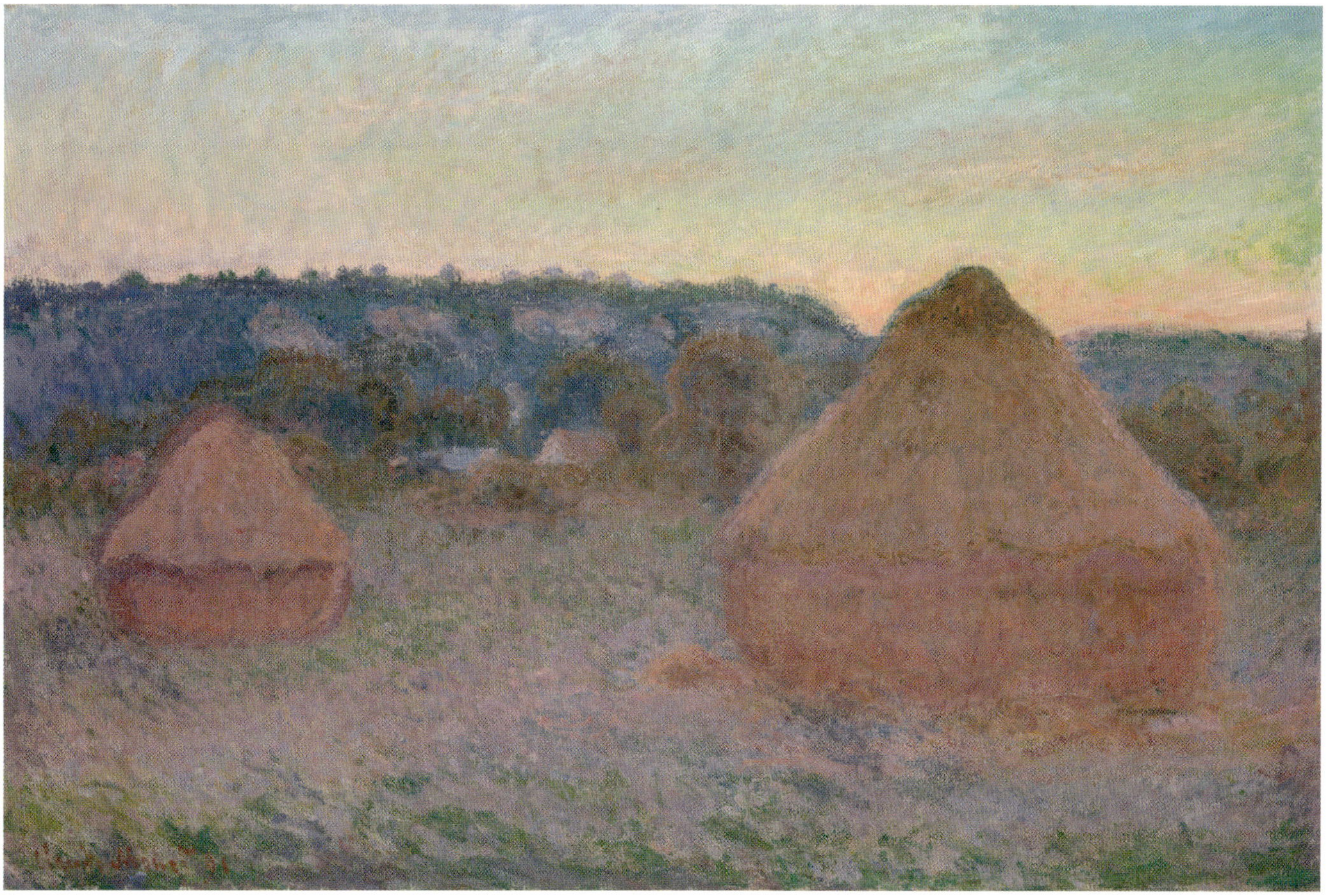

ABOVE: Claude Monet, *Stacks of Wheat (End of Day, Autumn)*, 1891. Oil on canvas, 65.8 × 101 cm (26 × 39¾ in).

UKIYO-E: THE INFLUENCE OF JAPAN

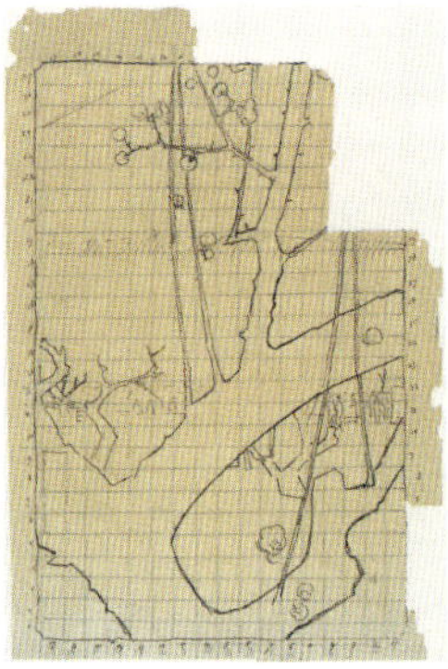

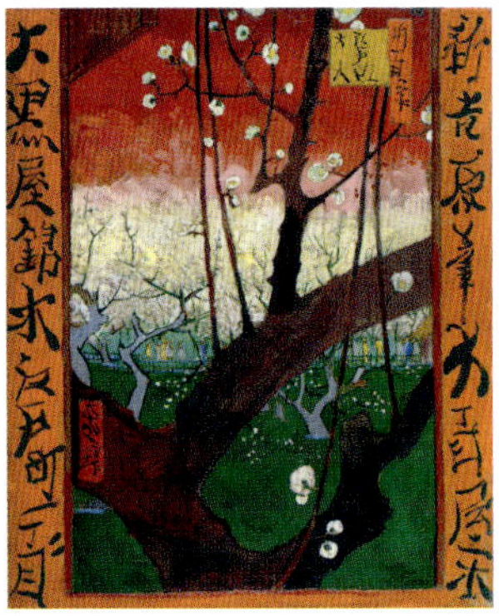

By the middle of the nineteenth century, Japan had been closed to foreign trade for more than two hundred years under the Tokugawa shogunate. The country slowly began to open up to the world again after the Kanagawa Treaty of 1854, which was agreed to after changing external factors and considerable pressure from the United States. For artists, the significant outcome of this regained contact was the appearance of Japanese prints that had a compositional style that differed considerably from the established European approach to picture making.

The relatively cheap woodblock prints in Japan largely depicted everyday themes – the theatre, actors, bathhouses and domestic interiors – in contrast to the imagery of Western history painting, such as mythological or religious topics, and subjects making allegorical allusion to matters of national importance. Yet the impressionist paintings of rapidly changing industrial landscapes and the leisure spaces of café and theatre were also a new kind of historical painting – history as it was being made. Seeing everyday scenes in these Japanese prints being treated with manifest technical skill and given due thematic weight was confirmation that such subjects could, indeed, be a proper focus for a serious artist.

By definition, Japanese art owed nothing to the tradition deriving from Classical Greek art that had shaped and continued to dominate the European academies. What it did do, however, was resonate strongly with an existing interest in art made before the Classical rationalism of the Renaissance exerted its grip that we see, for example, in the Pre-Raphaelites, and in the exploration of local craft skills in the various strands of art nouveau. Art historians Hugh Honour and John Fleming have emphasized that this 'art of the floating world', *ukiyo-e*, far from merely offering 'exotic' material for appropriation by the West, was immediately seen as art from which European artists could learn. Writer and critic Edmond de Goncourt was a prominent admirer of Japanese art, and wrote of its distinctive qualities in his journal:

> *Everything that [the Japanese] do is taken from observation. They represent what they see: the incredible effects of the sky. The stripes on a mushroom, the transparency of the jellyfish. Their art copies nature as does Gothic art.*[1]

Goncourt saw a stark contrast between this approach and that of the Greeks, whose art (with the exception of sculpture) he described as 'false and invented'.[2] Through a combination of surface line and blocks of flat colour, the absence of shadow, and the concentration on popular imagery, Japanese art provided both a lesson in compositional possibility and a validation of the European artists' commitment to the reality of their daily lives and the importance of their experiences of it. Honour and Fleming wrote:

> *Japanese prints dramatically affected the whole course of Western art in the latter half of the nineteenth century. They provided a catalyst which helped painters to throw off the spell of the Classical tradition, free themselves from the authority of the old masters and seek new conceptions in art, new ways of seeing.*[3]

ABOVE LEFT: Vincent van Gogh, tracing of *The Plum Tree Teahouse at Kameido (after Hiroshige)*, 1887. Pencil, pen and ink on paper, 38.3 × 26.2 cm (15 × 10⅜ in).

ABOVE RIGHT: Vincent van Gogh, *Flowering Plum Orchard (after Hiroshige)*, 1887. Oil on canvas, 55.6 × 46.8 cm (21⅞ × 18⅜ in).

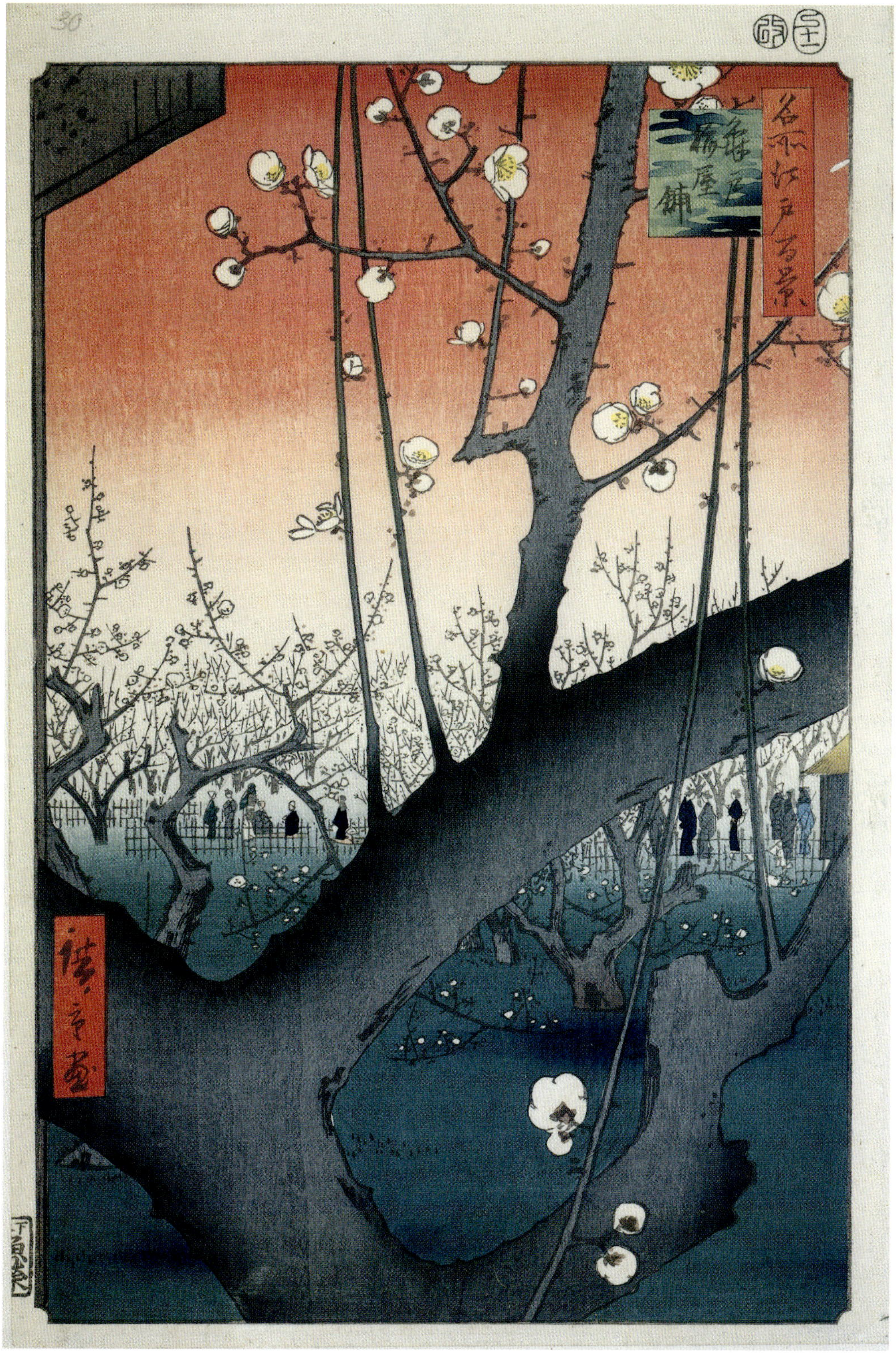

ABOVE: Utagawa Hiroshige, *The Plum Garden at Kameido Shrine*, 1857. Woodblock print, colour ink on paper (36.4 × 24.4 cm $14\frac{3}{8} \times 9\frac{5}{8}$ in).

If we are looking to find the room laid out in accordance with the normal rules of perspective, it can only appear distorted. But it is quite in keeping with Van Gogh's stated interest in the flat colours of Japanese print.

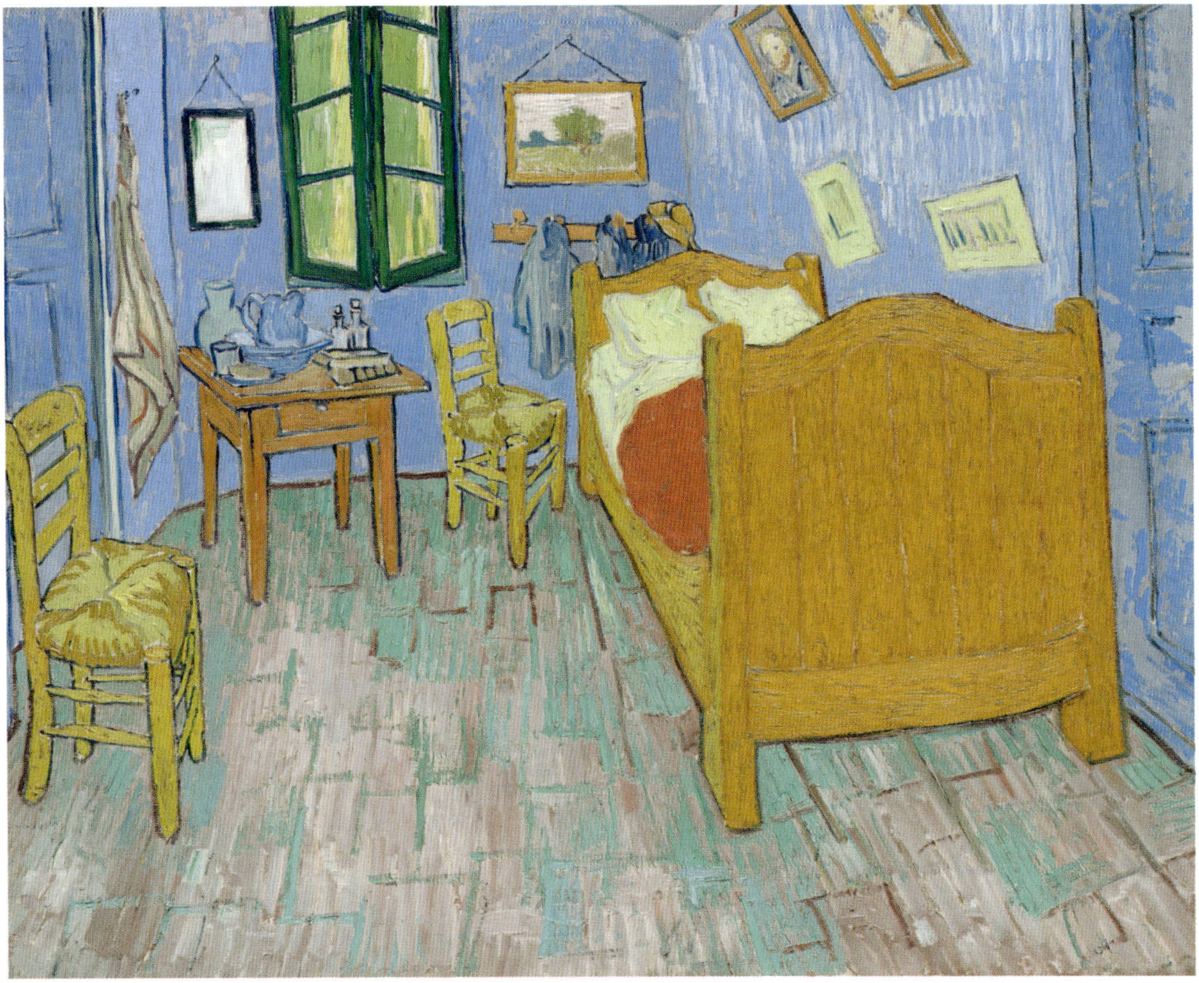

COLOUR JUXTAPOSED

Vincent van Gogh, the Dutch artist who would become known for his post-impressionist works, admired the unassuming compositional directness of Japanese prints: 'They do a figure in a few sure strokes with the same ease as if it were as simple as buttoning your coat.'[4] To assimilate the style, he painted his own versions of two works by Utagawa Hiroshige, *The Plum Garden at Kameido Shrine* (see page 37) and *Sudden Shower On the Great Bridge Near Atake*. In the latter, the gentle arc of the bridge rising from the bottom left corner is matched by the line of the far riverbank, which gradually descends towards the right-hand edge – neither the bridge or riverbank are horizontal. The rain from which the hurrying figures attempt to shelter themselves under umbrellas and coats is suggested by numerous, closely spaced black lines that run from the dark cloud at the top to the dark blue water at the bottom of the image.

Although a painting rather than a print, Van Gogh's faithful copy repeats the manner in which Hiroshige depicted the rain, while the water of the river, the trees on the far bank and the sky are done using his own characteristic short, strong brushstrokes. In the former, a tracing reveals how carefully he has copied Hiroshige's composition, although in Van Gogh's painting, the colours become much more vivid. An indication of the impact of the startling originality of Japanese prints is given in a comment by the French art critic Théodore Duret, one of the first to write seriously on the impressionists:

> *before the arrival among us of Japanese books, there was no one in France who dared to seat himself on the banks of a river and put side by side on his canvas a roof frankly red, a white-washed wall, a green poplar, a yellow road and blue water.*[5]

Compare this with van Gogh's own description of his painting *The Bedroom*, which was, he wrote to his brother Theo, 'painted in free flat tints like the Japanese prints':

> *The walls are pale violet. The floor is of red tiles.*
> *The wood of the bed and chairs is the yellow of fresh butter, the sheets and pillows very light greenish-citron.*
> *The coverlet scarlet. The window green.*
> *The toilet table orange, the basin blue.*
> *The doors lilac.*
> *And that is all.*[6]

If we are looking to find the room laid out in accordance with the normal rules of perspective, it can only appear distorted. But it is quite in keeping with Van Gogh's stated interest in the flat colours of Japanese print. All the planes, whatever our understanding of their actual orientation in the room, lie on and are part of the picture surface: the wall against which the bed stands does not recede but is pulled round across the top right quadrant of the canvas; the bed's footboard is skewed, counter to this, so as to match the flatness of the wall above it; the floor tilts vertiginously to run down the bottom half of the picture; chair seats and tabletop are pitched up such that their horizontality almost reads as verticality.

As Van Gogh said of the painting, colour was to do 'everything', and in simplifying the composition into this arrangement of contrasting and complementary areas, it would bring a 'grander style to things'[7] and convey the restfulness appropriate to such a setting.

OPPOSITE: Vincent van Gogh, *The Bedroom*, 1888. Oil on canvas, 73.6 × 92.3 cm (29 × 36⅜ in).

Mary Cassatt, an American artist who lived and worked in Paris, saw the exhibition of prints by Nishikawa Sukenobu and Kitagawa Utamaro in 1890. Both she and her friend Edgar Degas were struck by the simple boldness of line and colour in their work. Cassatt produced a suite of ten prints in response to her visit, but the exhibition had a broader impact on her work, allowing her to develop the handling of domestic and intimate themes in a way quite distinct from Degas or, indeed, from previous approaches. In his study of Cassatt's painting, art historian Frank Getlein suggests that while Degas saw bodies as 'forms in motion to be caught, miraculously, at point after exact point of surprising gesture, disposition of limbs, stretch of muscles', Cassatt's figures were all this but were also 'always human souls communicating with each other and themselves.'[8]

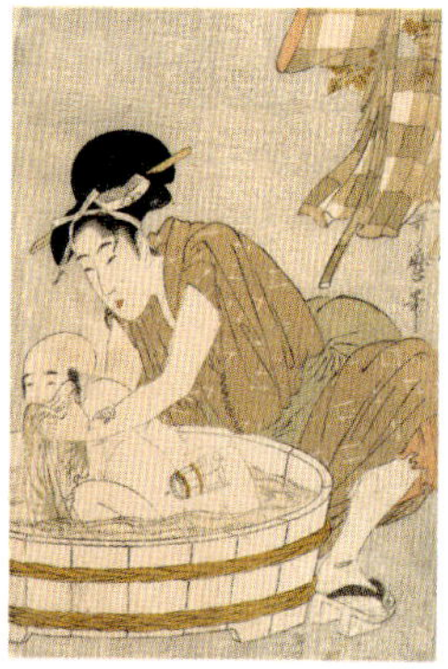

LEFT: Kitagawa Utamaro, *Bathtime (Gyōzui)*, *c.*1801. Woodblock print, colour ink on paper, 37.3 × 25.1 cm (14⅝ × 9⅞ in).

In the case of earlier treatments of domestic scenes, the contrast is equally strong. In Pieter de Hooch's 1663 *A Woman Peeling Apples*, for example, a mother sits, holding out a strip of apple peel to the daughter standing at her side. A large expanse of the mother's red dress is visible, since her white apron has been pulled back across her knee. The pointed tip of a shoe pokes out from beneath the hem. Similarly, her daughter's brown outer garment is hitched up in front to show the deep yellow dress below. If there is any innocence in this scene, it is a naiveté soon to be banished by the lessons of experience. The emotionally intense colour of the mother's dress, the suggestiveness of her peeping toe, the strip of peel – both snake-like and phallic – gently held by the daughter, and the apples themselves as signs of both knowledge and sin, give the painting an undercurrent of suppressed eroticism.

In Utamaro's *Bathtime*, a mother squats over a tub bathing her son. He holds his own miniature tub in one hand, gripping his mother's forearm with the other, while turning his head in an attempt to avoid having his face wiped with a cloth. There is a suggestion of a floral pattern on the cloth that echoes the leaves partially visible behind his kimono, which hangs above and behind them, being blown by a gentle breeze. Everything is cropped – the mother's left leg, the kimono, the bathtub – bringing the focus right in on the intimacy of the scene.

Cassatt's *The Child's Bath* shows the same act viewed from slightly above, a vantage point that flattens the carpet up against the picture surface. Behind the figures, both the floral wallpaper and the painted chest of drawers set against it provide two further patterned blocks that occupy the upper third of the composition. The broad pastel stripes of the mother's dress flow in a repeated serpentine curve down and across the canvas before they are cut off at the right-hand edge. The two heads touch in the top centre of the picture as they look down to watch as the mother washes the child's feet in a bowl. The bowl is glazed with concentric stripes of the same colour as the dress, and in the extreme right foreground stands the large jug from which the water has been poured to fill the washing bowl, cropped by the bottom edge of the canvas. The contoured curve of the jug's generous mouth, the loop of its handle, and the rings of the bowl's pattern capture and turn the falling lines of the dress, holding them within the frame of the painting and, as with the cropping of Utamaro's *Bathtime*, drawing attention to the quiet privacy of the moment and keeping it there. A further anchoring is accomplished through small details of the composition. Two pale pink highlights in the decoration on the chest of drawers in the right background resonate with the light shining along the child's shins in the left foreground; and the spray of flowers painted on the jug in the right foreground echo the wallpaper pattern in the left background.

In their studies of Cassatt's work, both Getlein and Griselda Pollock chose the word 'monumental'[9] to describe the effect of the child's body and the plain white towel around its waist set over and in contrast to the mother's patterned dress. No topic is unimportant, every subject is worthy of attention. In particular, the painting confounds any idea that the home, the domestic space with which society overwhelmingly places the lives and activities of women and children, is somehow of lesser importance.

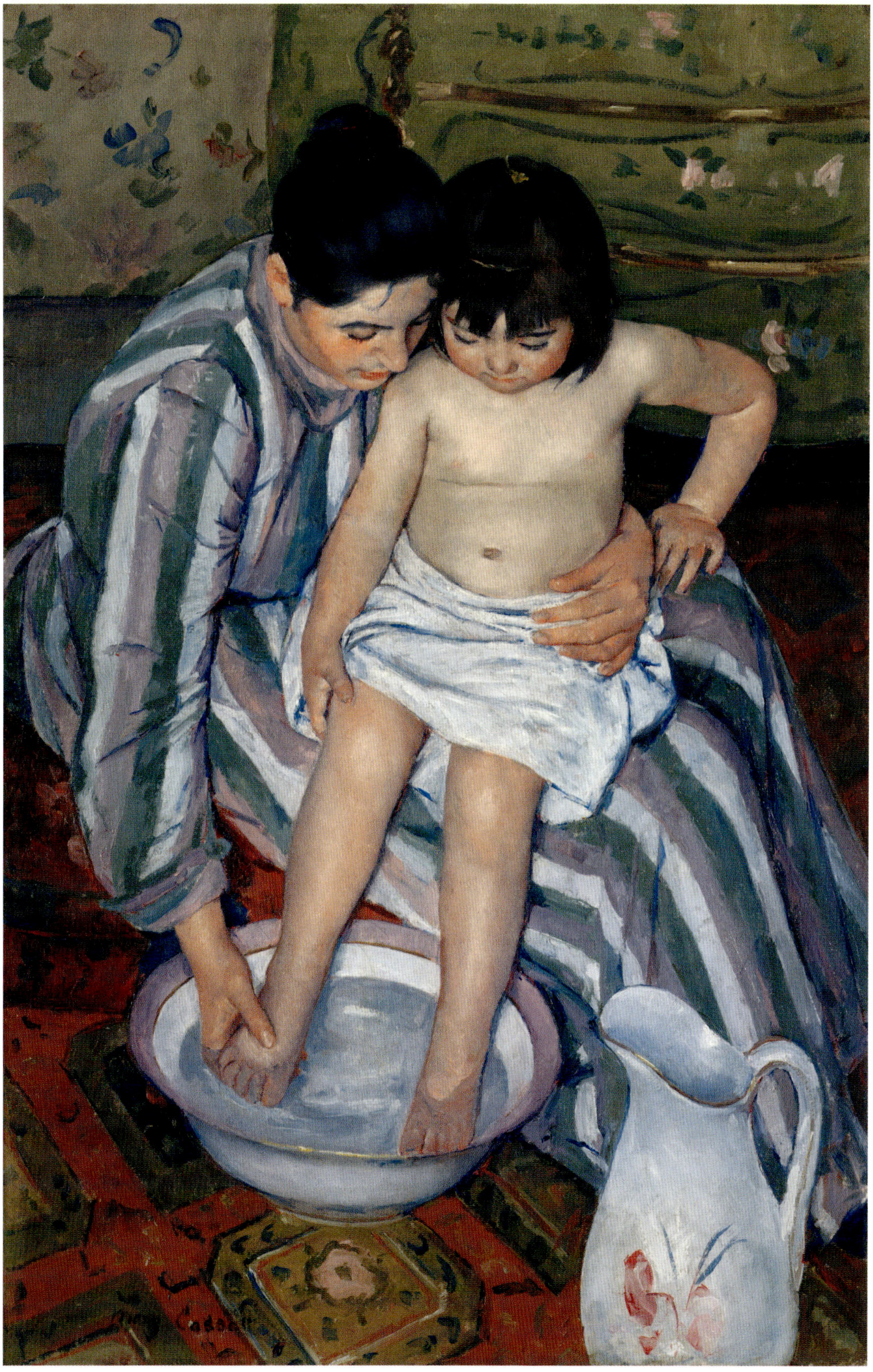

ABOVE: Mary Cassatt, *The Child's Bath*, 1893. Oil on canvas, 100.3 × 66.1 cm (39½ × 26 in).

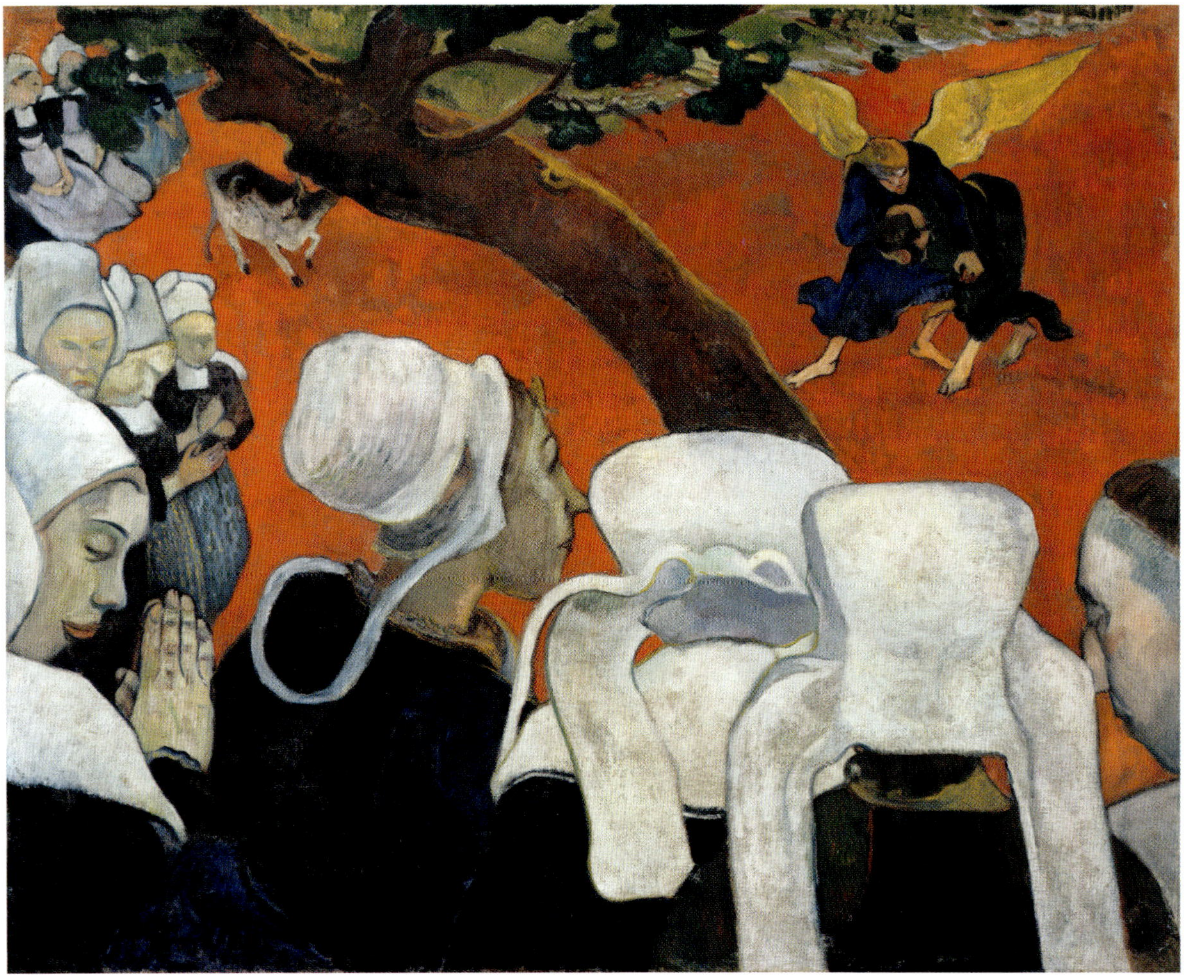

Setting a distance from the realism of Courbet and the impressionists, Vision After the Sermon *expresses the potential to find in the observable world a symbolic correspondence with the richness of our inner, spiritual lives.*

DREAM AND SYMBOL

Like Claude Monet, who began buying Japanese works in his teens and owned nine prints from Hokusai's series Thirty-six Views of Mount Fuji, the French post-impressionst artist Paul Gauguin was also a keen collector. 'Look at the Japanese', he wrote, 'who certainly draw admirably and you will see life in the outdoors and sunlight without shadows, using colour only as a combination of tones.'[1] In his own work, however, Gauguin was as concerned with his inner life as with the world under observation.

Offering some advice in a letter written in the summer of 1888, he cautioned, 'do not paint too much after nature'. Far from being a faithful rendition of a scene, art must always be an abstraction. 'Derive this abstraction from nature', he wrote, 'while dreaming before it'.[2] This was at the time in which Sigmund Freud was beginning his researches into dreams and the unconscious. The results of this research, published in 1900 as *The Interpretation of Dreams*, explore in depth the interrelationships between waking reality and the dream world. Gauguin's approach, which was closely aligned with similar interests among the symbolist poets in France, was to find a painterly means of bridging or linking the inner and the external world. Japanese art offered a way of synthesizing these twin realities through greatly simplified formal means. In the same year Van Gogh was in Arles painting *The Bedroom* (see pages 38–9), Gauguin made *Vision After the Sermon (Jacob Wrestling with the Angel).*

The rectangle of the picture is divided in two by the broad diagonal of the tree trunk, running from top left to bottom right and separating the white Breton bonnets of the onlooking women from Jacob and his antagonist. The composition thus presents two distinct realms: on the one hand, those of a real world in which the women exist, and on the other, an imaginative dreamscape in which the vision prompted by the sermon they have just witnessed plays itself out. They are distinct but united by the uniform red ground upon which all of the action, both real and imagined, takes place.

In terms of the flattening space, the juxtaposition rather than the mixing of colour, the banishment of any use of shadow, and the observation of nature, Gauguin shares much with the impressionists and the expressive post-impressionism of Van Gogh. For Gauguin, though, the impressionists retained 'the shackles of verisimilitude'.[3] As *Vision After the Sermon* already shows, no composition could achieve the creation of what the Belgian symbolist poet and critic André Fontainas, writing of Gauguin, called 'brooding wellsprings of surging emotion'[4] without acknowledging the productive power of one's dreamworld.

Poet Jean Moréas wrote in his 1886 'Manifesto of Symbolism' of a 'new vocabulary in which harmony is combined with colour and line'.[5] The rich interplay between the different sensory modes through which we apprehend the world suggested here by Moréas was certainly of interest to Gauguin. He asked us to consider 'the musical role colour will henceforth play in modern painting', and he wrote: 'amid the intoxicating perfumes of nature I dream of violent harmonies'.[6] This bringing together of sound, scent and colour echoes a line from Charles Baudelaire's poem 'Correspondances': '*Les parfums, les couleurs et les sons se répondent*'. (The perfumes, colours and sounds respond as one.) In the poem, Baudelaire speaks of nature as an environment where we proceed as through a 'forest of symbols'.[7] In setting a distance from the realism of Courbet and the impressionists, *Vision After the Sermon* expresses the potential to find in the observable world a symbolic correspondence with the richness of our inner, spiritual lives.

OPPOSITE: Paul Gauguin, *Vision After the Sermon (Jacob wrestling with the Angel)*, 1888. Oil on canvas, 72.2 cm × 91cm (28½ × 35⅞ in).

EXPRESSION

In *Self-Portrait with a Camellia Branch*, the German expressionist painter Paula Modersohn-Becker holds the branch of a camellia between thumb and index finger, up against her chest. Its centrally placed stem emphasizes the verticality of the unusually proportioned composition, while the leaves fan out to either side. Her head, which looks straight out at us, is framed by the pale blue-green background, with darker lines running through suggesting a curtain or drape. These lines extend down the canvas through the edges of her open cardigan/shirt. This has the effect of making the format even more tightly constrained.

The head is isolated by a large-beaded necklace that hugs her neck. Modersohn-Becker's use of colour and the development of a direct expressiveness through simplicity of form had been influenced by Paul Cézanne and Paul Gauguin, but she had also been studying the Egyptian collections in the Louvre, and *Self-Portrait with a Camellia Branch* acknowledges the Fayum portraits: images of the deceased placed on the breast of the mummy before burial. The Fayum portraits date from the Roman occupation of Egypt in the early centuries of the Common Era. Often cropped close in on the face, Modersohn-Becker appreciated the degree to which these formally simple and direct portraits could convey their subject's essential qualities. Writing of the influence of these portraits on *Self-Portrait with a Camellia Branch*, critic Anna McNay explained that they exemplify 'her tendency for tight cropping and framing, a technique that encourages the viewer to concentrate on the impassive, intense gaze, devoid of narrative or context'.[1] For Modersohn-Becker, 'feeling what I am experiencing inside is so much more valuable and important than what goes on outside'.[2]

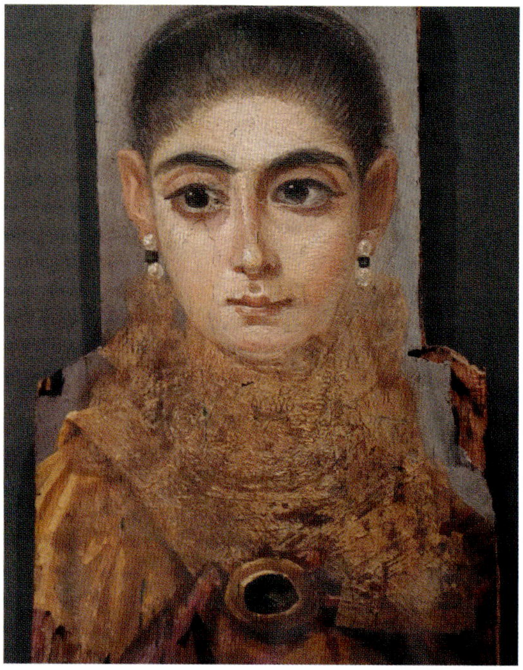

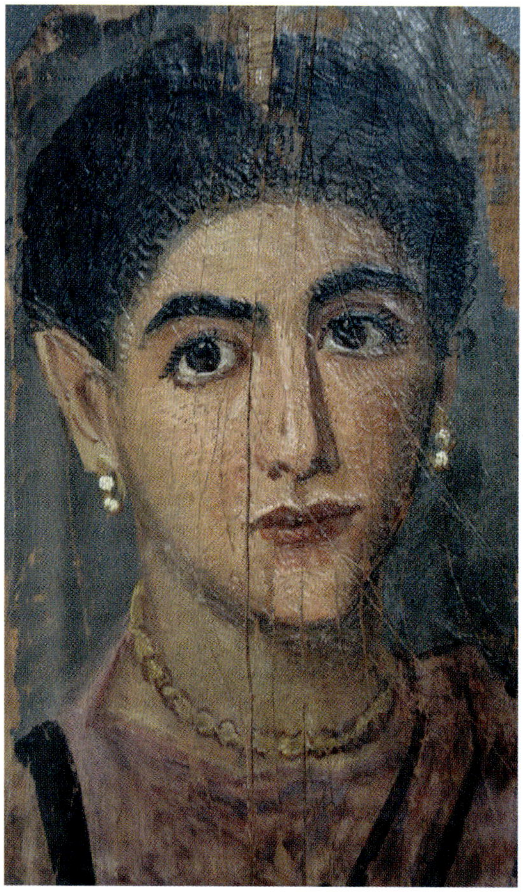

RIGHT, TOP AND BOTTOM: Portraits of young women from El Fayum. Encaustic painting on wood. Top *c.*160 CE 42.5 × 30 cm (16¾ × 11⅞ in) / bottom *c.*150–160 CE, 33 × 20 cm (13 × 7⅞ in).

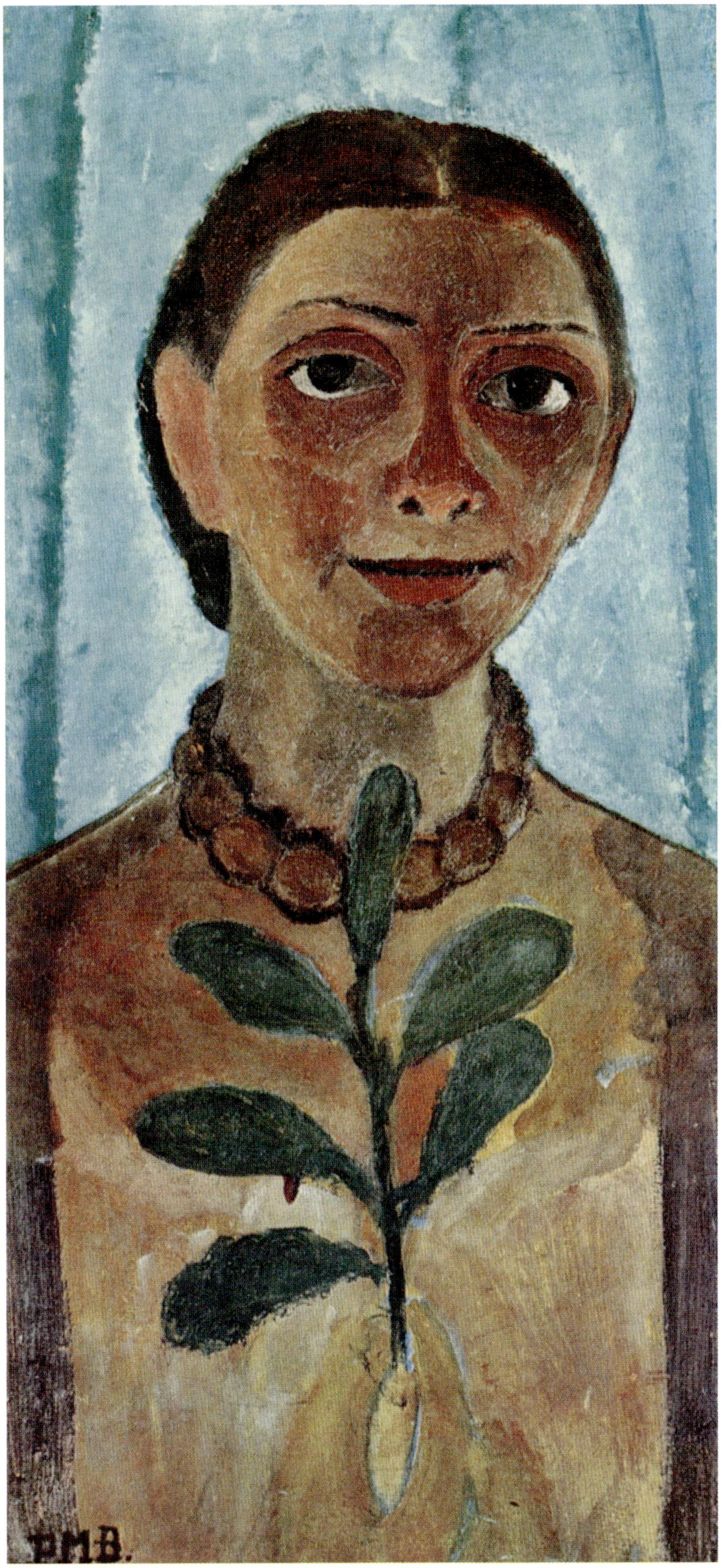

ABOVE: Paula Modersohn-Becker, *Self-Portrait with a Camellia Branch*, 1906–7. Oil on panel, 61.5 × 30.5 cm 24¼ × 12 in).

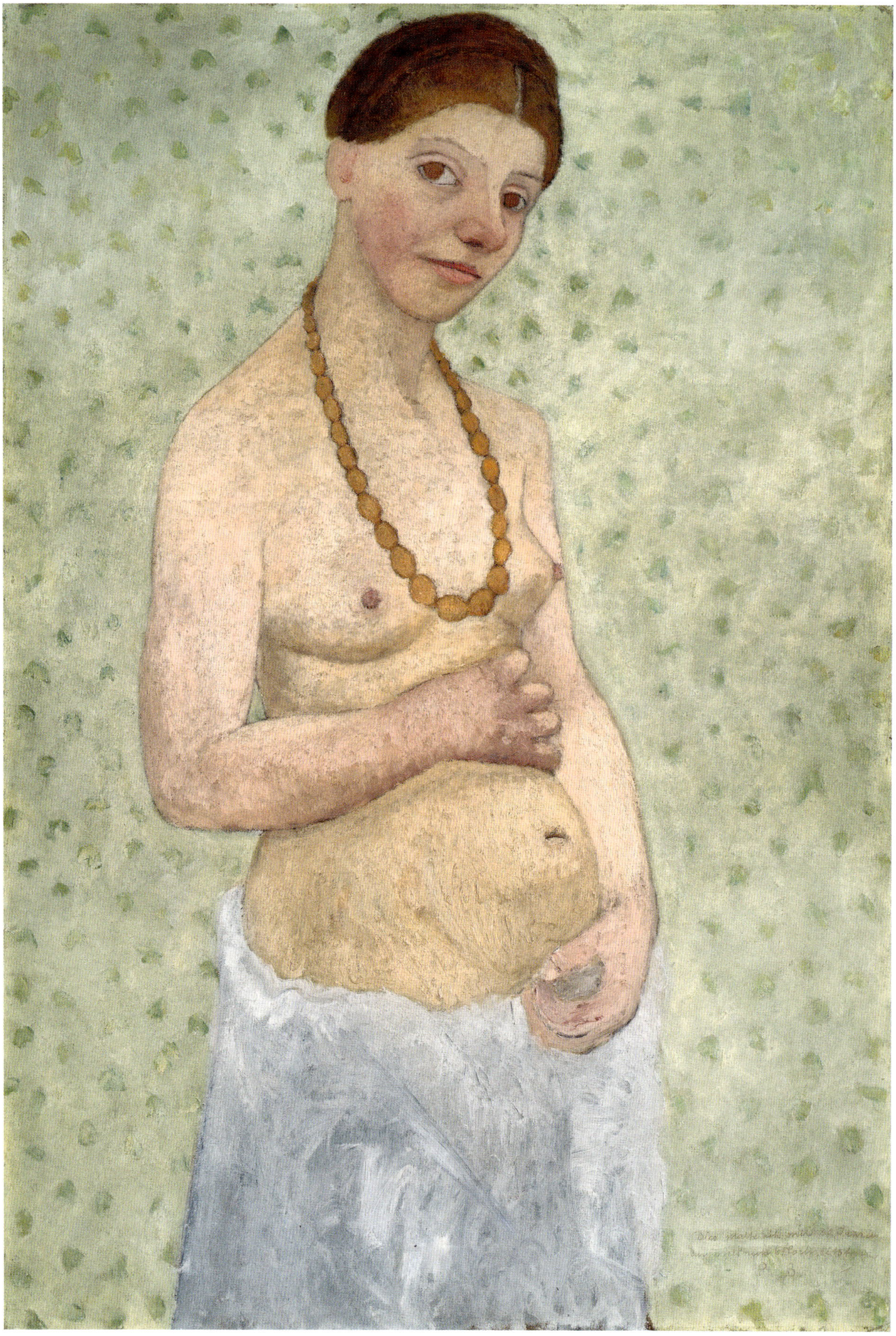

In 1906 she had left her husband, Otto Modersohn, in Worpswede, a village north of Bremen, Germany, and moved to Paris to concentrate on painting. In May of that year she painted a self-portrait in which she is seen against a stippled lemon-green background, standing in three-quarter profile but with her head tilted slightly and turned to gaze straight out at the viewer. A white cloth sits low on her hips, but she is otherwise naked apart from the amber necklace that loops down to hang between her breasts. Her right arm is held across her body under her breasts, while her left hangs down, the hand curling to gently cradle her belly. In some respects the composition is a traditional one, echoing as it does the pose of the suffering Christ seen, for example, in Lucas Cranach the Elder's *Ecce Homo* and a self-portrait drawing of the sick Albrecht Dürer in which he points to a wound in his side in imitation of Christ. Both of these artworks are located in Bremen, where Modersohn-Becker moved to when she was twelve, and almost certainly she would have known them.

However, over and above such reference to art historical precedents, there are two striking aspects to the painting. First, as stated, Modersohn-Becker shows herself naked, and second, from the full belly framed by her protective arms, she appears to be pregnant.

Modersohn-Becker inscribed the painting thus:

This I painted at age 30 on my 6th wedding day. P.B.

Modersohn-Becker was not, in fact, pregnant at the time of this painting. What she celebrates is her own possibility, both as a woman and as an artist. She had promised herself when only sixteen that she would have made of herself the artist she wanted to be by the time she was thirty. This portrait is the record of that achievement. The sixth wedding day is her fifth wedding anniversary, but she has signed it as Paula Becker, not under her married name (PMB) as she would do, for instance, in *Self-Portrait with a Camellia Branch*. *Self-Portrait on the Sixth Wedding Anniversary* is acknowledged as the first nude self-portrait by a woman in modern Western art. Painted as it is by someone who had parted from her husband in order to devote herself to art, it is a declaration of individuality and selfhood of remarkable assertiveness.

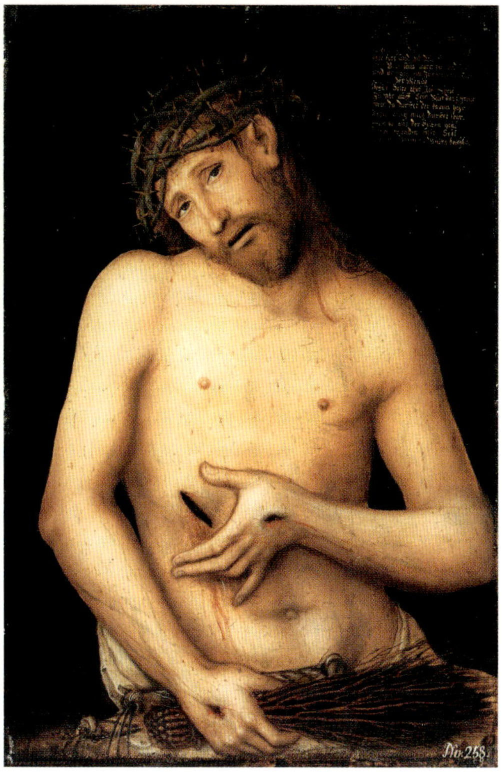

ABOVE: Lucas Cranach the Elder, *Ecce Homo, Christ as the Man of Sorrows*, *c.*1515. Tempera on panel, 51.2 × 34.5 cm (20⅛ × 13⅝ in).

Early in 1907 she returned to Worpswede and did, indeed, become pregnant. She gave birth in November that year and died shortly afterwards from post-partum complications. Rainer Maria Rilke, who visited Worpswede, was a close friend. The year after her death, he wrote 'Requiem for a Friend', which includes the lines:

And finally you saw yourself as fruit,
lifted yourself out of your clothes and carried
that self before the mirror, let it in
up to your gaze; which remained, large, in front,
and did not say: that's me; no, but: this is.[3]

OPPOSITE: Paula Modersohn-Becker, *Self-Portrait on the Sixth Wedding Anniversary*, 1906. Oil on canvas, 101.8 × 70.2 cm (40 × 27⅝ in).

Another, very different, self-portrait in which the artist's creativity is celebrated is the German Ernst Ludwig Kirchner's *Self-Portrait with Model.* A pipe-smoking Kirchner stands in the foreground wearing a boldly striped orange and blue dressing gown, its front partially open and revealing his bare legs and feet, suggesting that he is most likely naked underneath. The bright complementary colours and strong, simple pattern of the gown give a structural coherence to Kirchner's figure, which is effectively separated from the rest of the vivid-hued composition by a thick dark line surrounding the garment, and the complementary blue-orange gives way at only two points: the pink of his lips and the paintbrush – its bristles loaded with bright red pigment – held in his left hand and resting next to his groin. Kirchner faces towards us and away from the model seated behind him. Unlike Kirchner, her feet are shod. They are set slightly apart, but her thighs are together and held more securely so by the left hand reaching across to rest on her right knee. Art historian Frank Whitford describes the scene thus:

> *the frontal pose, the pipe and the young model almost cowering behind the masterful artist convey the impression of a robust bohemian life which for him (if not for the model) is enjoyable, relaxed, yet seriously creative.*[4]

Kirchner's feet, the palette held in his right hand and the top of his head are all cut off by the painting's edge, as if he considers the space simply too small to contain his overwhelming creative energy. The model is possibly Marzella Sprentzel, one of his favourites at the time. Another was Lena Franziska (Fränzi) Fehrmann, who is depicted in *Fränzi in Front of a Carved Chair*, made in 1910, the same year Kirchner originally painted his *Self-Portrait.* The rough brushwork in strong colours, the unnaturalistic tones – particularly the green of Fränzi's face next to the flesh pink of the chair – the inclusion of a carved object, and the unapologetic use of dark line to outline shapes and forms show a mixture of influences.

Kirchner was a dedicated promoter of his own work. A central figure in the Dresden artistic community the Brücke, founded in 1905, he wrote a chronicle of the group in which his own contributions to German expressionism are highlighted while those of fellow artists, particularly Max Pechstein and Erich Heckel, are somewhat downplayed. Later, he even invented a French critic, Louis de Marsalle, under which pseudonym he wrote and published six articles on his drawings, prints, sculptures and paintings from 1920–33. Anxious throughout his career to emphasize his originality, the connection of his work to essentially German traditions of high and vernacular art, and the absence in it of any significant debt to French art, a work such as *Fränzi in Front of a Carved Chair* nonetheless shows influence from the post-impressionism of Van Gogh, Gauguin and Edvard Munch, the colour palette of Henri Matisse and the fauves, African carvings, and woodcuts from both the high Renaissance in Germany and of popular culture.

Fränzi in Front of a Carved Chair and *Self-Portrait with Model* indicate two particularly problematic issues and attitudes. The first of these is the idea of 'primitivism'. The Brücke group took their name, meaning 'the bridge', from the statement in Friedrich Nietzsche's *Also Sprach Zarathustra* that 'what is great in man is that he is a bridge and not a goal'.[5] The bridge, 'a rope over the abyss', reaches from 'animal to Superman'.[6] At this time, African art was identified from within a Western colonialist mindset as 'primitive' work, regardless of the manifest skill of its makers and the unparalleled expressive quality of its forms. The attitude was pervasive and tenaciously held, so much so that even three-quarters of a century later, in 1984, the Museum of Modern Art in New York organized an exhibition entitled *'Primitivism' and Modern Art: Affinities of the Tribal and the Modern.*[7]

The second problematic issue is one of sexuality. In contrast to Modersohn-Becker's image of autonomy, independence and fecundity, Kirchner's male potency alone is expressed and, it seems, in relation to the female model whose own agency is compromised. A further aspect to the problem is that at the time these paintings were made Marzella was only fourteen and Fränzi ten. The aims of the Brücke, written by Kirchner, originally appeared on a woodcut print. The second of its three sentences states: 'As youth, we carry the future and want to create for ourselves freedom of life and of movement against the long established older forces.'[8] However proper or improper the relationships between these girls and Kirchner may have been – and this remains a matter of debate among scholars of the movement – it is nonetheless the case that their 'freedom of life' was found in, and perhaps at the expense of, the childhood innocence of others.

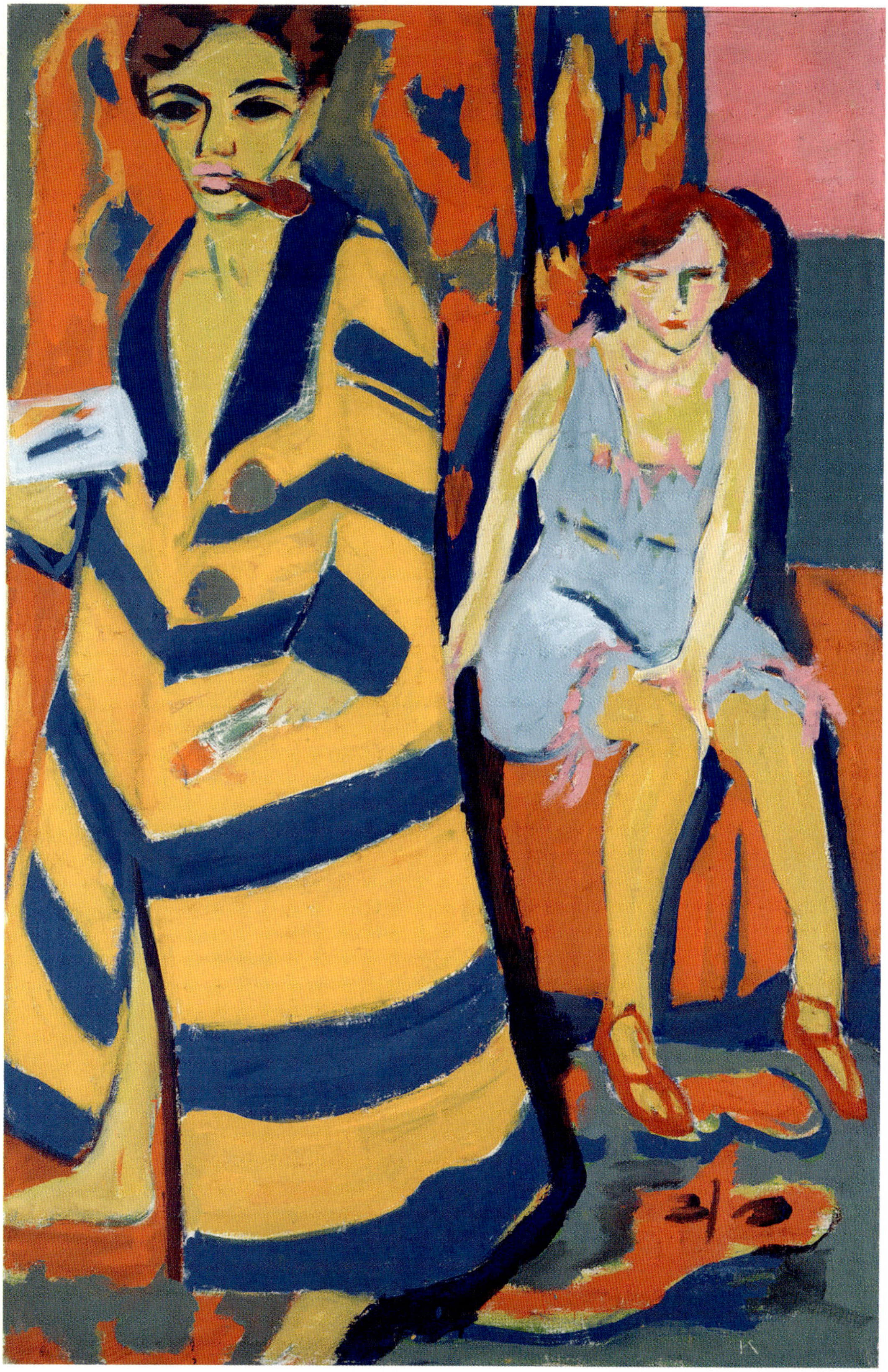

ABOVE: Ernst Ludwig Kirchner, *Self-Portrait with Model*, 1910 and 1926. Oil on canvas, 150.4 × 100 cm ($59^{1}/_{4}$ × $39^{3}/_{8}$ in).

OPTICAL COLOUR

***Le Chahut* – literally 'din' or 'pandemonium' – is another name for the cancan dance. The painting, by the French post-impressionist Georges Seurat, shows a line of alternating female and male dancers on stage performing their routine. In the foreground, his back up against the picture plane, is the bassist in the orchestra. To his left we can see the instrument and hands of the band's flautist, and the face and baton-wielding right arm of the conductor. To the bassist's right, an audience member looks admiringly up at the stage. The dancers are moving in unison, left legs on the ground and right legs aloft.**

Everything in this painting takes us upwards. The flying tassels on the shoes and shoulders of the women, the upswept moustache and coat tails of the men, the lines of mouth, eyes and nose on all their upturned faces, the conductor's baton, the flautist's fingers, the neck of the bass fiddle as it continues the diagonal begun in the player's right arm, the sweep of the dancer's skirt, caught up by a hand that also holds a closed fan: all of these details move our eye from the bottom of the canvas up the plane of the picture to the row of lights framed by the gentle curve of the proscenium running across its top edge.

The French poet and art critic Guillaume Apollinaire saw *Le Chahut* as 'a ballet full of grace, lyricism and good sense', and he described its painter, Seurat, as 'the founder and architect' of the 'elegant and modern city of neo-impressionism'.[1] As the name of the movement implies, it owes much to impressionism, especially in its continued emphasis on establishing visual effect through relationships between contrasting areas of pure colour. As Apollinaire's words suggest, however, Seurat's ambition was to find a set of principles by which this approach might be more rationally established. His pointillist technique, which juxtaposed dots of pure colour next to one another, was part of a careful, studio-based process of composition that necessarily moved his work away from the intuitive immediacy and *en plein air* practices of that group.

As well as engaging with key contemporary thinkers on colour such as Ogden Rood and Michel Eugène Chevreul (see overleaf), Seurat was also influenced by Charles Henry's theory on the ability of the line to convey emotion. A French mathematician and physiologist–psychologist who had developed theories of scientific aesthetics, Henry's essential idea, that lines directed upwards and to the right signified feelings of pleasure, and those moving down and to the left projected a more sombre mood, can be seen at work in *Le Chahut*. It is unquestionably a scene of enjoyment, but the gaiety comes courtesy of the frantic artificiality of urban entertainment. Seurat's use of Henry's pseudo-scientific ideas is satirical and ironic.

Seurat's meticulous compositional rigour was *sui generis*. He himself died young, and his stylistic experimentation did not develop further. This is not the case for divisionism more generally, which was important in a number of tendencies in the late nineteenth and early twentieth centuries, including symbolism, futurism and simultanism.

Rather than using paint mixed on the palette before application, the juxtaposition of small dots or lines of complementary pure colours allows mixing to occur in the eye.

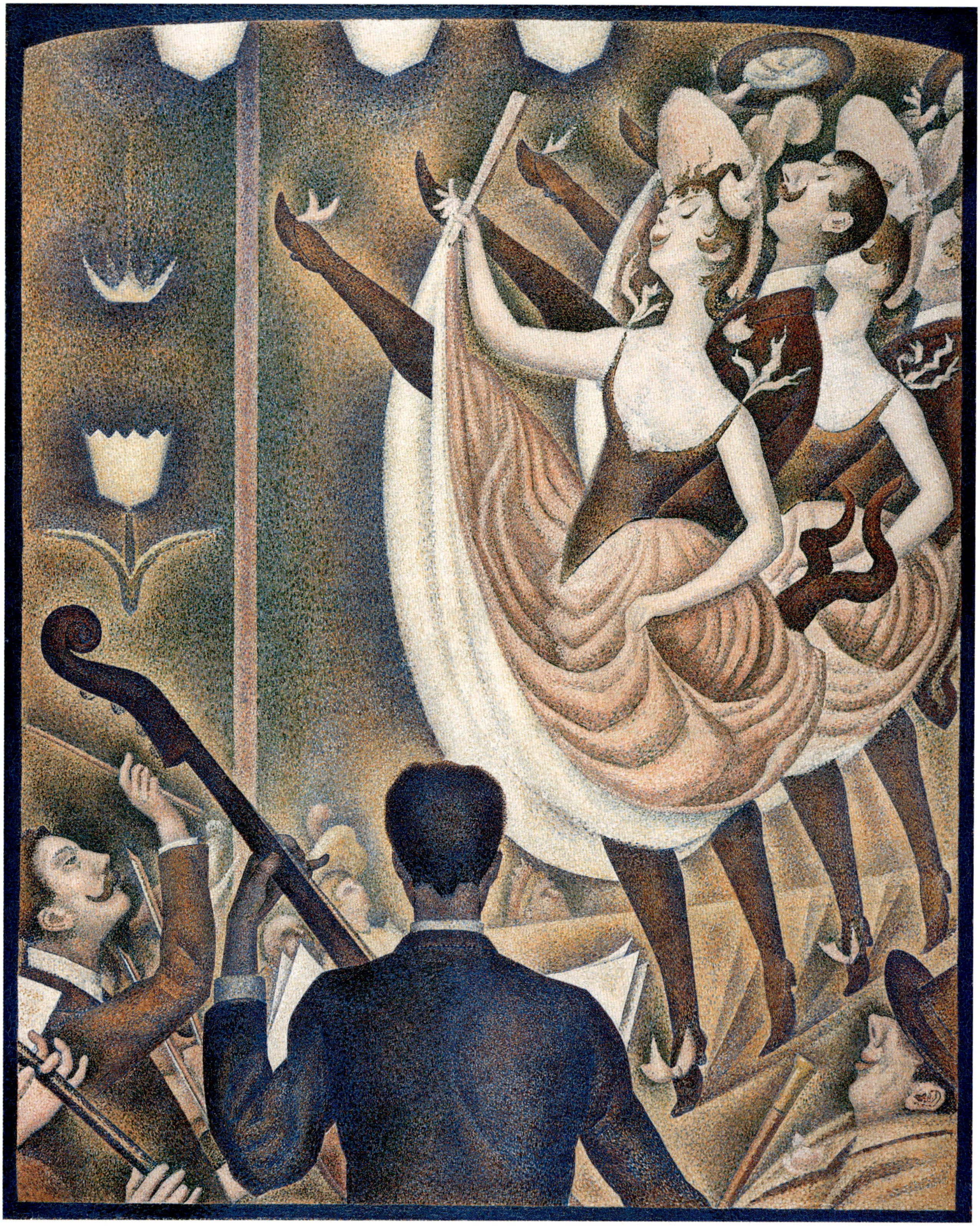

ABOVE: Georges Seurat, *Le Chahut*, 1889–90. Oil on canvas, 170 × 141 cm (67 × 55½ in).

HARMONIOUS CONTRAST

The French chemist Michel Eugène Chevreul wrote the influential book *De la loi du contraste simultané des couleurs (On the law of the simulaneous contrast of colours)*, which was first published in 1839, and further editions issued over the following decades. Accompanying it was an atlas of illustrations demonstrating his theories on the ways in which our perception of a particular colour is affected by the background on which it is set and the adjacent colours against which it is juxtaposed.

Chevreul outlines two systems of painting. The first of these is naturalistic representation, in which an object is modelled on a flat surface in such a way that the image 'makes an impression upon the eye of the spectator similar to that produced by the object itself'.[2] This method, with its reliance on the use of light and shade to indicate surface and volume, he calls chiaroscuro (from the Italian for light/dark), a term familiar since the Renaissance and used in particular in reference to the work of seventeenth-century painters such as Caravaggio and Rembrandt.

The second method, 'painting in flat tints', is seen by Chevreul as 'much simpler in its facility of execution':

> *It consists in tracing the outline of the different parts of the model, and in colouring them uniformly with their peculiar colours. There is no relief, no projections; it is the plane image of the object, since all the parts receive a uniform tint.*[3]

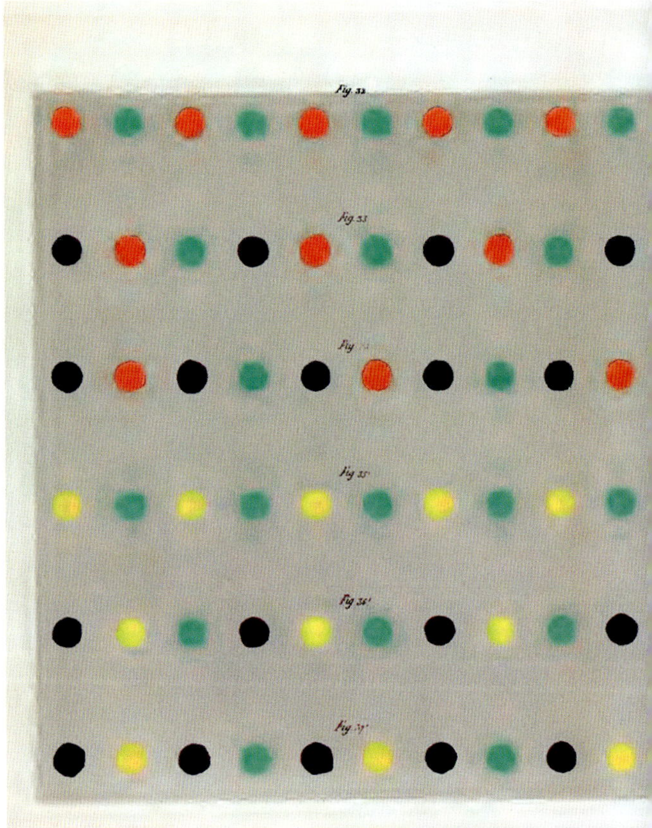

ABOVE: Michel Eugène Chevreul, colour contrast diagram from *De la loi du contraste simultane des couleurs et de l'assortiment des objets colore*, 1839.

In painting done by this method, there is no shading or blending together of colours, nor is the colour of an object altered in order to take account of how it might appear in a certain light. Because there is no reliance on tonality, each colour is vivid, and the 'simultaneous contrast' between two colours placed next to one another is as strong as possible.

Although the method of painting with flat tints is one that preceded the use of chiaroscuro to model form, Chevreul's insistence that this is no reason to consider it inferior lent theoretical support to artists in their exploration of ways in which best to represent both the external realities of their urban existence and the emotional and spiritual character of their inner lives. In painting, the theory of optical vibration derived from the use of flat tints and of the simultaneous contrast between two distinct juxtaposed areas of pure colour was termed divisionism. The technique of its application that we find in Seurat's studied application of Chevreul's ideas is referred to as pointillism. In his development of this technique, Seurat was also influenced by further work in this area by Ogden Rood, as laid out in his 1879 book *Modern Chromatics*. In more general terms, the significance of simultaneous contrast is evident in impressionism, in the post-impressionism of Van Gogh, in the symbolism of Gauguin, Maurice Denis and others, and in the efforts to represent movement and dynamism by the futurists. Specifically, too, we find Robert Delaunay's later systematic reading of Chevreul reflected in the name he chose for his own approach to painting: simultanism.

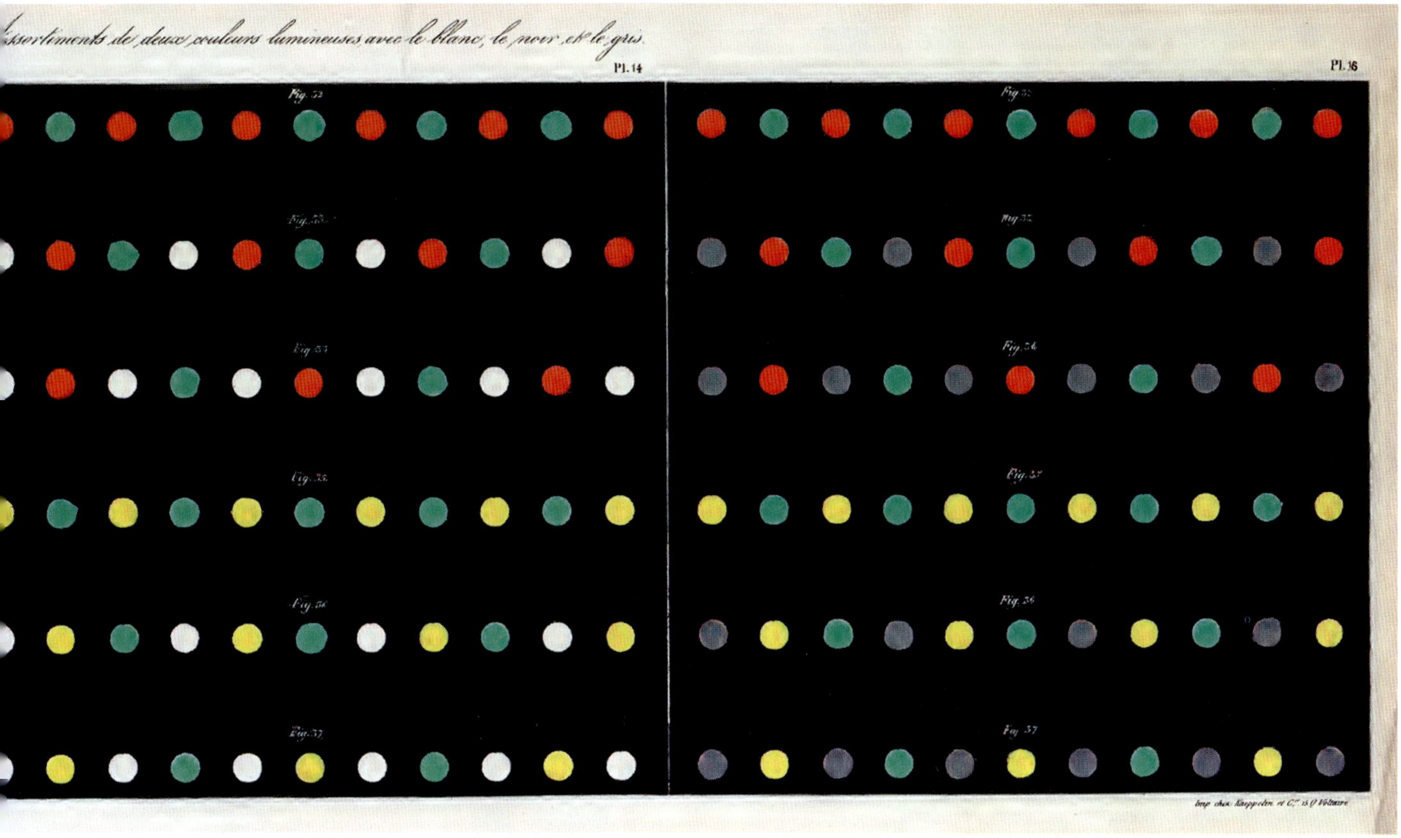

Because there is no reliance on tonality, each colour is vivid, and the 'simultaneous contrast' between two colours placed next to one another is as strong as possible.

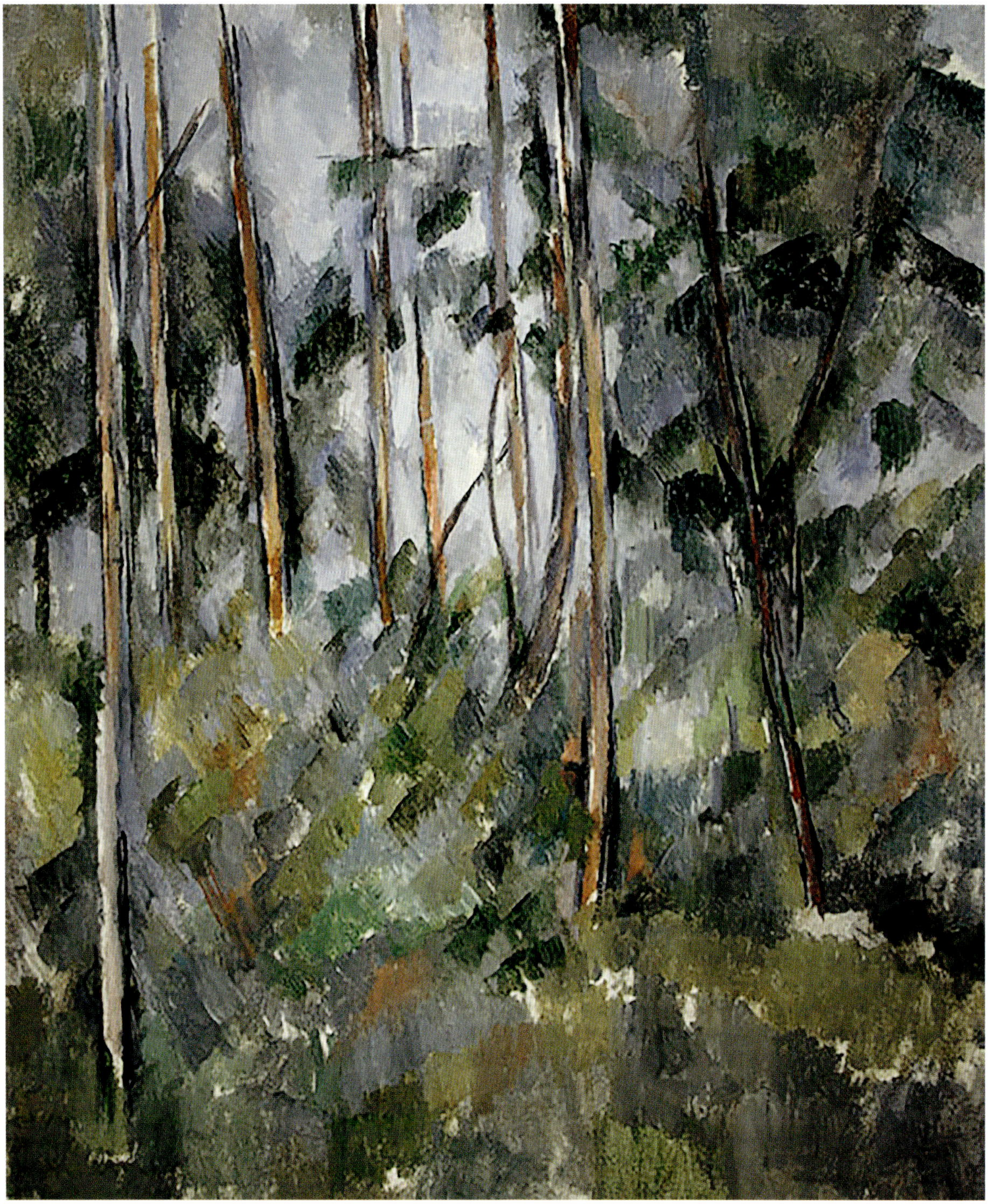

ABOVE: Paul Cézanne, *Sous Bois*, 1897–8. Oil on canvas, 54.4 × 46 cm. (21⅜ × 18⅛ in).

AFTER NATURE

In an essay on the French artist Paul Cézanne, published the year after his death, the painter and theorist Maurice Denis wrote that 'however much one admires Manet's *La Serre* ... the pictures of Cézanne seem like works of another period, no less refined but more robust than the most vigorous efforts of the impressionists'.[1] Cézanne himself had also noted that he wanted 'to make of impressionism something solid and durable', as solid and durable as the works to be found in the museums. But while the Louvre may be 'a good book to consult', to do so could only be a first step since 'the real and immense study to be undertaken is the manifold picture of nature'.[2] In a letter to his friend, the painter and critic Émile Bernard, he wrote:

> *Lines parallel to the horizon give breadth ... Lines perpendicular to this horizon give depth. But nature for us men is more depth than surface, whence the need to introduce into our light vibrations, represented by the reds and yellows, a sufficient amount of blueness to give the feel of air.*[3]

The lines of the tree trunks in *Sous Bois* reach the top edge of the canvas but extend down at varying lengths. The two longest – the one on the left and the one just to the right of the centre of the composition – establish a foreground, while the gentle arc of those in between these two is sufficient to bring that depth to the scene of which Cézanne speaks. Brushstrokes in varying greens, blues and reds describe undergrowth, foliage, sky and, importantly, that 'feel of air' – that sense in the body of the viewer of the spatial fullness of the woodland scene.

The light does not come from an external source – which is to say it is not lit by sunlight falling on it from one or other direction – but arises from the visual vibrations between adjacent strokes of differing colour laid on the white of the canvas. Cézanne has not completely covered the picture surface but instead, here and there, has left small patches of bare canvas visible. He acknowledged that this might give his paintings the appearance of being 'incomplete', but it was the necessary result of pursuing those 'sensations of colour which give the light'.[4]

As a consequence of his approach, Cézanne's paint marks do not attach themselves to specific objects, they do not perform the task of describing this or that aspect of a scene to the exclusion of contributing ambiguously to a more general sensation of light, space and material presence. Explaining this to Denis he said, 'there is no such thing as line, no such thing as modelling, there are only contrasts. When colour attains its richness, form attains its plenitude.'[5]

Brushstrokes [describe] that sense in the body of the viewer of the spatial fullness of the woodland scene.

At first sight it might appear that *The Basket of Apples* has similar distortions of perspective to those in Van Gogh's *The Bedroom* (see page 38). The basket in the upper left of the painting is 'tipped up', almost suggesting that the fruit spread across the table has spilled out, and we can see more of the top two rolls on the neat stack at the back of the table on the right than might be expected. But in this case there is no interest in a Japanese-inspired flattening. The folds in the cloth draped over the front of the table provide areas of light and shade, and the darker blue-grey brushstrokes on the tabletop to the right imply the casting of shadows due to the light falling from behind the viewer's left shoulder. Each fruit is identifiably distinct but does not have the precision of outline that would fix it as something seen from a single, static viewpoint. The philosopher Maurice Merleau-Ponty explained:

> *Not to indicate any shape would be to deprive the objects of their identity. To trace just a single outline sacrifices depth – that is, the dimension in which the thing is presented not as spread out before us but as an inexhaustible reality full of reserves. That is why Cézanne follows the swelling of the object in modulated colours and indicates several outlines in blue. Rebounding among these, one's glance captures a shape that emerges from among them all, just as it does in perception.*[6]

Furthermore, the rectangle of the tabletop is disjointed to a far greater extent than the seat in Manet's *La Serre*, as if the scene arranges itself anew within our perceptual field, depending on where we choose to direct our attention. Denis saw the impressionists' breaking up of the spectrum into its constituent parts in order to paint in pure colour as an essentially analytical approach to composition, and Cézanne's achievement of form through colour contrast as synthetic. The relationship between these two complementary procedures would reappear in a new context in the cubism that followed.

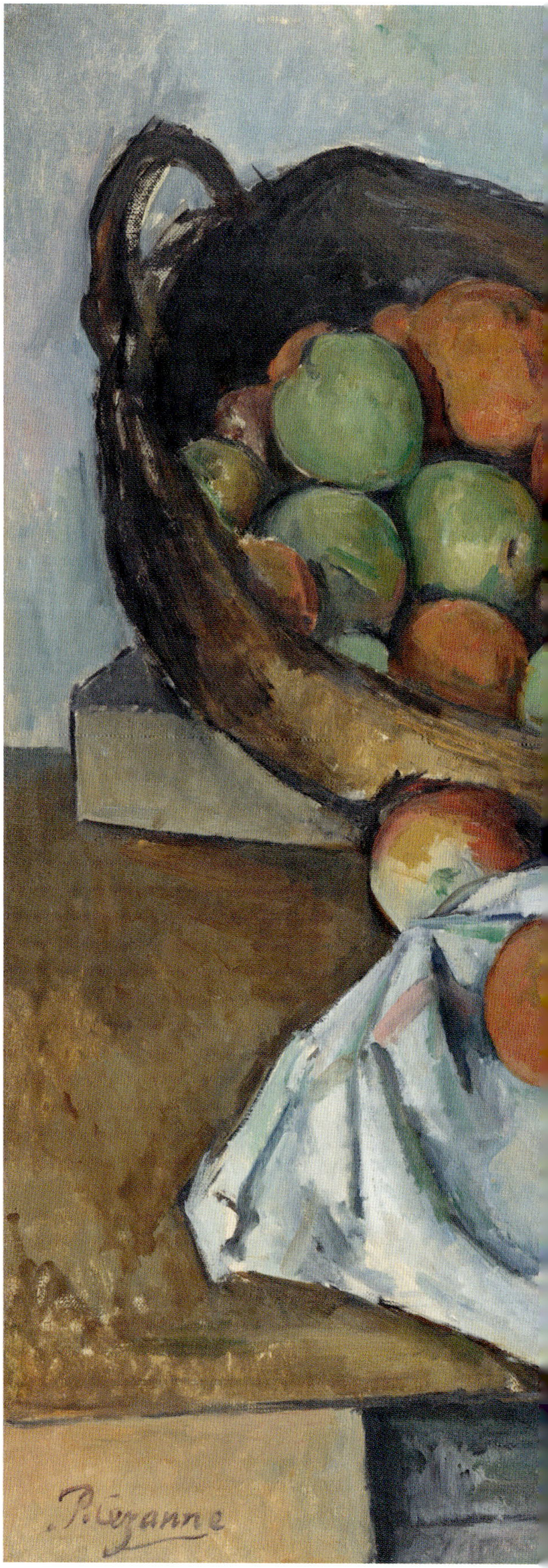

RIGHT: Paul Cézanne, *The Basket of Apples*, *c.*1893. Oil on canvas, 65 × 80 cm (25⅝ × 31½ in).

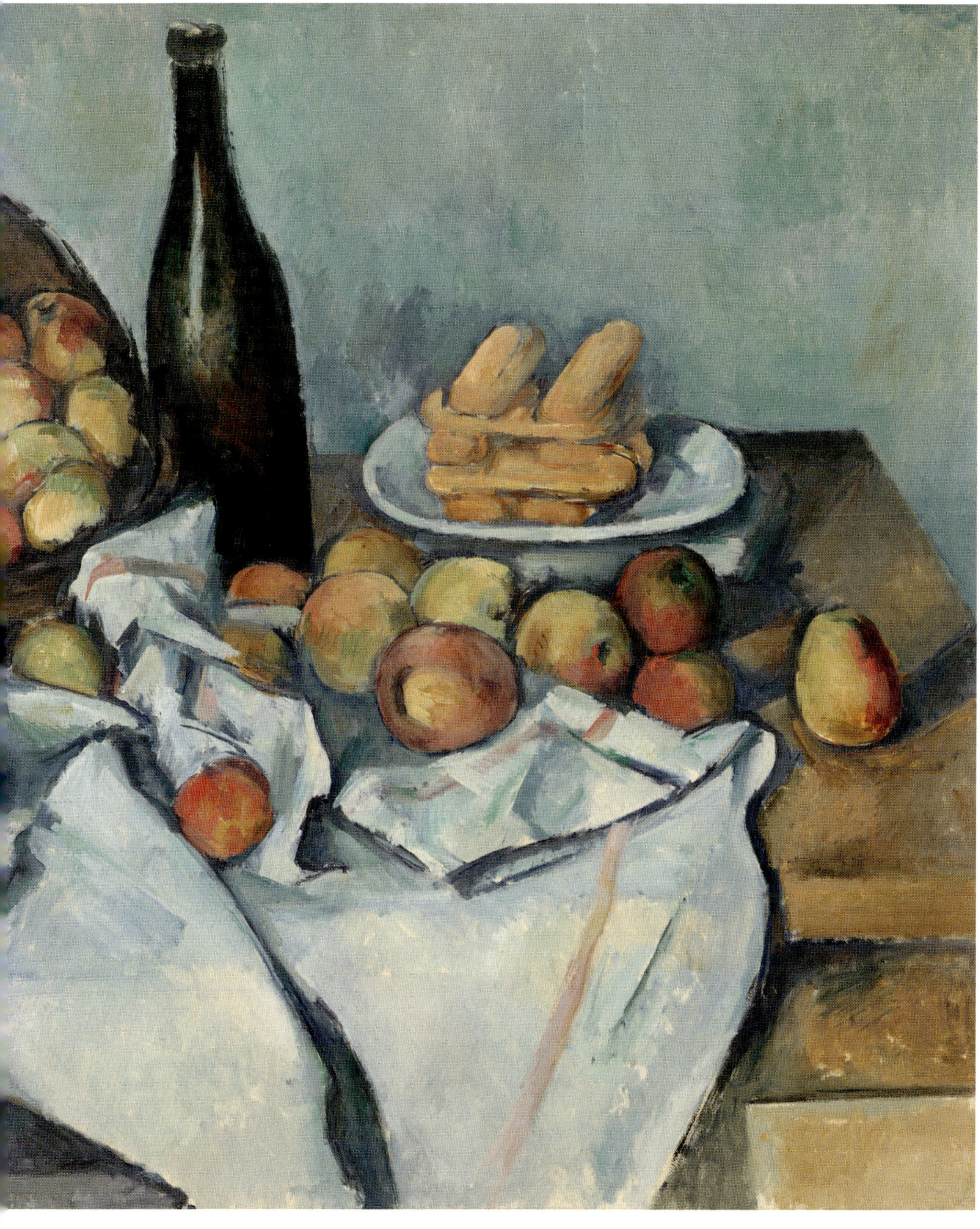

CHAPTER II:
A NEW REALITY

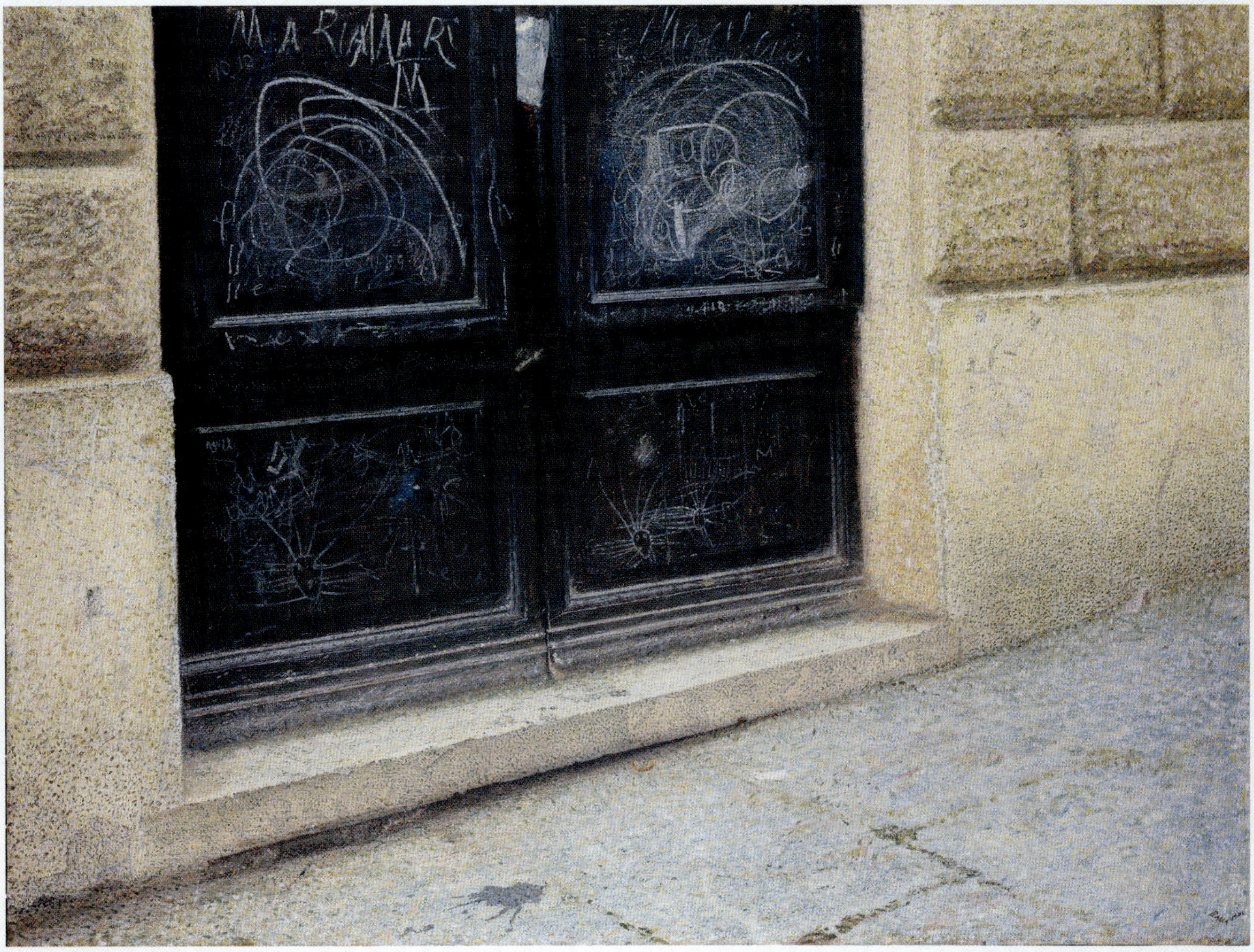

An early painting by the Italian futurist Giacomo Balla, called *Bankruptcy* (1902), shows the heavy double doors of a commercial establishment that have been closed and locked for the last time. Someone tried to deliver some final correspondence and, finding no one there, left it stuffed in the gap between these doors, and their dark surfaces became an ideal background upon which the inhabitants of the street could create their fantasies. Among these, a strange, ghostly death's head with weird rays shooting out in all directions has been drawn and redrawn. Abstract lines in white chalk curve repeatedly across two of the panels, describing nothing more than the bodily pleasure derived from the repetition of a sweeping gesture with the arm and hand. A girl's name – M A R I A, holy and pure but common, too – is fractured into its component letters and spread across the available space. On the pavement in front of the doors there is a dark stain, a splodge that looks as though someone has dropped a pot of ink and left the mess to dry rather than attempting to clear it up. The marks on the door and the pavement are, by turns, determined, intentional, idle, abusive, delicate, loving, indulgent, accidental, obsessive and much else besides. Above all, they are thrilling, and they are so because they bear witness to human presence. Something is over, but lots of other things have begun: the doors have closed and what is past lies in ruins, but this ruination is rich ground on which to go to work.

In considering this state of flux and promise, an intensification of that already identified by Charles Baudelaire and expressed in the works of the previous chapter, the historian Perry Anderson described modernism as a reality 'triangulated between three decisive co-ordinates'.[1] The first of these, a formalized academicism embedded in the structures of power against which artists could resist and from which they could assert independence, was a well-established factor in the compositional innovations of the nineteenth century. The second, a rapid emergence of new technologies, had a profound shaping role in the twentieth century. A world seen while walking or on horseback is not the world seen from a bus, train or motor car. A world viewed at ground level is not the world seen from an aeroplane several hundred feet up in the air. A discussion between two people in a room is not a discussion held at long distance over the telephone. An event witnessed at first hand is not a description and analysis of that event broadcast over the radio or read in a mass-circulation magazine.

The third of Anderson's coordinates is the 'imaginative proximity of social revolution'.[2] We might immediately think of the 1917 October Revolution in Russia, and the 1919 Spartacist Uprising in Germany, but the character of potential change in this period is far-reaching. Balla was part of the futurist group in Italy, and in their founding manifesto statement the poet Filippo Tomaso Marinetti praised war as 'the world's only hygiene'.[3] The glorification of conflict as an efficient means to remove unwanted and outdated institutions lasts only until the conflict arrives. The First World War is a traumatic disjuncture, refiguring both the sociopolitical landscape and the imaginative and emotional inner world that must work to accommodate its implications. The many innovations in composition during these decades reflect the effort to make that accommodation.

OPPOSITE: Giacomo Balla, *Bankruptcy*, 1902. Oil on canvas, 116 × 160 cm (45⅝ × 63 in).

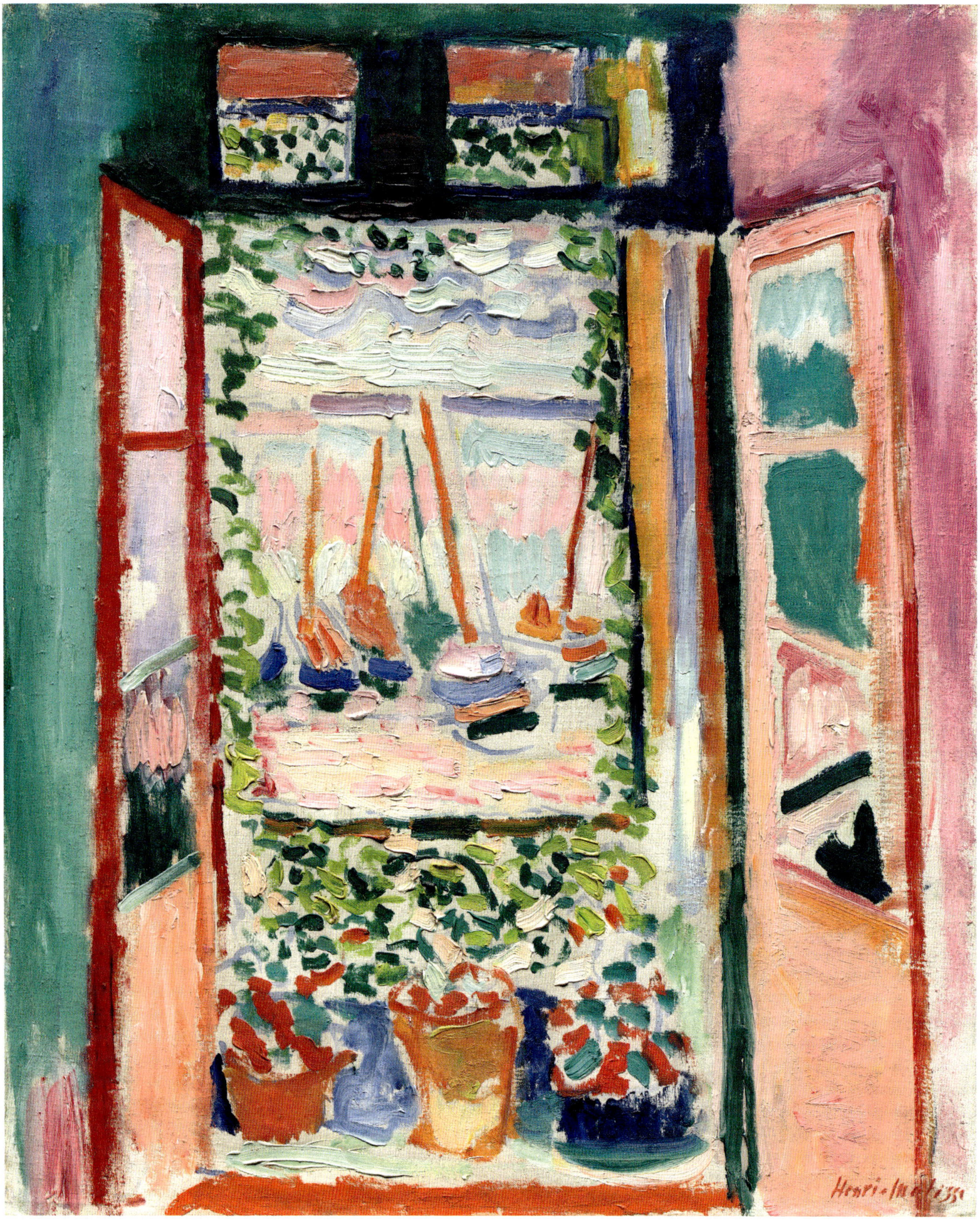

ABOVE: Henri Matisse, *Open Window, Collioure*, 1905. Oil on canvas, 55.3 × 46 cm (21¾ × 18⅛ in).

THE LAYERED FRAME

In his 'Notes of a Painter', the French artist Henri Matisse explained that it isn't in the emotion of a face or the violence of a gesture that we find expression. It is rather that 'the entire arrangement of my picture is expressive'. This conviction is what underpins the whole of his approach to composition:

> *Composition is the art of arranging in a decorative manner the diverse elements at the painter's command to express his feelings. In a picture every part will be visible and will play its appointed role, whether it be principal or secondary.*[1]

Open Window, Collioure was painted in the summer of 1905 and exhibited soon after at the Salon d'Automne in Paris in the same year. Half-glazed doors open onto a balcony, with plants in pots on the floor. Foliage twines through the railing and climbs up each side and across the top of the opening to form a second frame, through which the seascape beyond can be seen. Boats bob on the shoreline, their tilted masts making a loose screen in front of the sea. The thick purple line marking the horizon is broken in the middle, where the red mast of the nearest boat projects up through it. It is a nest of layered frames within frames: the rectangle of the canvas, the doorway and the balcony are the three main ones, but there are two skylights above the door, through which the ceiling and top edge of the balcony is visible. The two doors are themselves also frames, within which their three panes of glass reflect their surroundings in such a way that an additional column of abstract compositions provides a border to either side of the doorway. Again, in 'Notes of a Painter', Matisse expresses the view that precisely the thing that was of interest to the impressionists – the capturing of the sensations of a moment – was for him a sign of insufficiency:

> *A rapid rendering of a landscape represents only one moment of its existence. I prefer, by insisting upon its essential character, to risk losing charm in order to obtain greater stability.*[2]

Nonetheless the composition of *Open Window, Collioure* draws upon impressionism's innovations in the use of colour and its rejection of the modelling of space and depth through the use of shadow, as well as subsequent post-impressionist experimentations in flatness. The scene – in a literal realization of the time-honoured cliché of a painting as a window on the world – establishes a clear sequence of planes stepping back from the artist's viewpoint: room, balcony, beach, sea and horizon. But Matisse's use of colour and his handling of the paint both work against a simple reading of this spatial recession. The thinnest paint is the bands down the left and right edges of the canvas, the magenta, turquoise and green of the walls – the planes closest to us. By contrast, the blossom of the flowers on the balcony and, in particular, the clouds above the horizon are rendered in strokes and smudges of much thicker paint. In physical terms, the clouds, which are furthest away, are more prominent and project further from the canvas surface than anything else. The darker blues and greens of the window surrounds above the doors hold that area back, while the brighter red, orange and white details of the balcony on the far side shine through the window back into the room. In addition, there is red detail everywhere: the floor in the doorway, the flower blossoms, the door frames, the masts of the boats to right and centre of the picture, and the balcony ceiling, which holds the entire composition in its delicate network. In the composition as a whole, there are both smooth transitions and striking disjunctions of tone and hue. Explaining the colour relationships in his paintings, Matisse drew an analogy with musical composition. There, too, we find both harmony and dissonance, and recognize that it is as much in the resolution of the latter within the overall composition as in the direct appeal of the former that we experience enjoyment.

BUILDING A NEW REALITY

With Paul Cézanne we see clearly that a painting is a collection of marks on a surface. Furthermore, we begin to recognize that these marks can exist as much in and for themselves as they do for the purpose of representing something else in the world. We also see, after the impressionism and post-impressionism that would, in Paul Gauguin's words, 'do away with [shadows]', which are 'the trompe l'oeil of the sun',[1] that they appear again in Cézanne's compositions. What is built and given substance on the canvas surface is the space in which objects exist as much as the objects themselves.

This is equally true of cubism, the subsequent movement greatly influenced by Cézanne. In his book on the movement, Daniel-Henry Kahnweiler, the art dealer who exhibited cubism's two originators and primary proponents, the Spaniard Pablo Picasso and the Frenchman Georges Braque, wrote that the basic tasks of painting are 'to represent three dimensions and colour on a flat surface, and to comprehend them in the unity of that surface'.[2] This was not to be done by means of 'the simulation of form by chiaroscuro', or through 'pleasant composition', but in 'uncompromising, organically articulated structure'.[3]

In the stylistic experimentation of the preceding half-century, we witness a turning away from academic methods. Coupled with this is Maurice Denis's observation that before it is anything else, a picture is 'essentially a plane surface covered with colours assembled in a certain order'.[4] As disconcerting as those changes might have been, from the realism of Gustave Courbet to the vibrant colours and thickly applied paint of Matisse, the viewer was never left in doubt as to what the painting depicted. Faced with a cubist painting, however, the situation is more challenging. The French poet and art critic Guillaume Apollinaire wrote in his study of cubism that 'verisimilitude no longer has any importance'.[5] Instead of attempting to represent in some more or less adequate fashion a scene, object or person that existed in the world, the ambition was now to make something new through the act of painting since, as Apollinaire goes on to say, 'the artist sacrifices everything to the composition of his picture'.[6] The canvas provides a surface upon which a new reality is built.

In an echo of Maurice Denis's reference to the analytic and the synthetic aspects of painting in his theoretical writings, cubism is described as having two phases. In the first analytic phase, composition is focused on a visual disassembly of the subject – a person, collection of objects, a landscape – into its constituent planes, volumes and fragments of detail. In Picasso's *Portrait of Daniel-Henry Kahnweiler*, for example, we can see indications of the dealer's hair and facial features, clasped hands, and an adjacent bottle and fruit bowl set within a patchwork of interlocking and superimposed geometrical forms. In the latter, synthetic phase, these elements build into something independent of any pre-existing model in the world. The Spanish painter Juan Gris, associated most strongly with synthetic cubism, saw its earlier analytic phase as being primarily concerned with description. In describing his own synthetic approach, he said:

> *My aim is to create new objects which cannot be compared with any object in reality. The distinction between synthetic and analytical cubism lies precisely in this. These new objects, therefore, avoid distortion. My* Violin, *being a creation, need fear no comparison.*[7]

Braque's *Le Portugais*, painted in 1911, sits on the cusp between these two periods. Typically for cubism, and in contrast to the spectral range and strong hues of impressionism, post-impressionism and fauvism, Braque uses a severely restricted palette in order to avoid the possibility of optical vibration – which was so important to those earlier approaches – interfering with the painting's architectural structuring. The subject of the painting – the Portuguese referred to in the title – is a musician. The many small planes held within a strong overall pyramid anchored to the bottom edge of the canvas and reaching to the centre of its top edge allow us to construct for ourselves the figure of the guitar player and the café in which he is playing.

OPPOSITE AND OVERLEAF: Georges Braque, *Le Portugais*, 1911. Oil on canvas, 117 × 81.5 cm (46 × 32 in).

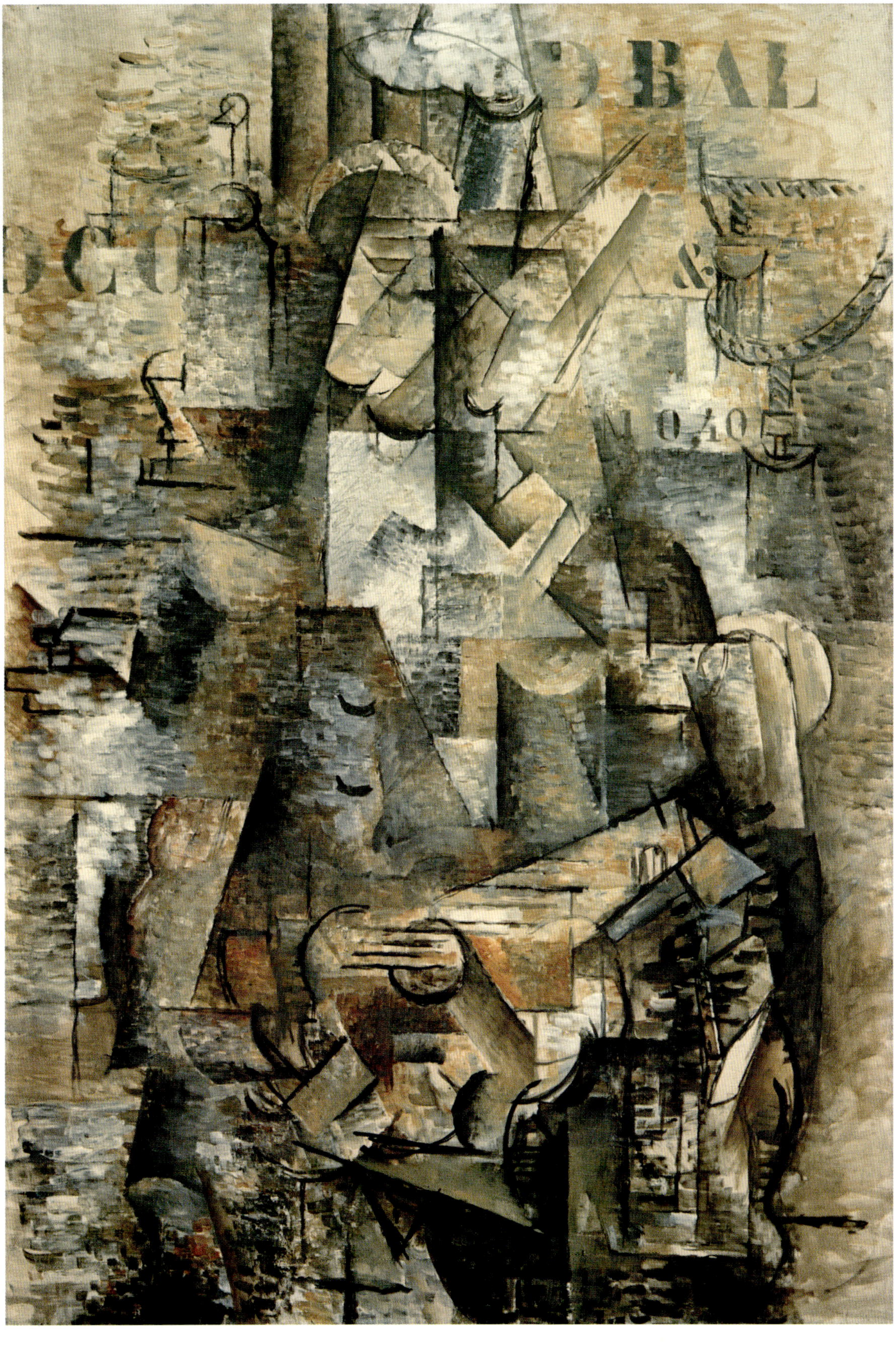
BAL
&
0,40

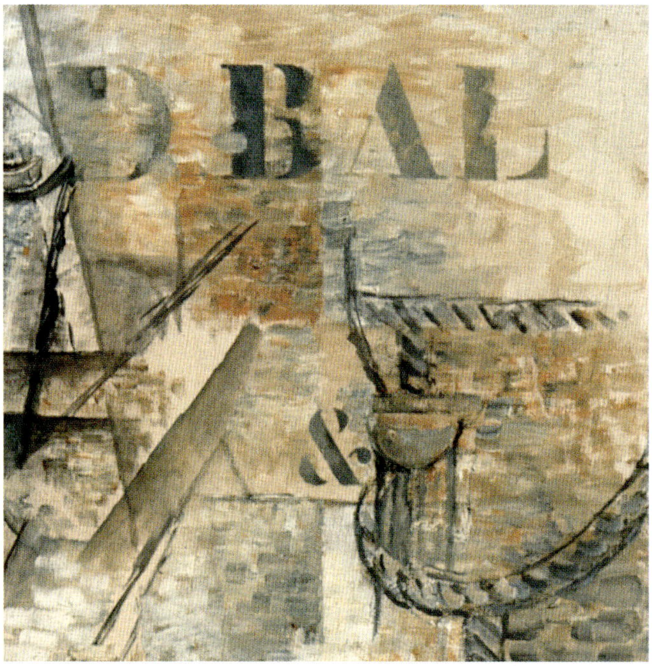

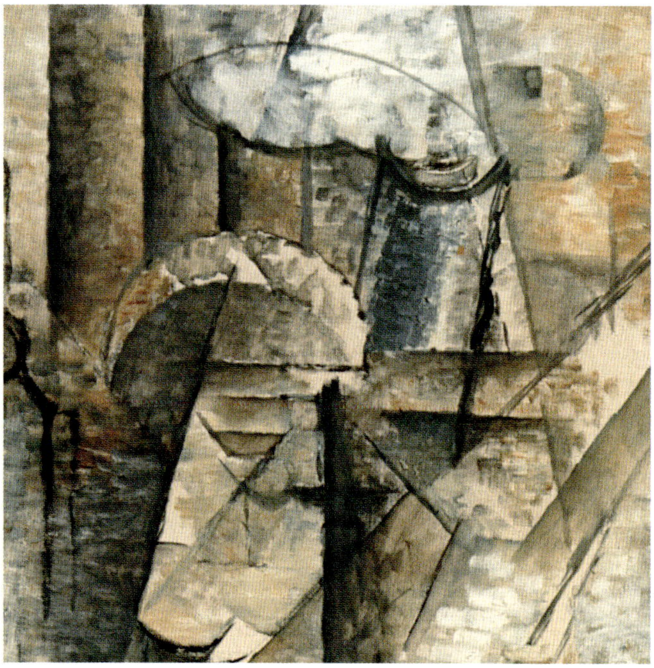

A combination of discs, curved areas and straight-edged planes give us his head, shoulders, torso and arms, while the shading along edges keeps each element sufficiently free from its neighbours to allow a sense of the man not as an image pinned down from a fixed viewpoint, but as someone existing in his own space. Details flesh out the scene: the sound hole and strings of the guitar sit at the lower centre of the composition, the tassel and rope of a curtain tie are to the upper right, while on the left there are bottles, perhaps on a shelf behind the bar.

From the fractured forms characteristic of cubist painting, we might infer that the movement constituted a deliberate step away from representational art towards abstraction. However, contrary to this idea, Braque understood his own work to be drawing on the exemplary realism of Courbet and Cézanne. 'As part of a desire to come as close as possible to a certain kind of reality', said Braque, 'in 1911 I introduced letters into my paintings'.[8] In the top right corner of *Le Portugais*, we can see four stencilled letters: D BAL.

In his 1909 painting *Violin and Palette*, Braque had painted a *trompe l'oeil* nail in the top of a canvas, complete with cast shadow, as a means to emphasize the independent reality of a painting as a created object. He would go on to use a house decorator's comb to produce a woodgrain effect, for example, in *Still Life with Playing Cards* (1913), but this first appearance of lettering is surprising, not least because of its clarity. The letters are real; they are themselves, not representations. They do not need to be fragmented or analyzed since, just like the canvas surface, they have only two dimensions. But then the letters in *Le Portugais* are also representations in that they are part of a poster on the café wall. This means that the musician's head, which – like the letters – is only paint on that same canvas surface, must be understood as sitting in front of the poster obscuring the letters GRAN. But there are other letters, too – OCO – as well as an ampersand and the numbers 10,40. These cannot be taken as arbitrarily placed marks, but as further elements within Braque's 'certain kind of reality'. We are on the pavement outside the café, looking through the window onto which the names of drinks (Chocolat, for example) and their prices have been stencilled.

Kahnweiler recalls that Braque and Picasso often referred to *'le tableau-objet'* when speaking of their work: the painting is as much an object as it is a picture.[9] The composition of *Le Portugais* repeatedly emphasizes the physical nature of the picture as paint on canvas, and at the same time builds, from the ground of the canvas, layer upon layer forward in its constitution of the three-dimensional scene.

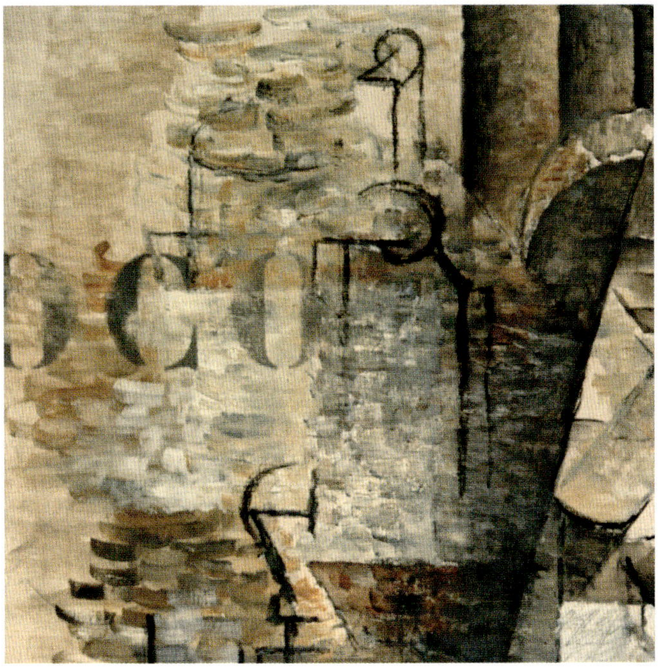 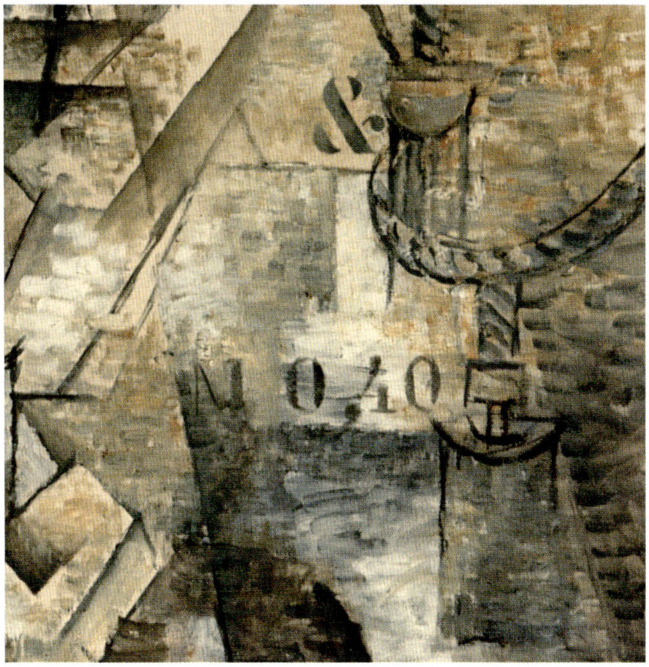

This first appearance of lettering is surprising … These cannot be taken as arbitrarily placed marks, but as further elements within Braque's 'certain kind of reality'.

THE DEATH OF TIME AND SPACE

In contrast to the restricted colour palette seen in the cubism of Pablo Picasso and Georges Braque, the Italian futurists championed the principles of divisionism and saw the optical vibrations produced by adjacent colours of different hue as the appropriate technique for representing 'the frenetic life of our great cities'.[1] In the 'Futurist Painting: Technical Manifesto', signed by Umberto Boccioni, Carlo Carrà, Luigi Russolo, Giacomo Balla and Gino Severini, the artists declared that an 'innate complementariness' was 'essential and necessary', and that 'painting cannot exist today without divisionism'.[2] This was written in 1910, before Boccioni encountered cubism and recognized the possibilities inherent in its fragmenting of forms. *The Street Enters the House*, from 1912, shows the fruits of this encounter.

This manifesto states: 'To paint a human figure you must not paint it; you must render the whole of its surrounding atmosphere.'[3] Here, a woman stands, leaning against the wrought iron railing of her balcony and looking down on the building site on the street outside. Whatever is being constructed – more accommodation for the city's growing population of workers, a new workshop – her neighbours on the left and right do the same. A forest of scaffold poles reaches up towards these onlookers while around and among them an army of labourers work on the foundations of the new building. The road reaches off into the distance at the top left of the canvas, where a cloud of factory smoke floats just inside the painting's top edge: 'Factories hung on clouds by the crooked lines of their smoke' is a line from 'The Manifesto of Futurism',[4] by F.T. Marinetti, the movement's founder. The facades of the buildings to the right, fractured into planes, curve over the scene, appearing at once both protective and threatening. The yellow earth of the street surface radiates across the front of the building nearest to us, and is also pulled over the back and arm of the watching woman. She is in her apartment as well as being in the street – and the street, in turn, is also in her. We sense through the reds, yellows, blues and purples that there is much noise and that this, too, spills into the apartment, filling it with shouts and hammer blows. Rather than the wet pavement, it is the woman's dark hair in the very centre of the composition that takes us deep into the earth. Here, again, is the 'Technical Manifesto':

> *Space no longer exists: the street pavement soaked by rain beneath the glare of electric lamps, becomes immensely deep and gapes to the very centre of the earth … Who can still believe in the opacity of bodies, since our sharpened and multiplied sensitiveness has already penetrated the obscure manifestations of the medium? Why should we forget in our creations the doubled power of our sight, capable of giving results analogous to those of the X-rays?*[5]

In writing these words, the artists echoed Marinetti's observation in his Manifesto that 'time and space died yesterday'.[6]

> *'To paint a human figure you must not paint it; you must render the whole of its surrounding atmosphere.'*
>
> **– Umberto Boccioni, 'Futurist Painting: Technical Manifesto', 1910**

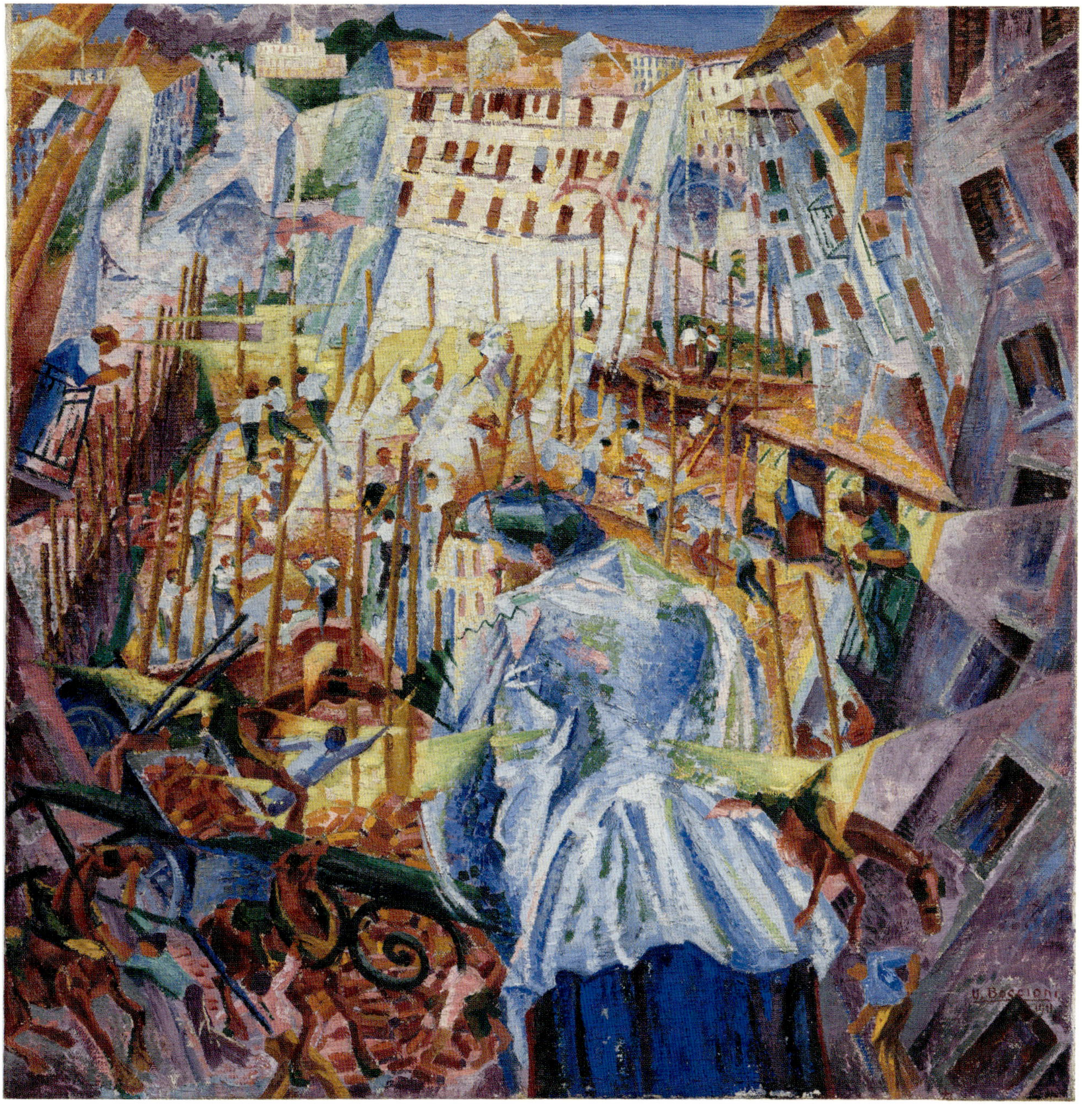

ABOVE: Umberto Boccioni, *The Street Enters the House*, 1911.
Oil on canvas, 100 × 100.6 cm ($39\frac{3}{8} \times 39\frac{5}{8}$ in).

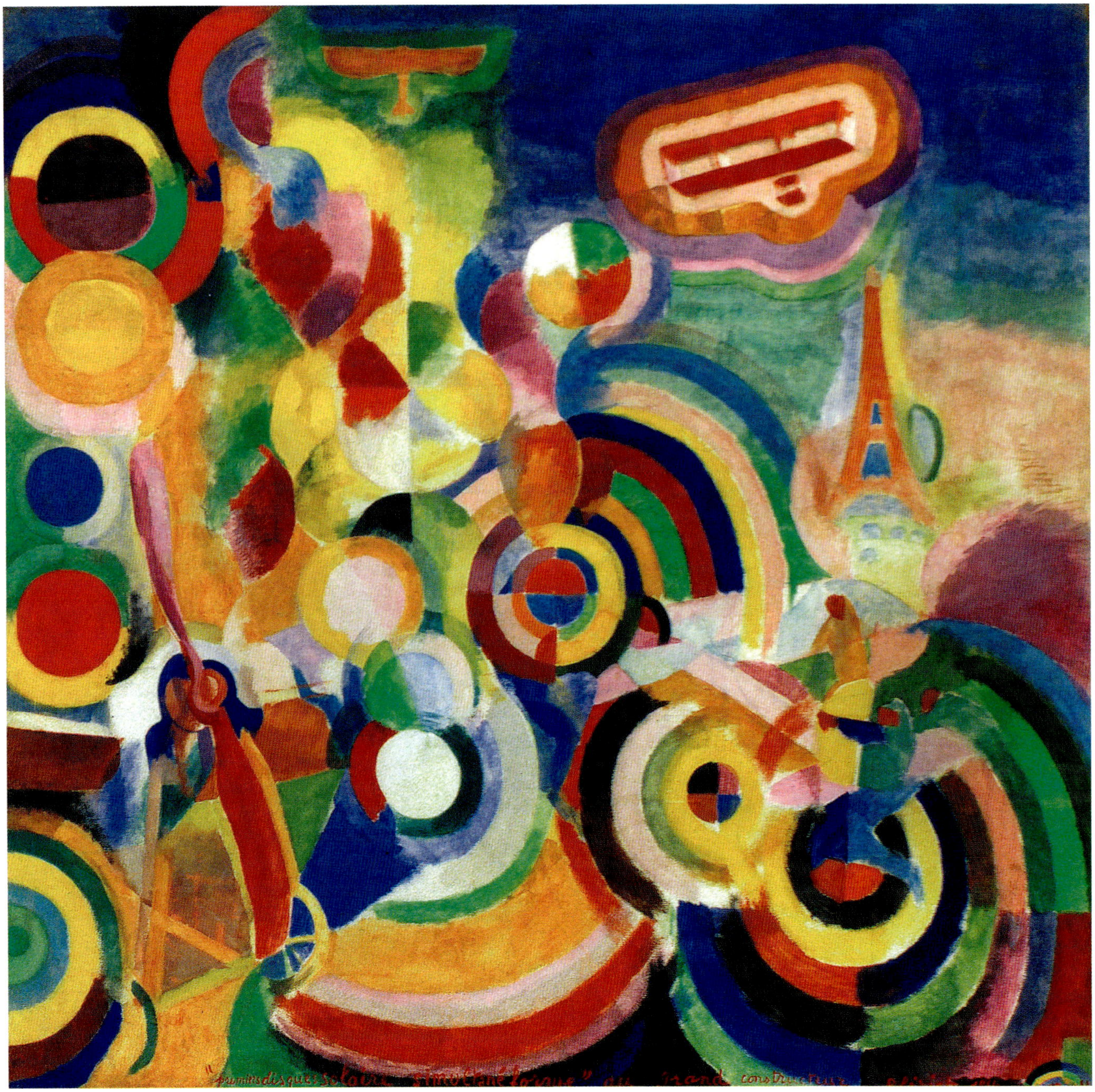

ABOVE: Robert Delaunay, *Homage à Blériot*, 1914. Glue tempera on canvas, 250 × 251 cm (98⅜ × 98⅞ in).

Like the futurists, and notably unlike the cubists in his own Parisian artistic circle, Robert Delaunay embraced the use of juxtaposed colours in his explorations of light and movement. Several decades later, he would write a note about his singular position:

> *I made paintings that seemed like prisms compared to the cubism my fellow artists were producing. I was the heretic of cubism. I had great arguments with my comrades who banned colour from their palette, depriving it of all elemental mobility. I was accused of returning to impressionism, of making decorative paintings, etc.*[7]

The surface of *Homage à Blériot*, painted in 1914, just before the outbreak of the First World War, and five years after the French aviator Louis Blériot's first flight across the English Channel, is composed primarily of overlapping discs of concentric, multicoloured circles. These cover most of the surface with the exception of a relatively clear triangular patch in the top right-hand corner. Among the pattern of circles an aeroplane propeller, part of its undercarriage and sections of wing, cut off by the left edge of the canvas, are clearly visible. To the right of this, a number of figures, perhaps playing football, move energetically around one another. In the top right sector is the distinctive outline of the Eiffel Tower, over which flies a biplane. In the top left, seemingly about to fly beyond the canvas's top edge, is a second plane or stylized raptor. The spirit of this ambition to ascend would be caught by the French writer Marcel Proust a few years later in *Sodom and Gomorrah* (1921) as his narrator recalls his first sight of a pilot in an aeroplane cockpit:

> *I felt that there lay open before him – before me, had not habit made me a prisoner – all the routes in space, in life itself; he flew on, let himself glide for a few moments over the sea, then quickly making up his mind, seeming to yield to some attraction that was the reverse of gravity, as though returning to his native element, with a slight adjustment of his golden wings he headed straight up into the sky.*[8]

As Delaunay said in his note, without colour there can be no sense of mobility in a painting. We could imagine that the bright primary colours of *Homage à Blériot* suggest the fracturing of light into its spectral hues by the spinning propeller blades, but Delaunay's vision is more all-encompassing. Perhaps more systematically than Georges Seurat and others in the previous century, he studied Michel Eugène Chevreul's colour theory (see page 52), even going so far as to borrow terminology from Chevreul's book, *On the Law of the Simultaneous Contrast of Colours* in describing the simultanism of his own approach. 'Simultaneous contrast', wrote Delaunay, 'ensures the dynamism of colours and their construction in the painting; it is the most powerful means to express reality.'[9] He saw these paintings, dependent only on the contrast of colours, as expressive of an experience developing over time but which would be 'simultaneously perceived at a single moment'.[10] The first of such works in this series, which would subsequently influence Paul Klee, he called Windows. It is as if the reality expressed through Delaunay's juxtaposed colours is one in which rapidly increasing speeds associated with new technologies seem to shrink distance to such an extent that we can imagine witnessing two things happening in geographically distinct locations at one and the same time.

In the years preceding *Homage*, Delaunay had made a series of Sun and Moon paintings, and the same cosmic scope animates the spinning discs of *Homage* that run in a string from the bottom right foreground to the top left and away. The Eiffel Tower, a frequent image in Delaunay's work, is symbolic of the totality he is seeking. Left as the only survivor from Paris's 1889 Exposition Universelle, it was at the time the world's tallest structure. To use his own words, it stands for him as a 'simulacrum' of the spatial harmony he sought, a harmony built through colour and that is dependent neither on post-impressionist 'effects' nor cubist 'objects' for its success.[11]

In the late 1990s, the British artist Bridget Riley began once again to use the curve in her paintings. It had been important in her early black-and-white op art compositions of the 1960s and continued to be present throughout the 1970s, but it was then largely absent for the next seventeen years until *Lagoon 2*. The structure of the composition is built from three basic elements: vertical lines forming bands of varying width, shallow arcs extending from the left-hand edge of the verticals, and diagonals rising from left to right. This last element, we remember, was the trajectory identified by Seurat as engendering a positive, uplifting emotional response in the viewer (see page 50). Riley had first encountered Seurat's pointillism and the divisionism of the futurists in the late 1950s.[12] There began her interest in colour, and her understanding that its use in painting presented a 'very complex, very difficult and, pictorially, a great challenge'.[13] In her black-and-white works – with the restriction between the two choices providing clarity – Riley saw herself dealing with 'a contradiction between stability and disruption'.[14] Once colour is introduced, all certainty disappears. If a red, which red; if a blue, which blue? What she was rediscovering, through Seurat, Claude Monet and Paul Cézanne, was that 'the basis of colour is its instability'.[15]

The advantage of the stripe is that it presents the longest possible boundary between one colour and another. A curve necessarily alters the breadth of an area, causing the dynamic interrelationship between adjacent colours to change as one travels along it. On the relationship between the vertical line and the curve, Riley refers to contrapposto, the ideal relaxed pose of the standing figure seen in Classical Greek sculpture and revived in the Renaissance. We see Michelangelo using it, for example, in his *David*, and playfully subverting it in portraying the drunken god in his *Bacchus*. 'If you think that contrapposto is the basic human movement', said Riley, 'the curve is very much connected to the standing human figure. The vertical line around which the curve moves is, in fact, the way the human body moves.'[16]

At the time, Riley was avidly pursuing every opportunity to visit exhibitions of Cézanne's work as part of what she called 'a sustained and considerable effort'[17] to study his painting. Riley acknowledged that the sense of space, air and movement in *Lagoon 2*, which results from the juxtaposed areas of greens, ochres, blues and violets, came from this study:

> *There was a feeling for cubism in my work – in the role of planes – and all of that came out of a study of Cézanne.*[18]

Although Cézanne provided the major orientation point for Riley in this work, Matisse is far from absent. Riley showed a slightly later painting, *Rêve*, to the British art critic David Sylvester. There are no verticals in the painting, just long, sinuous curves running the height of the canvas, with diagonals cutting across them to define areas of blue, green, and a light and dark yellow. It is full of movement and fluidity. Sylvester's response to the painting demonstrates that Matisse is a significant precursor.

> *[David Sylvester] came round, looked at* Rêve *and said 'It's very like Matisse' and then, after a pause, 'It's not like Matisse at all', and after another pause, 'But you might not have done it if you weren't aware of Matisse.' Then finally, 'It shows there's more than one way out of Matisse.'*[19]

Cézanne spoke of seeking what he called a 'little sensation',[20] a sense of space and presence in space built on the canvas through the placement of pigment and colour. In her compositions, Riley is seeking something similar. The feeling of space and movement, of nature, light and colour, and of the involvement of the body in interaction with all these is all the more palpable for the painting being unequivocally abstract. In connecting back so strongly to the compositional and colour explorations of the late nineteenth and early twentieth centuries – to the moment, in effect, before abstraction and non-representation had first appeared – Riley avoids so much of the debate in the years since the Second World War. By then, 'abstraction' had become a stylistic trope whose adoption – however tacitly, and however vehement the assurances that other approaches to painting were equally valid – was so often understood to carry a broader cultural, even a political message. Riley offers viewers a more direct experience:

> *People are entranced or enchanted; they are attracted, and they look with great care. They don't expect to find something, but they expect their eye to be caressed, as it were. They look for enjoyment and that's, in fact, what one would like to give them.*[21]

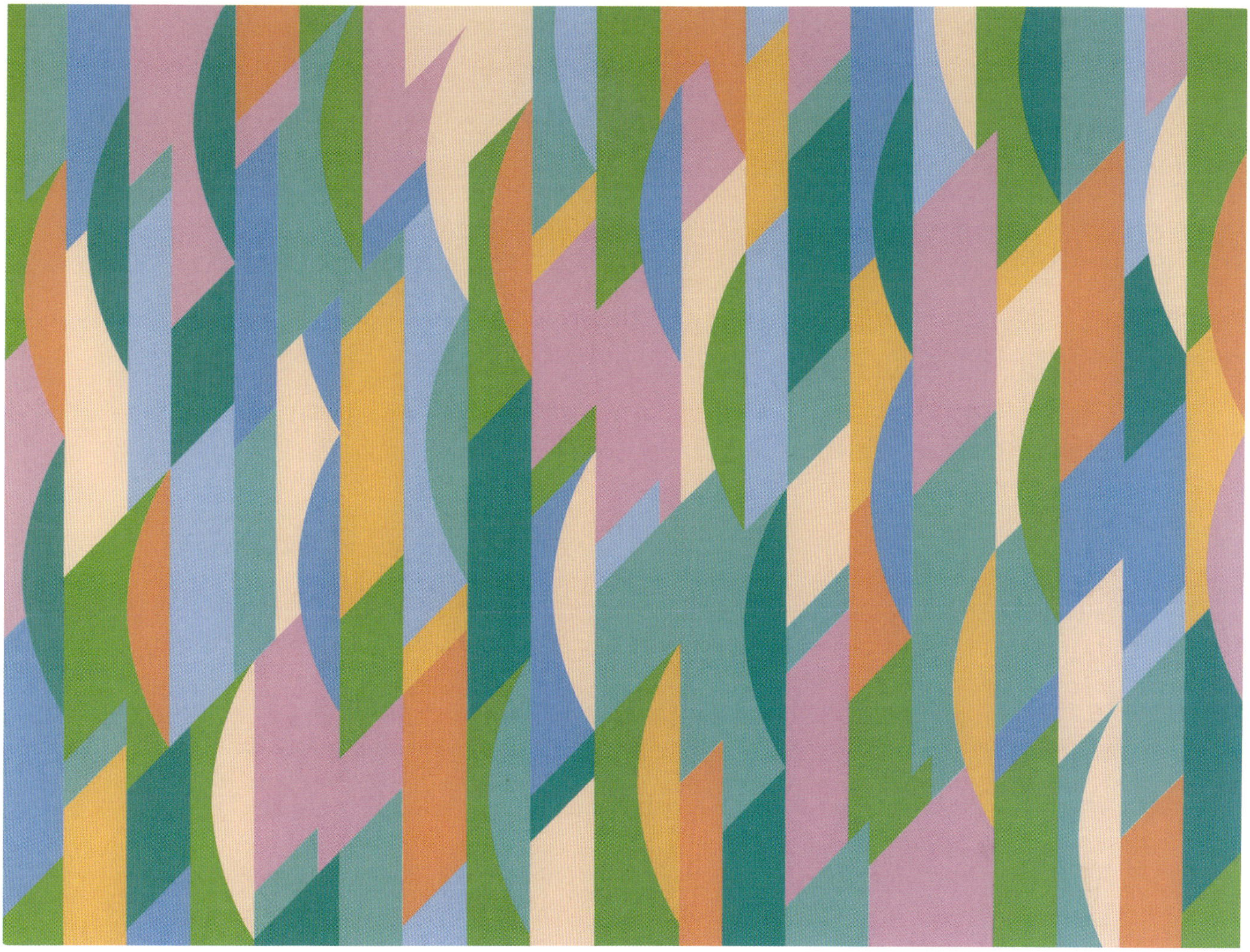

ABOVE: Bridget Riley, *Lagoon 2*, 1997. Oil on canvas, 147.3 × 199.4 cm (58 × 78½ in).

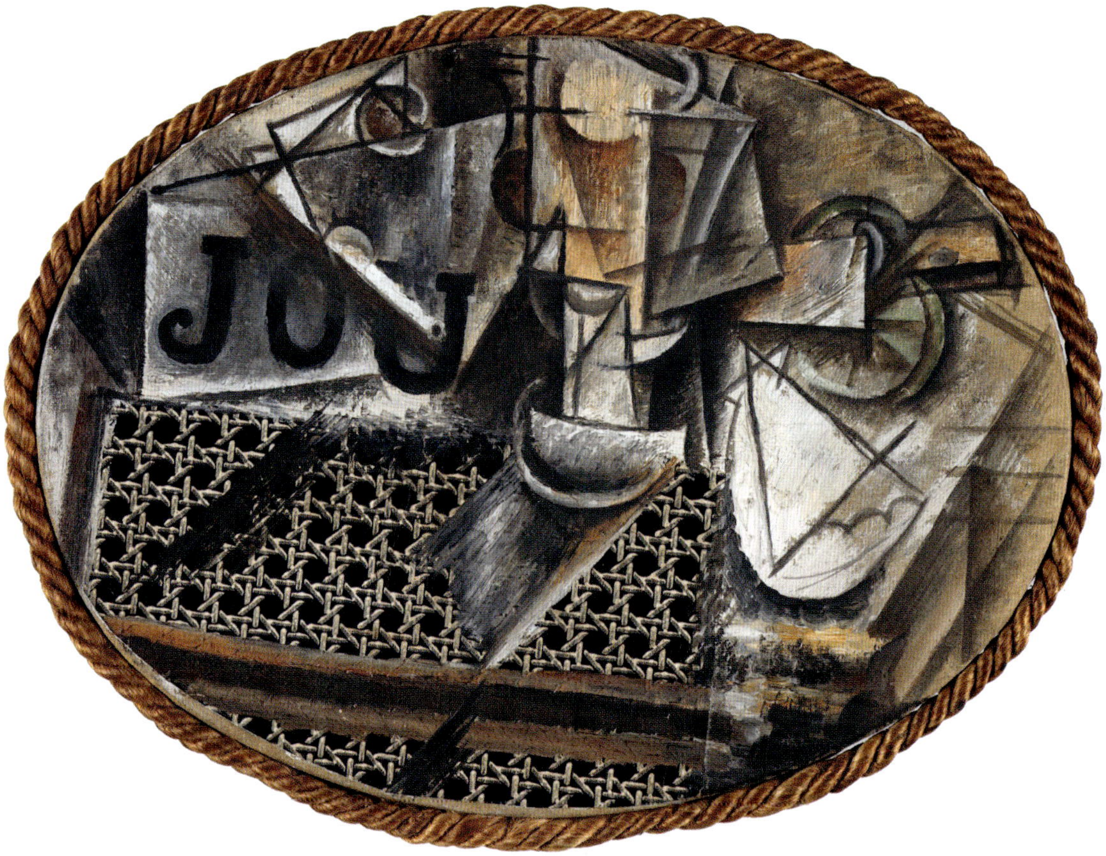

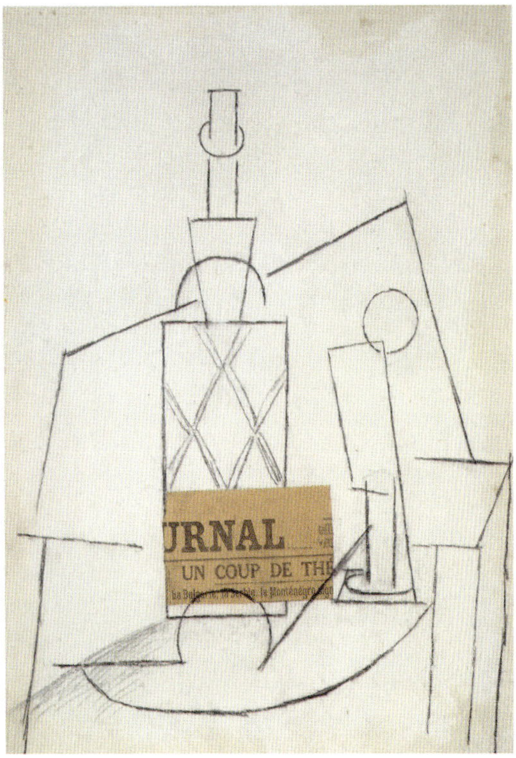

ABOVE: Pablo Picasso, *Still Life with Chair Caning*, 1912. Oil on oilcloth over canvas edged with rope, 29 × 37 cm ($11\frac{3}{8} \times 14\frac{1}{2}$ in).

LEFT: Pablo Picasso, *Bottle, Newspaper and Glass on a Table*, 1912. Charcoal, gouache, glued paper, 62 × 48 cm ($24\frac{3}{8} \times 18\frac{7}{8}$ in).

COLLAGE

Shortly after Georges Braque explored the interplay between real and representational elements in *Le Portugais* (see pages 62–5) both Braque and Pablo Picasso began to incorporate found or printed materials into their compositions. These are the first collages. Collage is emphatically a play with reality and representation in which the picture surface becomes a space where different juxtaposed and overlaid realities coexist. Sticking on a printed picture of an apple and a pear introduces a fruit bowl; a piece of newsprint literally places a newspaper in the composition while also representing the activity of daily news consumption and the world of events; a patch of wallpaper decorates the room in which everything is situated; some sheet music adds sound; and so on.

Picasso's *Still Life with Chair Caning* (1912) is an oval canvas, slightly broader than it is high. The painted forms down the right-hand third of the canvas and across its top half show various items on a table: a knife, some fruit, a napkin, wine glass, pipe and newspaper. The paper is clearly indicated by the three letters JOU (*Le Journal*). In the bottom left quadrant of the canvas, Picasso has pasted on a piece of oilcloth printed with a pattern of chair caning. The oilcloth is real, but the chair caning is not. It is an industrially produced printed image introduced into an otherwise hand-painted composition. It is at one and the same time the most real and the most unreal element there. Both the tabletop, on which the glass, newspaper and other objects are arranged, and the chair seat would be horizontal in real life. Here, however, we are disorientated by the fact that they are insistently vertical. To complete the work, Picasso has surrounded it, not with the kind of gilded frame one would expect for a piece of fine art, but with a length of rope. The whole composition is a complex of apparently incommensurable polarities: real and representational, high art and popular culture, paint and print, the handmade and the mechanically produced, the cheap and the expensive, depiction and illusion.

Cubist composition, at least that of Picasso and Braque – they had worked in tandem over the half dozen or so years leading up to the outbreak of the First World War – was essentially playful, a daily game (*jour/jou*) that we see exemplified in *Still Life with Chair Caning*. In another *papier collé* (pasted paper) collage, *Bottle, Newspaper and Glass on a Table*, Picasso uses a fragment that takes part of the paper's name (LE JO) URNAL underneath which is the first part of a headline UN COUP DE THÉ(ATRE). Again, there is a playful reference here, this time to the French poet Stéphane Mallarmé's late poem, 'Un Coup de Dés Jamais N'abolira le Hasard' (A Throw of the Dice Will Never Abolish Chance). Unlike the continuous narrative line of a newspaper article, Mallarmé set the words of his poem, printed in a variety of fonts and sizes, across the space of the page. Reading it thus requires the reader to become actively engaged in producing their own narrative journey, somewhat as Picasso invites us to synthesize the table with its bottle, glass and paper from the elements of the collage.

The advent of collage represents a significant enrichment to compositional possibility. Not least, it introduces a larger understanding of what it means to think of an image as a coherent whole. Henceforth, a variety of techniques and materials have licence to occupy the same surface. In the face of the destructive violence of the First World War, artists seized upon collage's ability to hold disparate realities within a single frame, both to reflect the brutality they witnessed around them and to offer the imaginative possibility of building a better world out of that chaos.

The First International Dada Fair was held in Berlin in the summer of 1920. By that time, dada, which had begun in Zurich in the middle of the First World War, was associated with groups in a number of European cities. Each of these had its own character, and the Berlin group, working in the aftermath of the Spartacist Uprising in 1919, was overtly political in outlook. The first line of the Berlin dada programme drawn up by Richard Huelsenbeck and Raoul Hausmann demanded 'the international revolutionary union of all creative and intellectual men and women on the basis of radical Communism'.[1] Publications critical of the government in the wake of the uprising were distributed, but as British art historian Dawn Adès noted, while some of the group were aggressively active, Hannah Höch remained 'primarily interested in showing what the world around her was like'.[2]

In a well-known photograph of the Dada Fair, Höch and her then partner Hausmann stand in front of a wall covered in their work. Two other participants, George Grosz and John Heartfield, had not wanted Höch to exhibit on account of her gender, but they finally agreed on Hausmann's insistence. In the photograph, behind Hausmann's right shoulder, is Höch's large photomontage, *Cut with the Kitchen Knife Dada through the Last Weimar Beer Belly Cultural Epoch of Germany*. Produced by the now familiar technique of cutting and pasting, Höch and the others were keen to draw a distinction between cubist collage and their own montage. Hausmann explained it thus:

> *We called this process photomontage because it embodied our refusal to play the part of the artist. We regarded ourselves as engineers, and our work as construction: we assembled (in French:* monter*) our work, like a fitter.*[3]

Höch had worked for some years prior to this at Ullstein Verlag, the publishers of the *Berliner Illustrirte Zeitung*, and it was in such popular and widely available papers and magazines that she found her imagery. Höch wrote of montage that it was 'a new, magical territory, for the discovery of which freedom is the first prerequisite'. However complex and jumbled its blizzard of image fragments might at first appear, however, its freedom did not indicate any lack of discipline since 'even these newly discovered possibilities remain subject to the laws of form and colour in creating an integral image surface'.[4]

Cut with the Kitchen Knife is organized into distinct zones, indicated with the text applied by Höch along with the photographic material. The figures in the top right portion constitute *die anti-Dadaistische Bewegung* (the anti-dadaistic movement). They are the bloated beer bellies of the culturally deadening Weimar government: Chancellor Friedrich Ebert, Gustav Noske (responsible for the suppression of the Spartacist Uprising by the Freikorps) and others. The head of the abdicated Kaiser Wilhelm II sits in the centre of this area, with his moustache provided by two wrestlers, and to his left is the head of German field marshal Paul von Hindenburg, sitting on the body of an exotic dancer. In the bottom left is *die grosse Welt Dada*, the great dada world, populated by the dadaists, or at least their heads. Hausmann is on a diving suit; Grosz and Wieland Herzfelde are balanced on a ballerina; an infantilized Heartfield is being bathed by the dancer Niddy Impekoven; and the German critic Theodor Däubler is back to front on the body of a baby. Karl Marx and the Russian revolutionary Vladimir Lenin can also be found there, along with more female athletes and dancers. Höch's own head appears in the bottom right corner, on a map of Europe showing those countries that had female suffrage. In the top left, Albert Einstein signals the importance of dada – 'He he, young man, dada is not an art style' – and offers some anti-capitalist financial advice: 'Invest your money in dada'. Below him are images of crowds, the general population, the proletariat, and in the midst is Karl Liebknecht, the murdered leader of the 1919 uprising, shouting *'tretet dada bei'* (join dada). This mass of imagery, set in motion by the cogs, wheels, gears and other bits of machinery animating the surface, circles around a relatively open central area in which the German dancer Niddy Impekoven pirouettes once again, but with her head replaced by that of Käthe Kollwitz, the first female artist to be awarded a professorship at a German art academy.

OPPOSITE: Hannah Höch, *Cut with the Kitchen Knife Dada through the Last Weimar Beer Belly Cultural Epoch of Germany*, 1919–20. Collage, mixed media, 114 × 90 cm (44⅞ × 31⅛ in).

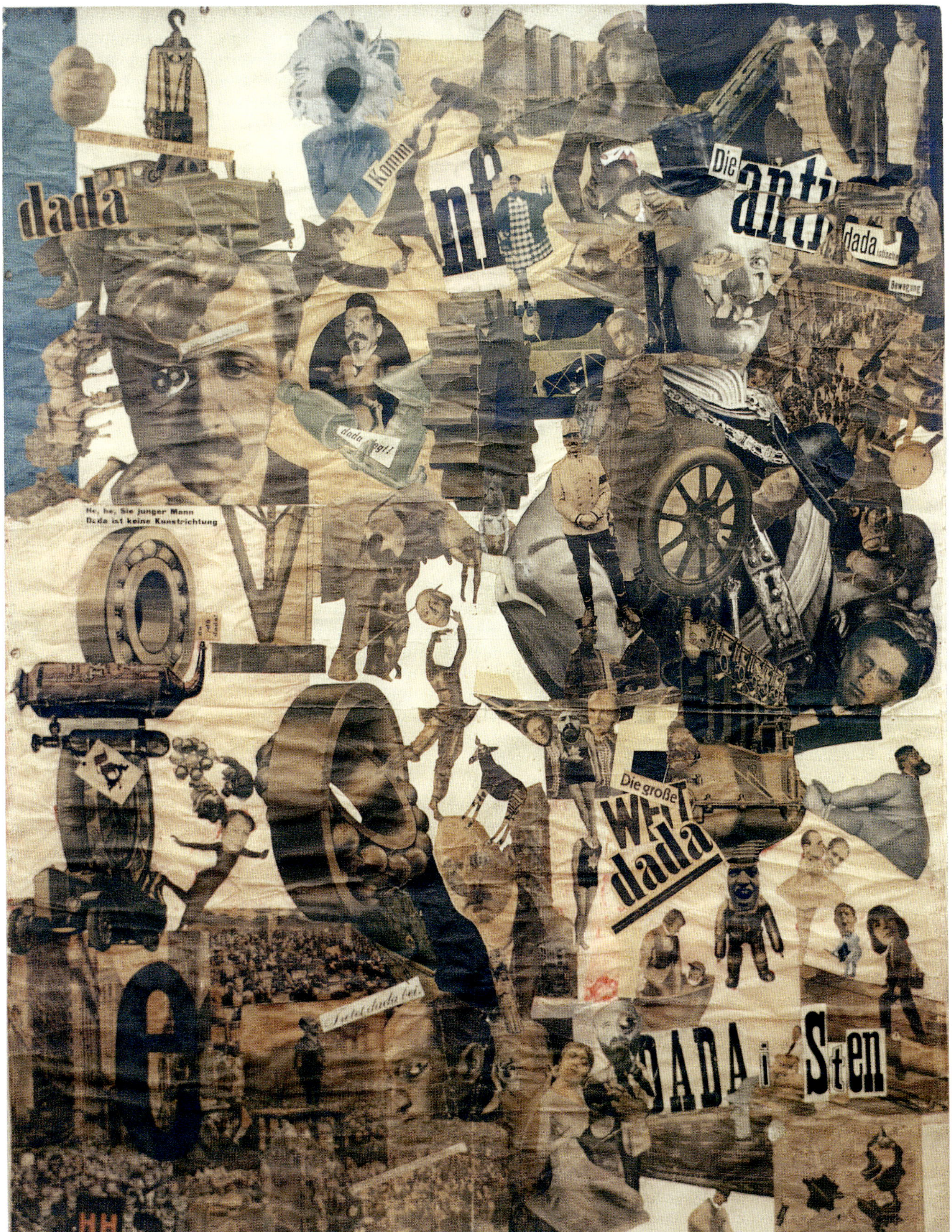
dada
Die
dada
Bewegung
He, he, Sie junger Mann
Dada ist keine Kunstrichtung
Die große
dada
DADA
HH

In the top left, Albert Einstein signals the importance of dada.

In the top right, we see the anti-dadaist 'beer bellies' of the Weimar government,

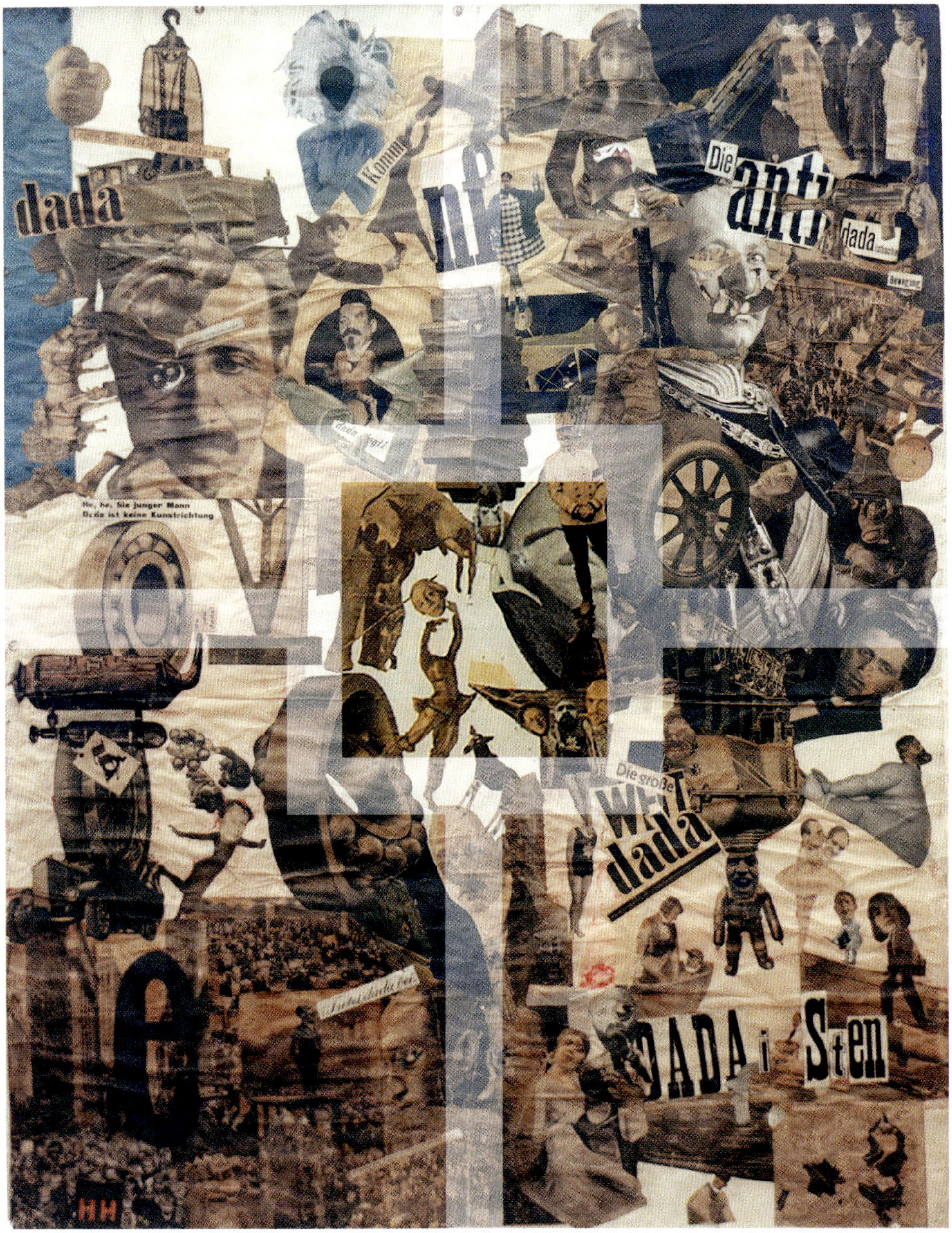

In the bottom left, crowds of proletariats gather, while the murdered socialist leader Karl Liebknecht encourages them to 'join dada'.

Käthe Kollwitz's speared head provides a central axis around which the composition revolves.

The bottom right showcases the dada world, featuring dada artists, Marx, Lenin, athletes and dancers.

In its approach to the experience of modernity, through the juxtaposition of fragments, the composition has an affinity with both Paul Cézanne and the cubists, as well as to the widely varied content of its material source, which came from between the covers of the mass publications of the time. Fifty years later, Höch would comment that her interest in making her photomontages essentially lay in wanting to convey a sense of what the modern world was like. They unashamedly engage with the social and political arguments of their time, and in forging a dynamic compositional coherence from their many pieces, they show themselves to be active agents in those debates. *Cut with the Kitchen Knife* is unquestionably a work made by a woman that speaks to the realities of women's lives. The title's 'kitchen knife', indicating that the montage originated from a domestic space overwhelmingly associated with women, the insistent use of female athletes and dancers as active, powerful cultural agents, the orientation of the composition around the exemplary creative combination of Kollwitz/Impekoven, and the map of female suffrage all bears witness to this.

A further element in the composition is that Kollwitz's head is transfixed by a spear held in the hand of a mahout standing next to his elephant. In this connection, with the spear acting as an axle around which the whole composition revolves, there is the spark of a critique of colonialism. Hitherto, as we saw in Ernst Ludwig Kirchner (see page 48–9), art from other cultures had met an enthusiastic reception primarily because it offered a counter to Western pictorial orthodoxy. What was not Western and 'civilized' was understood as 'primitive' and 'other', and it showed a way to break the grip that the academies and their rules exercised over artistic careers. Paul Gauguin's encountering objects from the Marquesas Islands and deciding to abandon his family to go and live there, Vincent van Gogh's curiosity about the displays at the 1889 Paris Exposition Universelle, and Picasso's interest in the African masks at the ethnographic museum in Paris's Trocadéro are all examples of this.

The problem is that all of this work had been appropriated as the spoils of imperialist conquer and was displayed as such. As we shall see, even the professed indifference to aesthetic judgement – is this beautiful? – in Marcel Duchamp's readymades (see pages 84–5) confirms the presumption that there could only be one definition of beauty. Höch's questioning was explored further in her subsequent series of montages, From an Ethnographic Museum. As Denise Toussaint, a German specialist on postcolonial theory and transculturality, said in her study of this series, where others 'used the primitive as material for their artistic reorientation … Höch unmasks this as an instrument of traditional hegemony and colonial legacy'.[5]

[Höch's photomontages] unashamedly engage with the social and political arguments of their time, and … show themselves to be active agents in those debates.

In the century since the beginnings of collage in cubist *papiers collés* and dadaist montage, it has persisted as a major compositional approach. As Höch's work has made evident, the technique operates in two opposing directions, involving both a dismantling, with a removal of elements from their familiar situation, and a reconstruction, with a reassembling of those elements into a new imaginative reality. Time and again this double orientation has offered the means to place personal expression within a critically examined political and cultural context. *Sunday After Sermon*, a collage made by the American artist Romare Bearden in 1969, fifty years after Höch's *Cut with a Kitchen Knife* (see pages 74–7), is divided into two rectangular parts by a clear vertical line running slightly to the right of centre. In the right-hand area, a group of men, women and attendant children gather in conversation. To the immediate left of the divide a girl sits with a cat, while a man stands in profile in the doorway behind. Everyone is wearing their Sunday best. The picture, made the year after the assassination of Martin Luther King Jr, revisits the spirituality and familiar rituals Bearden witnessed in Charlotte, North Carolina, the place where he was born and to which he made several return visits during his childhood.

In its overall composition, *Sunday After Sermon* recalls *Las Meninas* by Diego Velázquez (see page 11) – the large blank rear of the canvas to the left, the figures of the infanta and her entourage to the right, and the attendant in profile, backlit in the doorway to the rear. It also bears a strong formal resemblance to paintings by Pieter de Hooch, such as *The Courtyard of a House in Delft* and, especially, *Figures Drinking in a Courtyard* (both 1658).

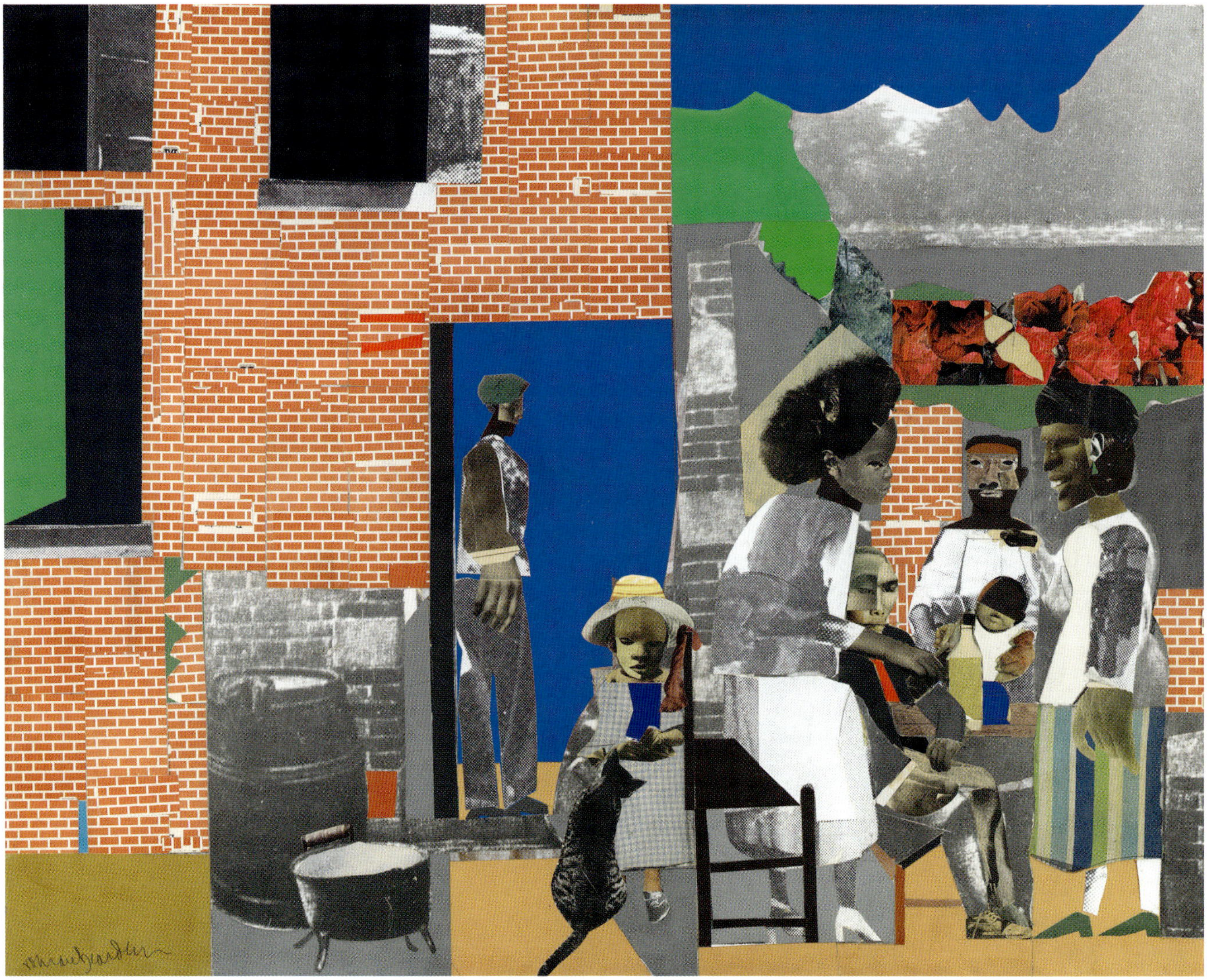

In his own writings on composition,[6] Bearden remarks on the lessons he learned from the thirteenth- to fourteenth-century Italian painters Duccio and Ambrogio Lorenzetti and the seventeenth-century Dutch painters Gerard ter Borch and de Hooch on the division of the canvas into large rectangles that, in turn, contained smaller ones. There are further compositional references both in the title, which resonates with Gauguin's *Vision After the Sermon* (see page 42), and in the similarity of the chair on the left of the figure group to the one in Vincent van Gogh's *The Bedroom* (see page 38). Furthermore, Bearden's interest in Chinese ink drawings, in particular their 'open corners', is mirrored in the ochre patch in the bottom left corner that provides a space through which the viewer can enter the picture and begin to contemplate its meanings. 'It is in matters of composition, especially', wrote Bearden, 'that the greatest painters studied their predecessors for solutions to their own problems.'[7]

Where the left portion of *Sunday After Sermon* is composed in clean, simple forms, the right is built from a tessellation of much smaller elements that echo the colours and patterns on the left. This is rhythmic and musical as much as it is visual, and jazz was a constant resource for Bearden:

> *I learned, I hope, a lot about painting from listening to Earl Hines. I listened and listened and listened … until I couldn't hear the music, only the silences – in order to pick up the intervals of his playing. All of this … comes from the drum.*[8]

He said this while talking about African art, which was for him the 'plastic expression' of the rhythms of the drum, the quintessential means of interpersonal communication.[9] The brick wall repeats in smaller patches on the right side, and the striped skirt of the woman on the far right picks up in muted form the blues, greens and ochres seen elsewhere.

For the faces in his compositions, Bearden would not usually lift one from a single photograph but would instead 'build them, for example, from parts of African masks, animal eyes, marbles, corn, and mossy vegetation'.[10] This is very different to the dada montage of Höch, in which we see an expression of a splintered, dizzying machinic existence. The Middle Passage slave trade in which millions of Africans were taken to the Americas left so many with fractured memories of their own communities, languages, myths and behaviour patterns. American artist Faith Ringgold, who remembers meeting Bearden when growing up in Harlem in New York City, talks of this history in relation to her use of quilting: 'slaves couldn't express themselves through the art that they would have made in Africa. They couldn't come to America and paint, carve sculptures or make masks, but they could make quilts.'[11] Working more from nature and ritualized daily habit than the machine, and in great affinity with activity such as the quilting bee, Bearden's collage works to assemble out of its initial fragments a coherent image of Black American identity and experience.

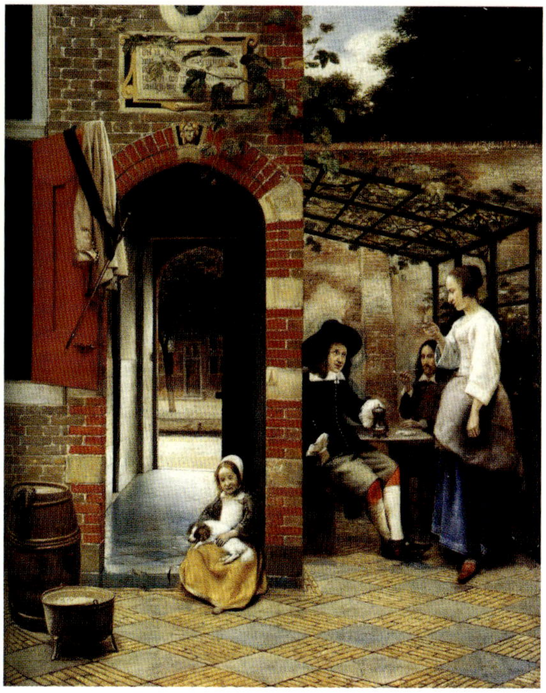

ABOVE: Pieter de Hooch, *Figures Drinking in a Courtyard*, 1658. Oil on canvas, 68 × 58 cm (26¾ × 22⅞ in).

OPPOSITE: Romare Bearden, *Sunday After Sermon*, 1969. Collage on cardboard, 101.6 × 127 cm (40 × 50 in).

In a 1967 essay, 'Art and Objecthood', the American art historian Michael Fried criticized minimalism for what he called its theatricality. Whereas a painting could be apprehended all at once, the viewer needed to spend time in the space with a minimal work. As the American artist Robert Morris demonstrated in his 1965 sculpture *Untitled (L-Beams)*, one's unfolding experience of even something as formally uncomplicated as a monochrome L-shaped box depended greatly upon how that box was positioned and oriented in the space with you. Instead of everything that mattered being in the painting, the experience of minimal work seemed to be guided as much as anything by external factors – how you felt, what kind of day it was, how the weather outside affected the light levels, and so on. Fried's essay ends with the short, assertive sentence: 'Presentness is grace'.[12] Although unaware of it when it was first published, the American artist Martha Rosler subsequently recognized presentness – what she describes as 'sharing an actual physical space with your audience'[13] – as something that she, too, was interested in at the time.

The achievement of presentness is that it 'smashes the modernist paradigm'.[14] The relationship between artist, viewer and artwork, and the place of that triangle of interconnections within society as a whole is called into question by such a sharing of space. Throughout the period of modernism – up to and including the experiments in 'non-composition' of post-painterly abstraction (see Chapter IV) – the studio where the painting is made, the gallery where it is exhibited, and the world outside of both of these could still be accepted as separate realms of creation, appreciation and context. Minimalism's 'theatricality' and pop art's preoccupation with the imagery of advertisements, television bulletins, sensation and celebrity that pervaded consumer society erased the boundaries (and we can see here that minimalism and pop are two sides of the same coin).

Talking about her House Beautiful: Bringing the War Home series, Rosler explained, 'When I understood what it meant to say that the war in Vietnam was not "an accident", I virtually stopped painting and started doing agitational works.'[15] She began in 1967, taking interiors from magazine spreads and advertisements, and introducing into them images drawn from, or alluding to the war in Vietnam. These collages were not destined for the gallery wall but were instead made as flyers to be copied and handed out at anti-war demonstrations. In one composition, *First Lady (Pat Nixon)* (*c.*1967–72), the wife of the US president stands in plush surroundings smiling at the camera. On the wall behind her is a large black-and-white image. Colour was for film and television, magazines and family photos, while black and white at that time was for the reality of newspaper reporting. However, the image on the wall is, in fact, of the American actress Faye Dunaway in the character of Bonnie Parker. It is a film still, taken from the final scene of *Bonnie and Clyde* (1967), in which the eponymous outlaws are being gunned down. While in other compositions in the series Rosler did use imagery taken from reportage of the war in Vietnam itself, on this occasion it is a dramatized, mediated, aestheticized rendering of violent death that intrudes into and commands the space. Here, Rosler's collage jolts the viewer into acknowledging both the degree to which television can similarly aestheticize scenes showing events in Vietnam and that it is all too easy for us to become inoculated against the truth of those brutalities in which we are all implicated.

Rosler's collages … insist that what we are typically assured is both spatially and experientially divided is, in fact, a single, interconnected whole.

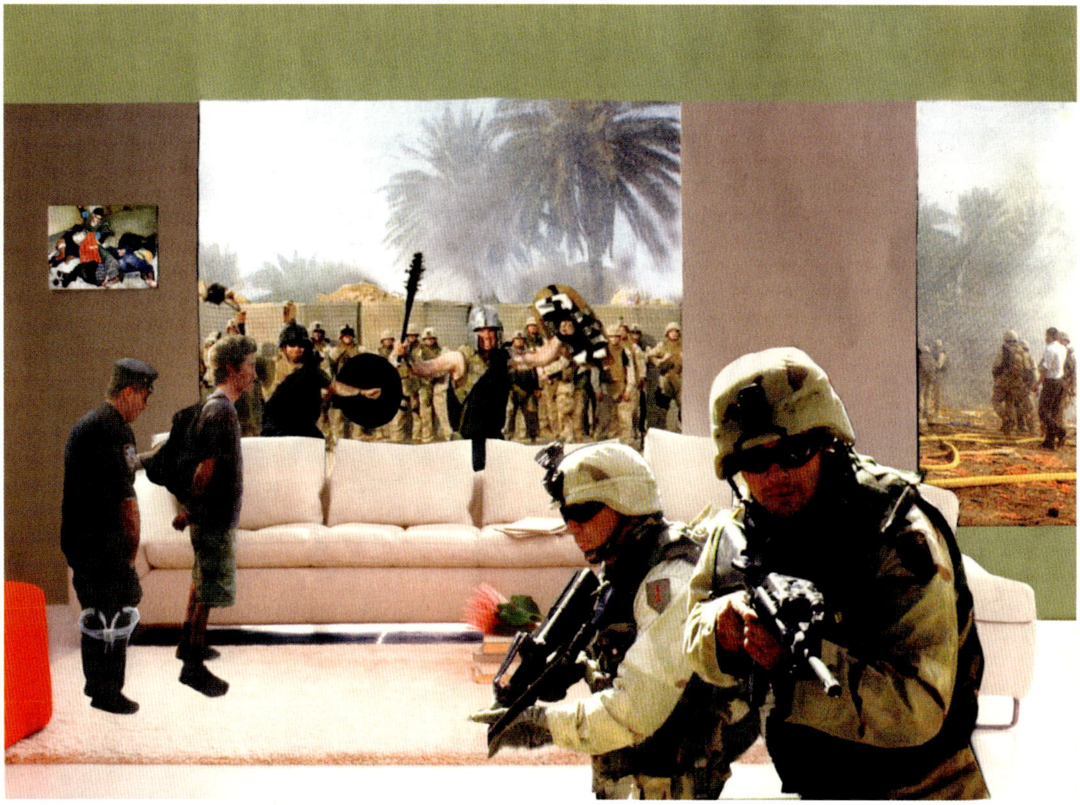

ABOVE: Martha Rosler, *Gladiators*, from the series House Beautiful: Bringing the War Home, new series, 2004. Photomontage, 50.8 × 61 cm (20 × 24 in).

Rosler's presentness is the immediacy of the street. 'Collage was obviously the medium of the twentieth century',[16] she said, though for her it was less dadaist montage than the coherent interrelation of pop cultural images within the single painting, such as in the work of American artist James Rosenquist that she found interesting. Unlike, say, Robert Rauschenberg, who introduced other materials into his compositions – the quilt and pillow in *Bed* (1955), the car tyre and stuffed goat in *Monogram* (1955–9), for example – Rosenquist brought his imagery, drawn from varied sources in advertising and the consumer capitalist lifestyle, into a wholly painted composition. Art historian Alexander Alberro observes a fundamental distinction between Rosler's approach to collage and that of earlier proponents of photomontage such as Höch and Heartfield. Whereas the dadaists employed the juxtaposition of disparate images as a way to fracture the sense of a coherent reality, Rosler's collages in the House Beautiful series worked to insist that what we are typically assured is both spatially and experientially divided is, in fact, a single, interconnected whole. The dominant narrative in the Western media explained the war in Vietnam as something taking place at a distance – 'over there' – in a location quite distinct from the comfortable and familiar domestic spaces of the homeland. Rosler's collages collapse that distance, erasing the distinction between 'here' and 'there'. The war pervades everywhere and implicates everyone. 'I was trying to show', she said, 'that the "here" and the "there" of our world picture, defined by our naturalized accounts as separate or even opposite, were one.'[17] On remaking the series for gallery exhibition some years later, Rosler explained, 'So much of my work involved the Vietnam War that it would have been obscene to show it in a gallery. But now, it's different; it's important to remember and to enable the young to discover what to some of us is still so present.'[18] The pervasiveness of which Rosler speaks persists across time. Struck by the parallels between Vietnam and continuing US military action, she produced a new series in 2004 and 2008, House Beautiful, Bringing the War Home: New Series. In *Gladiators*, as with other works in the series, the imagery intruding into the domestic interiors shows scenes from the second Gulf War.

While at college the Kenyan-born American artist Wangechi Mutu was puzzled by the reluctance among her peers to use the words beauty and beautiful. Modernism had consistently rejected the assumption that traditional standards of beauty were central to the production and appreciation of art. Time and again the labels attached to movements indicated critical rejection. From impressionism to fauvism, cubism to minimalism, the work associated with these tendencies is repeatedly judged as lacking some essential quality that would allow it to be fully accepted as art.

With his readymades (see overleaf), French artist Marcel Duchamp attempted to avoid such arguments by searching out objects to which one could remain completely indifferent: they were not beautiful but equally they were not ugly. In both cases, however – beautiful/ugly, beautiful/not beautiful – the ultimate measure of judgement remained 'beauty'. Everything was made and appraised in relation to a criterion that is unquestioningly presumed to be universal and thus universally applicable. Mutu explained her fellow students' avoidance of the term as the internalization of this immutable standard:

> *I believe the reason is because beauty was actually available to them, their culture decides for the whole world what is beautiful, how beauty should evolve, where it begins and ends. So they were rebelling against the very thing that had protected them.*[19]

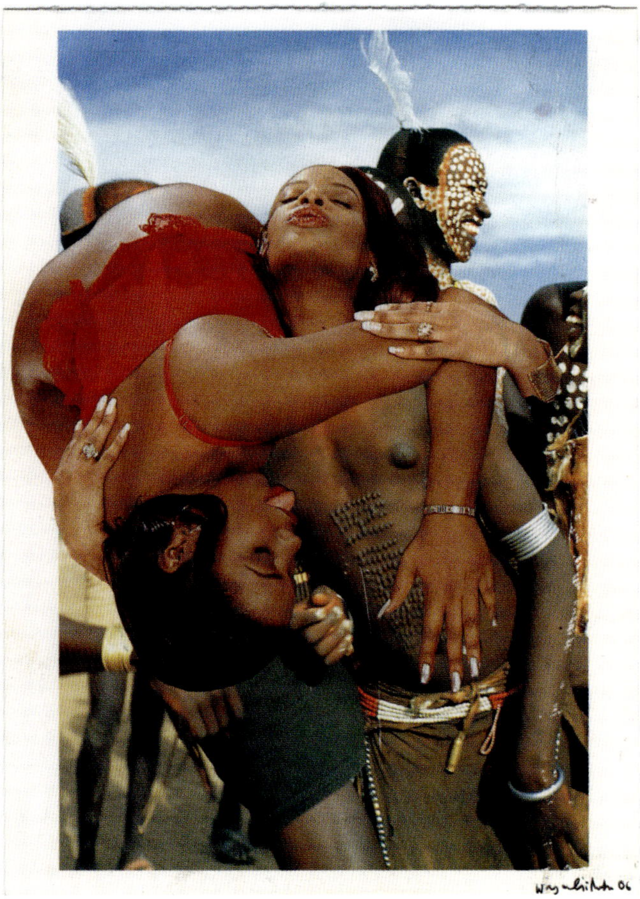

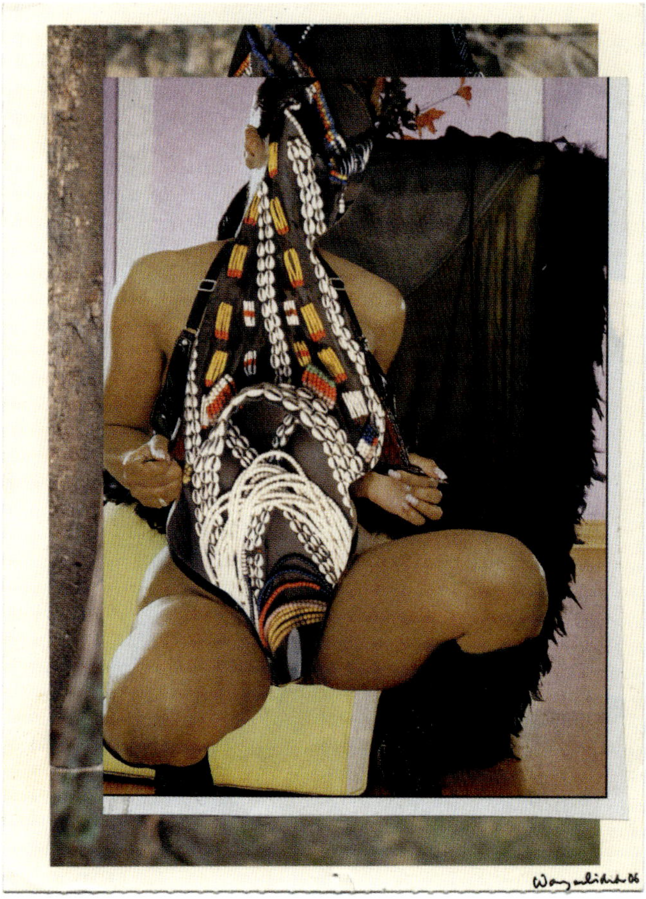

For her, however, judgements of beauty must inevitably reveal evidence of cultural relativism. The Ark Collection series of collages used photographs from the book *Women of the African Ark*. This was a book of postcards carrying images shot by two white photographers, the American Carol Beckwith and the Australian Angela Fisher, who had collaborated on many projects across Africa over several decades. The images show women from a number of different parts of the African continent, each wearing traditional costume in a pose and manner associated in the West with anthropological studies and feature spreads in publications such as *National Geographic*. Mutu's thirty-two collages keep to this postcard size, the format relating both to Beckwith and Fisher's book, as well as to the photo sequences in the porn magazines featuring Black women on which she also drew for the work.

Mutu likens the perusal of the newsstand to a naturalist studying the habits of an animal. 'If you want to know what an animal's system is about, you look at its shit, like elephant dung.'[20] The choice of elephant dung to illustrate her point might be taken as an oblique reference to British painter Chris Ofili's work. Ofili's *The Holy Virgin Mary* (1996) is a black Madonna on a vivid gold ground. The many butterfly-shaped collaged elements floating across the upper part of the picture are, in fact, images of women's buttocks cut from porn magazines and stuck onto the canvas. Mary's right breast is formed by a ball of elephant dung fastened to the picture surface, and rather than hanging on the wall, the work leans against it, propped up on two further balls of elephant dung. 'If you want to know where the animal has been and whether it's healthy', said Mutu, 'you sift through its stool. That's a little bit what it's like when I look at media.'[21]

Mutu was familiar with Picasso's cubist work and admired how he 'looked at things from different angles and they still ended up in one picture plane'.[22] Similarly, her own collages, although appearing flat, contain many dimensions and perspectives. Hair styles, grass, straw, foliage, water, flooring, jewellery, fabric patterns, cicatrice patterns on skin, fragmented bodies, reorientation and disorientation, inversion, silhouette, are all used in the construction of new women. The multitude of splintered images resonate, echo and blend in with one another, cohering into surprising and original figures that nonetheless retain aspects of the contrast between her disparate picture sources. Mutu views their composition as the outcome of many 'little surgeries'[23] that have been carried out by cutting into her starting images to 'find the truth, to find the humour, to find the sickness'. The collages are presented in vitrines, as if in a museum, and in their form and method of display there is a conscious reference to Höch's From the Ethnographic Museum series.

For people from countries that have experienced colonization, there is reluctance to reject the idea of beauty because it is not something over which they have yet been able to exercise any control. 'If your entire history of art and your language and your culture are considered to be primitive', said Mutu, 'maybe you'll fight for the idea of something being beautiful.'[24]

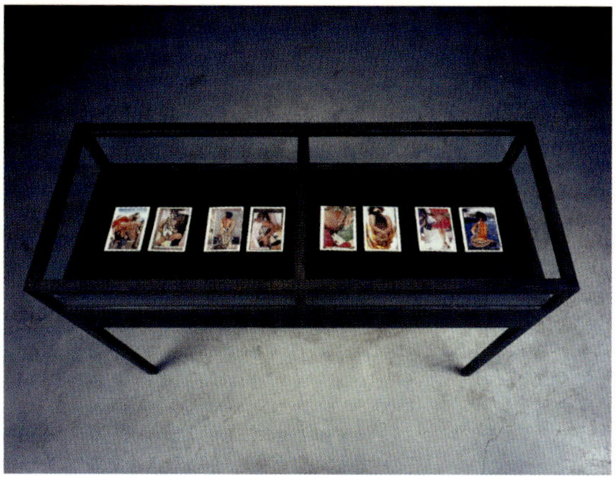

ABOVE: Wangechi Mutu, The Ark Collection, 2006. Installation view at Sikkema Jenkins & Co., New York.

OPPOSITE: Wangechi Mutu, details from The Ark Collection: Karo Woman, Hamar Woman, Hamar Woman, Hamar Woman, Surma Girl, Ogaden Market, Adari Girl, Maasai Girl, 2006. Collage on postcards, each 16.5 × 11 cm ($6^1/_2 \times 4^1/_4$ in); displayed in vitrines, each vitrine 101.5 × 157.5 × 58.5 cm (40 × 62 ×23 in).

THE READYMADE

If artists can now incorporate found material into a piece, is there any limit to the amount or proportion they can use? Does there need to be some painting or other intervention by the hand of the artist involved as well, or could a work consist of only found material? The French artist Marcel Duchamp's *Bicycle Wheel* is a perplexing object. As to what it is there is no mystery. It is the front forks and wheel of a bicycle upended and fastened to the seat of a four-legged stool. What this accomplishes is more of a puzzle.

It is not something to be looked at, but to be with – in other words, it is to be treated quite unlike all previous works of art.

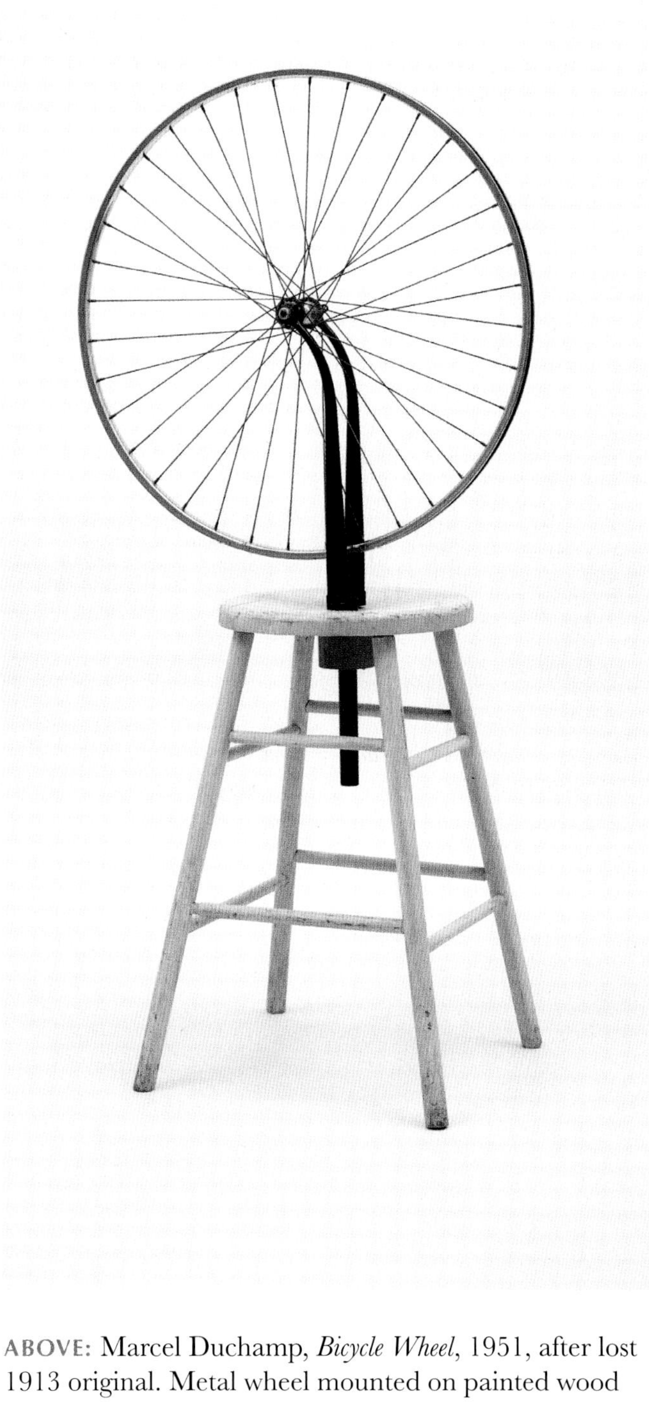

ABOVE: Marcel Duchamp, *Bicycle Wheel*, 1951, after lost 1913 original. Metal wheel mounted on painted wood stool, 129.5 × 63.5 × 42 cm (51 × 25 × 16½ in).

Duchamp would not use the term 'readymade' until 1915, but *Bicycle Wheel* is the first example of this kind of work. The stool and bicycle parts are mass-produced, proprietary items in whose design and manufacture Duchamp played no part. If there is anything we might consider an act of composition, it is only the bringing together of the two elements. But he said of this act:

> *When I put a bicycle wheel on a stool, the fork down, there was no idea of a 'readymade', or anything else. It was just a distraction. I didn't have any special reason to do it, or any intention of showing it, or describing anything.*[1]

Viewed in terms of traditional sculpture, we might see both the stool and the bicycle as plinths upon which a human figure could be placed. But one is static, the other movable; one is the right way up, the other is upside down; one is habitually encountered inside, the other outside. It confounds all accepted expectations of a work of art. It is not designed, shaped or fabricated by Duchamp. It is not unique, and insofar as it was conceived as a 'distraction', it does not ask to be looked at directly. Furthermore, it defies any effort to evaluate it according to the usual aesthetic criteria. Asked years later what guided his choice of 'readymades', Duchamp emphasized his effort to escape from any idea of beauty:

> *It's very difficult to choose an object, because, at the end of fifteen days, you begin to like it or to hate it. You have to approach something with an indifference, as if you had no aesthetic emotion. The choice of readymades is always based on visual indifference and, at the same time, on the total absence of good or bad taste.*[2]

The wheel can be spun and left to turn. It provides the kind of gentle, comforting movement in the periphery of one's vision that Duchamp likened to the flickering of flames in the fireplace. The work is diverting, an amusement, and something that quite consciously has no function. Indeed, it denies the functionality of its constituent parts. It is not something to be looked at, but to be with – in other words, it is to be treated quite unlike all previous works of art. Similarly, a few years later, in 1917, the French composer Erik Satie composed the first ambient 'furniture music' and was upset when the audience sat down to listen attentively rather than to continue circulating and conversing while it played. *Bicycle Wheel* is an object not to be attended to.

However much we might admire *Bicycle Wheel* as an object, now that we are at a distance of more than a century from its first appearance, it remains important for us to bear in mind the force of a gesture that achieved three things. First, it comprehensively undermined the idea that the defining task of the artist is to compose a work of art. Second, more emphatically than the multiple versions of scenes painted by Claude Monet such as his water lilies, it undermined the assumption that a work of art is a unique object. The object we look at today under the title *Bicycle Wheel* is not the thing that Duchamp constructed in 1913. That one was lost, as was its 1916 successor. Another was made in 1951, which is now in the collection of the Museum of Modern Art, New York. Duchamp licensed two further copies in 1961 and 1963, and then he supervised the production of a limited edition of fourteen further copies in 1964. So there are now multiple examples of *Bicycle Wheel* at large in the museums and galleries of the world. The third achievement of *Bicycle Wheel* is that it removed aesthetic judgement as the means to appraise a work of art. Henceforth, it was sufficient for an artist to designate something as a work of art for it to be accepted as such. Of course, more questions arise from this, two in particular being: first, how does one get to be recognized as an artist, and second, does context matter? Is it important for the wheel to be in a gallery rather than a bicycle repair shop? These questions will return later in the book.

CHANCE

The composition of Jean Arp's *Constellation According to the Laws of Chance* involves procedures he had been employing for more than a decade. Already by 1916, involved in the beginnings of dada in Zurich, the German-French artist had found a way to externalize compositional responsibility. In his account of the dada movement, artist and filmmaker Hans Richter describes Arp's working method at that time:

[Arp] also experimented with chance, putting on a piece of cardboard pieces of paper that he had cut out at random and then coloured: he placed the scraps coloured side down and then shook the cardboard; finally he would paste them to the cardboard just as they had fallen.[1]

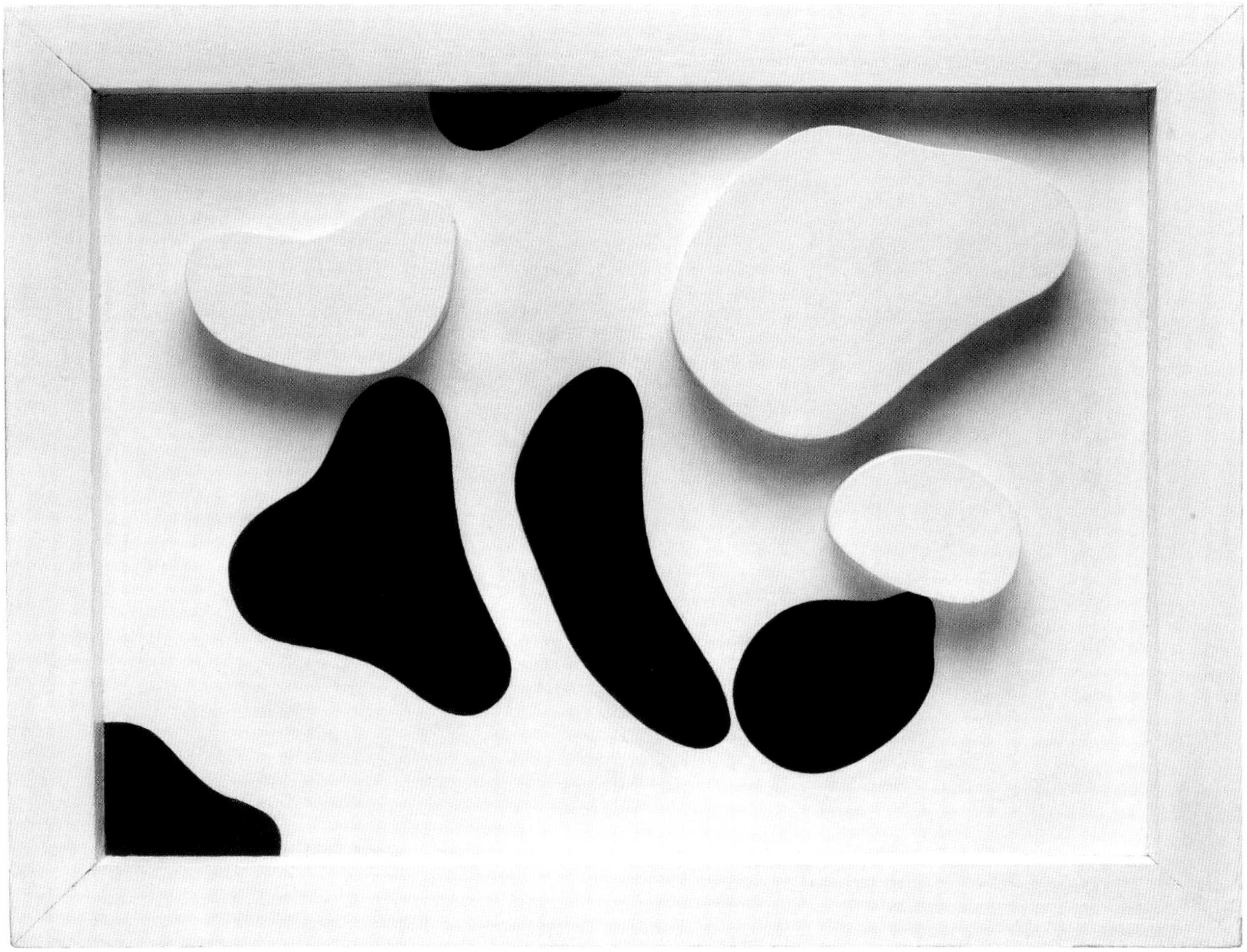

Constellation again involves Arp placing its various shaped areas and three-dimensional elements on a surface, in his words, 'automatically, without will'.[2] Strategies for bypassing conscious control of the compositional process become increasingly familiar in the first decades of the twentieth century. For the dadaists in the middle of the First World War, it was a means to counter what the Romanian-born French poet Tristan Tzara called the 'aggressive complete madness of a world abandoned to the hands of bandits, who rend one another and destroy the centuries'.[3]

Though earlier movements had rejected artistic orthodoxy, cubism and futurism had, in the dadaists' eyes, quickly become rigid in their own academies and as such were also to be condemned. 'We were all determined no longer to wrest pictures out of acts, still lifes, landscapes', wrote Arp.[4] What the dadaists desired instead was 'unlimited freedom'.[5] Arp saw his recourse to the use of chance as part of a search for an 'essential order':[6]

> *Chance opened up perceptions to me, immediate spiritual insights. Intuition led me to revere the law of chance as the highest and deepest of laws.*[7]

Positioning the different parts of a composition without design or intention might lead the viewer to see only chaos in the outcome. Arp was insistent that this apparent, superficial lack of order was only one aspect of dadaism, in that it failed to acknowledge the movement's fundamental seriousness. 'To speak only of dada's confusing unreality and fail to penetrate its transcendent reality, is to render only a worthless fragment of dada. Dada was not a farce'.[8]

In the development from the first collages that used only coloured paper to those that also incorporated shaped pieces of wood, Arp's compositions introduce us to the idea of a destabilization of categories. So much of what has been discussed so far has concerned itself in one way or another with the question of the picture surface's flatness. Thus, in Tzara's concise critique of Western art's reliance on the use of perspective:

> *Painting is the art of making two lines geometrically established as parallel meet on a canvas before our eyes in a reality which transposes other conditions and possibilities into a world.*[9]

Delaunay, in taking railway lines as epitomizing the cosmic totality for which he was striving, remains in thrall to this conception. Arp's *Constellation*, in contrast, confounds categories. It has three-dimensional parts, so it cannot be taken straightforwardly as a painting – it is an object in which the question of perspective is irrelevant. It is hung on the wall, so is not unquestioningly a sculpture. And it also has insistently two-dimensional parts, so is not simply a relief. In a further disruption of categories, in the Merz pictures and constructions of another dadaist, Kurt Schwitters, there is frequent use of found material. As with Duchamp's readymades, the idea of authorship and the importance of originality are rendered problematic. When considering a work of art, it is no longer a case of judging whether or not it is good of its kind – painting, sculpture, and so on – because those labels are restrictive and misleading.

OPPOSITE: Jean Arp, *Constellation According to the Laws of Chance*, *c.*1930. Painted wood, 54.9 × 69.8 cm (21⅝ × 27½ in).

ACCESSING THE UNCONSCIOUS

Here is a party game. As with so many innovations, the point of origin of this technique remains a matter of debate. The French writer André Breton, the primary voice and, to the discomfort of some, ultimately leader of surrealism, placed its inception as a surrealist procedure around 1925 in Paris in the house of the actor Marcel Duhamel, in which the painter Yves Tanguy and poet Jacques Prévert also lodged. Here, they would engage in what is, to all intents and purposes, the game of consequences. The early sessions were verbal, with the participants providing an appropriate part of speech in sequence to construct a grammatically correct sentence – article, adjective, noun, adverb, verb, etc. One of the early sessions generated the sentence, *Le cadavre exquis boira le vin nouveau* (the exquisite corpse will drink the new wine), from which the name Exquisite Corpse was taken to refer to all such creations.

What stimulated the surrealists about this technique was that it necessarily placed the act of composition beyond determination by any individual. It gave, as Breton explained, 'an infallible way of holding the critical intellect in abeyance'.[1] Because the eventual outcome could not be conceived by any of the contributors, each was free to indulge their imagination without needing to direct it towards the achievement of a particular goal. It heightened, for Breton, the possibility of revealing correspondences, those metaphorical linkages between inner life and the external world of which Charles Baudelaire wrote. It was also another way, unconnected to abstraction, to avoid 'the ridiculous activity of imitation of physical characteristics, to which a large and most questionable part of contemporary art is still anachronistically subservient'.[2]

This example, *Exquisite Corpse (Landscape)*, is a collaborative effort by four people: Valentine Hugo, André Breton, Tristan Tzara and Greta Knutson. Although it is true that it does not give up a simple message, its individual elements have a certain consistency: the chaise longue suggestive of daydreaming and the analyst's couch; the sleeping woman below whose head extends her dreamworld avatar in silhouette; the figure in the upper left that combines suggestions of flesh, mechanical function and a stoppered vessel, and which is, to all appearances, birthing the figure below; the voluptuous mouth at bottom left sporting dangerously sharpened teeth; the high-heeled, decorated and heavily laced boot at the bottom right; and so on. Freud, whose ideas on dream symbolism, fetishism and the functioning of the unconscious mind Breton greatly admired, could have a field day.

In his first 'Manifesto of Surrealism', Breton defines the means to access the unconscious mind as 'psychic automatism'. By relinquishing rational control over the process of drawing and composition, all filters are removed and the artist becomes a 'simple receptacle of so many echoes' of society's collective imagination, and a 'modest recording instrument' of its desires, anxieties and fears.[3]

It heightened … the possibility of revealing correspondences, those metaphorical linkages between inner life and the external world.

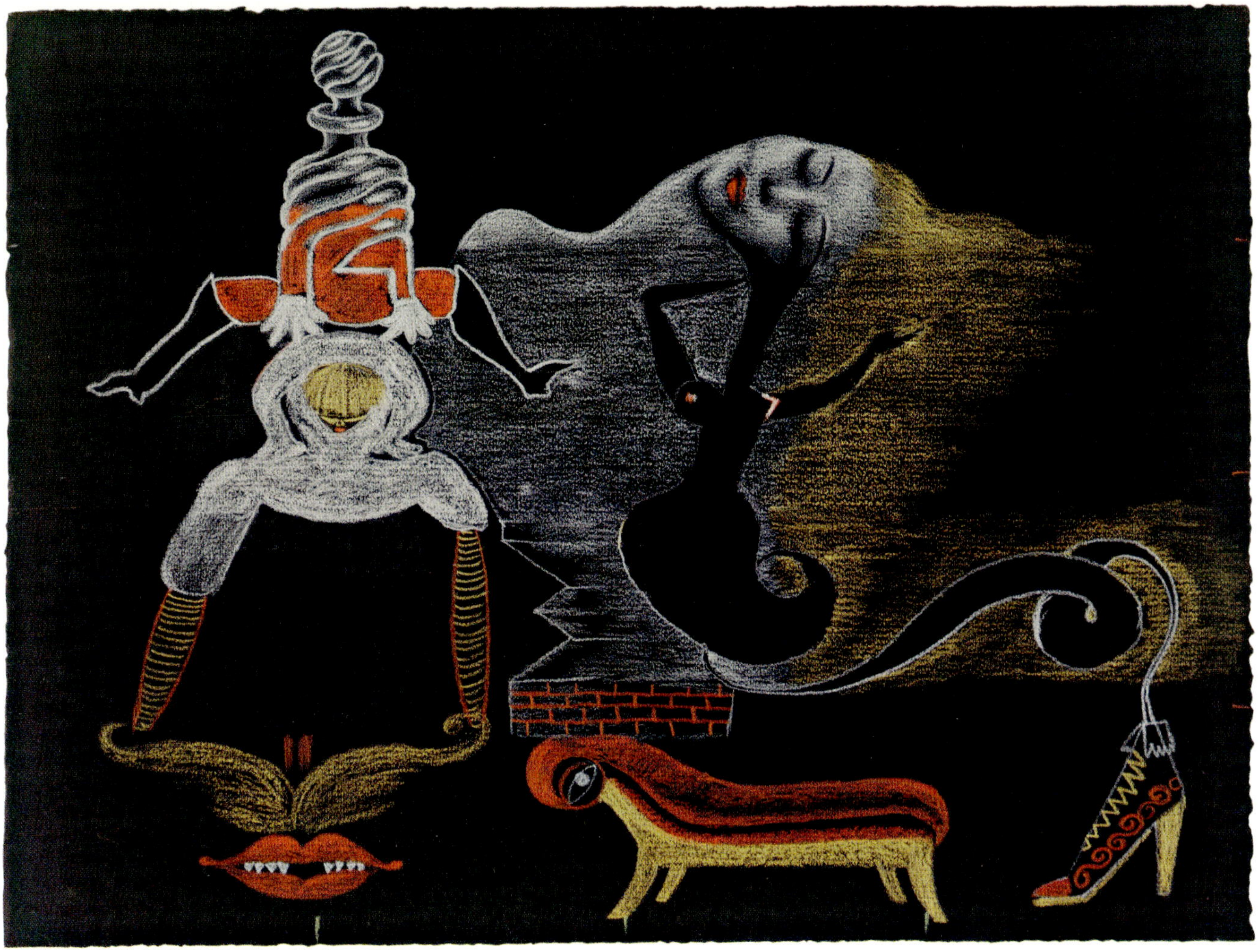

ABOVE: Valentine Hugo, André Breton, Tristan Tzara, and Greta Knutsen, *Exquisite Corpse (Landscape)*, *c.*1933. Composite drawing: coloured chalk on black paper, 24.1 × 31.7 cm ($9\frac{1}{2}$ × $12\frac{1}{2}$ in).

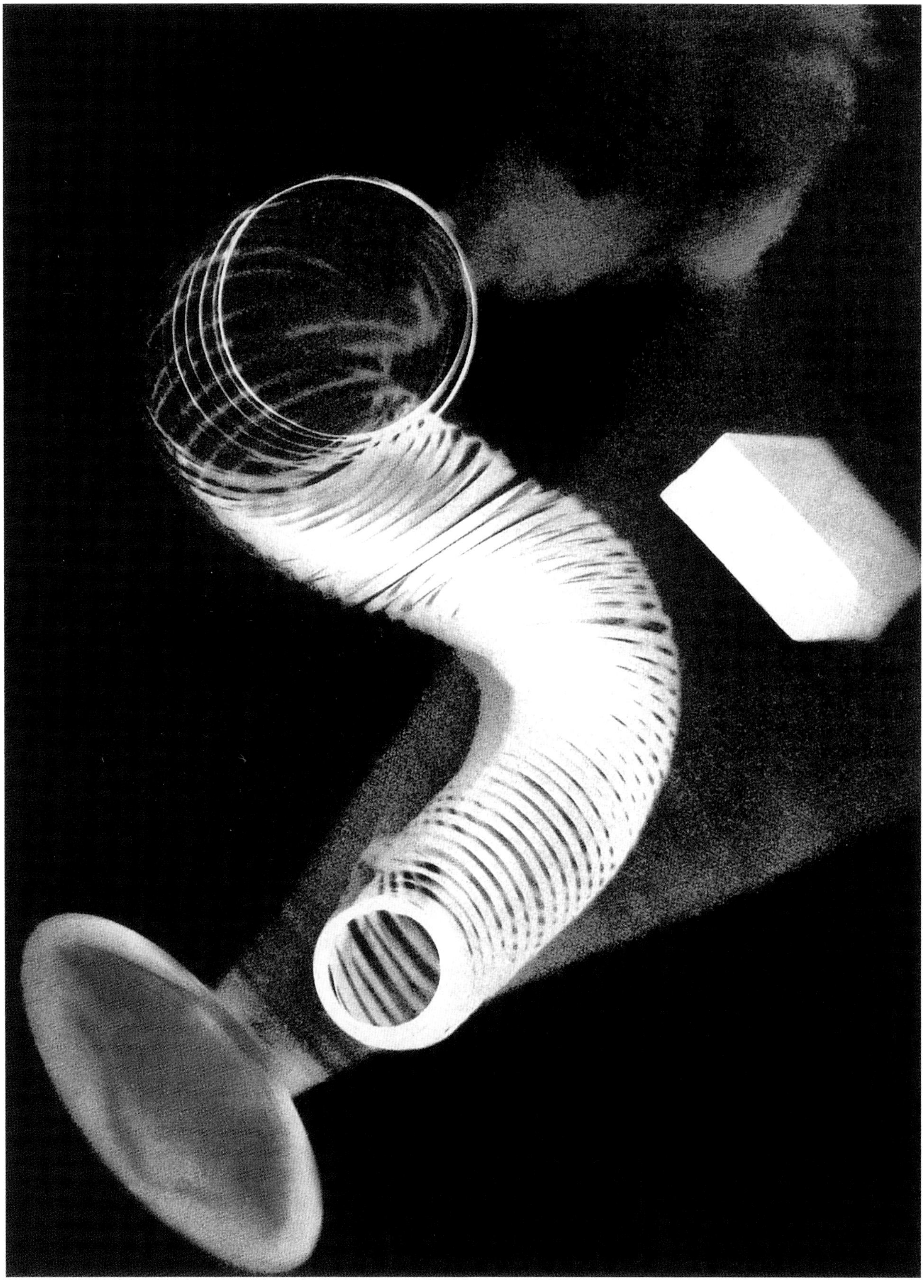

PAINTING WITH LIGHT

In his autobiography, the American artist Man Ray described the beginnings of his interest in the cameraless photograph. Appropriately, for a process that the Tristan Tzara called 'pure dada', it was an accident. During the course of developing some fashion shots taken for the French fashion designer Paul Poiret, an extra, unexposed sheet of paper got caught up and placed in the developing tray. Realizing that no image was going to appear, he placed some items of darkroom equipment on the paper and turned on the light. 'Before my eyes an image began to form, not quite a simple silhouette of the objects … but distorted and refracted … and standing out against a black background'.[4]

He made further prints using whatever small items he found lying around: a key, a handkerchief, some pencils, a brush, a candle, string and so on. When he later showed the results to Poiret, he explained that what he was attempting to do with light and photography was what painters do with pigment. The key feature of the Rayograph – the self-referential name he gave to the products from this process – is that they are made without the intervention of the camera. Unlike a conventional photographic image, which results when light from objects outside the space of the camera is directed by lenses onto a plate or film, the Rayograph image is tactile as much as visual. It arises not only from a chemical process stimulated by light, but also through contact between object and paper. It is immediate and intimate. Man Ray found the outcomes of the Rayograph process to be 'startlingly new and mysterious'.[5] Issuing, not from a view of the world made in the light of day, but out of the necessarily isolated interior of the darkroom, these images inevitably bring with them a sense of the unconscious and the dreamworld, that vital dimension for the surrealists.

Man Ray's allusion to the close relationship between painting and photography is in accord with the German critic Walter Benjamin, who notes in his 1931 'A Short History of Photography' that many of photography's early pioneers began as painters, turning their back on it only after attempting to bring its expressive resources 'into a living and unequivocal relationship with modern life'.[6] And after making this observation, Benjamin quotes Tzara on the brilliance of the darkroom light when set against the sparkle of the night sky:

> *When everything that called itself art was stricken with palsy, the photographer switched on his thousand-candle power lamp and gradually the light-sensitive paper absorbed the darkness of a few everyday objects. He had discovered what could be done by a pure and sensitive flash of light – a light that was more important than all the constellations arranged for the eye's pleasure.*[7]

OPPOSITE: Man Ray, *Untitled Rayograph*, 1922. Gelatin silver photogram, 23.5 × 17.8 cm (9¼ × 7 in).

Louise Bourgeois showed her Femme-Maison series in New York in 1947. Although she was French, she stated that it was only once she had moved to New York from Paris in 1938 that she could make the paintings. New York was a city she loved for 'its clean-cut look, its sky, its buildings, its scientific, cruel, romantic quality'.[8] All four works in the series are in the same tall, narrow, exaggerated portrait format and the same size. The first three are oil and ink on linen, and the fourth is ink alone. The figure in each is a naked woman whose upper body and head is encased within an architectural structure: a clapboard house, a classical building with columns supporting its pedimented facade, a high tower and a substantial villa of several storeys.

The building never completely encloses the woman. In the first work, a yellow figure stands in profile in front of a red backdrop extending three-quarters of the way down the canvas. She has no arms. The lower legs of a second figure are visible below the bottom edge of this screen or curtain. The house covers her head and shoulders, stopping just at the top of her breasts. Her hair streams out from the roof. Hair also escapes the roof in the second image, pictured opposite. Once again, the figure has no arms, but this time it is cut off at the knees. She is shown in full frontal, pale red against a background of orange-red above a broad white band. Her sex, much paler still than the rest of her body, is prominent. Three arms extend from the tower's upper windows in the third, and a small hand waves on the left of the fourth while another hangs down on the right. Of the fourth image, Bourgeois said:

> *There is sexual loneliness. She is dignified, but she is alone … she has no companion. The little hand is trying to call for help. She is not sexual at all. Her head does not know that she is naked. She has no hair or bosom … they are occupied by work.*[9]

By the time of making the Femme-Maison series, Bourgeois was a mother of three. She knew the surrealists both in Paris and in New York exile during the war, and in Femme-Maison we see a thorough rejection of the movement and its attitudes. While surrealism championed the revolutionary power of the unconscious, it did not consider that revolution reaching into the domestic space. As American art historian Mignon Nixon has pointed out, 'surrealism's fantasy of the feminine is child-free'.[10]

Bourgeois saw the composition of *Femme-Maison* as bringing together the two spaces: interior and exterior, private and public, personal and social. It is, she said, 'a symbiosis of one with the universe'.[11] The women, or woman, of Femme-Maison did not yet, as Bourgeois later wrote, 'have enough poise or objectivity'[12] to deal with the question, 'Are you male or female?' She could not at that time say, 'Don't ask me such a question!':

> *She does not know that she is half naked, and she does not know that she is trying to hide. That is to say, she is totally self-defeating because she shows herself at the very moment that she thinks she is hiding.*[13]

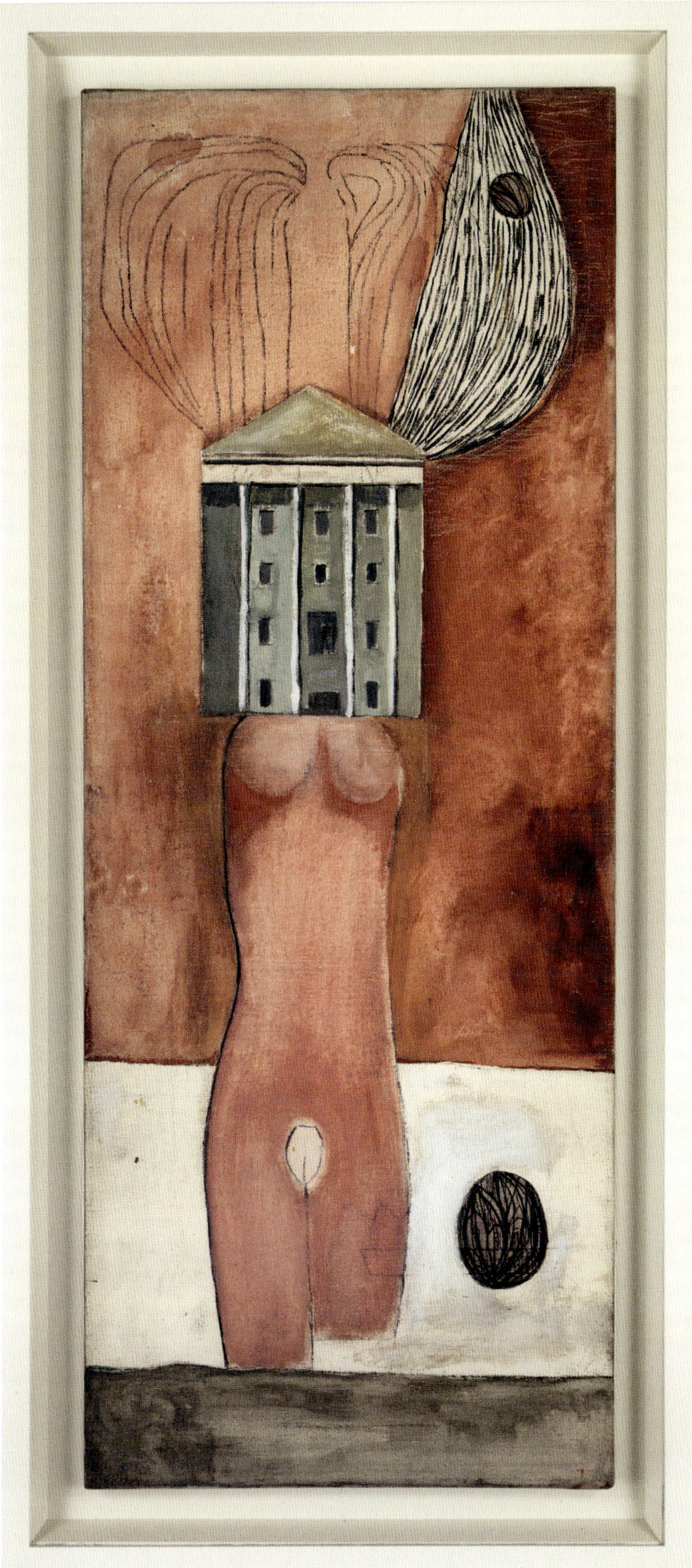

While surrealism championed the revolutionary power of the unconscious, it did not consider that revolution reaching into the domestic space.

LEFT: Louise Bourgeois, *Femme Maison*, 1946–7. Oil and ink on linen, 91.4 × 35.5 cm (36 × 14 in).

THE NEW TOTAL REALISM

In his study of *fin de siècle* Paris, the subject of his book *The Banquet Years*, the American author Roger Shattuck began his discussion of the French artist Henri Rousseau's paintings by considering the appropriateness or otherwise of attaching the description 'primitive' to the artist. In this case, the term is seen as interchangeable with 'naif', signifying a lack of both sophistication and of a proper understanding of the accepted rules of artistic composition. Rousseau undertook no substantial training, and received much criticism for this; the critic Guillaume Apollinaire described him as an autodidact who, notwithstanding the fact of his 'undeniable natural talents', was obviously without education and 'should have been no more than an artisan'.[1] For the Russian artist Wassily Kandinsky, however, it was Rousseau's perceived naiveté that was the appeal of his work. In describing him and his work, Kandinsky wrote:

> *The artist, whose whole life is similar in many ways to that of a child, can often realize the inner sound of things more easily than anyone else … Here lies the root of the new total realism.*[2]

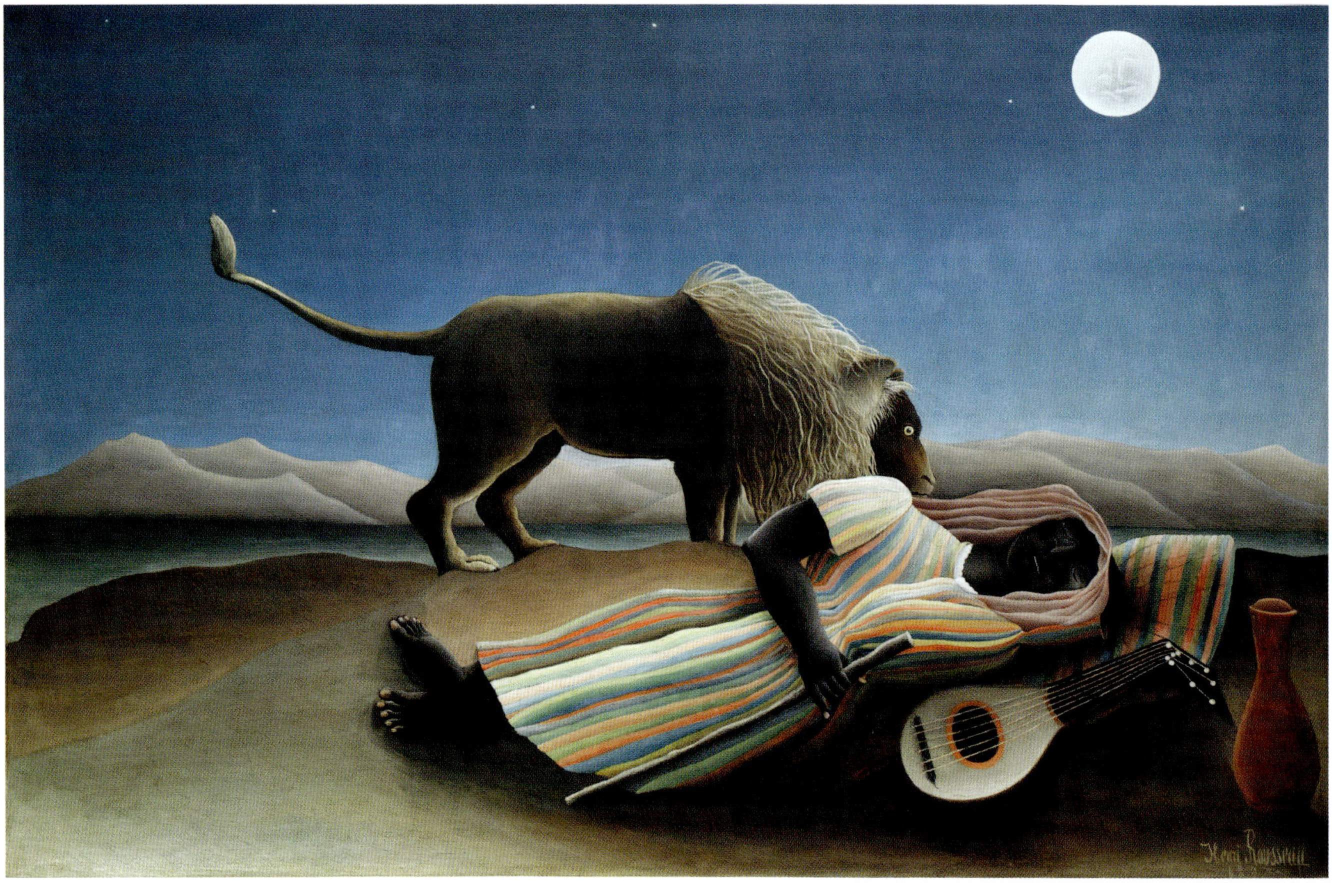

ABOVE: Henri Rousseau, *The Sleeping Gypsy*, 1897. Oil on canvas, 129.5 × 200.7 cm (51 × 79 in).

Rousseau's 1897 painting *The Sleeping Gypsy* depicts a woman stretched out in a desert landscape. Her right arm, bent at the elbow, rests across her body and she loosely holds a wooden staff. On the ground by her side are her mandolin and a jug of water. Behind her stands a lion, described by Rousseau thus: 'A lion wanders by, detects her and doesn't devour her.'[3] The lion is, nonetheless, alert. His eye, which stands out above the woman's shoulder, is wide open and his tail is erect. His mane is combed forward so that it continues the line from top left along the tail, across his back and down, over the woman's shoulder, round the neckline of her gown, and on to the neck and head of the instrument. The sense of flow is heightened by the narrow stripes of the woman's gown – paralleled by the mandolin strings – and the folds of the scarf that covers her head.

We have already seen a sensuous meander of this kind in Mary Cassatt, even down to the way in which the curves of a water jug are incorporated as suggestive of bodily form (see pages 40–1). What differs here is the way in which Rousseau's composition comprises a sequence of thin, flat layers. The position of the sleeping woman's feet imply that she is lying on her back, but her body is turned towards us so that we view her frontally. The sharp outline of her garments emphasizes this frontality, as does the distinct contour of the ground on which she is lying. While his back feet rest on this contour line, the lion's front paws are hidden behind it so that he is at once both right behind the woman and at a little distance. It is as if we are looking at a series of theatrical flats, one behind the other. The summits of the hills in the background stand out equally clearly as a third layer against the dark blue of the sky. Everything is clear, direct and unfussy: the woman, the lion, the arid landscape and the night sky. Everywhere, too, it sparkles with points of light: the lion's eye, the woman's teeth, fingernails and toenails, the tensioning pegs on the mandolin, the stars and, above all, the disc of the full moon. Kandinsky wrote:

> *In rendering the shell of an object simply and completely, one has already separated the object from its practical meaning and peeled forth its interior sounds. Henri Rousseau, who may be considered the father of this realism, has pointed the way simply and convincingly.*[4]

In its apparent innocence of style, Rousseau's composition reveals the rhythms at play in the scene as they resonate between woman, lion, landscape and sky. For Kandinsky himself, this was support for his own journey towards abstraction (see pages 108–9): 'The "representational" reduced to a minimum must in abstraction be regarded as the most intensely effective reality.'[5] The appeal of naiveté is pervasive at the turn of the twentieth century and can be recognized, as already mentioned, for example, in the revived interest in vernacular crafts in art nouveau design. One negative consequence, as Shattuck's questioning reveals, is to see non-European art as equally, and necessarily, lacking in sophistication. This conception of the 'primitive', so dominant in the art of the twentieth century, would prove hard to dislodge.

It is as if we are looking at a series of theatrical flats, one behind the other … Everything is clear, direct and unfussy.

French artist Niki de Saint Phalle began her Tirs performances in 1961 (from the French, *tirer*: 'to shoot'). Preparation involved constructing relief panels with a variety of objects, including dolls, religious items, fragments of crockery, toy cars and aeroplanes, and flowers, into which she fastened bags of paint. For the performance, she would shoot at the panel, causing the paint bags to burst and allowing their contents to spray and spill over the white surface. She explained that she shot because it was fun and it made her feel good. 'Men with their rockets, their atomic bomb, and all that filth they've dumped on us', she said.[6] 'Only a woman could use those destructive contraptions that man has imagined for a constructive end, and that's beautiful.'[7]

She had been taken aback when the American painter Joan Mitchell seemed to dismiss her ambitions, since Saint Phalle did not have commercial gallery representation and could therefore not be taken as a serious artist. Saint Phalle's position was perhaps also made more difficult by the fact that she had not been to art school. The French painter Jean Dubuffet had coined the term 'art brut' to refer to art made by those outside the established context provided by art schools, galleries and museums, but Saint Phalle, though lacking a formal art education, was very much an insider. When she showed the *Tirs* in New York, she involved her friends, the American artists Jasper Johns and Robert Rauschenberg, in the exhibition. Resonances with the work of both can be seen in the assemblage-like reliefs she constructed, as well as in her use of strong colour. There is, too, an affinity with Jackson Pollock's drip technique (see pages 146–7), and some criticism of her New York exhibition emphasized the view that her work was derivative. Donald Judd, for example, reviewing in *Arts* magazine, saw it as betraying the 'prevalent European failing' of mixing 'novel devices with very naive ideas about … past culture'.[8] But Saint Phalle was clear, both that her work was distinct and also that it arose from a quite different motivation: 'I wanted the world and the world then belonged to MEN … I felt jealous and resentful that the only power allotted to me was the power of attracting men' (she had worked as a model in the 1950s, appearing on the cover of *Vogue* in 1953).[9]

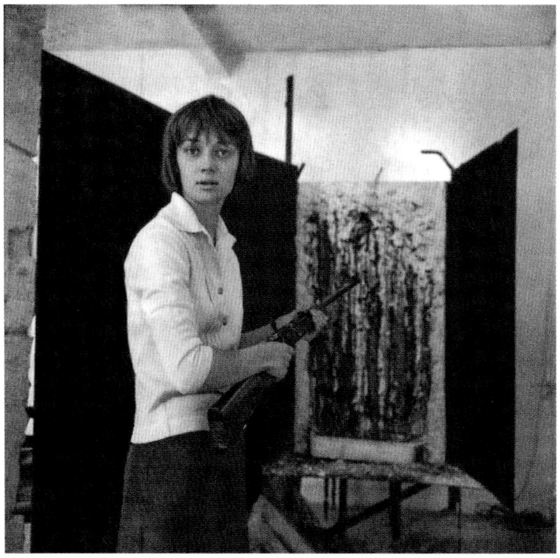

ABOVE: Niki de Saint Phalle performing Tirs at her *Feu à Volonté* exhibition, Galerie J, Paris, 1961.

After *Tirs*, Saint Phalle began making the large, exuberant sculptures that she collectively referred to as Nanas. These were initially inspired by the sight of her friend Clarice Rivers in the last weeks of pregnancy, and by Neolithic figurines of the fertile female form, such as the Venus of Willendorf figurine. With small heads, tapered limbs and rounded torsos, the Nanas are the antithesis of the slender, gamine look then coming into favour for fashion models. The brightly coloured patterning of their surfaces is a further contrast with the standards of beauty provided by Classical Greek statuary – although originally coloured, they were now being valued in their white marble state, an absence that has characterized much modern architecture and established the pretend purity of the white cube gallery. Saint Phalle had visited Barcelona's Park Güell, and had been impressed with the ceramic mosaics decorating the features designed there by the Spanish architect Antoni Gaudí. Gaudí's influence is evident in the all-over fractured colours of the Nanas' surfaces as much as in the colourful outcomes of the shot-at Tirs panels.

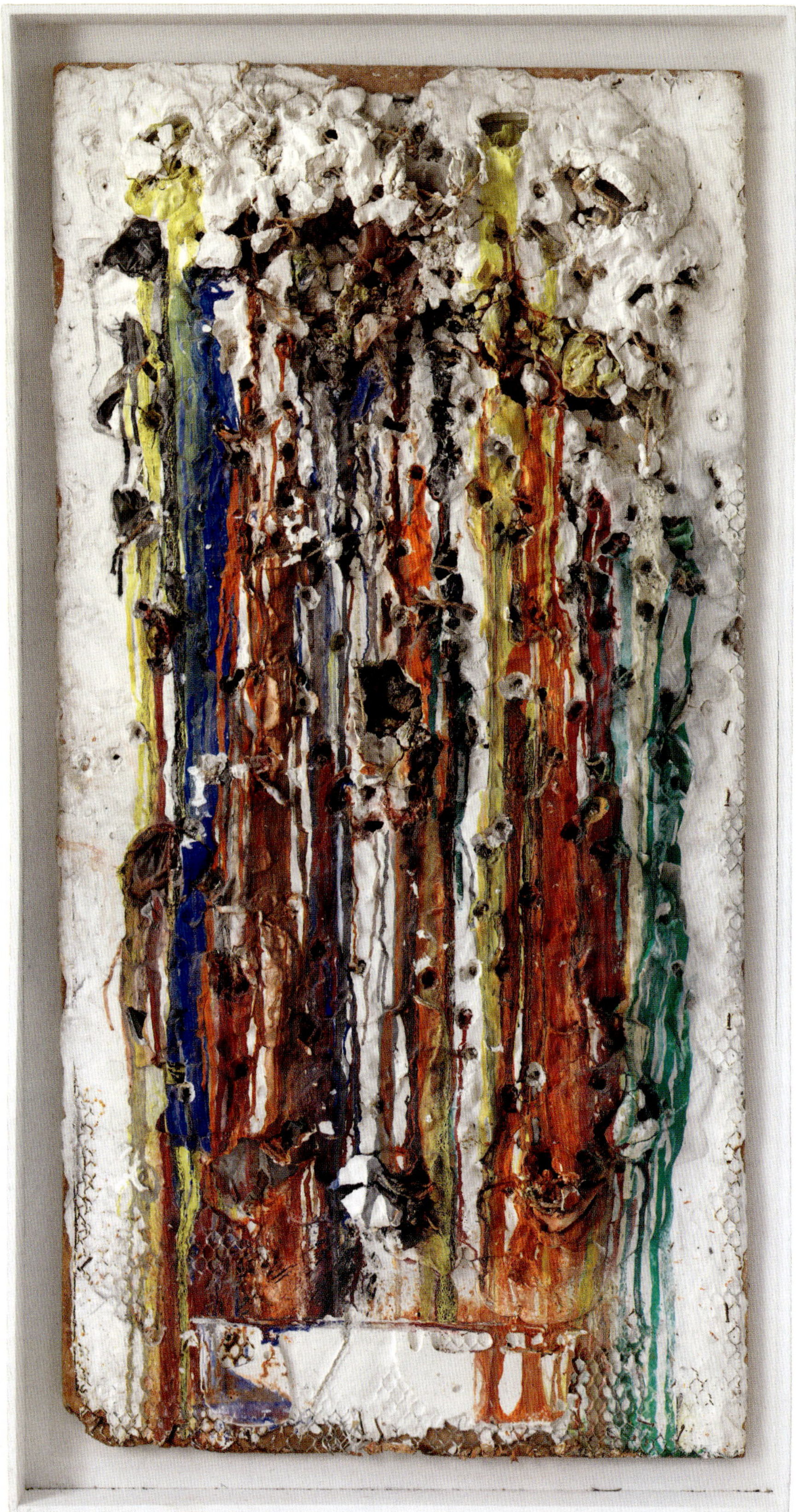

ABOVE: Niki de Saint Phalle, *Grand Tir – Séance de la Galerie J*, 1961. Paint, plaster, wire, fabrics, plastic on wooden panel, 143 × 77 × 7 cm (56¼ × 30⅜ × 2¾ in).

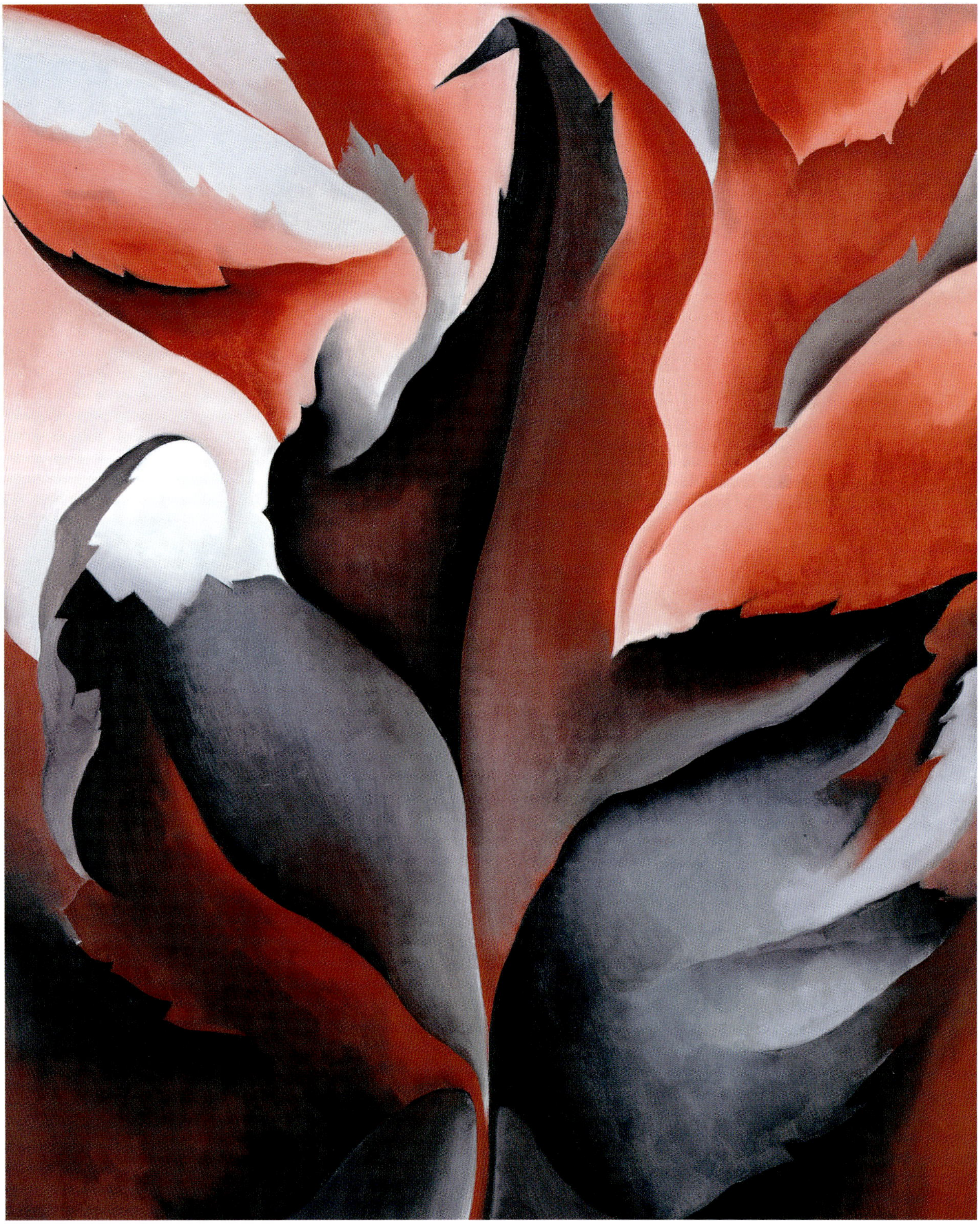

ABOVE: Georgia O'Keeffe, *The Red Maple at Lake George*, 1926.
Oil on canvas, 91.4 × 76.2 cm (36 × 30 in).

The basic triangular shape of *The Red Maple At Lake George* is akin to cubist composition. Predominant greys and dark reds in its lower portion continue up a sinuous central spine that divides the lighter reds, pinks and whites of its upper quadrants. A mix of undulating and sharply angled lines convey a strong sense of the serrated edges and curling planes of the tree's leaves. Unlike the cubists, whose broken planar forms built a reconfirmed reality, or Kandinsky, for whom exploration of line and colour led inexorably towards non-representation and abstraction (see pages 108–9), O'Keeffe saw these two paths as inextricable and mutually sustaining:

> *It is surprising to me to see how many people separate the objective from the abstract. Objective painting is not good painting unless it is good in the abstract sense. A hill or tree cannot make a good painting just because it is a hill or a tree. It is lines and colours put together so that they say something. For me that is the very basis of painting. The abstraction is often the most definite form for the intangible thing in myself that I can only clarify in paint.*[10]

For O'Keeffe, the process of abstraction is the process of composition. It allowed her to remove extraneous detail in rendering the essential qualities of a closely observed leaf or flower. 'One rarely takes the time to really see a flower', she wrote in a statement accompanying the first showing of *Black Iris III*, painted in same year as *The Red Maple Leaf at Lake George*, 'I have painted what each flower is to me and I have painted it big enough so that the others would see what I see.'[11] O'Keeffe was particularly interested in the work of the American photographer Paul Strand. His own interest in cubism prompted his studies of objects shot in extreme close-up, which saw them lose their identity as things and become a pattern of lines and shapes. O'Keeffe wrote to Strand, 'I believe I've been looking at things and seeing them as I thought you might photograph them.'[12]

O'Keeffe's position as a rare female artist among so many men exacerbated the struggle to establish an autonomy for her artistic identity. She fought against the intellectually and emotionally lazy tendency to characterize her art only in relation to that of those men – and hence as subordinate. In saying, 'a woman who has lived many things and who sees lines and colours as an expression of living might say something that a man can't',[13] she stressed that autonomy. O'Keeffe's work is its own thing and it could come only from her. Therefore her work should not be judged in comparison to the work of a male artist produced according to criteria instituted by men. Likewise, O'Keeffe would resist interpretations that took the similarity between her leaves, flowers, skulls or landscapes and the female anatomy as straightforwardly proto-feminist forms of expression that celebrated female sexuality. Holding such views might instrumentalize the paintings in the service of a wider battle, but they also suppress the immediacy of that close, analytical observation of the forms of the world that are at their centre.

One rarely takes the time to really see a flower … I have painted what each flower is to me and I have painted it big enough so that the others would see what I see.

– Georgia O'Keeffe, 1926

In his study, *The Cubist Painters: Aesthetic Meditations* (1913), Guillaume Apollinaire acknowledges the role played by the objects represented in cubist compositions. Their everyday familiarity means that they are not in themselves of any significance, but in compositional terms they are structurally essential:

> *The object, real or represented in* trompe-l'oeil, *is clearly called upon to play a more and more important role. The object is the inner frame of the picture and marks the limits of its depth just as the outer frame marks its external limits.*[14]

This idea of the thing depicted as an 'inner frame' is evident in the works by Georg Baselitz. It is a means to keep painting firmly in the realm of realism and representation, and to avoid abstraction. The eagle was one of the first motifs depicted by Baselitz when the German artist began painting his subjects upside down in 1969. He has continued to work in this way in the years since. Through this act of inversion, the subject remains subordinate to the act of painting itself. A viewer approaching the finished work with the question 'What is this a painting of?' will find their expectations thwarted. The canvas does not immediately offer its subject matter, enabling the viewer first to encounter the work as paint on canvas and to explore relationships between colours and marks across its surface.

Several years earlier Baselitz had written, 'Stand the topsy turvy world on its head', and the British art historian Richard Calvocoressi has suggested that 'the tilted, then upside-down, world' subsequently seen in Baselitz's paintings 'represents a vision of social disintegration, of madness, where moral values are threatened and upset'.[15] Born just before the outbreak of the Second World War, Baselitz's childhood environment was one of a destroyed physical, political and social order. His desire was not to restore that order, but instead to look at things from a position of ostensibly naive curiosity. Not least in establishing that position was a reconnection with the expressionism of the early twentieth century and that movement's own use of naivete, what it understood as 'primitivism', and vernacular form in resisting authority. Baselitz made inverted interpretations of works by Emil Nolde and other artists of the Brücke (see page 48), as well as others, including Rousseau's *The Sleeping Gypsy* (see pages 94–5) – the latter's influence can be seen in Baselitz's 1980 painting *Woman on the Beach: Night in Tunisia*. In this, Baselitz was only one among a number of German painters whose look back to that movement led to their being referred to as neo-expressionists.

His desire was not to restore that order, but instead to look at things from a position of ostensibly naive curiosity.

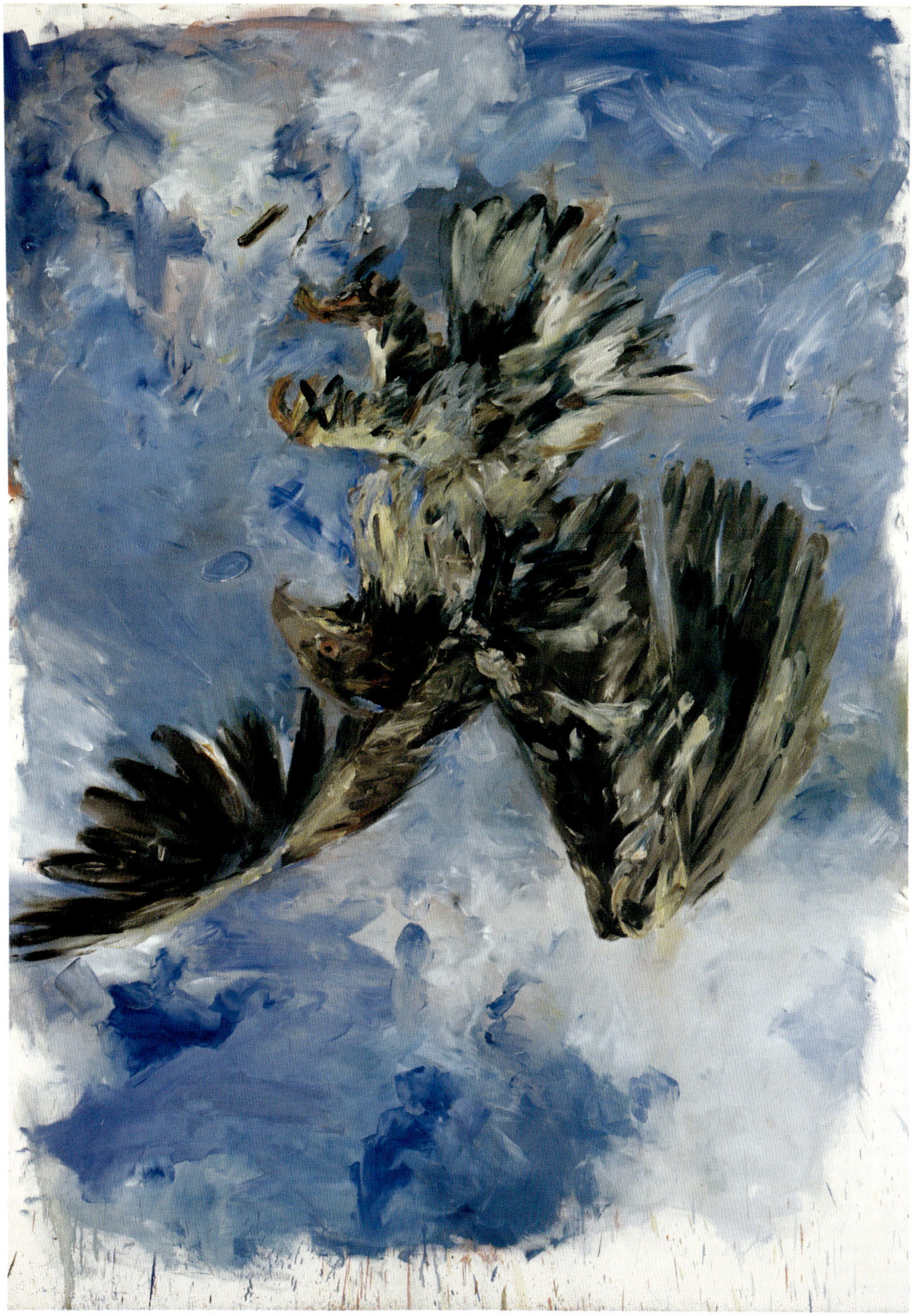

ABOVE: Georg Baselitz, *Finger Painting – Eagle*, 1972.
Oil on canvas, 249.5 × 180.3 cm (98¼ × 71 in).

CHAPTER III

A NEW MEANING

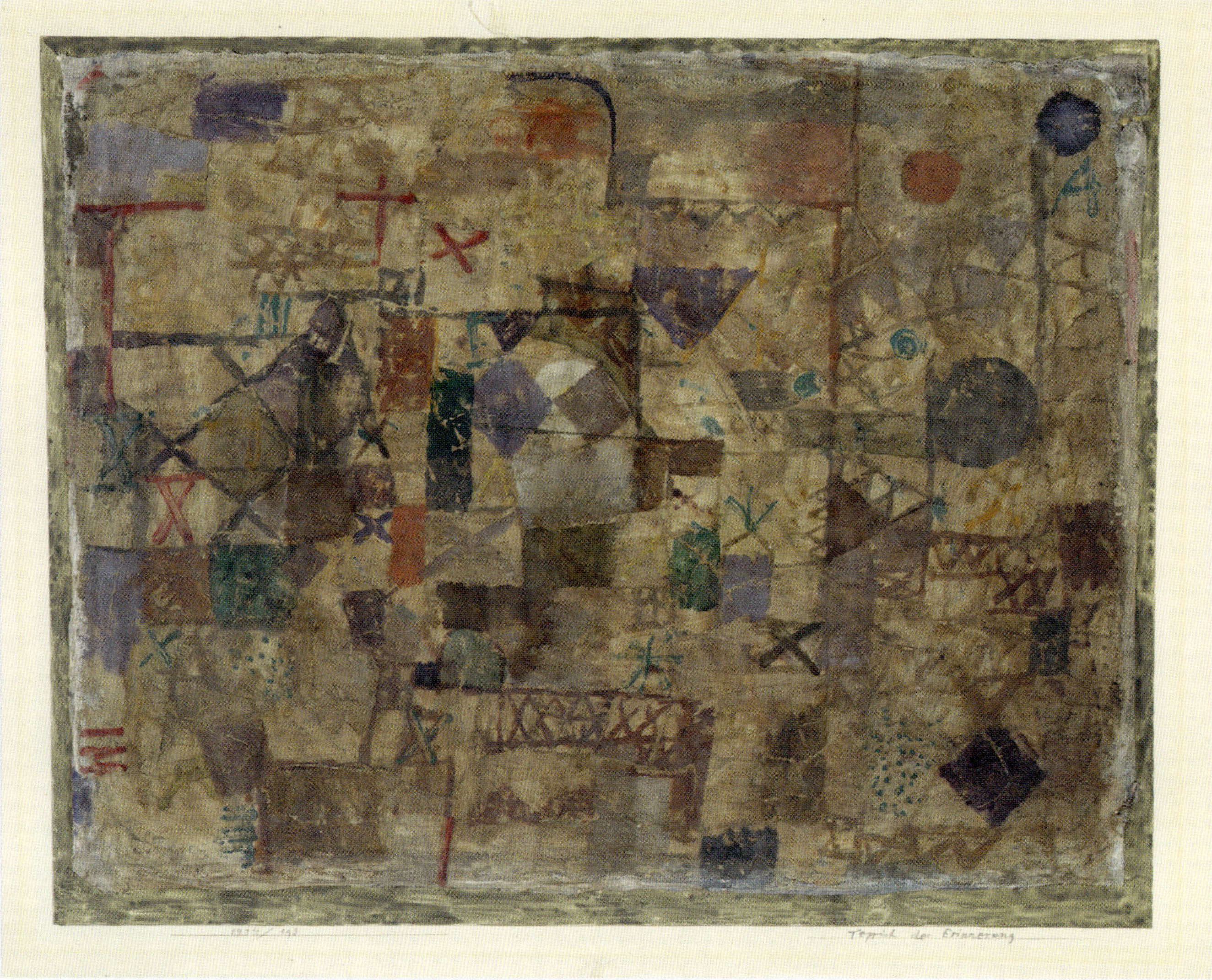

THE FABRIC OF REALITY

The Swiss-born German artist Paul Klee visited Tunisia in 1914 with fellow artists Louis Moilliet and August Macke, and the work Klee produced after this trip is marked by a shift in his compositional approach. Klee moved away from a placement of objects within the three dimensions of a depicted space towards a distribution of colour patches across the picture surface. Osamu Okuda, a Klee scholar from Japan, has described this pattern of distribution as carpet-like and, indeed, Klee has used the word in titling a number of compositions from this period. *Carpet of Memory* is one such work. Originally painted in a portrait format in 1914, Klee returned to the painting over the next few years, during which time he eventually turned the composition by 90 degrees to the left. Squares, lozenges, circles and oblong blocks of colour are placed across the picture surface within a scaffold of lines, crosses and arcs. Nothing is defined in representational detail; all is in the rhythm of colour patches and marks that are reminiscent of the architecture, colours, forms and landscapes seen on his North African journey without becoming descriptive.

In his 2010 study *Soul and Form*, the Hungarian critic György Lukács also used the image of the patterned carpet in explaining our efforts to comprehend the world of our experience:

> *There is an order concealed in the world of history, a composition in the confusion of its irregular lines. It is the undefinable order of a carpet or a dance; to interpret its meaning seems impossible, but it is still less possible to give up trying to interpret it. It is as though the whole fabric of fanciful lines were waiting for a single word that is always at the tip of our tongues, yet one which has never yet been spoken by anyone.*[1]

Various versions of abstraction appeared in the early decades of the twentieth century and all, in their various ways, have rested on a profound unease at the state of affairs in the world and signalled efforts to give form to possible alternatives. War, revolution, the physically and psychically disorienting impact of hitherto unfeasible speeds of travel, scientific and technical advances that enable us to see what the human eye cannot see and to penetrate the human body – all of these fuelled the search for a form of artistic expression that would take the viewer beyond the pragmatics of their prevailing circumstances. Forty years after the first appearances of abstract art, the American critic Clement Greenberg could still assert that, 'no one has yet been able to demonstrate that the representational as such either adds or takes away from the merit of a picture'.[2]

OPPOSITE: Paul Klee, *Carpet of Memory*, 1914 (cat. no. 193).
Oil on primed linen on cardboard, 37.8 × 50.3 cm (14⅞ × 19⅞ in).

AUTOMATIC COMPOSITION

In the 1890s, Swedish artist Hilma af Klint became one of the first women to attend Stockholm's Royal Academy of Fine Art. On graduating, she formed the group De Fem (The Five) with her fellow academician Anna Cassel and three other women. They were all interested in spirituality and the religious ideas behind theosophy. They conducted regular seances, and from these sessions emerged the collective sense of a dialogue with spirit personalities called 'The High Ones'. In a 1904 session, one of them, Amaliel, invited the women to engage in 'automatic' painting as a means to more fully access the spirit world with which they felt themselves to be in touch. Only af Klint took up this invitation.

Between 1906 and 1915, af Klint painted 193 works she collectively titled The Paintings for the Temple, and towards the end of this nine-year period she made *Group X, Altarpiece No. 2.* Its lower section comprises three triangles. Lines run from the bottom centre to a point two-thirds up the left- and right-hand edges of the canvas, forming an inverted isosceles triangle with right-angled triangles to either side. The outer areas are a figured deep red, except for a band of grey running across the bottom. They support the inner area so that, far from balancing precariously on its sharpest angle, we understand it to be expanding as it rises upwards. Lines from the bottom edge, at the centre, divide the central triangle into five sectors, which are themselves further subdivided by fifteen horizontals into regular segments. While the outer sectors are of a consistent dark colour, the central shaft is a column of ever-larger, double golden scrolls. In the upper portion of the canvas, a large golden disc rests on the tip of the highest scroll. A thin line, giving a sense of atmosphere and energy rather than substance, spirals round the disc and off the top of the picture.

As the overall name for the series implies, these paintings were intended not for exhibition in a gallery, but for installation in a religious space. Af Klint's journals show that she had both a chosen location and a developed idea on the structure of a temple. On the process of making her works, she wrote:

> *The pictures were painted directly through me, without any preliminary drawings, and with great force. I had no idea what the paintings were supposed to depict. Nevertheless, I worked swiftly and surely, without changing a single brushstroke.*[1]

She further noted that she did not consider herself to be proceeding in blind obeyance to the 'High Lords of the Mysteries', but that she felt them always by her side.[2]

These paintings were intended not for exhibition in a gallery, but for installation in a religious space.

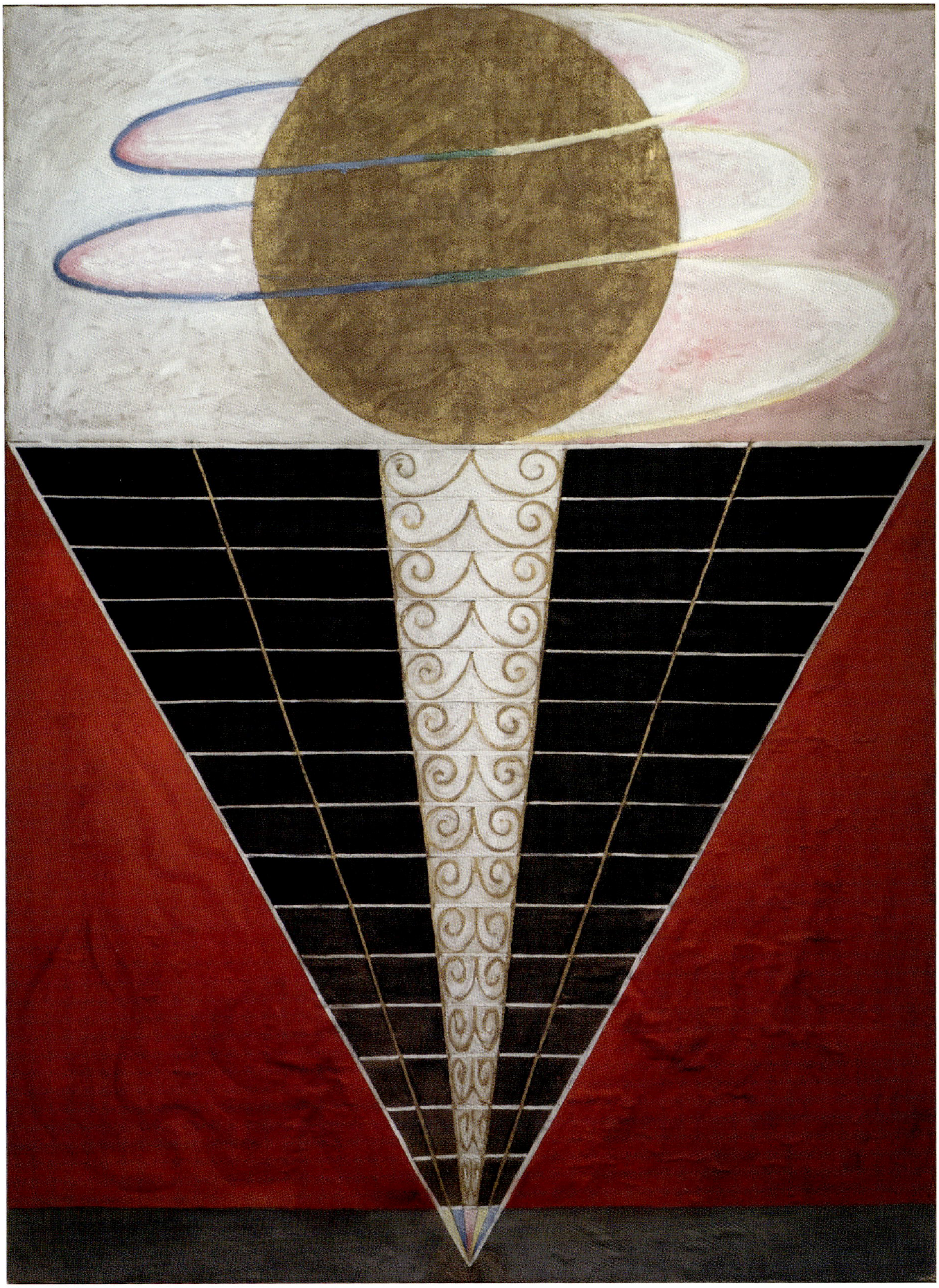

ABOVE: Hilma af Klint, *Group X, Altarpiece No. 2*, 1915.
Oil and metal leaf on canvas, 238 × 179 cm (9³⁄₈ × 70³⁄₈ in).

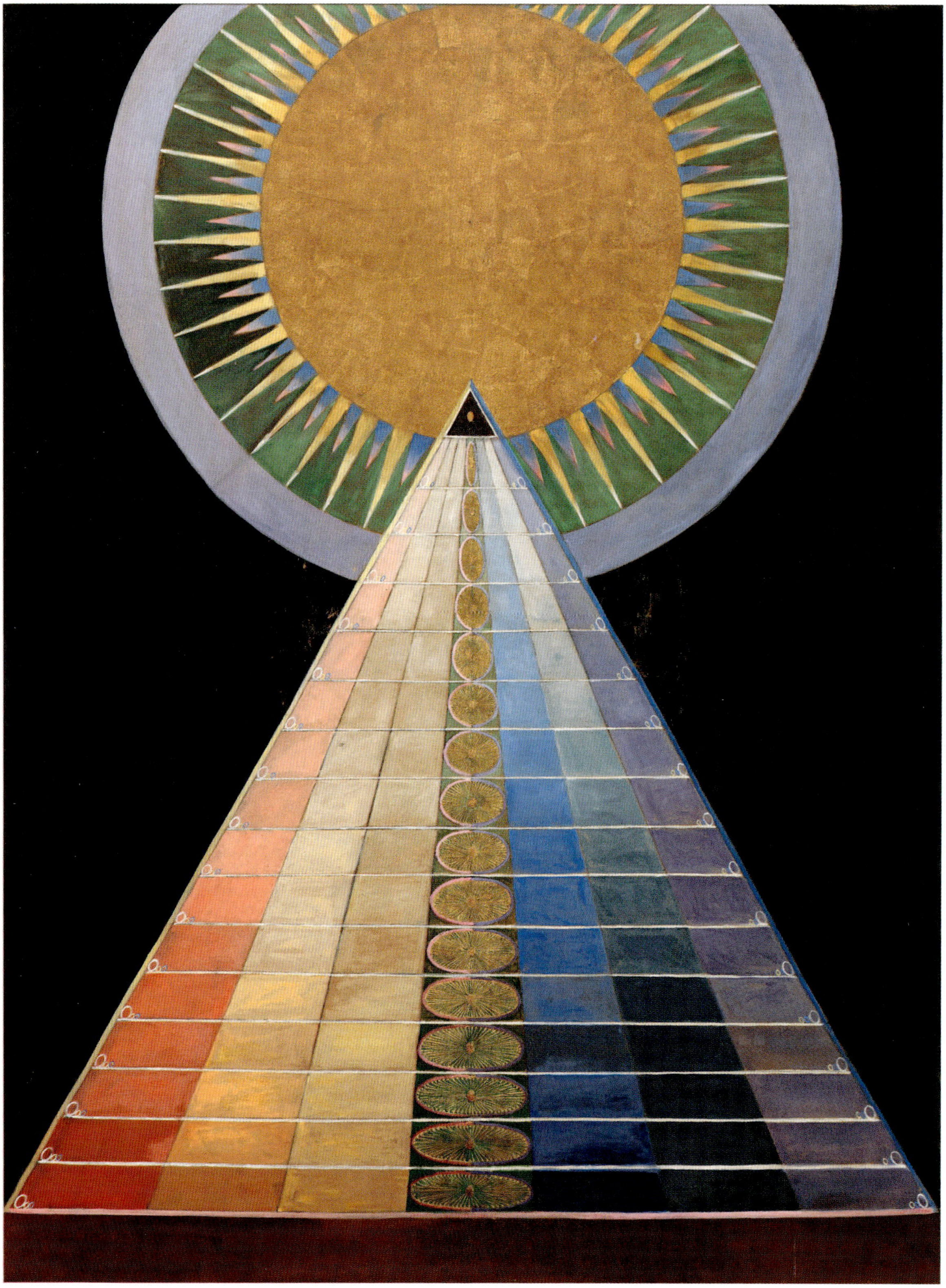

ABOVE: Hilma af Klint, *Group X, Altarpiece No. 1*, 1915. Oil and metal leaf on canvas, 237.5 × 179.5 cm (93½ × 70⅝ in).

Along with much else, the 1890s saw the discovery of the electron, electromagnetic waves and radiation. All of these coupled with elements already being shown through photography, brought an awareness of how much in our lives remains invisible to us. Just as people nowadays might think of physicists looking for a grand unified theory of electromagnetic, gravitational, strong and weak nuclear forces, the popular imagination at the time held a strong notion of an 'ether' in which all of these otherwise invisible forces and realities might coexist. There was the belief that above a physical plane on which we conduct our daily lives existed an astral plane where all the opposing elements we experience can come together in unity. In af Klint's paintings, the spiral occurs repeatedly as an image of a potential ascension to such an enlightened state. The bottom of the central triangle in *Group X, Altarpiece No. 2* has sectors of blue and yellow, as does the upper spiral. To af Klint, yellow signified male and blue female. What was being striven for was a state of non-gendered unity.

Standard histories of modern art explain the emergence of abstraction with reference to artists such as Wassily Kandinsky and Piet Mondrian, both of whom were also interested in theosophy and ideas of spirituality. It is clear that The Paintings for the Temple, begun in 1906, show that af Klint had been producing abstract compositions for a number of years before either of them. With this knowledge, however, we cannot simply place her retrospectively at the head of an otherwise unchanged timeline. Apart from a small number of paintings shown at a convention on spirituality in London in 1928, af Klint did not exhibit any of this work in her lifetime. Furthermore, she left an instruction in her journal that nothing should be shown until twenty years after her death. She died in 1944, so it was not possible to consider showing this work to the public until the mid-1960s, and, in fact, it was only in 1985 that it was shown. If anything, what af Klint's compositions present us with is a challenge to reconceive what a history of art might be.

THEOSOPHY

At the turn of the twentieth century, there was a rise in new spiritualities such as theosophy – a philosophy promoted by the Russian mystic Helena Blavatsky, British socialist Annie Besant and former British priest Charles Webster Leadbeater – as well as the anthroposophy of Rudolf Steiner. An Austrian-born spiritualist who was originally also an adherent of theosophy, Steiner wrote in his book on the subject:

> *The soul and spirit worlds are just as real as the sense-perceptible world; in fact, they are real in a much higher sense … How these soul and spiritual phenomena become perceptions by means of our inner senses is analogous to how certain processes in space are perceived as colours.*[3]

Despite the fact that an 1887 experiment by the American physicists Albert Michelson and Edward Morley had already cast serious doubt on the existence of a hypothesized light-carrying medium, the luminiferous ether, Besant and Leadbeater spoke of it as something 'now comfortably settled in the scientific kingdom' in the opening section of their 1901 book, *Thought-Forms*. Along with mesmerism and the German scientist Wilhelm Röntgen's rays (hypnosis and X-rays), it gave the impression that science was speculating on 'invisible presences' and attempting to find 'rational explanations' for observed phenomena by contacting the 'astral plane'.[4] Their book is illustrated with a series of abstract coloured forms identified as embodying emotional states. Steiner, along with Besant and Leadbeater, associated specific colours with particular emotions, a tabulation that would be of importance in the developing abstraction of af Klint and Kandinsky. In broader terms, the positing of an accessible spiritual realm alongside our mundane reality was given serious attention by many developing abstract approaches to composition.

THE SPIRITUAL IN ART

In 1911, Wassily Kandinsky wrote *Concerning the Spiritual in Art*. In laying out his thoughts on form, colour and composition, the essay argued the case for abstract art. His argument started with an explanation of 'the movement of the triangle'.[1] As in the case with af Klint (see pages 104–7), it is a segmented form, and through its layers we progress from a solid base up towards a fully enlightened awareness at its peak.

However, the triangle is also a basic, stable organizational structure that we can see in innumerable paintings – in Raphael's *Madonna and Child* (see below), for example, just as clearly as in a Paul Cézanne or a cubist work. Given the universality of such an underlying geometric schema, the artist is free to bring this aspect of their composition forward to our attention and to concentrate less on the material presence of the objects and people depicted. Thus, we can see that 'the abstract idea is creeping into art … Its gradual advance is natural enough, for in proportion as the organic form falls into the background, the abstract ideal achieves greater prominence'.[2]

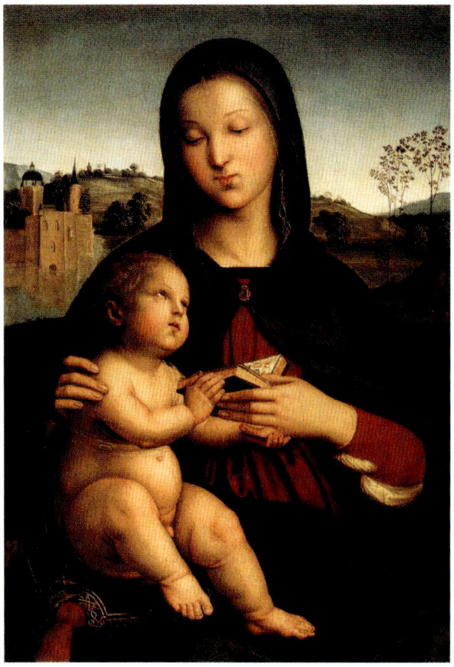

Cossacks, which Kandinsky began in late 1910, shows him in the midst of this advance towards abstraction. Viewed from one perspective, *Cossacks* is a rhythmic play of line and colour. Kandinsky's understanding of line had developed through his study of and work in German woodcut, and his use of colour was influenced by his encounter with post-impressionism and fauvism on visiting Paris. The composition allows both to exist and operate independently of one another: line does not bound and restrict colour, and colour is not asked to perform the task of filling out a prescribed form. Held within the space formed by the thick, jagged black diagonal in the bottom left and the gently curving blue line on the right, a host of black lines and arcs, along with patches of bright colour, animate the surface. A central rainbow bridging the two main diagonals is echoed by interlinked black arcs above and more repeated black curves to its right. Along the top of the composition there are two lilac streaks surrounded by sharply angled lines. All of these abstract elements can resolve themselves into a scene of battle. In the top left, two Cossacks on horseback clash with cutlasses, while in the bottom right there are three more soldiers, two holding lances and the third also with a sword. Above the brow of the hill, where they stand, is a castle. The sky is filled with birds.

While clearly considered a painting in its own right, the arrangement of lines and colours in *Cossacks* also forms the left half of a larger work, *Composition IV*, which was painted early in the following year. Here, the thick black lines of the soldiers' lances divide the canvas vertically, and although they and the two fighting on horseback are still evident, the details of the earlier fragment are now considerably simplified. The castle has no internal detail and, like the landscape and other figures, is just outlined in black. Two lying figures provide an insistent diagonal in the newly extended area on the right, while what is now the middle hill becomes more than anything an intense blue centre to the composition. The birds are absent and the sky, as much as the landscape, has become a patchwork of intense colour.

LEFT: Raphael, *Madonna and Child with Book*, *c.*1502–3. Oil on panel, 55.2 × 40 cm (21¾ × 15¾ in).

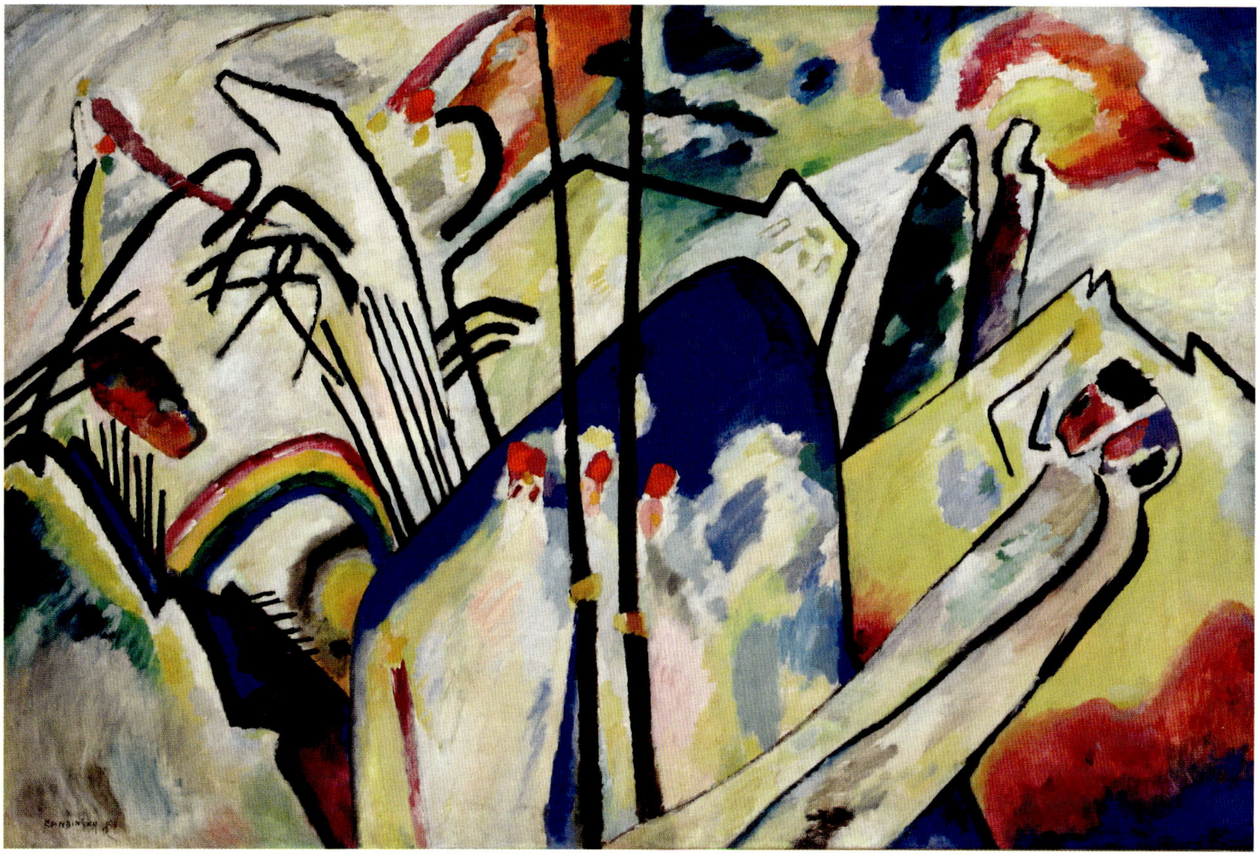

ABOVE: Wassily Kandinsky, *Composition IV*, 1911. Oil on canvas, 159.5 × 250.5 cm (62¾ × 98⅝ in).

By this time, Kandinsky was already using the word 'composition' to describe and title his paintings. This – along with the related descriptor 'improvisation' and his frequent references to the search for harmony and rhythm in his writings – makes plain the degree to which music sat at the heart of his thinking and approach. 'Sound is the soul of form',[3] wrote Kandinsky in an essay printed in a Munich-based expressionist publication he co-edited with German painter Franz Marc (see pages 110–11) in 1912. Synaesthesia, the apprehension of correspondences between the senses, was an important idea, and in this spirit Kandinsky wrote a play, *The Yellow Sound*. In some ways it can be seen as a continuation of the German composer Richard Wagner's idea of his operas as *Gesamtkunstwerke* (total works of art), in that they required input from all of the sensory and creative modes – music, movement, lyrics, colour and scenography – for these works to be realized.

Much later, in 1935, Kandinsky wrote to his dealer asking him to locate an unexhibited work he had made that same year (1911), which he considered to be the first ever abstract painting. As we have already seen, however, this claim remains at the very least debatable.

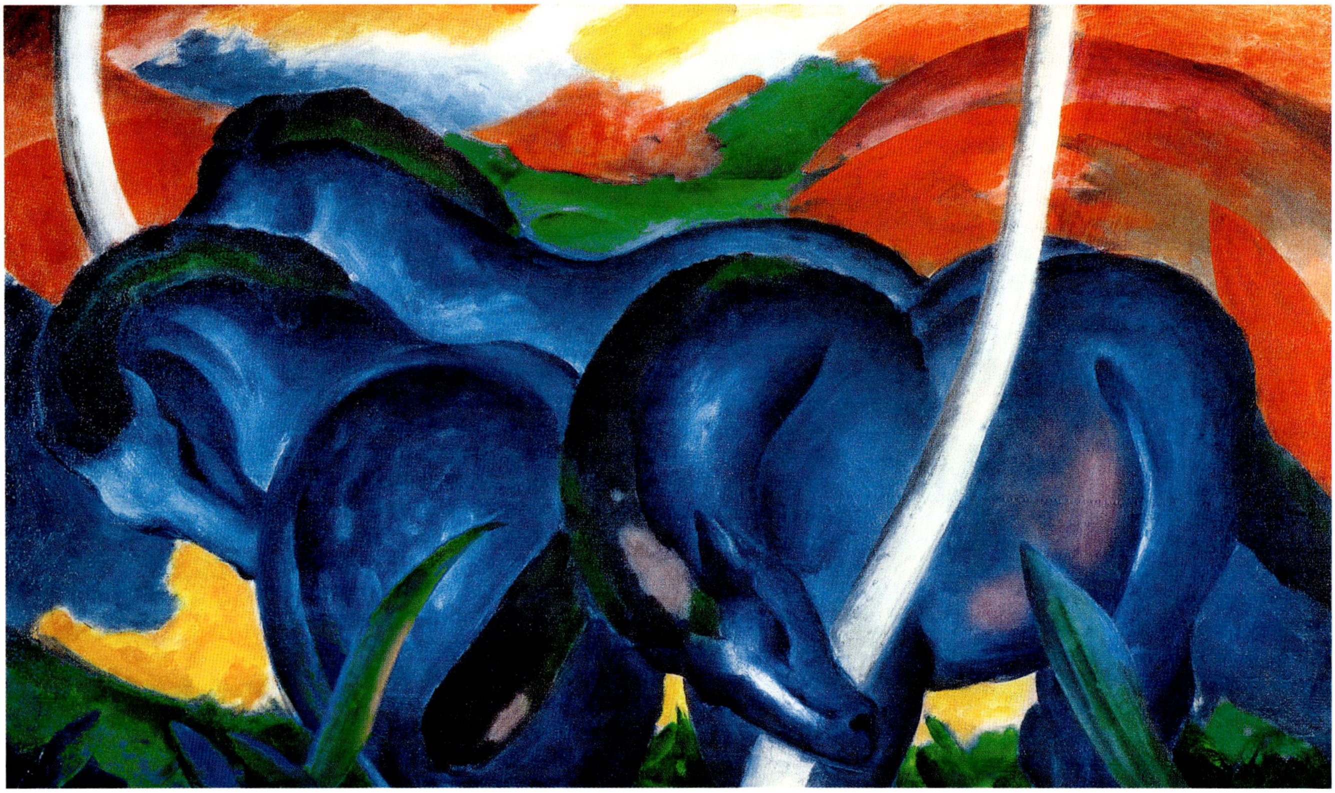

ABOVE: Franz Marc, *The Large Blue Horses*, 1911.
Oil on canvas, 105.6 × 181.4 cm (41⅝ × 71⅜ in).

We should … ask ourselves how the animal itself experiences that landscape. We must 'contemplate the soul of the animal'.

In his aphorisms concerning truth in painting, the words of Franz Marc closely paralleled Wassily Kandinsky's search for the spiritual essence behind the facade of external appearance: 'We finger the shell without reaching the kernel, … the mask of things so blinds us that we cannot find the truth.'[4] If abstraction was the process of discovering appropriate forms in which to express this truth, where for Kandinsky it made non-representation possible, for Marc it was understood as a means to avoid imposing the painter's consciousness onto the scene being depicted. 'Does it make sense to paint an apple and with it the window sill on which it lies?' he asked. 'If you say it is a problem of "sphere and plane", the concept "apple" really falls by the wayside.'[5]

Placing animals into a landscape depicted as we see it is no more than a 'poverty-stricken convention'.[6] What we should do instead is ask ourselves how the animal itself experiences that landscape. We must 'contemplate the soul of the animal' in order that we 'divine its way of sight'.[7] The creatures in Marc's paintings are simplified and somewhat abstracted, but their appearances were developed from a sustained study of animal form, first while he was living in Munich and subsequently, after moving to Berlin, on frequent visits to its zoo. *The Large Blue Horses* is a collection of curves and arcs. The backs, rumps and bent heads of the animals sit in the foreground, their undulating forms echoed by the hilly contours of the land behind.

Primary colours predominate, and Marc saw each of these as possessing particular qualities, as he laid out in a letter to his friend, the German artist August Macke:

> *Blue is the male principle, stern and spiritual. Yellow the female principle, gentle, cheerful and sensual. Red is matter, brutal and heavy and always the colour which must be fought and vanquished by the other two.*[8]

Although the desire to attribute particular characteristics to different colours is familiar, Marc's ideas rested, as he told Macke, more on his own intuitive feelings about colour than on adherence to any established theory. His own blue = male/yellow = female distinction, for example, is the exact opposite to af Klint's usage (see page 107). The horses in this painting are blue, and the background hills are largely red. Yellow ground under the animals establishes their collective and individual presence in a space defined by the white trunks of two trees, one in the right foreground, the other to the rear on the left. Large green leaves spike up from the bottom edge on either side of the central horse's head, establishing the extreme foreground and pointing towards the fields and trees in the near distance. For Marc, it was not the work's 'conventional exterior' that mattered so much as the 'inner life' of the composition to which those features gave access, and which 'guaranteed its truth'.[9]

LINE AND COLOUR

Originally influenced by the symbolism of late-nineteenth century and the fauvism of the early-twentieth century, Piet Mondrian was a Dutch painter whose early work is noted for its expressive use of colour. Having moved to Paris and encountered cubism, he painted a series of trees from 1908 to 1912, in which the organic individuality of his subject is progressively reduced in favour of concentration on the fundamental and essential qualities of the form: the verticality of the trunk and the horizontality of the spreading branches.

The First World War began while Mondrian was visiting his father in the Netherlands, and he remained there throughout the hostilities. During this time, he met and was influenced by the mathematician and philosopher M.H.J. Schoenmaekers, whose ideas were closely allied to the theosophy of Helena Blavatsky, Jiddu Krishnamurti and Annie Besant (see page 107) and the anthroposophy of Rudolf Steiner. Schoenmaekers saw the expression of a positive mysticism as being important in the creation of style in art, and the title of his book *Het nieuwe Wereldbeeld* (The New Worldview) was transposed by Mondrian when he gave a name to his approach to art making: *nieuwe Beelding* (neo-plasticism).

Mondrian created a series of monochrome works from 1915, collectively titled Pier and Ocean, composed of short vertical and horizontal black lines that suggest, without actually quite representing, the surface of a calm sea. Only a greater preponderance of vertical over horizontal lines in the bottom centre of a picture allows us to infer the presence of a pier jutting out into the water. On the rectangle of the canvas, the horizontals and verticals are distributed more or less evenly within a centrally placed oval area, leaving all four corners empty. This avoidance of corners is familiar in cubist composition as a means to ensure the structure remains firmly anchored on the picture surface and does not fall into the danger of 'sliding off' the canvas edge.

However, Pier and Ocean was only a staging post. Mondrian remained dissatisfied with cubism's interest in representing volume – which is to say, with expressing three dimensions on a two-dimensional surface. It was his belief, as he stated, 'that this very space has to be destroyed'.[1] Instead of volume there would be the plane, established by means of horizontal and vertical lines, and in order that the plane did not itself then become a settled, immutable presence on the canvas surface, he needed to go further still: 'I came to making only lines and brought the colour within the lines. Now the only problem was to destroy these lines also through mutual oppositions.'[2] Wassily Kandinsky's abstraction was a process of moving from nature towards its essentials (see page 108–9), but for Mondrian this in itself was insufficient. 'Abstraction alone is not enough to eliminate the naturalistic from painting. Line and colour must be composed otherwise than in nature.'[3]

In Mondrian's characteristic works from the early 1920s onwards, such as *Composition No. II: Composition with Yellow and Blue*, this understanding of abstraction is realized. Black lines are no longer distilled from natural forms – a tree, a pattern of waves – but are fundamental expressions of the world (horizontal) and all that exists upon it (vertical). The colours Mondrian used are restricted to the primaries: red, yellow and blue. More than simply pure colours, they are the entirety of colour itself. Between them they can be mixed to make any colour, but for Mondrian to do so would be to specify and deny all other possibilities in that instance. Each area of colour is held within horizontal and vertical black lines, forming a part of a single, unified picture plane. If the colours were unconfined and able to float freely, they would necessarily be seen as laying upon the picture surface, thus reintroducing the illusion of space.

Composition with Yellow and Blue is regular but not symmetrical. The large area of yellow in the top left is balanced by the much smaller, but darker, denser and optically heavier area of blue on the middle right-hand side. The upper right-hand white square might be pulled down by this blue and retreat against the brightness of the yellow, but it is larger in area next to the narrower base of the yellow rectangle, and the thicker line underneath the blue supports and holds it in place. The four areas of white in the lower part of the canvas contribute further to the complex rhythm of the composition. All of the areas work in relation to and in equilibrium with each other. The canvas is square, so there is no stress on either the horizontal (a landscape format) or the vertical (a portrait format), and all of the relationships work within the composition rather than in relation to the overall area that contains it.

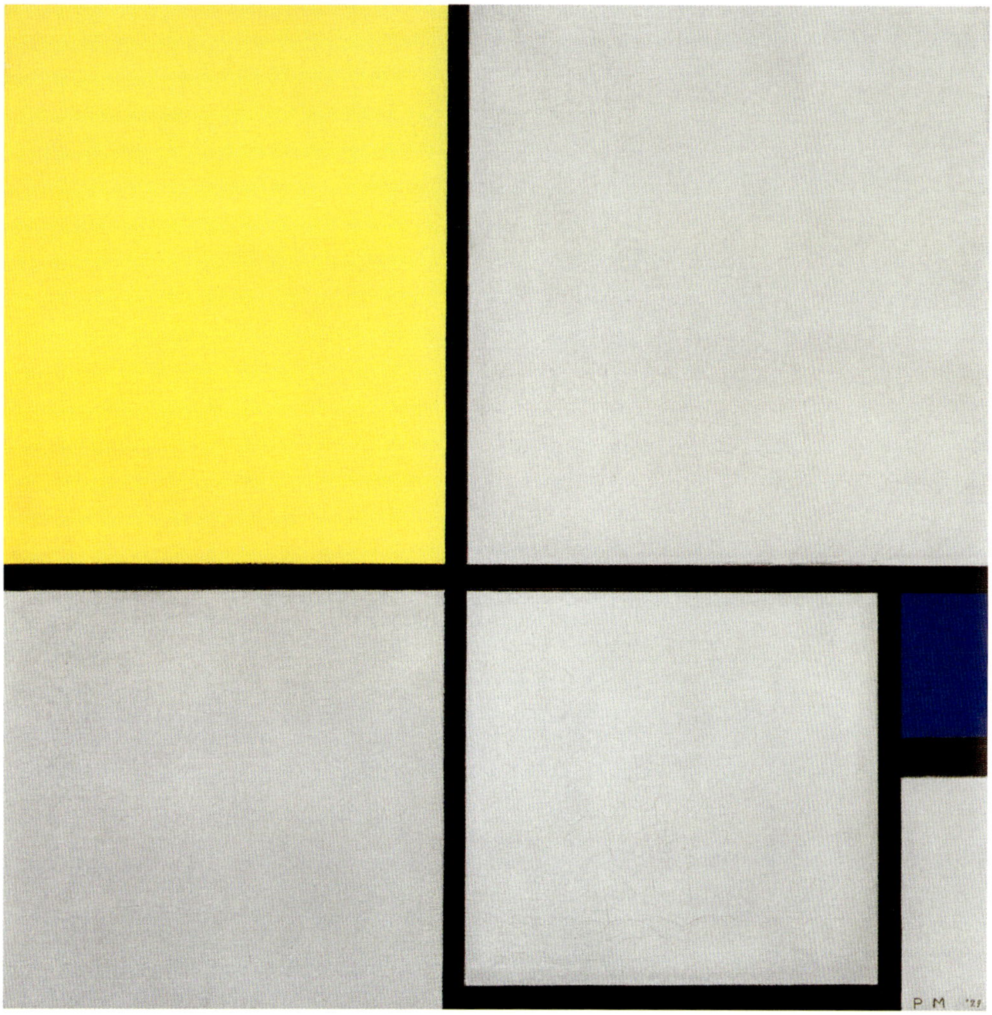

ABOVE: Piet Mondrian, *Composition No. II: Composition with Yellow and Blue*, 1932. Oil on canvas, 52 × 52 cm (20½ × 20½ in).

Mondrian's placement of the lines was intuitive rather than determined according to a mathematical formula. There is, too, an implicit sense that the lines, far from ending at the canvas's edge, extend far beyond it. Nonetheless, each composition is a painting in its own right. The principles of Mondrian's neo-plasticism were espoused by a group of Dutch architects, designers and artists towards the end of the First World War, collectively known as De Stijl (The Style). The author of its first manifesto, architect-designer Theo van Doesburg, in keeping with Mondrian's borrowing from Schoenmaekers' language, speaks of the 'new plastic art' that succeeds by 'excluding natural form'.[4] Mondrian made clear to van Doesburg, however, that he did not see his own art as interior design for this new architecture. Later, van Doesburg would also make use of the diagonal line in his design, something which Mondrian thoroughly rejected. Mondrian did, however, compose a number of paintings, including his last, unfinished work, *Victory Boogie Woogie*, on a square canvas set at 45 degrees. This format is a distinct echo of the hatchments placed high up on the pillars in the light-filled church interiors painted by Mondrian's seventeenth-century compatriot Pieter Saenredam.

'What is painting?', asked the American artist Barnett Newman. 'Is it really circles? Is it really nature? What are we going to paint? Surrealism? Cubism?'[5] In 1948, searching for answers to these questions, he covered a relatively small canvas – 70 × 40 centimetres (27½ × 15¾ inches) – with an even red brown, except for a strip of masking tape running vertically down its centre. Using a palette knife, he scraped a lighter red orange over the tape. His original intention was to remove the tape, leaving a negative vertical stripe defined by feathered marks of the red orange, and to then complete the painting. In the end, after much consideration and hesitation, he decided to do nothing else and leave the over-painted tape in place.

This work titled *Onement I* was the first painting to feature the vertical stripe that Newman later referred to as a 'zip', and the beginning of what he considered his mature style. Only a few years earlier he had written about the problems he saw with the abstract art being made in Europe.

> *The present feeling seems to be that the artist is concerned with form, colour, and spatial arrangement ... The whole attitude of abstract painting, for example, has been such that it has reduced painting to an ornamental art whereby the picture surface is broken up in geometrical fashion into a new kind of design-image.*[6]

What is more, this art of balance and equilibrium concerned itself with the 'unworldly' rather than the more pressing realities of the immediate post-Second World War years.

The American critic and curator Thomas B. Hess observed that *Onement I* marks a departure from this approach. There was a distinct relationship to Mondrian's work, who had spent his last years in New York, and who also used tape to mark the lines with which he articulated the picture plane, defining areas of colour, but that was where the similarity ended:

> *By using symmetry, by placing the zip dead centre in the painting, the constricting apparatus of composition was wiped away at a sweep. By achieving what composition aims for – balance, harmony, scale, order – symmetry makes the whole elaborate, academic ritual obsolete.* [7]

Newman understood that his avoidance of composing as an act of balancing elements constituted a complete break with Western European traditions. Symmetry continued to be a central aspect of his art for the rest of his career, with the placement of the zips in large fields of colour often establishing, or implying, a central square with balancing areas to either side. One consequence of escaping the need to compose was a greater freedom to explore and use colour. Newman's colour fields were large. *Vir Heroicus Sublimis* (1950–1), for example, is nearly 2.5 metres (8 feet) high and 5.5 metres (18 feet) wide. During its first showing, he gave instructions to the work's viewers that they should not stand back in an effort to bring its entire expanse into their field of vision, but instead remain close to, thereby becoming enveloped by the colour.

Towards the end of his life, Newman painted four canvases using only primary colours. Unlike anything he had done before, he began the first with the desire to make something asymmetrical and 'off balance'.[8] The major proportion of the canvas was first built up in red, and it was only after doing this that 'the problem of colour became crucial',[9] because he recognized that the only other colours that would work with this large central area were yellow and blue. However, by this time, these primary colours were carrying a lot of ideological baggage. The Soviet artist Aleksandr Rodchenko (see pages 122–3) had declared them the limit beyond which no artist need go, while for Mondrian, who had spent his last years in New York at exactly the time Newman was struggling to shrug off the dictates of European art, they were the only colours one needed. They were, in a sense, his colours. Hess laid out Newman's dilemma succinctly:

> *Newman wanted to use the primaries and Mondrian was saying, Good! Wonderful! You must use the primaries, so Newman could not use the primaries, but why not use them anyhow, and attack the totem as much as he had attacked the taboo?*[10]

In acknowledging that the dilemma existed, and in declaring his decision to confront it, Newman named the series Who's Afraid of Red, Yellow and Blue? With it, the primaries become available again, unshackled from any further need to pay dues to Mondrian and the painters of high modernism before doing so.

LEFT: Barnett Newman, *Who's Afraid of Red, Yellow and Blue III*, 1967–8. Oil on canvas, 245 × 543 cm (96 × 214 in).

As Newman directly addressed Mondrian in his Who's Afraid series, the Guyanan-born British artist Frank Bowling explicitly refers to Newman in *Who's Afraid of Barney Newman* (1968). This is one from a series of Map paintings made while he was living in New York in the late 1960s and early 1970s. For this series, the ground upon which Bowling poured, pooled and moved his paint was prepared with tracings of countries and continents, notably South America and, from within that, Guyana. The outlines – made with the aid of an epidiascope (a type of projector) borrowed from the American painter Larry Rivers – follow those used in the Mercator projection for making maps, which exaggerates the size of countries in the temperate zones and diminishes those in the tropical and equatorial regions. The left side of the canvas is green, while the right is red. A broad band of yellow running down the centre of the canvas completes a composition which consciously refers to Newman's first zip painting, *Onement I*. Although Bowling has said that he was unaware of the specific meaning of the colours at the time, they are those associated with Rastafari: red for the blood of those who have died in the cause of freedom, green for the natural promise of the land, and gold for the rich resources of Africa.

While the colours of *Who's Afraid of Barney Newman* are well-defined and distinct, those in *Night Journey* are more complex and layered. The outlines of South and Central America and Africa are visible across the central portion of the canvas. Both the left and right areas of the canvas use a range of reds, though on the right a broad blue area veils Africa and the spaces above and below it on the canvas. There is some green in the upper left, as well as in the central area, where it sits under a yellow streak running down from the upper edge almost to the bottom. This yellow band fills the space of the Atlantic Ocean. A bright red line of thicker paint along the left bottom edge supports the darker area above it and resonates with the white shadowing along the Pacific coastline of Central America and the green jutting down from the top edge. The composition is a rich mix of staining, pouring and brushing, a process which Bowling has described thus:

> *I would say the idea with my work is to fill up the space and to try to get a picture. There are various areas where I've emptied the pots of acrylic paint or water or ammonia or whatever, the various liquids I work with, and rested them on the surface of the canvas, and the marks they make become structural elements … All these bleeds of paint, these marks – they're not pre-determined. All I can say is that the paint is pooling and flowing and at the corner of the canvas – with the canvas laying on the floor – I might turn the pot differently … That's not accidental.*[11]

Bowling's map paintings disrupt all attempts to categorize them. If they offer comment on American post-painterly abstraction and colour field painting they do so not from the outside but by being part of it, by contributing to it. The appearance of the South American continent and of his country of birth, Guyana, grounds an experience that is both personal and, by fact of history and circumstance, postcolonial. The yellow stripe in *Night Journey* can undoubtedly be seen to highlight the space of the Middle Passage across the Atlantic forcibly taken by so many Africans sold into slavery, but Bowling did not see the map paintings as making a direct political statement. To take them as such would be to ignore the primary fact that they are, above all else, paintings. As Bowling said:

> *It is easier to say than to paint the thesis that works from Black hands and psyches have a distinct stamp. The measure of honesty an artist brings to his work cannot be too much stressed.*[12]

When he was in London among his Royal College of Art peers, Bowling used photographs as source material, like many who were a part of pop art. He has subsequently remarked, however, that rather than the film stars and pop idols favoured by his peers, he was looking more at the press coverage as Europe dismantled its colonial empires in the first half of the twentieth century. In particular, he focused on the abduction and murder in 1961 of Patrice Lumumba, the first prime minister of the newly independent Congo. What, he later wondered in an interview with curators Okwui Enwezor and Olu Oguibe, was so different in this from the other stories of death and disaster, the plane crashes, electric chairs, race riots, lynchings, suicides and atomic explosions that, for example, so preoccupied pop art proponent Andy Warhol?

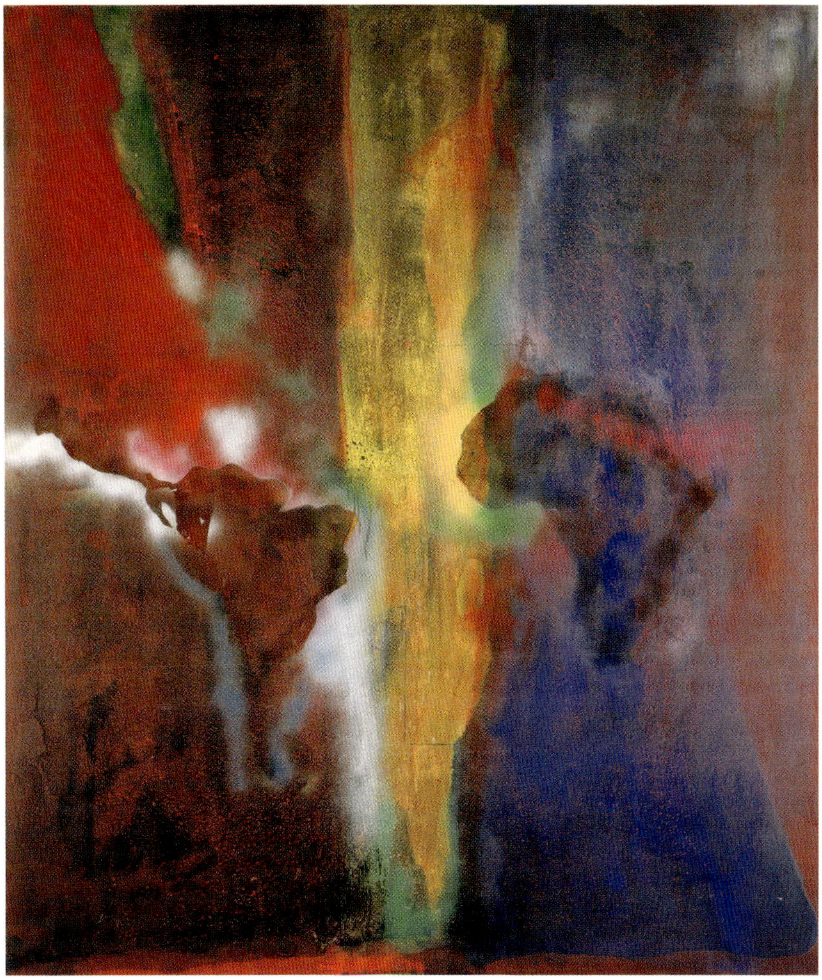

ABOVE: Frank Bowling, *Night Journey*, 1968–9. Acrylic on canvas, 212.7 × 183.2 cm (83¾ × 72⅛ in).

Alongside his painting, Bowling also wrote for *Arts* magazine during his stay in New York. Among his contributions was a series of six essays on the experience of Black artists and the less than adequate ways in which the art world was acknowledging their presence and contribution to contemporary art. 'I believe the Black soul, if there is such a thing', he said later, 'belongs in modernism'.[13] In other words, the postcolonial experience is a central aspect of the broader modern experience in the world. Bowling's time in New York taught him, as he said after returning to the UK, that while there is 'something which is very distinctively Black … there is no Black art'.[14] To categorize works as 'Black art' is to apply an implicit separation from other works which would just be called 'art'. This chimes with Georgia O'Keeffe's insistence that while her experience as a woman enabled her to make a unique contribution, her work should be recognized as art, not female art or women's art (see page 99). Bowling explained in his interview with Enwezor and Oguibe:

> *I think that we brought a sensibility to abstraction as a new way of making art. A new way of making painting. It evolved with the generation after 1945, with Pollock and all these people. But by the time we, the Black guys got on the scene, I think we brought a new sensibility to painting that was no longer a question of bridge-building at all. We were going with the flow, and I think that we brought a very original edge to the post-painterly abstraction and colour field painting which is not recognized.*[15]

When Anwar Jalal Shemza came to London in the mid-1950s, he was already a successful artist and author in Pakistan. He enrolled at the Slade School of Fine Art, determined to familiarize himself fully with the modernism to which, as an established artist and published writer with a national reputation, he understood himself to be contributing. However, in a lecture given at the Slade by Ernst Gombrich, in which the Austrian author of the hugely successful art historical survey *The Story of Art* characterized Islamic art as 'functional', led Shemza to a crisis of identity:

> *I remember leaving the room for a few minutes before the lecture finished, and sitting on a bench outside. As the students came out, I looked at all their faces; they seemed so contented and self-satisfied. I went home and looked again in the mirror. This time I couldn't find any familiar face at all, neither the beginner at the Slade nor the 'celebrated artist'.*[16]

The basic forms of the square and the circle that Shemza frequently used can be related to an interest in the abstraction seen in the works of Mondrian and Paul Klee, but the expression of this interest occurred in the context of a grounding knowledge of calligraphy and Mughal architecture gained in Lahore.

Shemza's painting *The Wall* has four distinct areas. An uneven white band down the lower half of each side and along the bottom is matched by a similarly U-shaped area running along the top and halfway down the left and right edges. This upper area, scraped and brushed over a darker ground, is predominantly a broken golden yellow shading to terre verte on the right. These form a frame around two further areas, which are similarly figured patterns in black and yellow of gridded squares containing semicircles and double semicircles. The painted image is not a Mondrian-like plane, since the black and yellow squares are as much on, as they are a part, of the picture surface. There is space behind or beyond the grid, and the squares of this grid diminish in size as it rises towards the top edge of the canvas, implying a recession into distance that introduces a different sense of spatiality. 'My art', noted Shemza in one of his sketchbooks, 'is based on the simplification of the three dimensional solid, architectural reality and the decorative element of calligraphy'.[17]

The Wall is fruitfully ambiguous in its composition. The solid white U-shaped area within which the grid is framed might itself be the wall of the title, but the pattern is also that wall. The suggestion of something existing beyond it implies, not least, a pierced screen behind which things are less easy to see, but through which sound, light and atmosphere can freely pass. Shemza understood calligraphy as giving the 'means to convey your feelings and also produce some aesthetic response'.[18] As British art historian Kobena Mercer has written in relation to Shemza's work, in contrast to Western art in which the line is subordinate to the appearance of things in the world, 'the calligraphic line in Islamic arts of inscription is the holy word itself'.[19] Far from merely 'ornamenting a prosaic message', the calligraphic line is spiritual and devotional.[20] Shemza studied Klee's work in depth, and the affinity between the two artists stands out clearly when we compare Mercer's observation with a remark by Klee from his 'Creative Credo':

> *Since infinity has no definite beginning, but like a circle may start anywhere, the idea may be regarded as primary. 'In the beginning was the word'.*[21]

'the calligraphic line in Islamic arts of inscription is the holy word itself'.

– Kobena Mercer, 'The Longest Journey: Black Diaspora Artists in Britain', *Art History*, June 2021

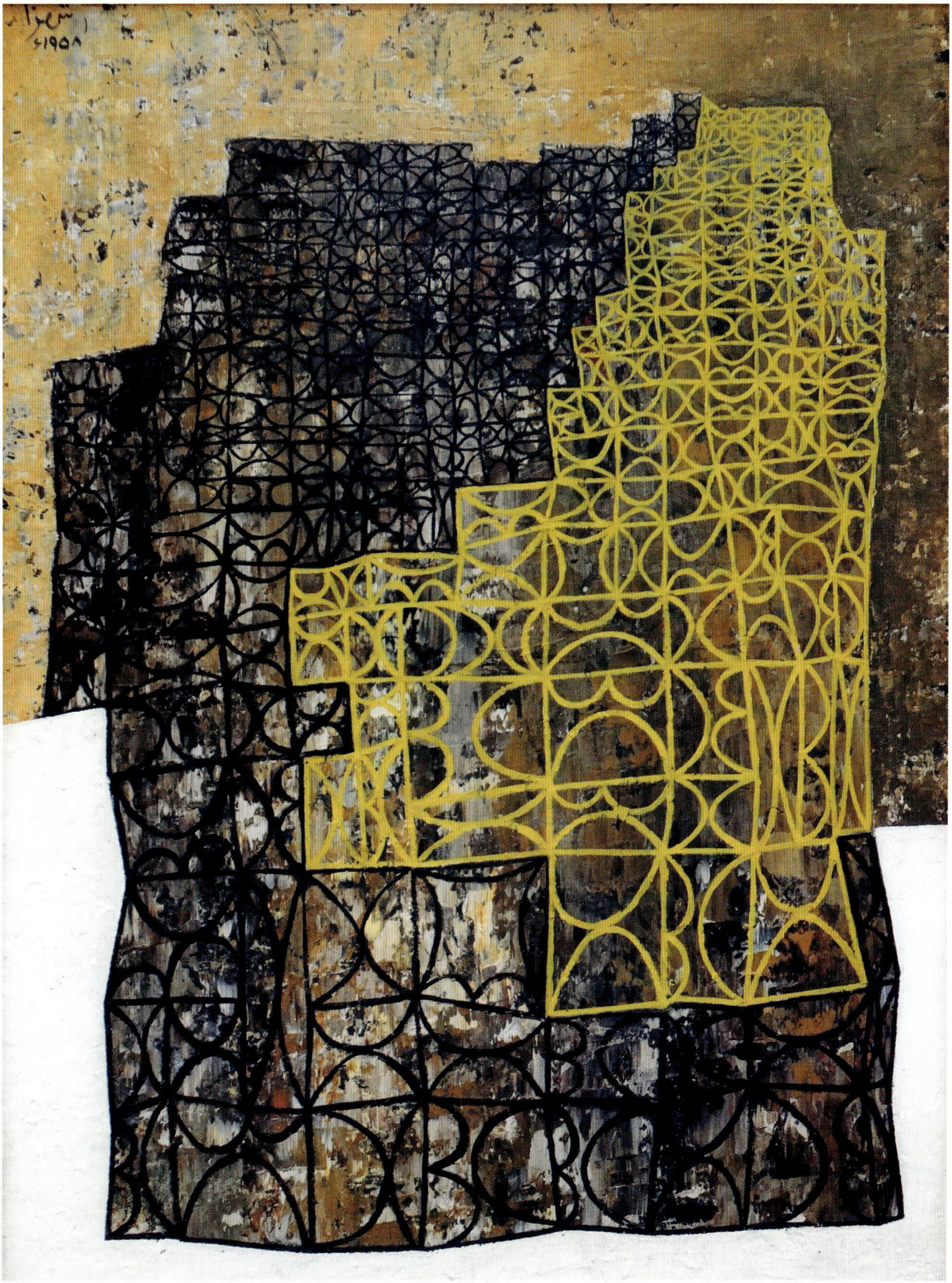

ABOVE: Anwar Jalal Shemza, *The Wall*, *c.*1958–85. Oil on board, 60 × 44.5 cm (23⅝ × 17½ in).

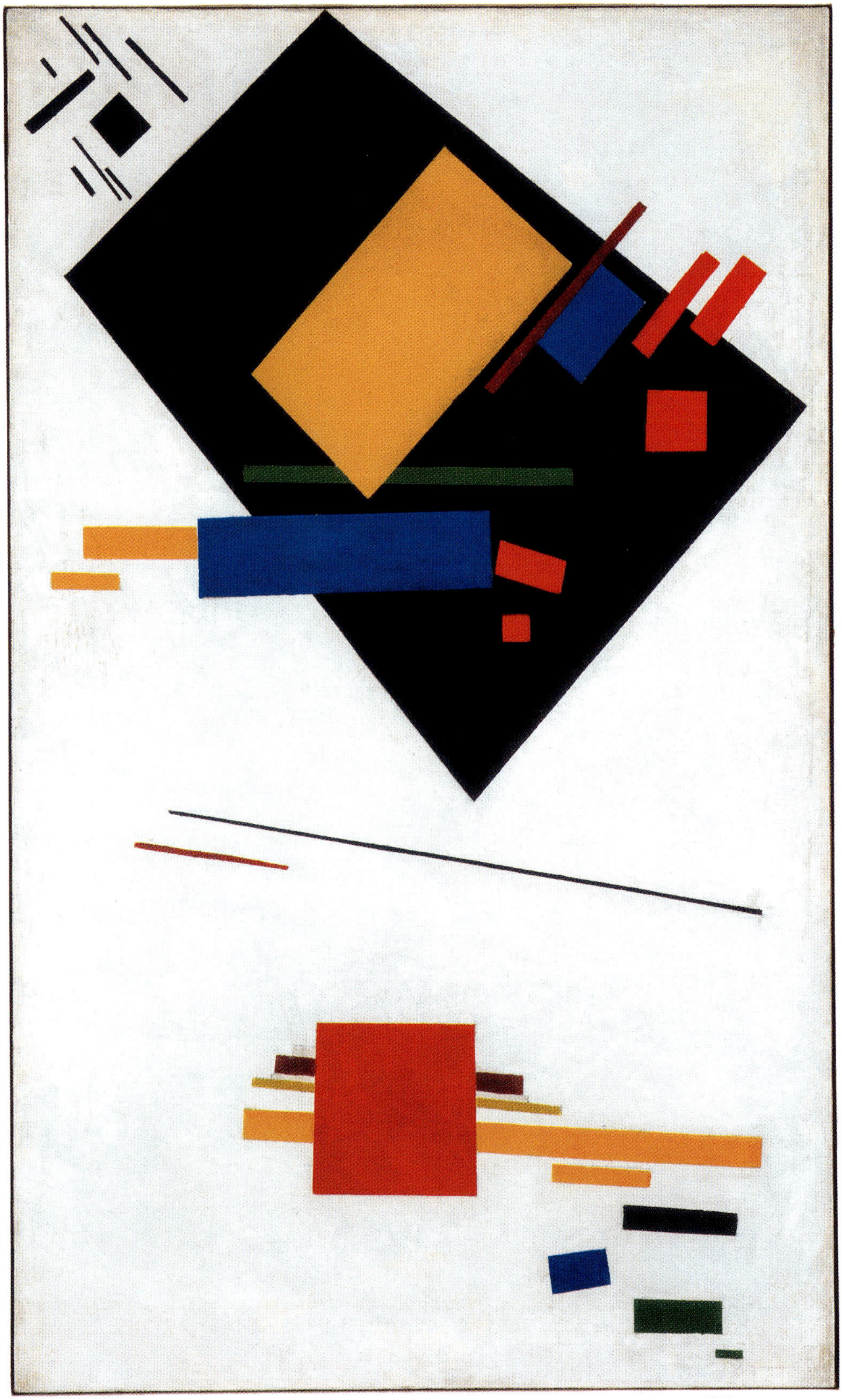

SUPREMACY

Approaching abstraction as a journey through the appearances of the natural world towards the perception of an inner reality, Wassily Kandinsky talked of the physical fact of the picture surface as the place upon which the ideal can be realized. As Kandinsky wrote in his book *Concerning the Spiritual in Art*, 'attempts must be made to bring the picture onto some ideal plane which shall be expressed in terms of the material plane of the canvas'.[1]

This 'new form of composition' in which the ideal and material planes are combined requires us to destroy the idea of 'one single surface' that is both the starting point and compositional goal for a painter such as Piet Mondrian.[2] It also contrasts with the Ukrainian painter Kazymyr Malevych, for whom 'the artist (painter) is no longer bound to the canvas (the picture plane) and can transfer his compositions from canvas to space.'[3] Malevych sees in the work of artists such as Raphael, Peter Paul Rubens and Rembrandt nothing more than 'a conglomeration of countless things'.[4] Our preoccupation with what is represented blinds us to the feeling that gave rise to such paintings in the first place. In Malevych's 'nonobjective' art, form has no requirement to describe any object in the visible world. It is like the symbols of the earliest humans 'which represented, in their combinations, not ornament but a feeling of rhythm.'[5]

The first example of what Malevych called suprematism was a black square on a white ground. Malevych's description is terse: 'the square = feeling, the white field = the void beyond this feeling'.[6] He exhibited it at *The Last Exhibition of Futurist Painting 0.10* in Petrograd (St Petersburg) in 1915. It was positioned high up across a corner of the gallery in the place traditionally held in a Russian household by a religious icon. Executed only a couple of years before Russia's October Revolution, it is quite unlike anything that had been made before.

Suprematist Painting (with Black Trapezium and Red Square), shown alongside the black square in that exhibition, has a number of forms within the void. The upper portion, marked off by a thin sloping straight line beginning just in from either edge of the canvas, shows a strong diagonal running from the top left corner. Dominating this area is the large black trapezium, whose shape, placement and orientation give a sense of movement from a distance towards us as much as from top downwards. Shapes of various colours – not only the primaries, red, yellow and blue, but also the secondaries green and purple – lay over and extend beyond the trapezium, adding to the understanding that we are seeing movement in space. Below the thin line, which prevents the onrushing forms above it from overwhelming us, there are further coloured shapes. While none are horizontal, they run from side to side, providing a dynamic balance upon which the upper forms are held. A bright red square, slightly to the left of centre, anchors everything. There are no curves in the composition; all lines are straight. Malevych explained:

> *I call the additional element of suprematism 'the suprematist straight line' (dynamic in character). The environment corresponding to this new culture has been produced by the latest achievements of technology, and especially of aviation, so that one could also refer to suprematism as 'aeronautical'.*[7]

There is no attempt to reintroduce the spatiality of a world that can be rendered through the use of perspective. Instead, the aim is to present something new, in line with the scientific propositions and technological advances of the time that recast everything in terms of the four dimensions of space-time.

OPPOSITE: Kazymyr Malevych, *Suprematist Painting (with Black Trapezium and Red Square)*, 1915. Oil on canvas, 105 × 65.7 cm (41⅜ × 25⅞ in).

PUT TO WORK

Kazymyr Malevych saw suprematism as an art that was both 'pure' and 'unapplied'.[1] It served no purpose beyond itself. In contrast, the constructivists, for whom 'efficacious existence is the highest beauty',[2] saw the potential for art to contribute to the actual rebuilding of a post-revolutionary society. Three women – Aleksandra Exter, Liubov Popova and Varvara Stepanova – and two men – Aleksandr Vesnin and Aleksandr Rodchenko – took part in the *5 × 5 = 25* exhibition held in 1921. Stepanova wrote at the time:

> *Composition is the contemplative approach of the artist in his work. Technique and industry have confronted art with the problem of construction as an active process and not a contemplative reflection. The sanctity of a work as a single 'entity' is destroyed. The museum which was a treasury of this entity is now transformed into an archive.*[3]

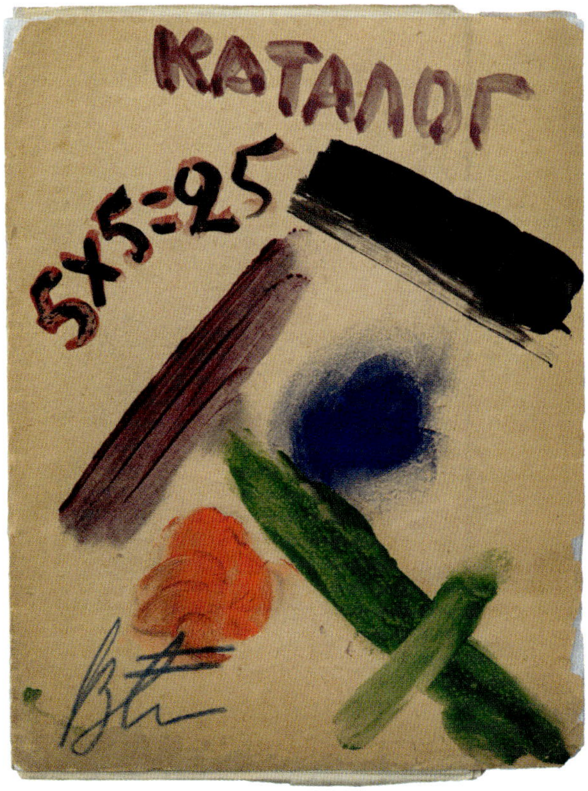

Stepanova worked in theatre design and in textiles. She was appointed professor of composition in the textile department at VKhUTEMAS, the Higher Art and Technical Studios in Moscow, and she saw the department's task as the educating of people to work, like herself, as 'artist–constructors' in the textile industry.[4] The aim was not to adapt imported and outdated designs, but to invent new styles appropriate to the post-revolutionary society and its conditions. The constructivist lexicon of clear lines, bold, contrasting colours and simple shapes was a rich resource, and the implicit infinite extensiveness of a repeat pattern was entirely in tune with the new understanding of both space and surface. This coherence is what Stepanova and her husband Rodchenko, in their 1921 'Programme of the First Working Group of Constructivists' refer to as *faktura*: 'material consciously worked and expediently used'.[5]

Alongside Stepanova's experimentation directed towards the needs of production, part of Rodchenko's contribution to *5 × 5 = 25* constituted a valediction to painting. Three of his works were monochrome panels: one red, one yellow and one blue. Quite unlike Piet Mondrian, for whom these primaries provide endless new possibilities, Rodchenko saw this as a reduction of painting to its limit and titled the three panels 'Last Painting'. The same year he and Stepanova wrote their 'Productivist Manifesto', which includes the slogan: 'Down with the conservation of artistic traditions. Long live the constructivist technician'.[6] He had earlier assisted the sculptor Vladimir Tatlin with his decoration of the interior of Moscow's Café Pittoresque. Abstract forms in cardboard, metal and wood broke out from the walls, shaping not only the architecture but also the space within. What began as a container and a contained volume became a dynamic, energetic exchange between the two inseparable halves of a single entity.

LEFT: Varvara Stepanova, cover of *5 × 5 = 25 (An Exhibition of Painting)*, 1921. Illustrated book, page (each): 17.8 × 11.7 cm (7 × 4⅝ in).

The constructivists ... saw the potential for art to contribute to the actual rebuilding of a post-revolutionary society.

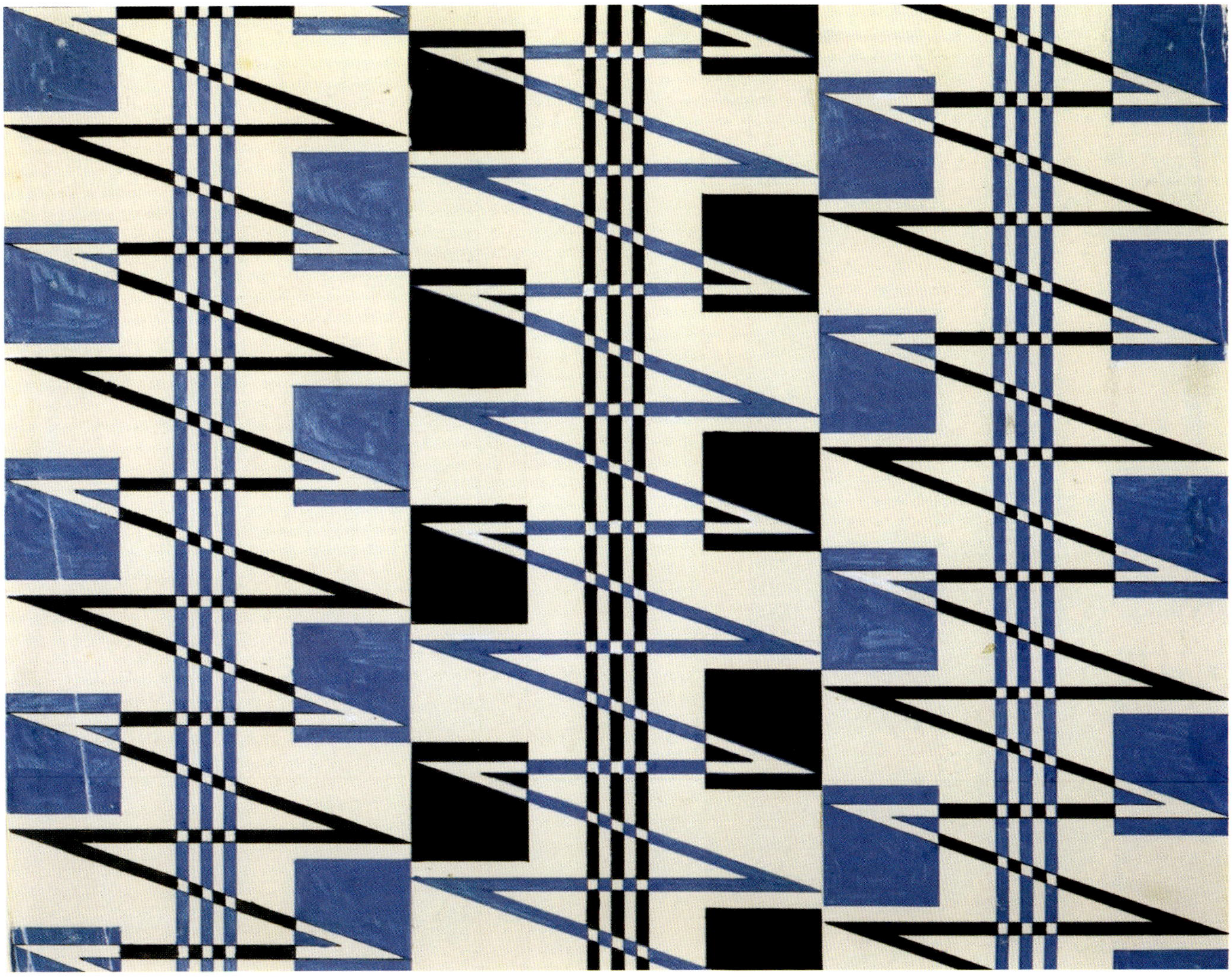

ABOVE: Varvara Stepanova, *Fabric Design*, 1924. Gouache, 21 × 27 cm (8⅜ × 10⅝ in).

In a 1925 essay, 'A and Pangeometry' (A being an abbreviation for Art), the Russian artist El Lissitzky discussed the fate of perspective in painting. Perspective, he said, is a means to 'define' space, to 'make it finite' and ultimately to 'enclose' it. 'Perspective has comprehended space according to the concept of Euclidean geometry as a constant three-dimensional state.' Composing according to the rules of perspective sees the world 'fitted into a cube'.[7] The picture plane forms the base of a pyramid whose apex is either in front, in our eyes, a method he ascribes to Eastern pictorial tradition, or at a vanishing point on the horizon behind the painted surface, the preferred solution in the West.

In the nineteenth century, mathematicians Bernhard Riemann, Carl Gauss and Nikolai Lobachevsky had developed new geometries beyond Euclidean space and, in parallel to these scientific advances, from the development of impressionism onwards, artists had loosened their dependence on the perspectival rendering of pictorial space. In particular, the cubists 'transposed the space-confining horizon to the foreground and identified it with the area being painted'.[8] From this moment the artwork starts to build out from the plane of the canvas and encroach upon the space of the world inhabited by the viewer. Pablo Picasso's constructions and, subsequently, Tatlin's counter-reliefs exemplify this new spatial treatment.

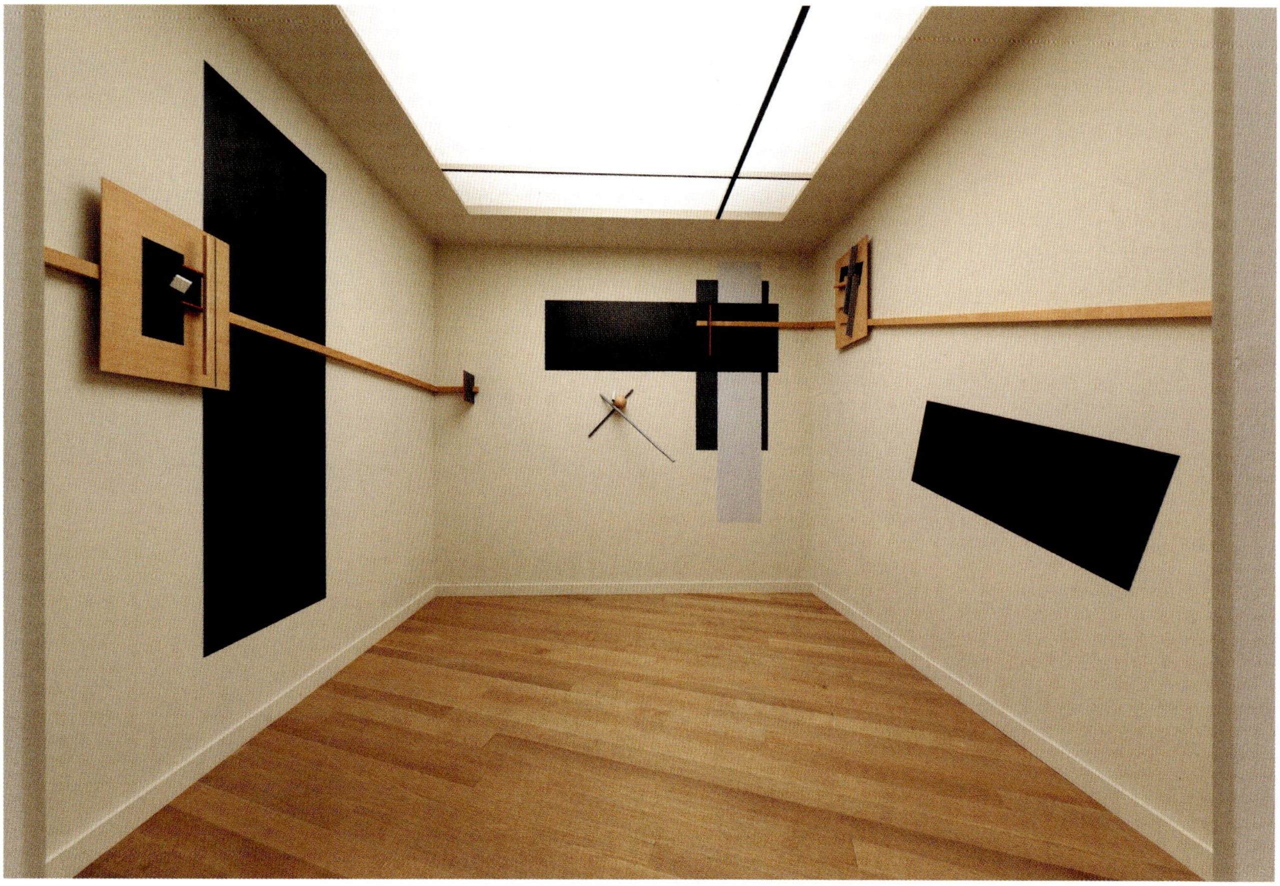

ABOVE: El Lissitzky, *Proun Room*, 1923 (reconstructed 2010). Mixed media, 300 × 300 × 260 cm (118⅛ × 118⅛ × 102⅜ in). Installation view, The Museum of Modern Art, New York.

El Lissitzky had worked with Malevych in Vitebsk, Belarus, and saw suprematism as fundamental to the new conception of space in art. Going beyond futurism, which only showed the vibrations of movement, suprematism revealed the dynamic equilibrium of forces in tension. In drawing a relationship between scientific and artistic advances, El Lissitzky stressed the importance of irrationality. In mathematics, we can see it symbolized in $i = \sqrt{-1}$ – an 'imaginary thing' – and in art we can find it in suprematism, which has 'swept away the illusion of three-dimensional space on a plane, replacing it by the ultimate illusion of *irrational* space with attributes of infinite extensibility in depth and foreground'.[9]

The logical outcome of the progression from pre-impressionist perspectival space to cubist and constructivist reliefs is that composition pushes further out from the wall and becomes fully realized as a dynamic environment that engages the viewer rather than being a static object to be quietly contemplated. El Lissitzky talked of the possibility of now being able to imagine multidimensional spaces 'into which one can go for a walk without an umbrella'.[10] He gave the word 'Proun' to his own compositions. Although never fully defined, it is generally accepted to be an acronym signifying 'project for the affirmation of the new', and El Lissitzky further referred to it as 'an interchange station between painting and architecture'.[11] For the most part, these works were two-dimensional – drawings, prints and paintings – but for a 1923 exhibition in Berlin, El Lissitzky constructed a *Proun Room*. A suite of lithograph prints from the same year includes a plan for this room showing basic forms and flat areas of colour connected by lines and bars. The elements are distributed over all surfaces of the space: walls, floor and ceiling. El Lissitzky explained that his exhibition room was 'designed with elementary forms and materials; lines, flat surfaces and bar, cube, sphere, and black, white, grey and wood; and surfaces which are spread flat on to the wall (colour) and surfaces which are placed perpendicular to the wall (wood)'.[12] There are two reliefs that provide a 'problem situation', and which constitute a 'crystallization'[13] of the relationships between the fundamental forms of cube and sphere and the interconnecting bars of the whole area. To avoid any confusion about the character of the space, El Lissitzky explained, 'this is not a living room'.[14] It is not a mere extension of our everyday world but a space of potential and possibility, from whose elements and with whose energy a new, post-revolutionary reality can be realized.

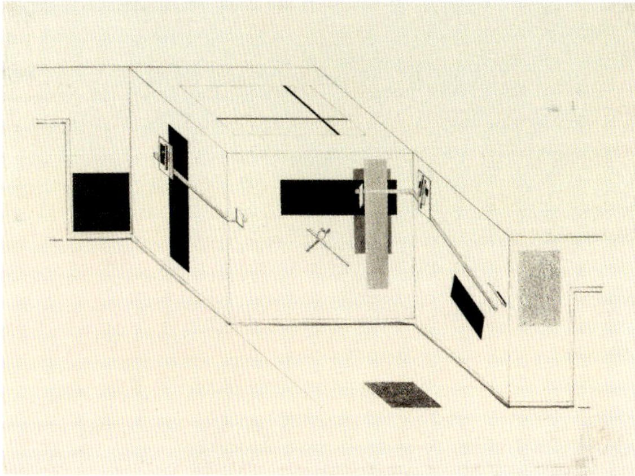

ABOVE: El Lissitzky, *Proun Room*, 1923. Lithograph, 60.5 x 43.5 cm (23⅞ x 17⅛ in).

INTO THE SURFACE

The state of 'aggressive, complete madness',[1] to which the German-French artist Jean (Hans) Arp had responded, returned with a vengeance only two decades later after the Second World War. The despairing fear voiced by the German philosopher Theodor Adorno, that there can be no poetry after Auschwitz, is pervasive. For Lucio Fontana, who had moved from Argentina, where his Italian parents had immigrated, back to Europe after the war, modern art lay destroyed in the fallout from the atomic bombing of Hiroshima. Fontana wrote a series of manifestos in the later 1940s, and in the earliest one, the 'White Manifesto' (1946), he expressed in plain terms the need for a new direction in art. 'We live in a mechanical age', he said, where 'painted canvas and upright plaster no longer have a reason to exist'.[2] Meeting the challenge of the new reality called not only for art to find new forms, but also for it to abandon established categories: 'We need to go beyond painting, sculpture, poetry and music. We need a greater art in harmony with the requirements of the new spirit.' Following the Italian futurists in 1909, for whom 'time and space died yesterday', and the Russian constructivists in 1921, for whom 'time and space are reborn to us today', Fontana announced that, having 'abandon[ed] the practice of all the forms of known art, we commence the development of an art based on the unity of time and space'.[3]

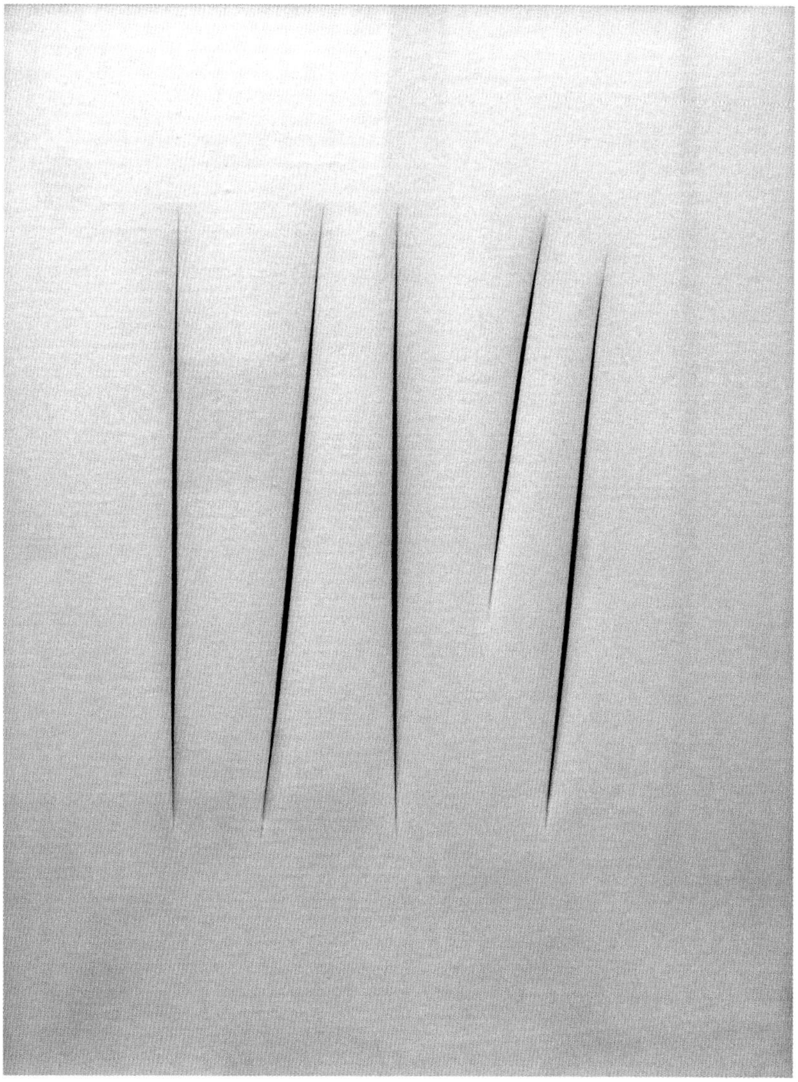

From this period, Fontana began a series of paintings in which the monochrome surface is punctured by a number of holes. As Iranian-born art historian Jaleh Mansoor noted in her study of post-war Italian art, the plane of the painting, with its bright, saturated colour, presented for Fontana 'nothing less than suffocation, limit, and restriction'.[4] Subsequently, Fontana would slash the canvas with one or more cuts. Throughout all the shifts in compositional approach over the preceding century, the picture surface had remained, both physically and conceptually, as the artist's primary ground. Whatever happened on the surface might change considerably, but the surface itself was immutable. More than anything, as Mansoor observed, 'for Fontana the surface cannot be taken as a given; it is a historically determined part of European culture – a Europe to which he returns at the moment of its dissolution'.[5]

Concetto Spaziale (*Spatial Concept*) is the title Fontana gave to a series of works comprising a monochrome or unpainted surface interrupted by one or more vertical slashes. We might anticipate that the cuts would reveal the wall behind, but there is a black backing to the frames, which turns our expectation of a banal reality into a view towards that unknown future moment in which the unity of time and space for which we are waiting will be achieved. The cuts are not marks on the surface; they are a gesture that both affirms the physical presence of that surface and compromises it. As a destructive gesture with broad cultural implications, made in the wake of the atrocities of the Second World War, it has an affinity with other works such as *One for Violin Solo* (1962) by Japanese-educated Korean Nam June Paik. In his Fluxus performance, in which a violin is raised above the head and smashed down onto a table, not just the instrument is destroyed but, by implication, the whole system of Western music (see page 137).

Likewise, the auto-destructive art performances of Gustav Metzger, who escaped to the UK from Nazi-occupied Austria in 1939, refused the Western aesthetic tradition. Metzger's own 'Auto-Destructive Art Manifesto', written in 1960, as Fontana began the *Spatial Concept* series, begins:

> *Man in Regent Street is auto-destructive.*
> *Rockets, nuclear weapons, are auto-destructive.*
> *Auto-destructive art.*
> *The drop drop dropping of HH bombs.*
> *Not interested in ruins, (the picturesque)*
> *Auto-destructive art re-enacts the obsession with destruction, the pummelling to which individuals and masses are subjected.*[6]

There has been cutting before, of course, in the cubist collages of Georges Braque and Pablo Picasso, and in the photomontage of Hannah Höch and her fellow dadaists, but in those cases it is carried out in order to shape elements for subsequent attachment to a coherent surface. It will occur again, for example, in the shaped canvases of Frank Stella and the abstract compositions of Ellsworth Kelly, for whom the preparation of each monochrome shaped element was a way to detach that shape from the rectangular canvas that would otherwise have held it captive. Unlike any of these, however, Fontana's cut is a self-sufficient gesture which, in its productive destructiveness, constitutes that rejection of illusion of which he speaks in the 'White Manifesto'.[7]

OPPOSITE: Lucio Fontana, *Spatial Concept White*, 1962. Acrylic on canvas, 102.5 × 83. 5 cm (40⅜ × 32⅞ in).

BEYOND THE CANVAS

'Everything has already been made, everything has been done!'[1] recalled the German artist Imi Knoebel, in reference to the problem facing him and his fellow artists when arriving at art school in the 1960s. Lucio Fontana had slashed the canvas in Italy, the French artist Yves Klein had settled upon a signature colour – the vibrant International Klein Blue – through which he embodied his desire for the infinite void, and Kazymyr Malevych had painted the *Black Square* to signal a new beginning. What could be done now that these radical steps have been taken?

Knoebel studied under Joseph Beuys in Düsseldorf, sharing a studio with his then collaborator, Rainer (Imi) Giese, and two other German painters, Jörg Immendorff and Blinky Palermo. Both he and Palermo made early work that re-examined Malevych's dynamic arrangement of form, though in their case the placement of works energized the architecture of the exhibition space rather than keeping that energy contained within the four sides of a canvas. In 1968, Knoebel made and exhibited a small stretcher without any canvas – a painting beyond painting, and a painting before all painting. Originally working in black and white, he first used colour in 1975 with *Green Heptagon.* He thought green 'the most necessary, the most correct, the most natural, indeed the most existential colour', yet though he and Palermo conducted a thorough search of all the paint suppliers, he couldn't find the right green. So *Green Heptagon* was actually pink, not green. Compositionally, Knoebel saw the heptagon as the most basic form unhindered by associations:

> *There's the square, the quadrilateral or the right angle, then comes the pentagon, that also has a regularity, the hexagon just as much. But the heptagon, that is a free, completely free story. The heptagon is the first polygon that is free.*[2]

Palermo died two years later, and in homage to his friend, 'the master of colours', Knoebel made *24 Colours – for Blinky*. The work comprises twenty-four large, irregularly shaped polygonal wooden panels, none containing a single right angle, and each painted a different monochrome colour in acrylic. Twenty-one of the panels are hung on the wall at a sufficient distance from one another to enable each to be seen as a separate entity when looked at straight on. The remaining three, a pale yellow, a pink and a pale blue, rest on the floor, stacked one in front of the other hard up against the wall. The panels have substantial depth, so moving slightly to the side reveals that the colour, which is only on the front surface and does not extend round to the edges, stands away from the wall. The arrangement of the work is dependent on the space in which it is installed. Each has to be allotted a place within the gallery, of course, but the sequence is such that the colours and shapes retain their specificity and individuality, and the viewer is unable to identify any ordering principle linking one to the next.

The key compositional shift in this work is the bringing of colour off the wall and into the space. El Lissitzky had been explicit in characterizing his *Proun Room* as somewhere disconnected from the everyday world within which a new reality might be created (see pages 124–5). Likewise, Knoebel's work makes it evident that the gallery space is to be recognized as a sociopolitical as much as an aesthetic environment. In contrast, a few years before Knoebel made this work, the American conceptional artist Michael Asher had scraped the walls, floor and ceiling of the Galeria Toselli in Milan back to bare plaster and concrete. What would normally be experienced as a 'white cube', separated from the rest of the world in order to allow time and space for aesthetic contemplation, had been disenchanted and revealed as just another part of our everyday cityscape.

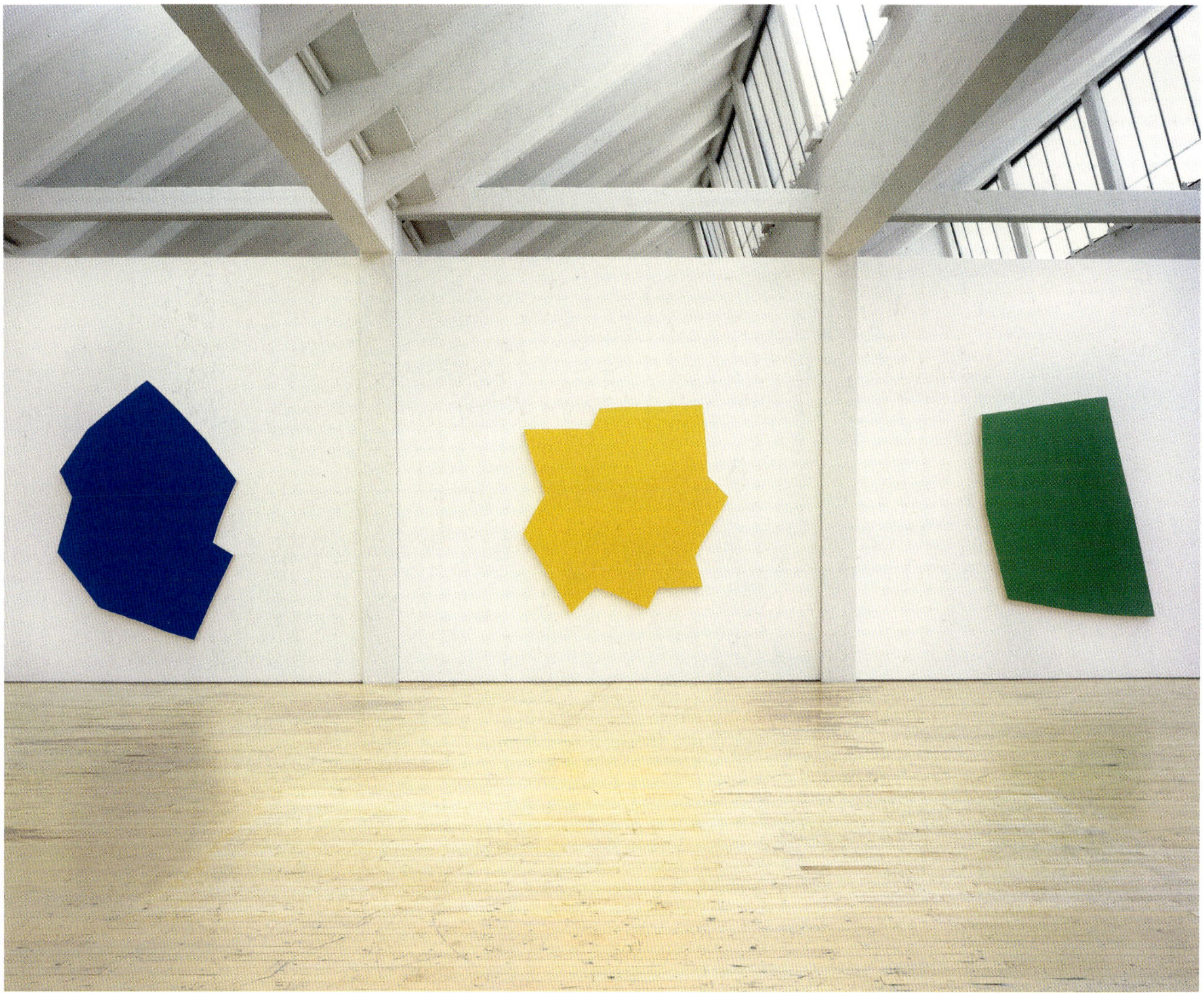

ABOVE: Imi Knoebel, *24 Colors – for Blinky*, 1977.
Installation view, Dia:Beacon, New York, 2014.

The placement of works energized the architecture of the exhibition space rather than keeping that energy contained within the four sides of a canvas.

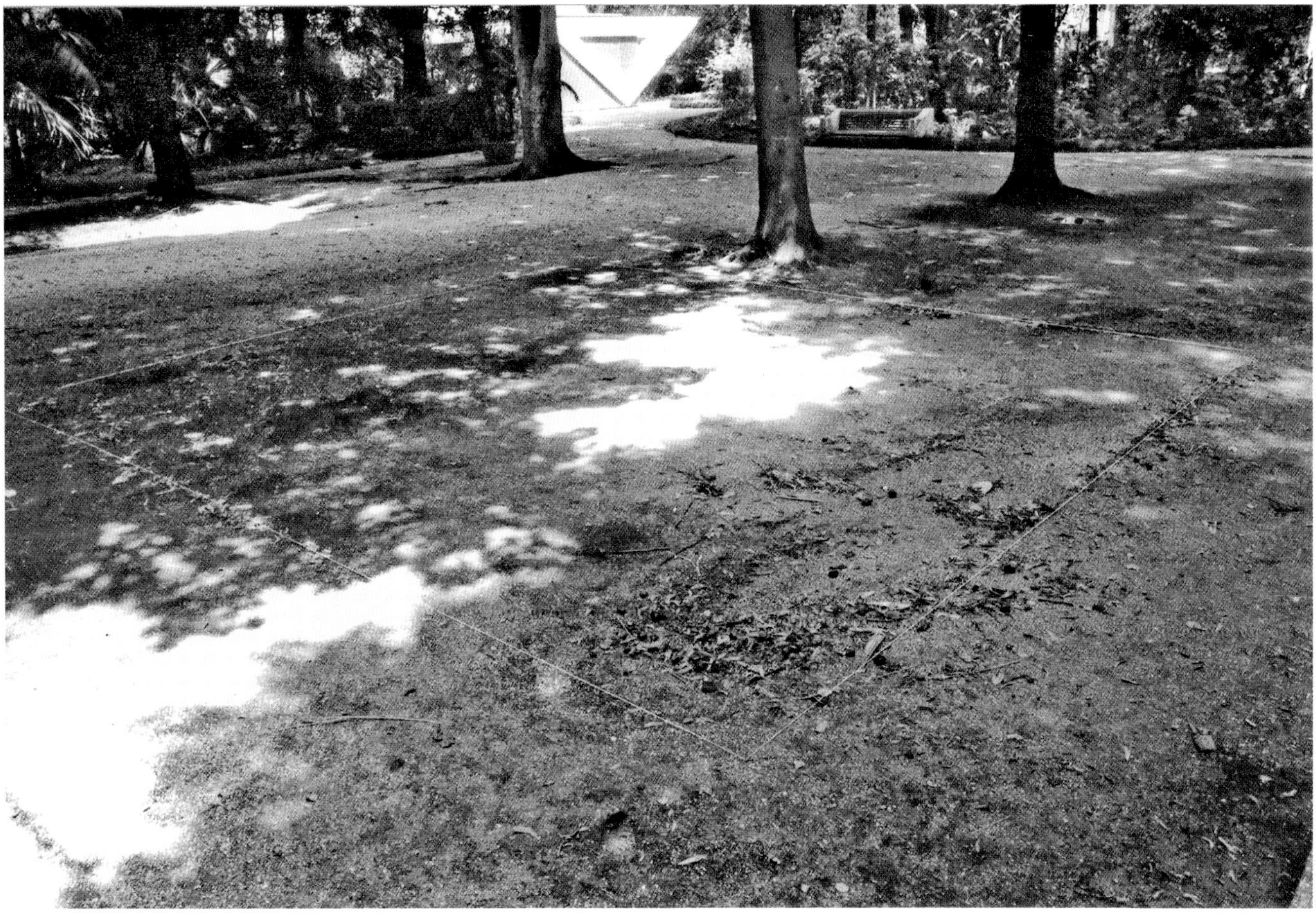

ABOVE: Robert Irwin, *String Drawing – Filtered Light*. Site-determined installation, courtyard of the US Pavilion, Venice Biennale, 1976.

Irwin's answer to the figure–ground problem was to stop painting and to work instead with the totality of an environment.

TOTAL ENVIRONMENT

The American artist Robert Irwin started his essay 'Notes Toward a Model' with the statement, 'I began as a painter in the middle of nowhere (L.A.) with a few questions'.[1] He would spend the decade between 1960 and 1970 trying to answer those questions. What is the mark on the canvas and the image it is perceived as making? How and why is it that this image becomes the focus of our attention? What is the status of the frame, the delineated space that contains that image? What is the significance of the canvas edge that defines the 'beginning and the end' of what is perceived? Working through these questions, said Irwin, 'I slowly dismantled the act of painting to consider the possibility that nothing ever really transcends its immediate environment'.[2]

In the years immediately prior to this, and in response to his discovery of abstract expressionism in 1958, he had been making abstract compositions, their thick paint laid on in bold strokes. What struck him, however, was that these paintings soon came to look 'arbitrary', and that, as he wrote, 'six months after the "emotion" of my involvement much of what I had done just seemed unnecessary'.[3] As Irwin well understood, the questions this realization led him to ask were in many ways the same ones that had been addressed throughout the preceding century. They concern what he referred to as 'the figure-ground problem': what constitutes the primary object of attention in a painting, what provides the context for that object, and how do these inter-relate within the frame of the overall image? Modernism's solution, as we have seen, had been to flatten the picture space until image and canvas surface become to all intents and purposes one and the same. Irwin's answer to the figure-ground problem was to stop painting and to work instead with the totality of an environment.

Irwin described his art as arising in sites that he 'conditioned'. In characterizing it thus, he was drawing a distinction with the more widely used designation for work conceived for a particular location: 'site specific'. Relinquishing the familiar certainty of a painting's physical presence within the gallery might give cause for concern to some artists, but Irwin viewed his move quite differently:

> *The wonder of it all is that what looked for all the world like a diminishing horizon – the art object's becoming so ephemeral as to threaten to disappear altogether – has, like some marvellous philosophical riddle, turned itself inside out to reveal its opposite. What appeared to be a question of object / nonobject has turned out to be a question of seeing and not seeing, of how it is we actually perceive or fail to perceive 'things' in their real contexts.*[4]

For his exhibition at the Venice Biennale in 1976, Irwin made *String Drawing – Filtered Light*, a site-determined installation situated in the courtyard in front of the US Pavilion. In physical terms, it is as slight as could be – a square area of ground marked out with string under the courtyard's trees. Throughout the day this patch of ground is home to a constantly shifting pattern of light and shade as the sun moves across the sky and breezes agitate the leaves above. 'With such economy of means', wrote author and museum director Hugh M. Davies, 'Irwin had defined this subtle, two-dimensional canvas, and through the simple act of framing, he revealed a delightful naturally occurring event, one that would otherwise have remained unseen'.[5]

This was not a kind of sanctuary in which the individual could remain in isolated contemplation ... but an exchange between exterior and interior conditions.

INTERPERSONAL AND GEO-SOCIAL ENACTIONS

Maria Nordman explores a radically different approach to the interrelationship between artist, earth, sun and what we might habitually think of as a viewer. The central importance of this network of connections between we humans, our environment and the cosmos is reflected in her concept of 'Geo-Aesthetics' within which all her work sits. In 1979, Nordman contributed to a series of exhibitions mounted by Berkeley Art Museum, California, under the overall title 'Space as Support'. The work's title provides us with salient facts – the location and the time frame – and indicates unambiguously that the constitutive elements are the earth, the sun and anyone present:

> *6/21/79 5 a.m.–9 p.m. pre- sun-up to post sun-down terrestrial/solar co-authoring of a site with any person arriving U. C. Berkeley Art Museum – Bancroft Way*

Nordman's exhibition lasted for a single day, on 21 June, the summer solstice and the year's longest day. The doors to the museum were unlocked at 5 a.m., just before sunrise, and the building remained open until 9 p.m., shortly after sunset, some sixteen hours later. In preparation for the day, Nordman had covered the gallery's floors with an adhesive matt white vinyl so that, instead of being absorbed by the dark concrete, all light falling on the material would be reflected back into the space. All coverings on the skylights were removed so that as much sunlight as possible could enter the museum. While all steps had been taken to maximize the amount of natural light within the building, no spotlights, strip lights or any other artificial light source was used at any point during the day. Those arriving at either end of the day would, therefore, experience the building in crepuscular half-light, and those visiting over the middle part of the day would see it in full sun. Coloured filters – red, blue, green and, in one case, black – were stretched over the glass doors, all of which, including emergency exits, were unlocked and accessible. The entire museum was open and available to visitors, who were free to go wherever they wished.

As the Italian curator and critic Germano Celant observed, Nordman had established not so much an environment as a set of conditions in which the public can act.[6] On another occasion she commented that it would be inappropriate to think of a work as an installation, because 'the sun & the person cannot & will not be "installed"'.[7] The same applies here. Nordman's interest is in the social, interactive potential of the situation. In his 1980 study, *The Practice of Everyday Life*, the French theorist Michel de Certeau called a space 'a practiced place'. 'Space', he wrote, 'is composed of intersections of mobile elements. It is in a sense actuated by the ensemble of movements deployed within it'.[8] Nordman referred to her intervention as a 'prepared place', a description that anticipates activation in the manner de Certeau describes. Her preparation of the Berkeley Art Museum created what she saw as a 'perpetual condition of co-presence'.[9]

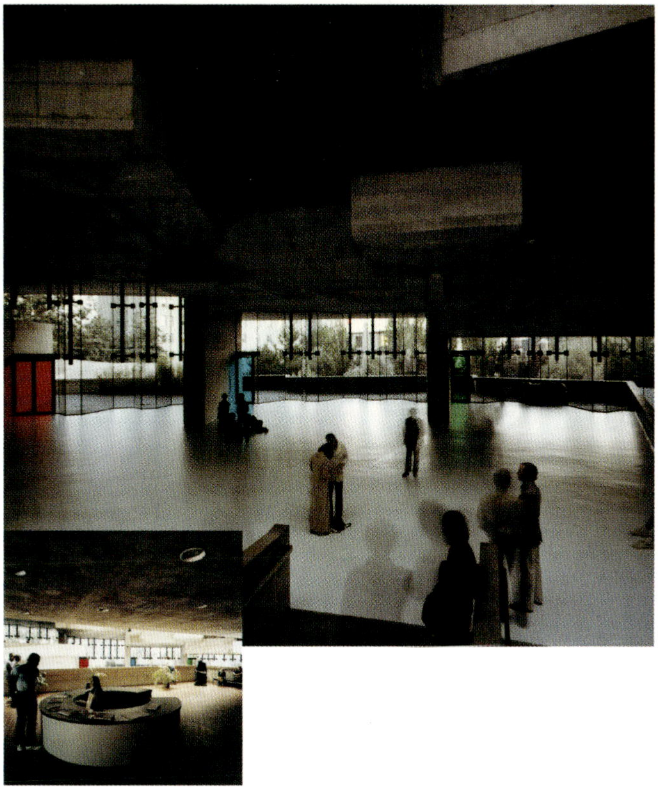

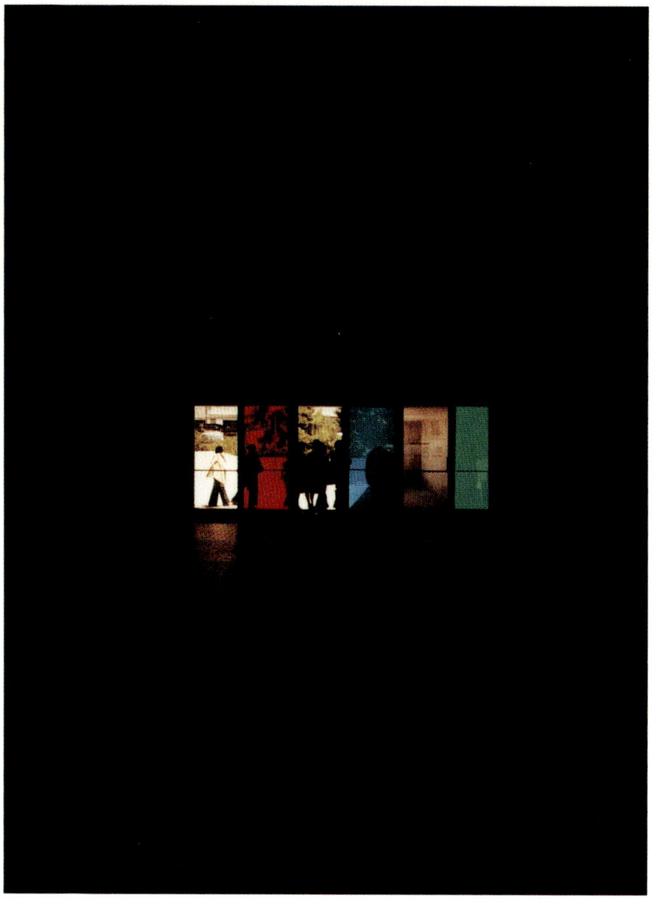

ABOVE: Maria Nordman, *6/21/79 5 a.m.–9 p.m. pre- sun- up to post sun-down, terrestrial/solar co-authoring of a site with any person arriving. U. C. Berkeley Art Museum – Bancroft Way,* 1979.

This was not a kind of sanctuary in which the individual could remain in isolated contemplation, but an exchange between exterior and interior conditions within which multiple viewers – whatever their age, background and distance of travel – constitute what she called 'a public instance':

> *I propose to give the unknown speaker the first word. The work could be of any person who is present. Any person in the presence of any other person. (The possible presence of one or more unknown persons is a public instance.)*[10]

Those visiting the museum on that day were not coming to see a work that had been installed for their viewing pleasure, but were themselves each the active agents in the realization of a work. Being fully open to its surroundings, the museum is unequivocally a part of its urban context. In making it so, Nordman initiated the possibility of a work for any who were present. Whatever the work may have been, it was contingent upon their presence, and upon the movements, actions and decisions they chose to make in conjunction with the movement of the sun.

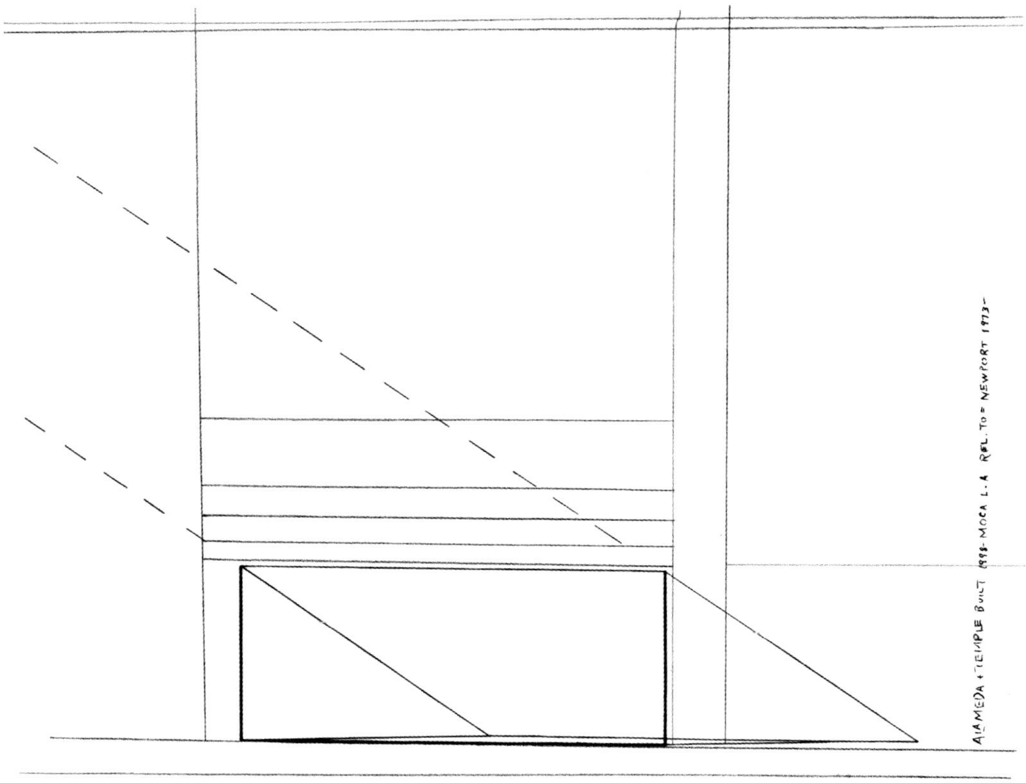

Throughout Nordman's work, the sun and its light are crucial participants in the composition. 'It is the sun', as she has explained, 'creating the aesthetics of the time construction – not myself.'[11] We can see this, for example, in a later work in downtown Los Angeles, *Alameda & Temple* (1995). An open doorway allows sunlight into a space. For four months each year, and at a certain time in the sun's passage each day, its light will fall for a handful of minutes so that it forms a unity with the room's own angles and planes, projecting them into a place of light and shadow for anyone present.

> *Into an open back door at a sidewalk: solar architecture moving into conjunction and disjunction with a given building occurring with variations in the earth's orbital speed and a specific concrete extension of the given walls … For any person arriving by chance from any direction in concert with the sun.*[12]

ABOVE: Maria Nordman, *ALAMEDA & TEMPLE 1995–PRESENT SOLAR INFLUX / 10:00 a.m. 11/1/95 annually 4 months – In Continuous change / (A 100 Year minimum Neighborhood Existence) / Solar Projections into a Rectangular Opening – Loading dock of David Geffen MOCA. L.A.*; Shown by MOCA in concert with LACMA in 2000. Connects with: *11:30 a.m. 2/28/72, 2 months Newport Harbor Art Museum Pacific Coast Highway Alley*. (now OCMA – Costa Mesa).

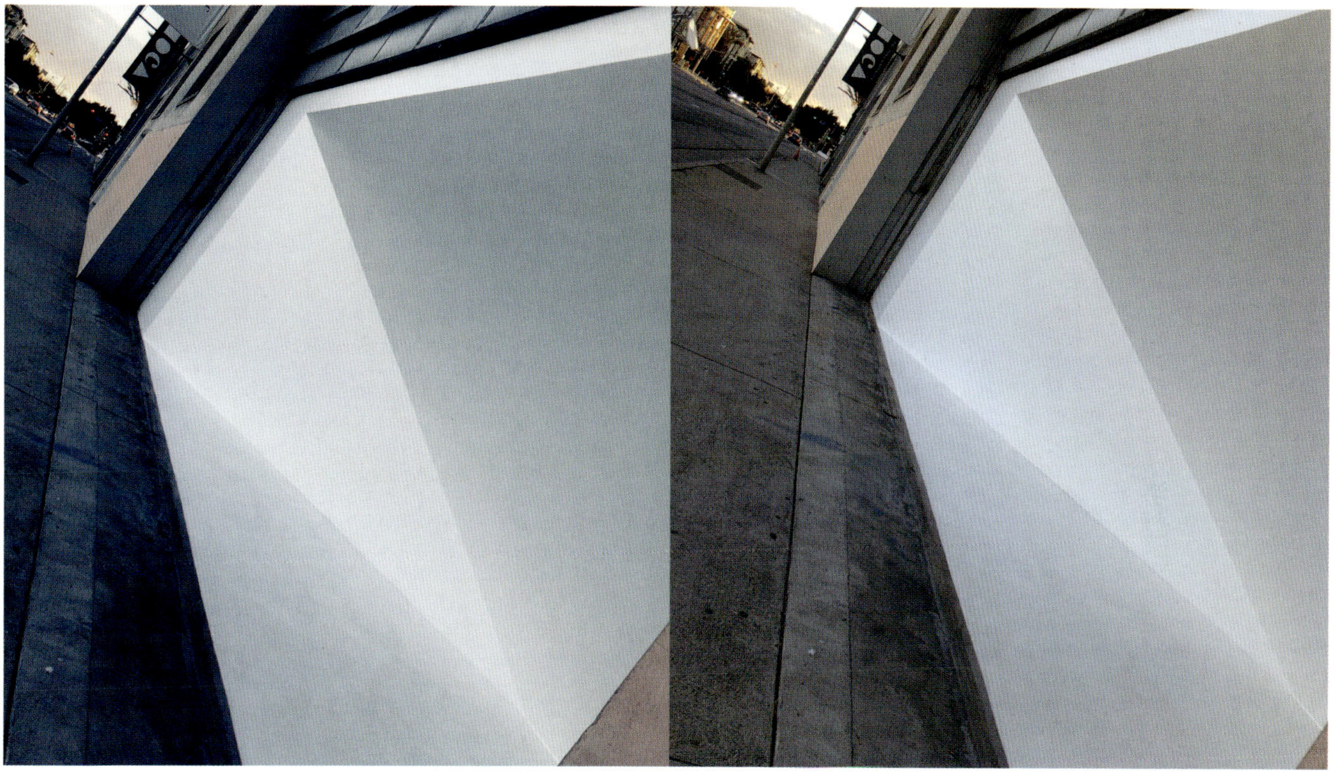

ABOVE: Maria Nordman, *Alameda & Temple*, 1995–present.

'Would a work emplaced directly into an intercultural neighborhood give access to any person arriving in a port city – from any place on the earth – each person potentially engendering a new meaning from the personal social and geo-specific memory?'

– Maria Nordman, 2022

THE DIGITAL CONTEXT

It's reported that on first seeing a photograph around 1840, the French painter Paul Delaroche exclaimed, 'From today, painting is dead'.[1] Eighty years later, Aleksandr Rodchenko again told us that painting is finished.[2] However, contrary to such pronouncements of its demise, painting has remained both possible and actively present. The American artist Donald Judd (see pages 184–5) and others can reject the idea of illusion, or of composition as the relating of parts within the boundaries of the overall canvas, but what this leads us to is a question of context.

Composition persists, if not as that arrangement of parts within the defining rectangle of the canvas, then as organization within enlarged and redefined parameters. Photography has expanded the range of representational techniques open to us and at the same time introduced questions of the truth to be found in the visible world. Motorized transport shifted an understanding of space, our occupation of, and movement through it; flight quite literally brought a new perspective on the world to be represented. Telegraphy and telephony increased our reach across space; radio and television – hearing and seeing things at a distance – changed the relationship that has existed between ourselves and the world. These technologies were not merely a set of new tools, but an expansion and enrichment of lived space. If anything has passed away, it is the set of circumstances experienced by Delaroche and Rodchenko. Reaching for something incontrovertibly false in his study of certainty, the Austrian-British philosopher Ludwig Wittgenstein settled on the statement that one had been on the moon. Humanity has now been to the moon, and we have seen the image of Earth as a blue marble floating in endless dark space. Our world is no longer the one Delaroche and Rodchenko, or indeed Wittgenstein, inhabited.

In a short text from 1966, 'Cybernated Art', Nam June Paik drew the distinction between art made using new technology (cybernated art), and art that is appropriate for a life in which advanced technology is a shaping presence.[3] Both are important, but the latter, art for cybernated life, is the more important of the two. Such art does not itself require advanced technology. Paik went on to talk of the cathode ray tube as an invention that ran counter to the great run of history, throughout which it has habitually been the strongest force that has prevailed. In this invention, it is the minuscule electron that has triumphed.

Paik began working with portable video equipment as soon as it became available in the mid-1960s, and he quickly became engaged in developing a synthesizer that would mix distorted live video imagery with electronic signals. He said of the machine that it would:

Enable us to shape the TV screen canvas
As precisely as Leonardo
As freely as Picasso
As colourfully as Renoire [sic]
As profoundly as Mondrian
As violently as Pollock
As lyrically as Jasper Johns[4]

It was another form of collage, layering images, incorporating multiple perspectives and situations. As such, it was the antithesis of what Paik termed 'vuzak', the visual equivalent of elevator muzak. It allowed the viewer the opportunity to relate in an active manner with the medium of television rather than to simply receive its messages in a passive state.

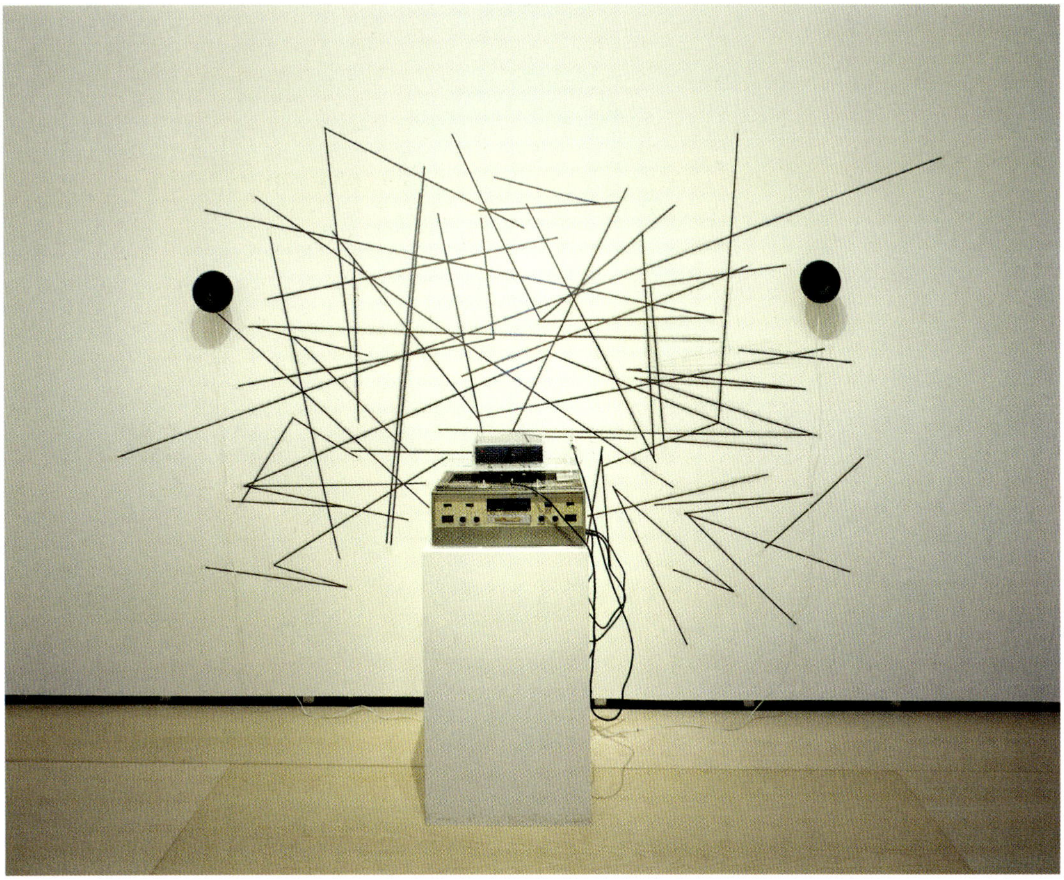

ABOVE: Nam June Paik, *Random Access*, 1963 (2000 version). Strips of audiotape, open-reel audio deck, extended playback head and speakers, variable dimensions. Installation view, Guggenheim Museum Bilbao, 2001.

Paik trained as a musician, and his first use of technology was audiotape and tape recorders. From the outset, he was interested in challenging the apparent fixity of categories, as is clear in a piece such as *One for Violin Solo*, where the destruction of an individual instrument highlights its role as the representative of an entire musical system. Western music, its scales, rules of harmony, established compositional forms, and performance protocols was the restrictive frame from which it was necessary to escape. *Random Access* is an open, apparently arbitrary network made from strips of magnetic audiotape of varying lengths stuck directly onto the gallery wall. In front of it, a tape recorder and speakers are set up. The arrangement is straightforward except for the machine's playback head, which has been removed but has remained connected to the machine by a long wire. Rather than merely looking at this arrangement, viewers are invited to interact with the work by picking up the head and rubbing it along whichever strips of tape they wish. Whatever sounds have been previously recorded onto the tape, before it was cut up and stuck to the wall, will play through the speakers. The content of the recording on the tape strips is not of particular importance. There is no requirement to decipher a message, and the choice of which strip or strips to rub and the order in which to do so is entirely up to the viewer. *Random Access* offers a set of circumstances within which the viewer can become the essential agent in the making of their own composition.

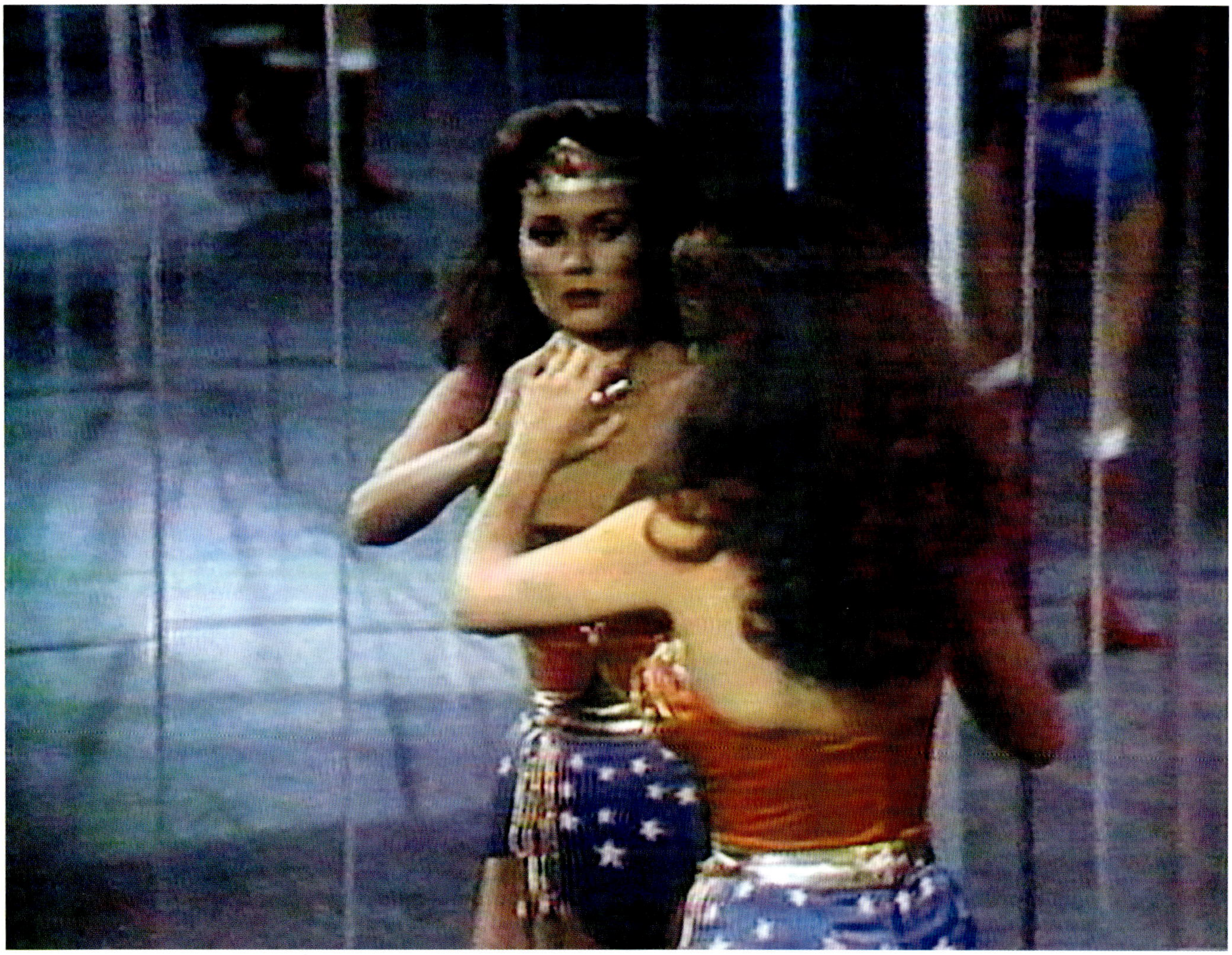

TRANSFORMING TECHNOLOGY

Where Paik was interested in newly available video technology for the access it gave to a medium otherwise controlled by corporate and government interests, the medium was also of particular importance to female artists, since its use avoided their having to follow the heavily male-dominated histories of painting and sculpture. Everyone using video, irrespective of gender, was a beginner. Everyone could experiment and test the potential and the limits of the medium free of expectations since there simply had been no previous practitioners to establish any rules.

American artist Dara Birnbaum's *Technology / Transformation: Wonder Woman* manipulates imagery taken from the Wonder Woman television series. Scenes in which the actress Lynda Carter spins round to change in a flash from her day-to-day existence as a secretary into Wonder Woman are repeated throughout the video. More recently, the gif format has become a ubiquitous aspect of what we view in our everyday life, and the slow-motion replay is now such a part of watching sport that we can be frustrated that it is not available when attending a live game. However, in Birnbaum's case, repetition has a more direct effect: it disrupts the normal television-watching experience, slowing down and suspending the image flow that is characteristic of the medium. We are held within this suspension, able to view the screen action as a number of unfolding moments rather than a narrative thread to be followed.

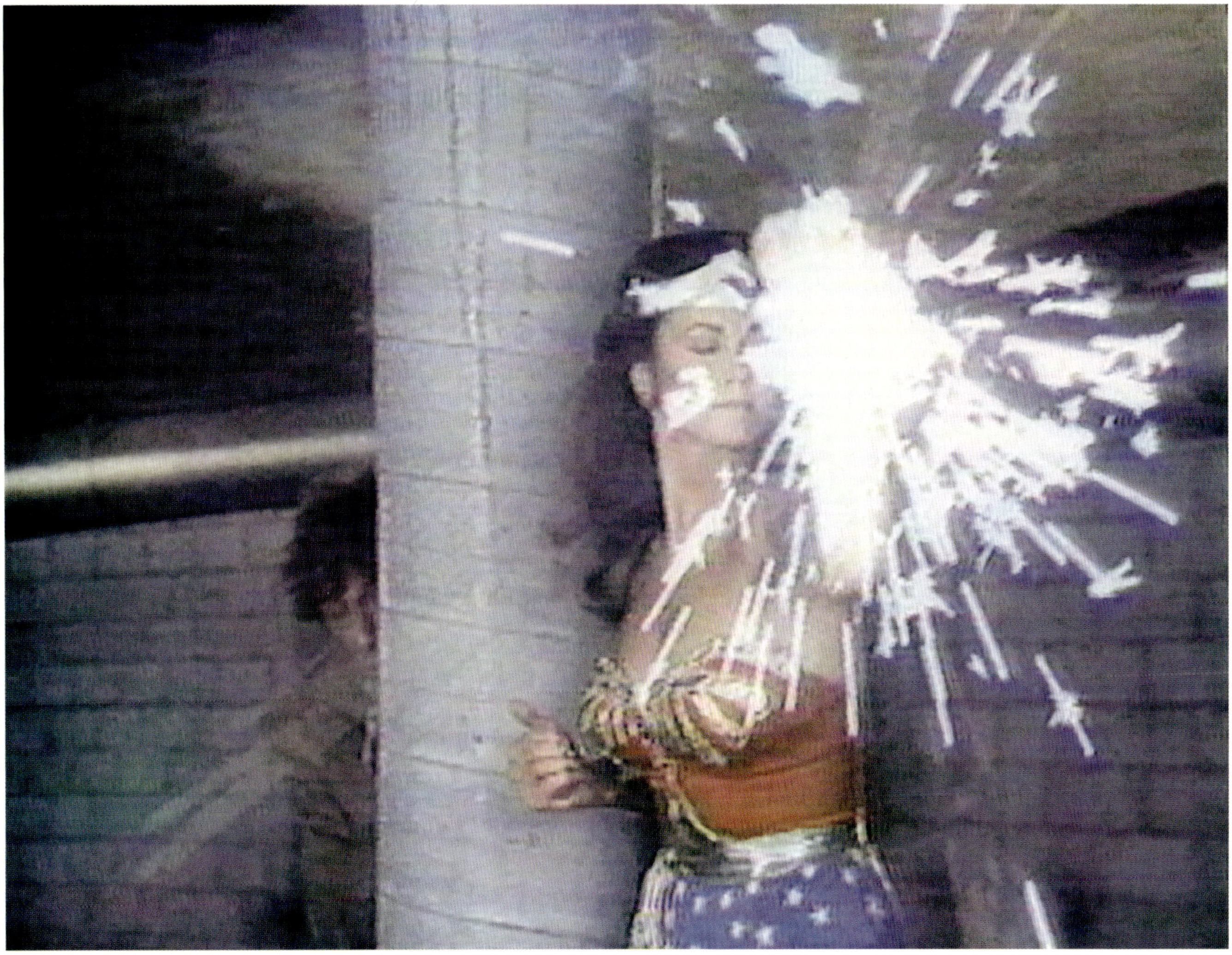

Walter Benjamin noted that we do not give the screen our undivided attention, and instead watch the action taking place upon it in a state of distraction.[5] But in *Technology / Transformation: Wonder Woman* we are brought back to the kind of attentive state in which we look at a painting and are able to see more clearly what is going on. Wonder Woman/Lynda Carter is seen in a variety of indoor and outdoor settings, indicating the mutability and unfixedness of roles. On those occasions that a man appears in the clip, he is weak and hesitant. In one instance, for example, the man cowers behind a pillar while Wonder Woman fends off a hail of bullets with her magic bracelets. The sequence of repeated clips begins and ends with a multiplied explosion, after which the screen fades to blue and *Wonder Woman Disco* by the Wonderland Disco Band – a group only brought together in order to exploit the popularity of the television series – plays while the lyrics scroll up the screen. We see in the end that the special effect of the flash and puff of smoke as just that – an illusion masking the fact that the woman in the office and Wonder Woman are one and the same person. There is a transformation, but also there is not.

OPPOSITE AND ABOVE: Dara Birnbaum, *Technology / Transformation: Wonder Woman*, 1978–9. Single-channel video, colour, sound, 5 min. 50 sec.

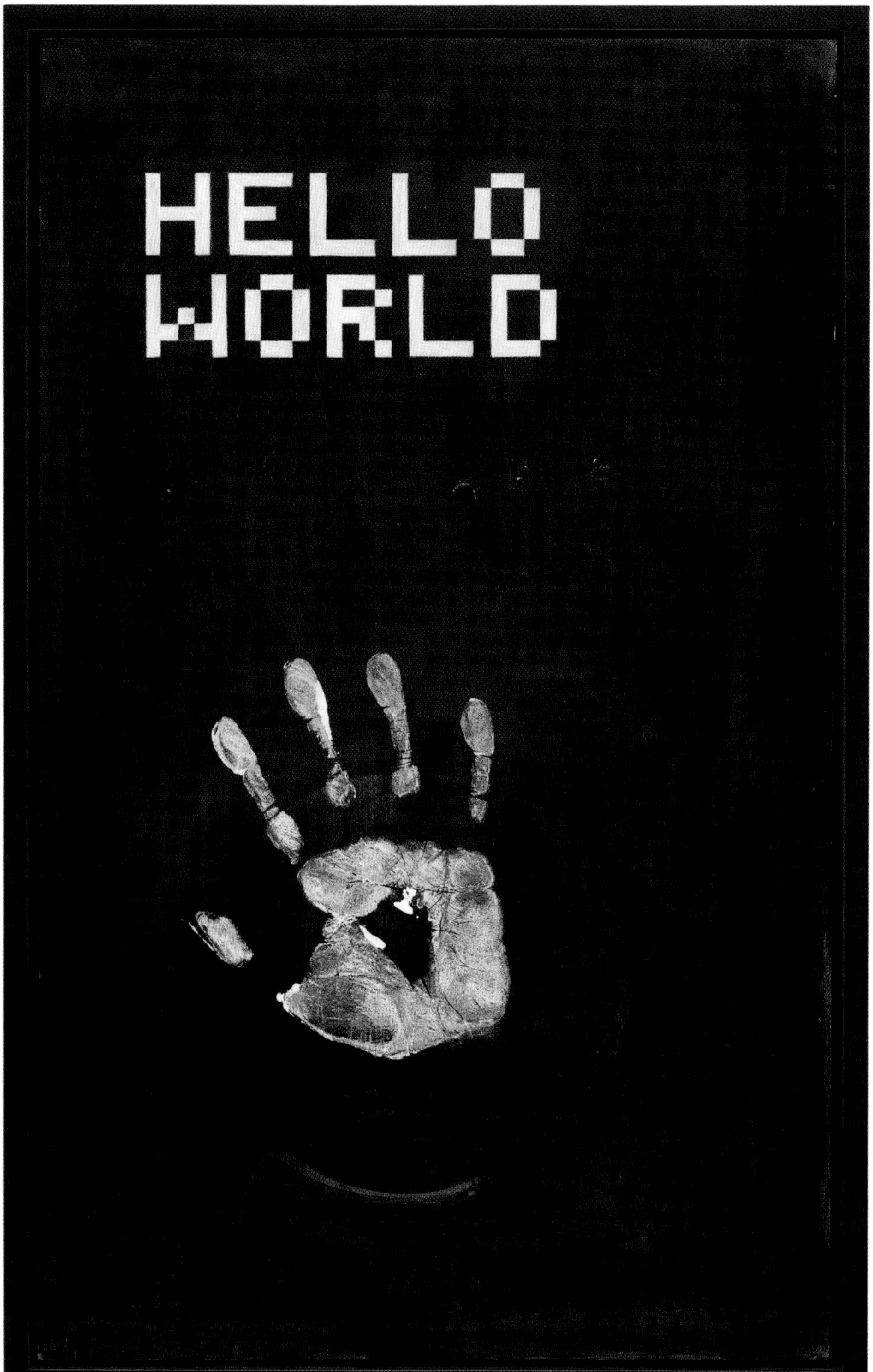

ABOVE: Keith Tyson, *Artmachine Iteration No. 1.1: Hello World*, 1991. Mixed media on metal panel, 64.1 × 42 cm ($25^{1}/_{4}$ × $16^{1}/_{2}$ in).

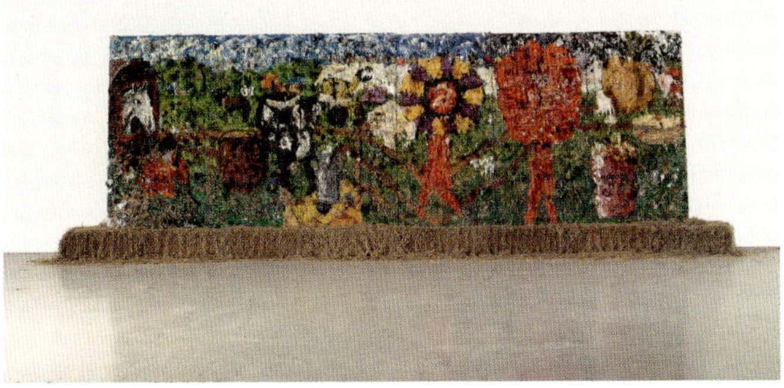

ABOVE: Keith Tyson, *Artmachine Iteration No. 136: Country Fair with Prize Tent*, 1999. Oil, silicone and wood on straw bales, 300 × 960 × 60 cm (118 × 378 × 23⅝ in).

What colour? What scale? Which materials? These are all basic questions that have to be answered in the making of an artwork. Where Georges Braque and Pablo Picasso look to the represented object as the provider of an inner frame on which to build compositional order, the British artist Keith Tyson is preoccupied with the possibility of generating an artwork that would not involve him in tendentiously selecting from the overwhelming blizzard of facts, sensuous impressions, thoughts, encounters and exchanges that constitute daily existence, since all of these things mattered equally.

The financial world's big bang of 1986, which saw share dealing move from noisy stock exchange trading pits to the online world, also saw theorists attempting to analyze ways in which computer technology's ability to handle large quantities of data at high speed would transform the working environment. 'Organizational leaders', wrote American scholar Shoshana Zuboff, 'recognize the new forms of skill and knowledge needed to truly exploit the potential of an intelligent technology.'[6] In developing his Artmachine, Keith Tyson implicitly acknowledged that in such a transformed economy it makes no sense to pretend that art could be the one area of human endeavour not affected by the incursion of information technology into our lives. Artmachine was a set of algorithms or precise sequence of specific instructions programmed into a computer that would generate an outcome in the form of a proposal for an artwork. The output would give indications on size, material, subject matter and other parameters, which were then adhered to in the work's production.[7] *Artmachine Iteration No. 136: Country Fair With Prize Tent*, for example, is a six-panel work depicting the scene of the title. It sits on the floor, leaning against the wall and surrounded by a barrier of straw bales. Viewed from a distance, the scene is relatively clear; but when seen from close up, the image dissolves into the hugely mountainous, globby paint surface resulting from an instruction that it be 45.7 centimetres (18 inches) thick.

The first Artmachine work was *Hello World*, a painting with two main elements rendered in white on a dark ground. The top half of the metal panel is taken up with the text of the title in the kind of cyber font familiar from early digital displays. Underneath it, in the bottom half of the painting, is a hand print. To anyone who has done any coding, the text here will be instantly recognizable. It is the outcome of the first exercise in a widely popular primer on programming, designed to introduce the novice coder to their computer.[8] The task is to write an algorithm that will result in the screen displaying the greeting, 'Hello World'. As British mathematician Hannah Fry explained in the preface to her eponymously titled book on the way algorithms are increasingly shaping our lives, this simple message helps to establish the relationship between the computer and the human who interacts with it. The 'world' indicated in the greeting is not only our day-to-day reality, from which the machine receives its instructions, to which it delivers its output, and of which it has become a part, but also the digital space within the computer itself, which the programmer can now begin to explore. *Hello World* is the technology that has expanded our current space for action, and it is also the palm print on the cave wall, emphasizing the continued importance of touch and intimate connection to the world that art represents to us.[9]

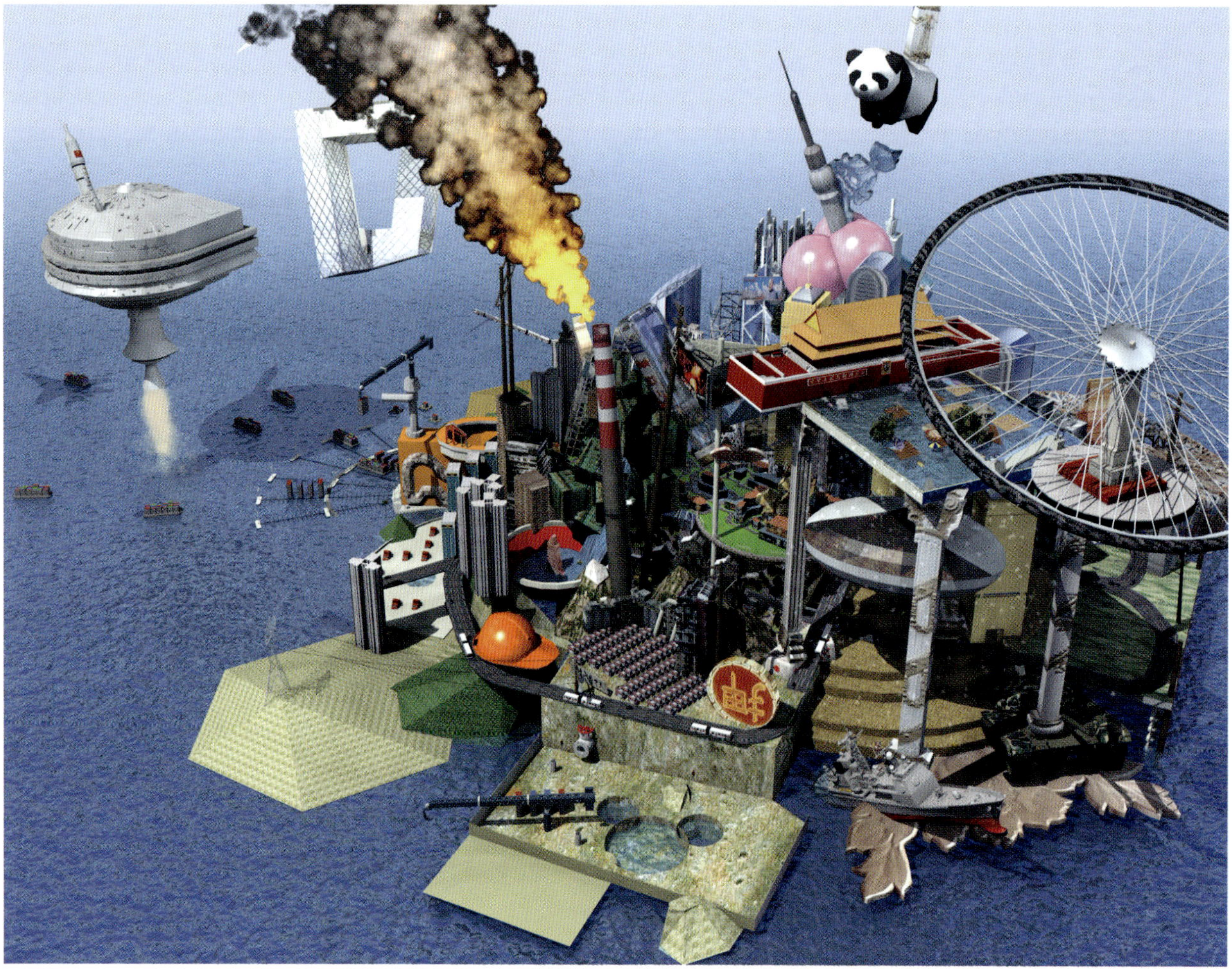

ABOVE: Cao Fei (SL avatar: China Tracy), *RMB City: A Second Life City Planning*, 2007. Machinima, Single channel video, 4:3, colour with sound, 5 min. 57 sec.

'Hopefully there's a new possibility in our electronic second life.'

– Cao Fei speaking as China Tracy

The inseparability of *Hello World's* two otherwise distinct territories – the one figured through coding, the other sensed through bodily presence – is brought home in the Chinese multimedia artist Cao Fei's adventure into a fully realized digital realm. Her motivation for developing a functioning, habitable virtual environment came from the conviction in the first decade of the twenty-first century that 'virtual reality will be the future'.[10] There was, she felt, a pressing need to construct a digital space in which all those activities currently associated with the gallery and museum system could be reconfigured. This space would '[transcend] geographical and material boundaries', and would '[encourage] institutions and artists to realize projects that cannot be realized in our physical reality'.[11] She refers to this space as a 'digital utopia', and we should understand this through the original meaning of the word utopia = no place rather than as an ideal location in which everything is wonderful.

Everything, however, is not wonderful in Cao's digital utopia of *RMB City*, an environment constructed using the then-popular online platform Second Life. Running between 2009 and 2011, it was, in fact, as much a dystopia as anything else, a strange collage built from twisted features of contemporary China: a rusted version of the bird's nest stadium constructed for the Beijing Olympics, the Three Gorges Dam, Shanghai's Oriental Pearl TV tower, supersized malls, water flowing into giant toilets on the container piers of the Pearl River Delta area, travelling through the sewage system, and out into an ocean on which float statues of Mao Zedong. Cao inhabited *RMB City* – named after the Chinese currency, the *renminbi* – with her avatar, China Tracy. As Tracy, she said:

> *Flee from the twilight of the real world ... stab through the protection of reality with the sword of virtuality. This time, the once-invincible real is the defeated one.*[12]

In the nature of the platform, *RMB City* was a public realm. People in the know could visit to explore and to witness the various organized events, but others might come upon it by accident. Residencies were also run in the city for other artists during its two-year lifetime. Conceived as 'interventions' into the city, they used the virtual environment as a space in which to explore the everyday realities for those building the new cities of China at breakneck pace, and those working in its factories. The Hong Kong-born artist Yam Lau, for example, took the opportunity to consider how a character from Chinese folklore, already a figure of imagination as much as flesh and blood, might exist and continue to offer an example in this new world.[13]

There is much talk of reality and virtuality in discussion, not only of Cao's work but also more generally of work based online. These two terms mark a distinction, or separation, between the tactility and material presence of our world and the distant, abstract appearance of the online environment. A different way of considering these two domains was suggested by the French philosopher Gilles Deleuze, who drew the distinction between the virtual and the actual in his 1966 book *Bergsonism*, recognizing both as being a part of the real.[14] Looking back on *RMB City* several years after the end of the project, Cao acknowledged the necessary reciprocal connection between these aspects. 'What the city nowadays lacks is a sense of cohesion and intimacy, which all may have been snatched by these online platforms.'[15]

As ever, questions concerning the frame – what constitutes the frame, what is contained within it, how its contents are organized, what transgresses its limits – remain central in considering a composition as multivalent and layered as *RMB City*. Second Life provided the platform on which to compose the location, and also the tools with which to undertake the construction. Once done, this location was itself a context in which other works could take place. But none of this occurred in an isolated realm. What counted was the interpenetration of the 'second' life with the 'first'.

CHAPTER IV
A NEW FRAMEWORK

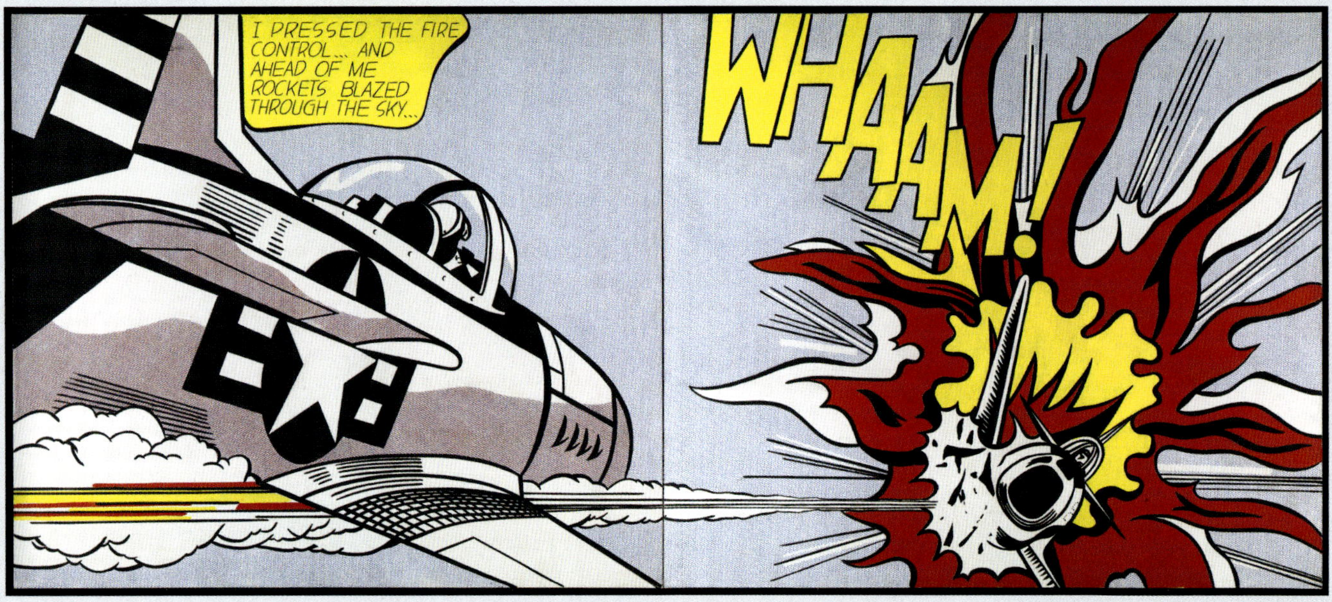

ART AFTER PAINTING

Roy Lichtenstein's *Whaam!* is a complex painting. At a casual glance it appears to be a straightforward transcription of two frames taken from a comic-book story. The assumption that this is all there was to paintings of this kind lay behind early criticisms of pop art as being an art style that insufficiently transformed its source material. But as the American artist himself insisted, 'transformation is a strange word to use. It implies that art transforms. It doesn't, it just plain forms'.[1] Lichtenstein referred to abstract expressionism as 'ground-directed', in which a mark is put down on the canvas and then other marks are made in relation to it until the composition is complete. His work may seem to be 'object-directed' insofar as we see in it a representation of something that exists in the world, but he is adamant that it 'is still ground-directed; the fact that it's an eyebrow or an almost direct copy of something is unimportant'.[2] Sizes and positions of elements in the source image are adjusted, details are altered and flattened, onomatopoeic words are given graphic form that echoes their meaning, and lines indicating the sound, as well as direction of travel of rocket and exploding aeroplane fragments.

Time passes across the diptych – from the release of the rocket in the left-hand panel to the explosion of its target in the right. But this temporal passage is disrupted by the speech bubble in the top left, which places the event we are witnessing in the past. And yet, notwithstanding the startling difference between pop art's embrace of the imagery of the consumer society and the gestural intensity of abstract expressionism, there were underlying continuities, too.

The American art historian Robert Rosenblum – who had been enthusiastic about Lichtenstein's work from the outset – recalled that the American art critic Clement Greenberg stated with conviction, after the artist's first show in 1962, his name would be forgotten within a decade. Pondering the appalled rejection of this new painting, he pointed to the similarity between this situation and the criticism that greeted Gustave Courbet when he first showed at the Salon in Paris (see pages 20–1). Lichtenstein's use of Ben Day dots, so reminiscent of nineteenth-century divisionism, to create the blue sky in which *Whaam!*'s aerial battle takes place, as well as in the shading on the attacking fighter's fuselage, provides further connections. Rosenblum asked of Lichtenstein's adoption of this style:

> *Were the bizarre human beings in Seurat's* Le Chahut *or* Le Cirque *not the ancestors of Lichtenstein's equally strange, bodiless creatures who played out comic-strip dramas or helped to sell refrigerators in newspaper ads?*[3]

Keeping this in mind, we should not allow our surprise at finding ostensibly lowbrow imagery in an art gallery to divert us from appreciating the subtlety of a composition.

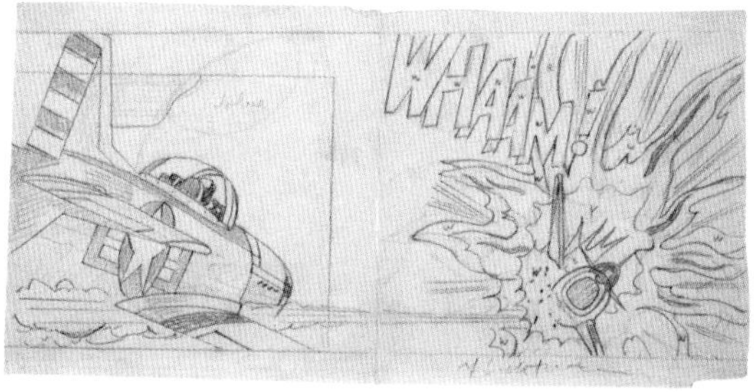

OPPOSITE: Roy Lichtenstein, *Whaam!*, 1963. Acrylic paint and oil paint on canvas, 172.7 × 406.4 cm (68 × 160 in).

ABOVE: Roy Lichtenstein, Drawing for *'Whaam!'*, 1963. Graphite on paper, 14.9 × 30.5 cm (5⅞ × 12 in).

FREEING THE LINE

However much ideas had shifted and broadened in the century since Gustave Courbet's *A Burial at Ornans* (see pages 20–3), the question of composition in painting had, to a significant extent, remained one of understanding the relationship between figure and ground. It was the case with cubism, where the canvas surface provided a ground upon which the facts of a painting could be built – the glass, newspaper, bottle, musician and so on – and in so doing established itself as the rear limit to the space within which the facts of the composition could exist. Even where the surface can be read as space rather than ground, as in the suprematism of Malevych (see pages 120–1), the coloured oblongs, trapezoids, lines and squares of his compositions move as distinct entities through this limitless environment.

Writing in the early twentieth century, however much the German art historian Wilhelm Worringer saw a line beginning as an inherently abstract gesture, it was from there that it took a journey towards a 'semblance of organic aliveness and natural likeness'.[1] Ultimately, a line could always be seen to mark an outline, to set a limit or to establish the surface of a form. Yet, in Jackson Pollock's 1948 painting *Number 1A*, line does none of these things. The American artist had spent time at the British printmaker Stanley Hayter's Atelier 17 studio in New York, where he met the French surrealist artist André Masson and became acquainted with the automatic drawing technique. The American art critic Bernice Rose observed:

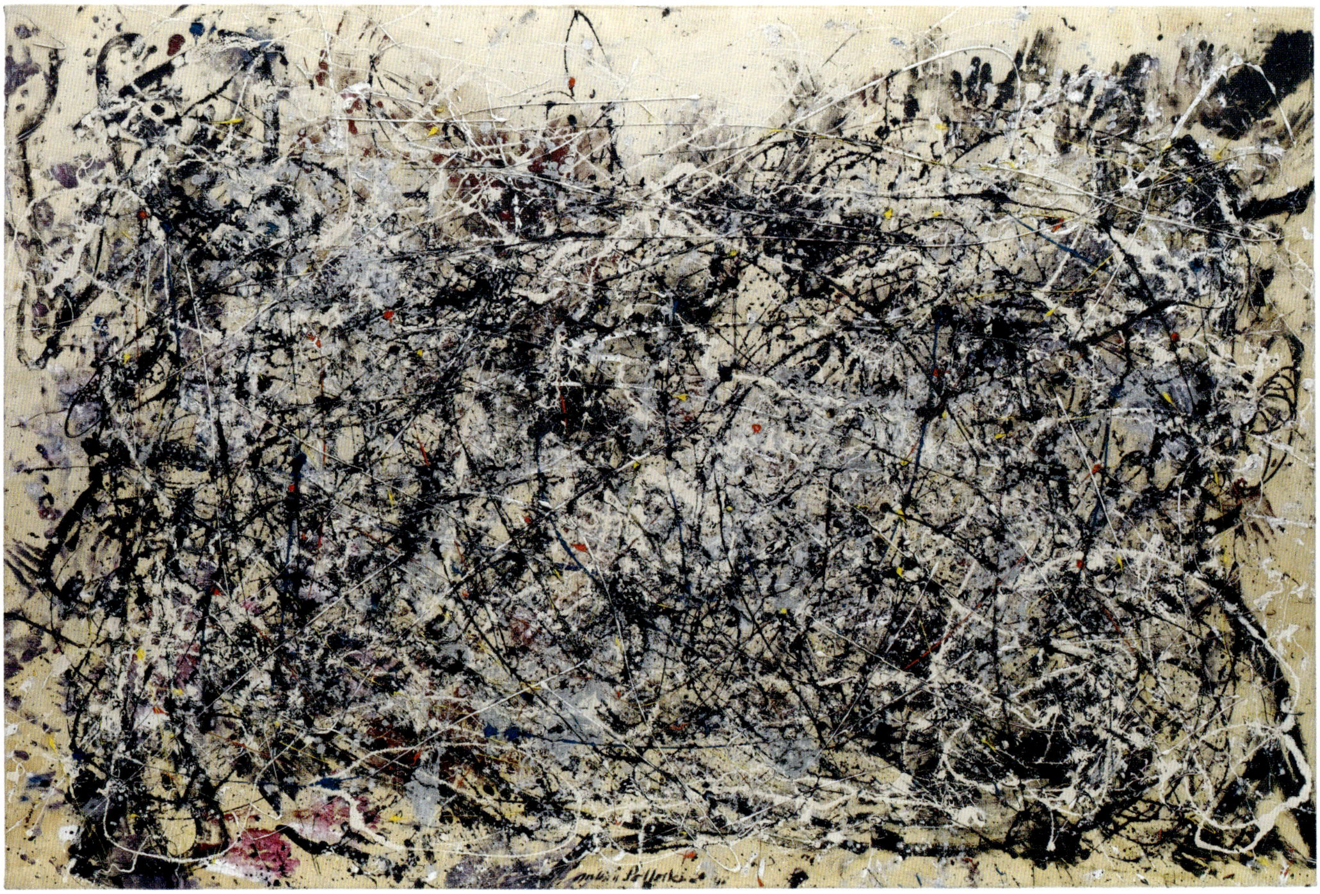

ABOVE: Jackson Pollock, *Number 1A*, 1948. Oil and enamel on unprimed canvas, 172.7 × 264.2 cm (68 × 104 in).

> *The importance of Pollock's discovery of automatic drawing cannot be overstressed; automatic drawing released the images in his psyche to his hand, it then enabled his hand to free him from the dependence on those images. It is in the transference of the freedom of automatic drawing to automatic painting that Pollock's style is created.*[2]

He worked on a large piece of unstretched canvas tacked to the studio floor so that he could, in his own words, 'walk around it, work from the four sides and literally be in the painting'.[3] Such an approach was, as Pollock observed, similar to the method of the Native American sand painters of the western United States. Rather than the artist's standard oils, he preferred working with more fluid industrial paints, which can be dripped from the end of a stick moved above the canvas instead of being laid on with a brush.

Working in this way instead of addressing a stretched canvas propped or hung vertically, using the whole area with equal intensity in a manner referred to at the time as 'all-over', dripping the paint in lines and skeins laid through rhythmic movement, working from all four sides and sometimes stepping onto the painted area – all of these mark *Number 1A* as a different kind of painting from all those that had preceded it. Pollock's line is not descriptive. It does not outline form, does not serve to structure the painting as a conventional space within which incident can be understood to be taking place. The paint lines, their rhythmic repetitions, *are* the incident and the form. Where they run over one another they do not create the illusion of spatial depth. They are all acting on the surface of the canvas, implacably and unmistakably so.

The size, too, is significant. Taking inspiration from the Mexican muralist David Alfaro Siqueiros, the decision to work at this scale established the painting as being at home in a gallery for public viewing rather than something to be found in a domestic interior. The American art critic Harold Rosenberg spoke of Pollock's canvas as 'an arena in which to act' – hence the term Action Painting in referreing to the approach. He goes on to say that the canvas 'was not a picture but an event'.[4] This idea of the work of art as an event would become increasingly more important in the latter half of the twentieth century.

Pollock's line is not descriptive. It does not outline form, does not serve to structure the painting as a conventional space within which incident can be understood to be taking place. The paint lines, their rhythmic repetitions, are the incident and the form.

Pollock's place as an exemplary figure among the group of his contemporaries referred to as abstract expressionists and the remarkable quality of his innovation in painterly composition has led to his approach being appropriated as a stylistic symbol, both for abstract expressionism itself, and for American, or more generally Western culture as a whole. As examples of the former, the spaghetti in James Rosenquist's multipanel composition *F-111* (1964–5), or the loops and swirls marking the sunlit water surface in *Peter Getting Out of Nick's Pool* (1966) by the British artist David Hockney, can be recognized as cool, perhaps ironic, representations of Pollock's freed line. In regards to the latter, during the Cold War, the United States organized travelling exhibitions in the 1950s to promote its culture, pitting what it saw as its progressive abstract expressionism against the representational socialist realism of the USSR. Forty years after the first forays into abstraction by Hilma af Klint, Wassily Kandinsky and others, it was becoming much harder to accept it as pure non-objectivity. Our familiarity with abstraction as a stylistic and compositional possibility meant that it was now recognizable simultaneously as both nonrepresentation and the representation of nonrepresentation.

In their own, later, investigation into painterly practice, the British group Art & Language playfully brought these two antagonistic positions together. Having perfected a convincing imitation of Pollock's style, they used it to replicate well-known photographs of Lenin. Art & Language imagine four kinds of viewer for their Portrait of V.I. Lenin in the Style of Jackson Pollock series. If you know neither Pollock nor Lenin, you see a jumble of lines; if you know only Lenin, you see an idiosyncratic portrait of the Soviet leader; if you know only Pollock, you see a passable attempt at his style; and if you know both Pollock and Lenin, you may be able to shift between the two in the way we do with the familiar drawing of the duck/rabbit. When Ludwig Wittgenstein discussed the duck/rabbit drawing, it was to argue that we can never view anything as what it purely is, but must necessarily always see what we are looking at *as* something – we can see the line as a duck or as a rabbit, but not both at the same time. Although Art & Language's composition is a simple conflation of two predetermined elements, the way in which the two work against each other makes for a multifaceted result. As well as being a genuine attempt to reproduce Pollock's style, it is also an ironic quotation of that style. Similarly, the picture functions as a portrait and as a sardonic reference to the portrait it reproduces.[5]

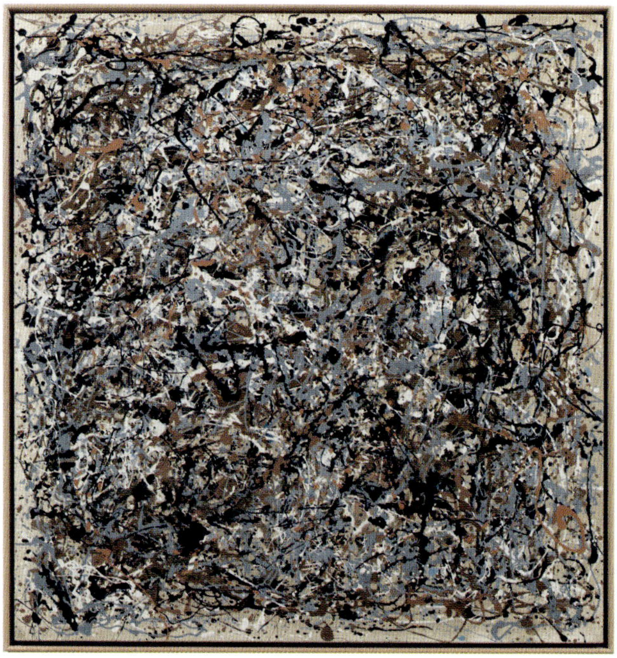

It is because Pollock's line is unencumbered by the requirement to outline or describe that there is force in calling it into descriptive use.

ABOVE: Art & Language, *Portrait of V.I. Lenin in the Style of Jackson Pollock VII*, 1980. Enamel on canvas mounted to board, 105 × 100 cm (41⅜ × 39⅜ in).

OPPOSITE: Gordon Bennett, *Myth of the Western Man (White Man's Burden)*, 1992. Synthetic polymer paint on canvas, 175 × 304 cm (69 × 120 in).

Pollock's drip painting style is also quoted by Australian artist Gordon Bennett in his painting, *Myth of the Western Man (White Man's Burden)*. In this instance Bennett, who was of indigenous Australian and Anglo-Celtic parentage, is referring to Pollock's *Blue Poles*, which was purchased by the Australian state in 1972. As a symbol of the government's ambition to signal the country's engagement with the best of culture, the painting quickly came to stand as a rebuke to the creativity of indigenous Australians. In his composition, Bennett has reduced the five blue 'poles' of Pollock's composition to a single one being planted in the centre of the canvas by a settler. This wind-buffeted figure is surrounded by a swirl of blue patches, each of which carries a date of significance in the history of the country and of the struggle against the colonization and oppression of the indigenous population. At the bottom of the pole is '1788', the date on which the flag was raised and the colony established. At the top is '1992', the year of the Mabo High Court decision in which the continent's status as Terra Nullius – an empty land available for exploitation as the settlers saw fit – was finally overturned. A further dimension to *Myth of the Western Man* is the overall pale blue field into which are set the dated blue flags, and over which the Pollock-like black lines are laid like whiplash welts and scars. This field is rendered in the repeated small dot technique associated with the Papunya Tula artists of the Western Desert in Australia's Northern Territory (see also pages 168–9). Pollock's allusions to Native American Navajo ground painting also interested Bennett and impacted his practice. In his artist journal in 1992, Bennett explained:

> *My reason for dwelling on Pollock's 'style', or rather his development for the annals of art history, is because one of his major influences in the development of action painting was indigenous American sand painting, the ritualistic and ceremonial aspects of which have strong parallels with Aboriginal Australian ground painting ceremonies.*[6]

Both Art & Language and Gordon Bennett made use not only of Pollock's general drip painting style but also of this essential aspect of the freed line. It is because Pollock's line is unencumbered by the requirement to outline or describe that there is force in calling it into descriptive use. It becomes multilayered, being Pollock's line and a representation of it, as well as the outline of a domed forehead, a bearded chin or the scarred skin of the indigenous body.

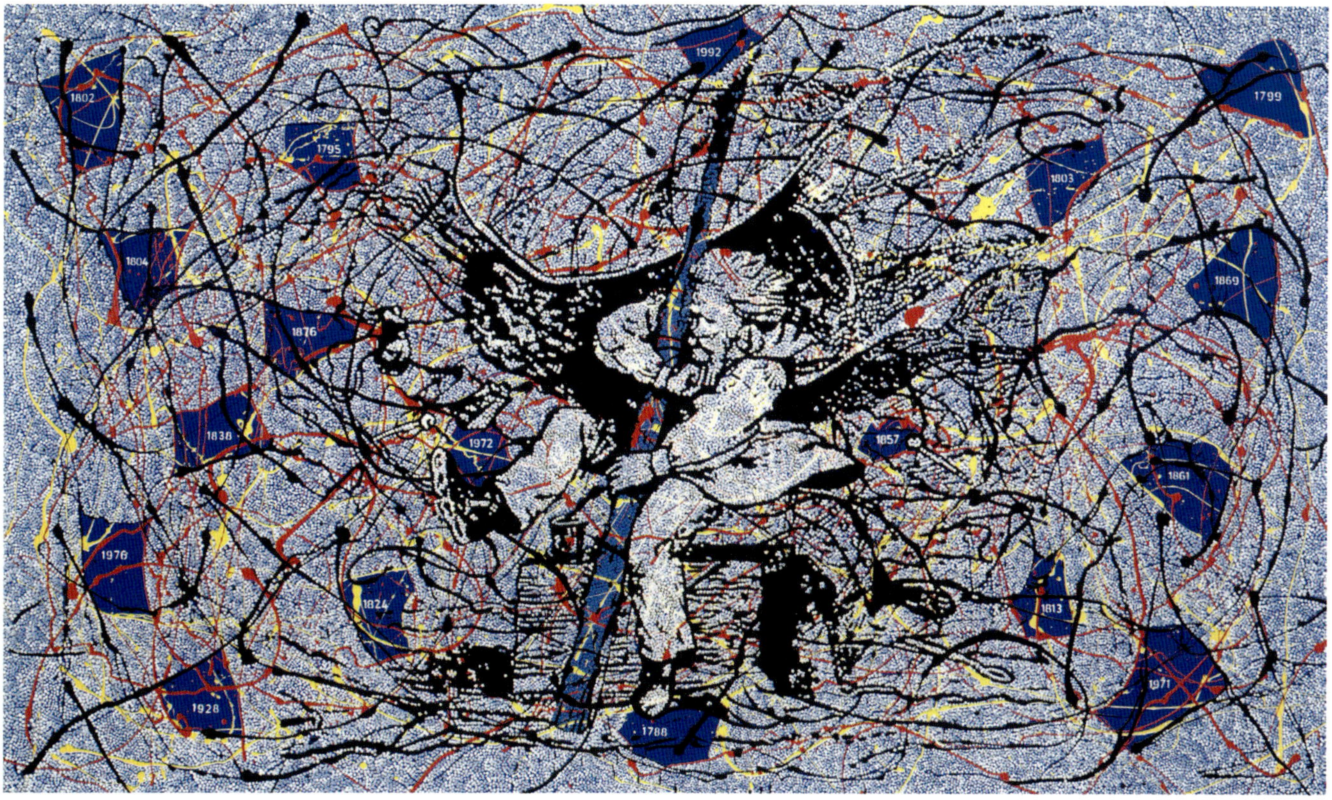

NOT COMPOSING?

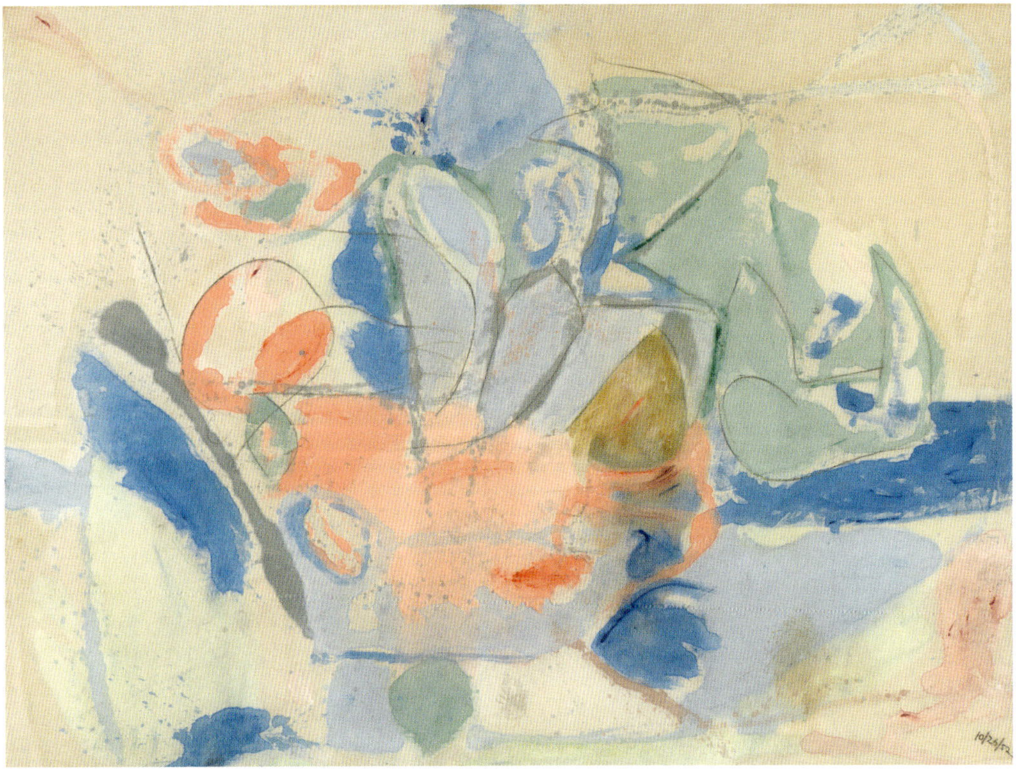

ABOVE: Helen Frankenthaler, *Mountains and Sea*, 1952. Oil and charcoal on unsized, unprimed canvas, 219.4 × 297.8 cm (86⅜ in x117¼ in).

Is it possible to produce a painting without composing it at all? In the United States in the late 1950s and early 1960s, the discussion of this idea was symptomatic of the desire to distance American painting from European antecedents. Marcel Duchamp had already opened one possible solution with his proposal of the readymade (see pages 84–5), and it was taken up by the American artist Jasper Johns in 1954 when he made a painting of the American flag. Its pattern of stars and stripes and its use of the three colours red, white and blue are all given components. Johns is entirely relieved of the need to decide what to paint where, and when the painting is complete, what it represents – a flat rectangle of cloth bearing a familiar, definitive pattern – is exactly what it is. The image and its object are congruent.

Clement Greenberg's narrative of the development of modernist art describes it as a journey towards the realization of a medium's fundamental properties. In the case of painting, he saw these properties as twofold: the rectangle of the picture plane and the flatness of the picture surface. In 1953, the American artist Morris Louis saw Helen Frankenthaler's *Mountains and Sea*, a large canvas in which areas of colour had been achieved by applying thinned paint and thereby staining the unsized canvas. Frankenthaler, an American abstract expressionist painter, said of her technique:

> *When I first started doing the stain paintings, I left large areas of canvas unpainted, I think because the canvas itself acted as forcefully and as positively as paint or line or colour. In other words, the very ground was part of the medium, so that instead of thinking of it as background or negative space or an empty spot, that area did not need paint because it had paint next to it. The thing was to decide where to leave it and where to fill it in and where to say this doesn't need another line or another pail of colours. It's saying it in space.*[1]

The piled-up central forms of *Mountains and Sea*, and the areas of both thinned and more intense blue redolent of tumbling and spreading water, certainly give a strong visual sense of the title's subject matter. More than this, however, those basic orientations of the loosely depicted land- and seascape – verticality and horizontality – are thoroughly bound up in the techniques and processes employed in making the painting. While the staining of the unprimed, unsized canvas would necessitate its placement on the studio floor, the charcoal lines that chart and articulate those stained areas suggest its being worked on in an upright position.

Frankenthaler's example was transforming for Louis, showing him, as he said, 'a bridge between Pollock and what was possible'.[2] Louis's series of Unfurleds such as *Alpha-Pi* are composed of lines of acrylic paint – then still a new medium for artists – poured onto unstretched canvas. When subsequently fastened to a stretcher, the resulting painting shows irregular stripes, each of a different colour, running in rough diagonals from both sides down to the bottom edge. Each stripe is of pure colour and for the most part does not mix with its neighbours. The central space, a truncated V of unpainted canvas, might leave us to get lost in its blank immensity, but the strong, multicoloured diagonals anchor the sides to the bottom and strengthen the overall rectangle of the painting. The American painter and critic Walter Darby Bannard wrote:

> *Louis suddenly, so it seems, discovered that pictorial coherence could be strongly established by reversing the assumption cubism ... had forced on painting: that visual integration of the picture is achieved by putting the visible parts of the painting together. Instead of accommodating the edges of the picture, and fussing with the factors of design they imposed, the 'unfurleds' throw the parts of the painting* against *the edge, and forced the edges to do the job of holding the picture together.*[3]

While the paint is being poured, the surface is of indeterminate dimension, so the question of composing by placing one element in relation to another within a defined rectangular space remains an impossibility. The decision on how the stained canvas will be cut and fitted to a stretcher, thereby fixing the limits of the rectangle and establishing it as a painting, comes later. In Greenberg's terms, Louis's Unfurleds are as unremittingly flat and as implacably rectangular as it is possible to be. However, the perception that they arrived out of an apparent lack of interest in the idea of composition on Louis's part is erroneous. In a May 1965 letter to the journal *Art International*, Greenberg addressed two statements: one made by Guggenheim curator Daniel Robbins, who claimed that Louis had a 'calculated concept of un-compositional painting', and the other by Lucy Lippard, who noted his 'much discussed principles of non-composition', and 'his supposed lack of interest in formal relationships to the extent that he refused to decide the final dimensions of his canvases'.[4] Greenberg replied:

> *I knew Louis well enough, and long enough, to be able to say that 'calculated concept of un-compositional painting' would have struck him as inane, whether applied to his own or anybody else's art. It mattered very much to him whether his colour ran down an inch or half an inch; and he would have as little dreamt of refusing 'to decide the final dimensions of his canvases' as of letting someone else paint on them.*[5]

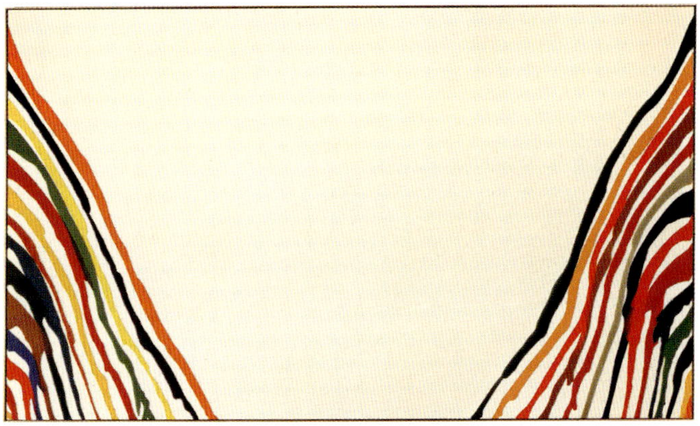

LEFT: Morris Louis, *Alpha-Pi*, 1961. Magna on canvas, 260.4 × 449.6 cm (102½ × 177 in).

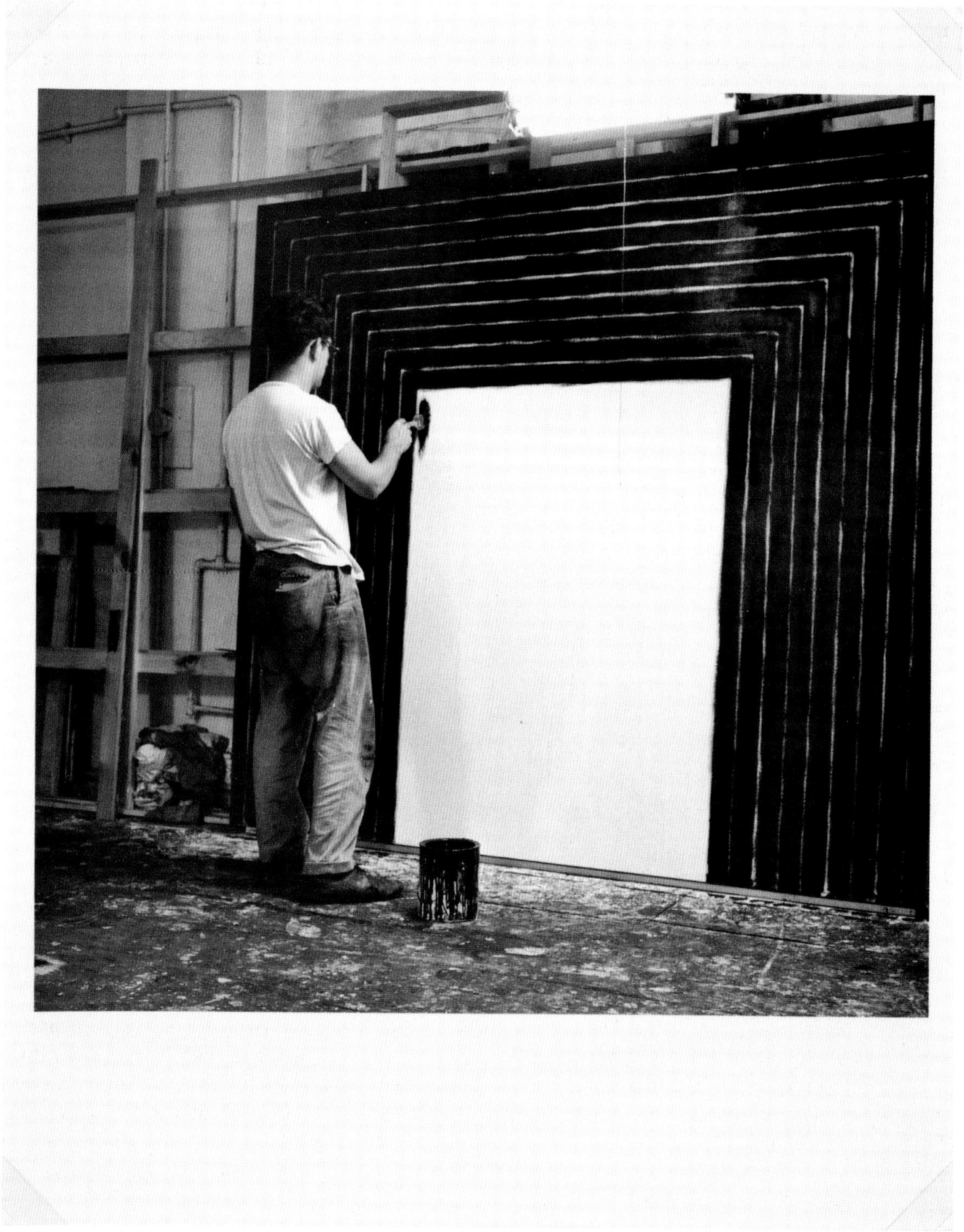

ABOVE: Hollis Frampton, *#27 painting Getty Tomb* from The Secret World of Frank Stella. Neg. 1958–62; print 1991.

In 1958, the American artist Frank Stella began a series of paintings with surfaces filled with even, concentric black stripes. In one of the simplest, *Getty Tomb*, for example, the stripe runs up the right-hand edge, across the top and down the left-hand edge of the canvas. Others in the series are similarly straightforward, using permutations on a very small number of initial choices: first, either bisecting the surface with a single horizontal or vertical line or using both a horizontal and a vertical line to divide it into quadrants; and second, orienting the stripes either parallel or at a 45-degree angle to the canvas edges.

A sequence of photographs taken by the filmmaker Hollis Frampton shows Stella at work on *Getty Tomb*, gradually covering the canvas with further stripes parallel to the first. What is evident in the images is that the outcome is to all intents and purposes determined from the beginning. Once he has begun to paint, Stella makes no further decisions about what he will do. In other words, composition – in the usually understood meaning of a process involving the balancing of various elements within the rectangular space of the painting – seems to have little or no relevance here.

In the majority of cases, an important moment in the making of a work comes when the artist decides that no further additions, subtractions, adjustments or rebalancing could improve things. By implication, this judgement means that the work is 'finished', although a change of heart and a feeling that one could work on it a little more will always remain a possibility. This is a very different kind of terminus to what is happening with Stella's stripe paintings. In his case, there is not and cannot ever be any doubt as to when the painting is finished, and this is true of all the stripe paintings he made during the first half of the 1960s. In each case, there is a congruence between the physical fact of the stretched canvas and the painted image on its surface.

Stella invariably used deep stretchers and did not continue the painting round onto the edges. Explaining this in a 1964 interview he said:

> *When you stand directly in front of the painting it gives it just enough depth to hold it off the wall ... it makes it more like a painting and less like an object, by stressing the surface.*[6]

And yet this slight increase in the surface's projection into the space of the gallery has the added consequence of emphasizing the physical presence of the painting. In the same interview, he also says:

> *My painting ... really is an object. ... All I want anyone to get out of my paintings ... is the fact that you can see the whole idea without any confusion ... What you see is what you see.*[7]

Despite this, it would be a mistake to think that the work was isolated and disconnected from either the history of art, or the wider world. Robert Rosenblum pointed out that Stella's stripe itself could be linked to its use in a 1941–4 painting by the American abstract artist Robert Motherwell, as well as to the pattern of the American flag, the readymade composition that appeared in the work of Jasper Johns in 1954. Moreover, the titling, which can perhaps be seen as a way of situating the work and providing it with context, is always significant. In addition to rectangular and square formats, Stella began from 1963 to use shaped canvases. Two from that year are trapezoidal, and their shape, their colours and their titles – *Valparaiso Flesh* and *Valparaiso Green* – refer directly to a painting of Valparaiso harbour in Chile with boats furling their sails by the nineteenth-century American painter James Abbott McNeill Whistler, *Crepuscule in Flesh Colour and Green: Valparaiso* (1866). The horizon line cuts Whistler's canvas in two, and both the sea in the lower half and the light clouds lit by the setting sun in the upper, are rendered in large part through use of the colours of the title. Set parallel to the canvas surface, the boat's main sail in the centre of the picture hangs limp, its shape a distinct trapezium. Stella took these elements – the bisected canvas, the two colours and the trapezium – to make his pair: each in a single colour; both trapezoidal, one the inverse of the other. The Irish art critic Brian O'Doherty wrote in his 1986 book, *Inside the White Cube*, that Stella's large, shaped paintings bring home the point that such work is no longer made for people to purchase and hang in their homes, but instead exists to provide the opportunity for a photograph of their installation in a museum or gallery.[8]

The idea of abstraction – and what it meant to say that anything to do with something as material and practical as painting was abstract – posed a problem for the American painter Pat Steir. 'I couldn't intellectually translate the idea of abstraction', she said. 'It seems to me, when you put down a line, there is a line. How could that line be abstract?'[9] The line is real and exists because paint has been applied to the canvas. And if there is an image, it is there because it is in the paint: 'The paint makes the image', Steir explained, 'the paint and the image are the same thing'.[10] In the wake of abstract expressionism, Roy Lichtenstein had taken that movement's quintessential symbols and rendered them in his signature style derived from the comic strip. The exploding rocket in *Whaam!* (see pages 144–5), and his several versions of the flamboyant stroke of a paint-laden brush, for example, present us with the sign of expressiveness. When we encounter gestural paint handling, we understand that we should see it as emotionally involving.

Steir was similarly interested in the brushstroke, but she approached it from a very different angle: 'My idea was to make the dripping brushstroke the icon of abstract painting, to make the picture become figurative.'[11] The brushstrokes in her Waterfall series are applied in paint thinned to an extent that allows it to flow freely under the inevitable and inexorable force of gravity down the canvas surface. The work of gravity is constitutive, and it needs no assistance or helping hand once the paint has been applied. 'The thing that I always have to force myself to do', confessed Steir, 'is let the paint hit the canvas, walk away and let it do its thing.'[12] As well as being directly applied, paint is flicked and thrown, with the movement of Steir's arm giving shape to the paint in the air before it reaches the canvas. The results leave far behind the purist concern with flatness that so preoccupied the debate around painterly and post-painterly abstraction in the 1950s and 1960s. The Waterfalls are waterfalls both in the way they are made and in how they look. They are moments on a flat surface, but they also have depth. They are an image of what they are and at the same time they are what they are.

Steir has long studied Chinese painting and has related the way the viewer experiences the scale of her works to compositional techniques found there:

> *Look at the relation of the mountain and the monk. In the Zen painting the monk is looking at the moon. Everything is huge except the monk, who is a tiny little black dot. Because in the picture we are seeing what the monk is seeing from his point of view: he is a small part of the universe. Which to me is the same as my mountain paintings, or my sky paintings. I am the painter looking from a huge distance at the huge sky and the mountain looming.*[13]

This comment is made in relation to other series, but is of equal relevance to the Waterfall paintings, which are made as though the falling water were right in front of the eyes. 'I'm trying desperately to make chaos', Steir said, 'but I make order. I try to make the chaos within the work; that's why I depend on gravity to leave a lot of space for accident. For chaos'.[14]

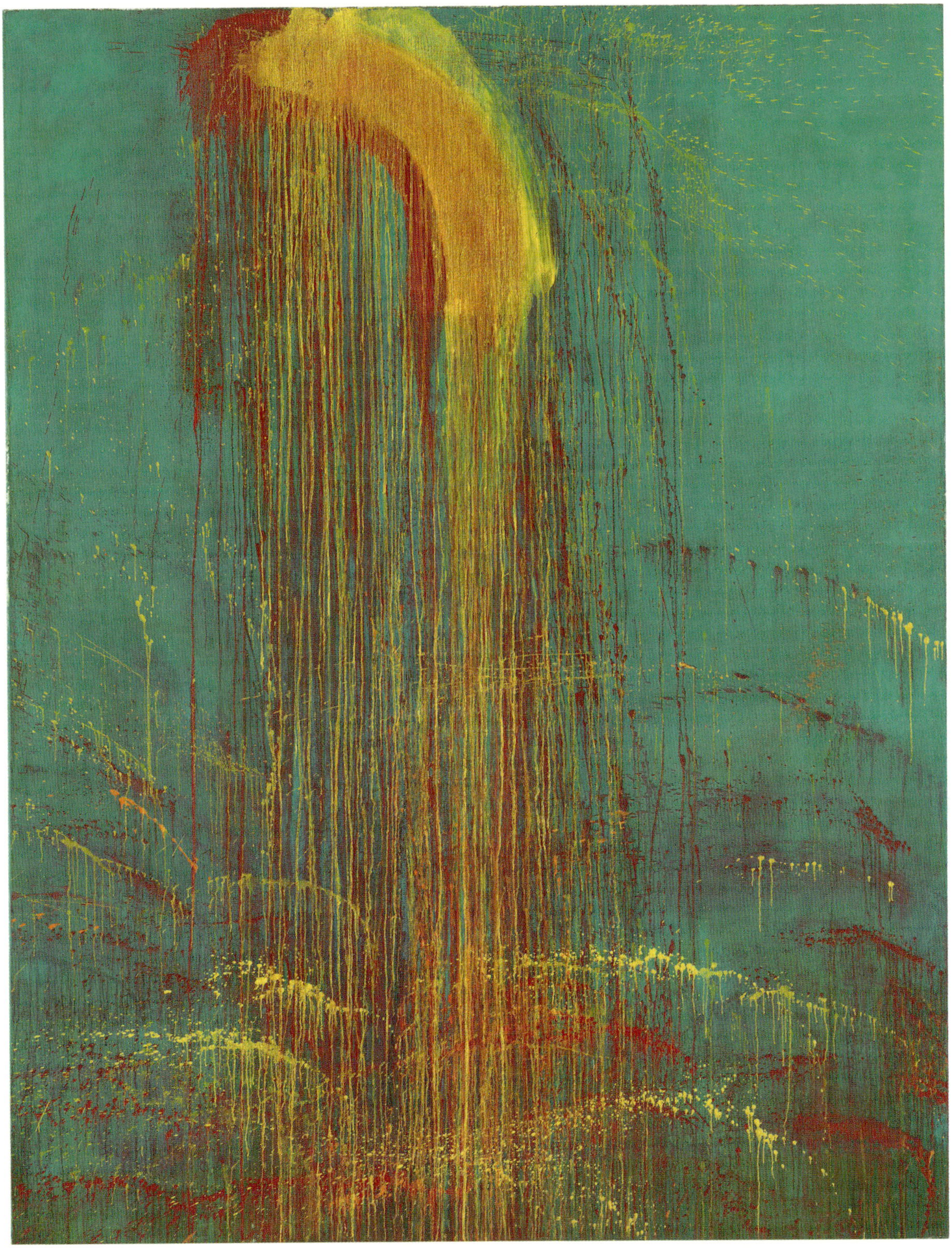

ABOVE: Pat Steir, *Middle Lhamo Waterfall*, 1992. Oil on canvas, 292.1 × 229.9 cm (115 × 90½ in).

BORROWING

For a long time, copying the old masters was considered to be the best training for an artist. Go to the museums and galleries, study what those who came before you have done, and attempt to emulate it. In a culture of mass production, however, the act of copying becomes something altogether different. The rhetoric of the avant-garde emphasized originality as a quality to be prized in a work of art, and the search for newness was symptomatic of the ever-strengthening grip of the market. If something was unique, it could command a good price, whereas if it appeared to be an echo of something already seen, the demand for it would be considerably reduced. In this context, copying took on new significance.

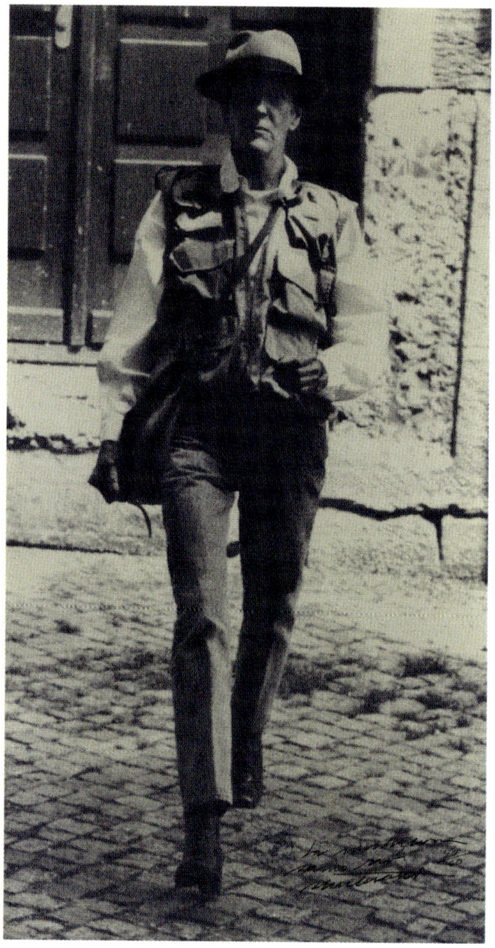

ABOVE: Sturtevant, *Beuys. La Rivoluzione siamo Noi*, 1988. Screenprint on paper, 95.3 × 50.9 cm (37½ × 20 in).

The American artist Elaine Sturtevant, latterly known simply as Sturtevant, began in the early 1960s to make works that looked rather like those of her male peers, including Jasper Johns, Frank Stella, the sculptor George Segal, and pop artists Tom Wesselmann, James Rosenquist, Roy Lichtenstein, Andy Warhol, and Claes Oldenburg. They were never exact copies, albeit on one occasion Andy Warhol gave her one of his own screens to make a Marilyn Monroe painting. Instead, Sturtevant used the characteristic style and familiar imagery of each artist to compose what at first sight might be taken for an example of his work. What aided this possibility of false recognition was that Sturtevant's first exhibitions were staged in galleries that spectators were not allowed to enter, thus meaning that they could only be viewed from the street like a shopfront window display of tempting goods. As she later said, 'it was not about the objects – it was about a totality … it was about thinking'. She further commented, 'Pop only dealt with the surface. I started asking questions about what lay beneath the surface. What is the understructure of art? What is the silent power of art?'[1]

A casual glance at one of these works might lead us to mistake it for an 'original', but once this misapprehension is recognized, the issue for the viewer is to wonder how it functions in its context. Dealers and some artists were hostile to Sturtevant's work and, following adverse critical reaction to an exhibition focused on Marcel Duchamp and Joseph Beuys in 1972, Sturtevant withdrew from art making for a decade. It was only in the 1980s – when, in quite different circumstances, the idea of copying and borrowing gained currency – that Sturtevant's work was reappraised. Her version of Joseph Beuys poster work, *La Rivoluzione siamo Noi (We Are the Revolution)* was created at this time. In Beuys' work, we see him dressed in his trademark felt hat, fishing jacket, boots and jeans, striding towards the camera. In *Beuys. La Rivoluzione siamo Noi*, a similarly dressed Sturtevant replicates Beuys stride for the camera. By using an existing work by another artist as a starting point, Sturtevant removed any idea of representation – which is to say, the idea that an image has to have an origin – as a necessary consideration in the process of composition and artistic production. She summed this up succinctly shortly before her death:

> *What is currently compelling is our pervasive cybernetic mode, which plunks copyright into mythology, makes origins a romantic notion, and pushes creativity outside the self. Remake, reuse, reassemble, recombine – that's the way to go.*[2]

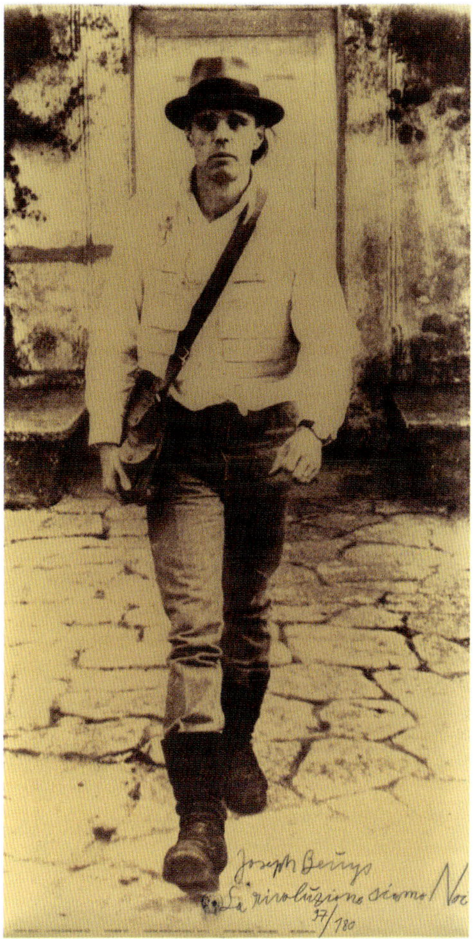

ABOVE: Joseph Beuys, *La Rivoluzione siamo Noi (We Are the Revolution)*, 1972. Silkscreen with handwritten text and stamp, 191 × 100 cm (75⅛ × 39⅜ in).

By using an existing work by another artist as a starting point, Sturtevant removed any idea of representation … as a necessary consideration in the process of … artistic production.

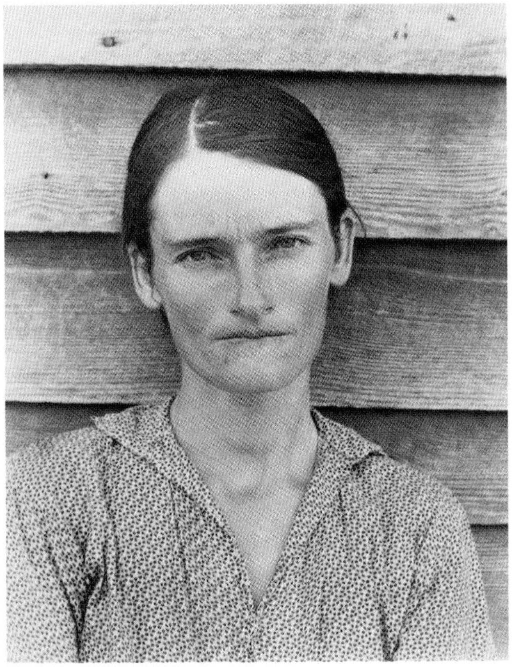

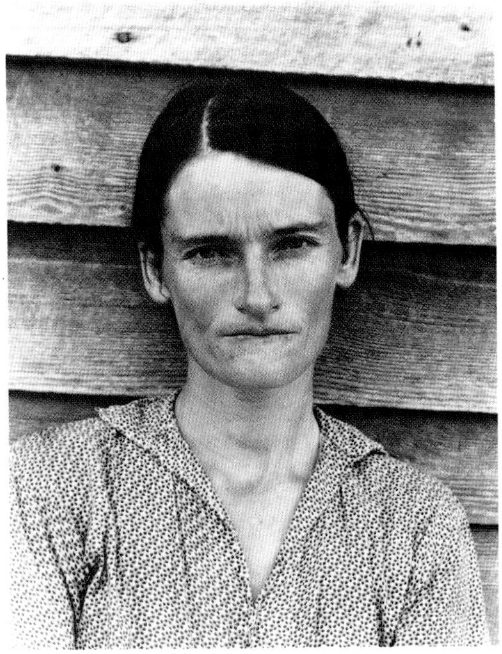

ABOVE LEFT: Walker Evans, *Alabama Tenant Farmer Wife*, 1936. Gelatin silver print, 20.9 × 14.4 cm (8¼ × 5⅝ in).

ABOVE RIGHT: Sherrie Levine, *After Walker Evans: 4*, 1981. Gelatin silver print, 12.8 × 9.8 cm (5⅛ × 3⅞ in).

APPROPRIATION

One feature of much mainstream art of the 1980s was the open and deliberate reference to previous artworks, objects and styles. It preceded the widespread availability of material via the internet, and it is symptomatic of a questioning attitude towards the standard narratives of stylistic development in the arts. The story told by American museum director Alfred H. Barr, most clearly shown in the diagram he produced to accompany his 1935 *Cubism and Abstract Art* exhibition at New York's Museum of Modern Art, paralleled Clement Greenberg's charting of painting's progress in the twentieth century (see page 15). But Greenberg's story came to a halt with the post-painterly abstraction of Morris Louis, Kenneth Noland and Jules Olitski in the 1960s, and the subsequent decade would run on empty.

Just as in other contexts, the practice of copying – for example, in the studying of the old masters as a means to developing one's own skills – was differentiated from the idea of repetition. Here, however, copying was understood not as borrowing but as what was more usually referred to at the time as appropriation – a reverse of the normally understood relation between the precedent and its subsequent re-creation. There was no requirement to justify borrowing. Rather than being subservient to the precedent, appropriation could take over and turn the work to the artist's own ends. As far as the act of composition was concerned, it could be seen in the decisions made on what materials to appropriate and how they were presented. One example is the use of patterns associated with late 1950s and early 1960s op art in the distorted grids of Victor Vasarely, the repeated black-and-white lines of Bridget Riley (see pages 70–1) – by New York City-based painters such as Philip Taaffe, Ross Bleckner and Peter Schuyff. However legitimate or otherwise, there was a view that the visually disconcerting rhythms of op art represented the last gasp of modernism, and to re-create the look of this work with the aim of discovering further expressive possibilities within it, was to signal a dogged refusal to give up and accept that everything was over. Such compositional tactics had significant impact in the social setting of the 1980s and '90s in which AIDS was taking the lives of so many.

Another, very different instance was the series of photographs made by the American photographer Sherrie Levine. In many respects, they appear not to be hers at all, given that the images are all well-known photographs by such famous predecessors as the American photographers Walker Evans and Edward Weston. In Levine's case, we are apparently looking at, say, Evans's portrait of Allie Mae Burroughs, a cotton sharecropper's wife in Alabama. In reality, Levine photographed Evans's image as a flat shot from the page of a catalogue in which it has been reproduced. What we are looking at, therefore, is a print of the representation on a page of a mass-produced book of a photograph of a print taken from Evans's original negative. Just as Jasper Johns took the readymade pattern of the American flag as a template for the organization of paint on canvas, using a well-known photograph as the subject of a photograph removed any suggestion that compositional choice was central. What Levine was looking at is the system of representation, reproduction and distribution.

Turning back upon the artefacts produced within a system enables us to see the workings of that system itself. One major aspect of Levine's act is that she, a woman, was the one behind the camera on this occasion. In rephotographing an image of high cultural status, she issues an explicit challenge to the traditional view of art history that overwhelmingly privileges and reinforces the assumed naturalness of art arising from moments in which a male artist looks upon a female subject. In looking at Levine's *After Walker Evans: 4*, certain states of affairs become visible to us and we understand how they came to be accepted. It is, however, quite possible to remain comfortably contained within that same system. What has happened in the years since is that the existence of other, alternative ways of looking at and structuring the world have come into play. Where such alternatives have made their presence felt, the question of composition is further problematized.

If the art object was 'dematerialized' … wouldn't that make it difficult to sell?

DEMATERIALIZATION

So much of what we have seen throughout the past century has involved, in one way or another, questioning the frame within, or in relation to which, the artwork can be understood to exist. What, then, might be the consequence of doing away with any kind of reliance on the frame altogether?

In 1973, art critic and curator Lucy Lippard published *Six Years: The Dematerialization of the Art Object from 1966 to 1972*. The book is a collection of artworks, statements, interviews, critical comments and chronology of exhibitions charting the development of conceptual art along with the related factions of minimalism, land art and post-minimal anti-form or distributional art. For a later edition, Lippard included a new introductory essay, 'Escape Attempts', on the attitudes and practices of that time and their subsequent appearances over the succeeding three decades. Central to much conceptual art was the desire to operate in such a way that the art world could not appropriate an artist's work, treat it as a commodity and market it for financial gain. If the art object was 'dematerialized' – as an idea, a short descriptive text, a set of instructions, or coloured light instead of paint on canvas fastened to a wooden stretcher – wouldn't that make it difficult to sell?

Lippard begins Part II of 'Escape Attempts' by quoting the American artist Robert Barry:

> *For years people have been concerned with what goes on inside the frame. Maybe there's something going on outside the frame that could be considered an artistic idea.*[1]

Barry pursued this idea in his own work. On one occasion, for example, he kept a gallery closed for the duration of his exhibition there so that visitors could only look for and think about art while locked out of the space in which they usually expected to find it. And in contradiction to a critic such as Clement Greenberg, for whom all that was germane to the evaluation of a painting was what could be seen held within the rectangle of the canvas, Barry proposed almost the opposite with his text work, ALL THE THINGS I KNOW BUT OF WHICH I AM NOT AT THE MOMENT THINKING – 1:36PM; JUNE 15, 1969.

The American artist Lee Lozano made pop-related paintings in the early 1960s. Her sexualized images of tools on an imposing scale – *Hammer* (1963), for example, is 239 × 254 centimetres (94 × 100 inches) – confronted the stereotypically gendered expectations associated with the abstract expressionism of the 1940s and 1950s, with its rhetoric of muscular, almost heroic risk-taking in the application of paint to canvas. Later in the decade, Lozano embarked on a series of works that pushed ever further beyond the limits of the frame. She noted that as an artist she wanted to 'seek the extremes', because 'that's where all the action is'.[2] The Art Workers' Coalition (AWC) formed in New York in 1969 with an initial focus on artists' rights and the under-representation in museums of Black and Puerto Rican artists. When invited, along with many others, to support the aims of the AWC, Lozano made the following statement:

> *For me there can be no art revolution that is separate from a science revolution, a political revolution, an education revolution, a drug revolution, a sex revolution or a personal revolution. I cannot consider a program of museum reforms without equal attention to gallery reforms and art magazine reforms which would aim to eliminate stables of artists and writers. I will not call myself an art worker but an art dreamer and I will participate only in a total revolution simultaneously personal and public.*[3]

Simply adding a few extra artworks to a few collections would be pointless if the institutions within which they were to be displayed and interpreted, and the social and economic structures that supported and maintained those institutions, were not also fundamentally reimagined. Everything had to change or nothing would change. As she made this statement, Lozano began her *General Strike Piece*, in which she would

> *Gradually but determinedly avoid being present at all official or public 'uptown' functions or gatherings related to the 'art world' in order to pursue investigation of total personal and public revolution.*[4]

Next to this description of the piece in her notebook, Lozano wrote that it would go on at least through the summer of that year (1969), but in the end it continued for the remaining thirty years of her life. Although it was a refusal to contribute, the strike retained a notional connection to that which was being avoided. What it became for Lozano, by the following year, was a complete withdrawal from New York and its art world. Her notebook entry reads:

> *IT WAS INEVITABLE, SINCE I WORK IN SETS OF COURSE, THAT I DO THE <u>DRO**POUT**</u> (NOTE PUN) <u>PIECE</u>. IT HAS BEEN CHURNING FOR A LONG TIME BUT I THINK IT'S ABT TO BLOW. <u>DROPOUT PIECE</u> IS THE <u>HARDEST</u> <u>WORK</u> I HAVE EVER DONE.*

In the emphasis on the 'pout' of 'dropout', we can understand Lozano's sense of frustrated disappointment with circumstances. While Marcel Duchamp famously announced in 1923 that he was ceasing to make art, he nevertheless carried on playing the fully integrated, thoroughly present dilettante for the rest of his career. He relied on the art world to certify that he had given up making art (albeit he was, in reality, secretly continuing to do so all the time).

Lozano's *Dropout Piece* is, to use her word, much more extreme. Conceptualism's fate shows that in the end, the market can find a way to accommodate every artistic gesture. A photograph or a typewritten sheet of paper can ultimately be bought and sold as easily as a painting. Even a set of instructions can be marketed if it is accompanied by a certificate stating that its owner is the only person authorized to carry out those instructions as a legitimate artwork. And when there is no product to sell at all, the market will make the artist themselves into the commodity, requiring them in one way or another to perform their role as aesthetic worker. For Lozano, by withdrawing altogether, she made it impossible for the market-driven art world to co-opt either her work or her own self to its purposes. She would not become another commodity.

The quick way out at this point would be to decide that Lozano had just decided to give up making art and thereby ceased to offer anything for us to look at or consider. But as she said in her notebook, '<u>DROPOUT PIECE</u> IS THE <u>HARDEST</u> <u>WORK</u> I HAVE EVER DONE.' It is not the cessation of all activity but the start of a prolonged period of labour. In a short text, the British conceptual artist Keith Arnatt had wondered whether it might be possible for him to 'do nothing'[5] as a contribution to an exhibition, only to conclude that even doing 'nothing' was doing something.

The life Lozano lived from 1970 until her death in 1999 might not immediately be perceived, or be perceivable as the work of an 'art dreamer', but her invisibility need not lead us to conclude that it was not. Art historian Jo Applin observed: 'Once Lozano quit her activities within that art world and went silent, she gave up her standing as a voice to be reckoned with'.[6] It was thus only towards the end of her life, when it became possible once again to organize the exhibition of her work, that the strength and significance of Lozano's withdrawal could be recognized. The year before she began *General Strike Piece*, land artist Robert Smithson remarked in his essay, 'A Sedimentation of the Mind: Earth Projects', that 'If art is art, it must have limits'.[7] In working at the extremes, 'where all the action is',[8] Lozano went beyond the limits, and in doing so posed the question as to how we might now understand anything we see or encounter as a composition.

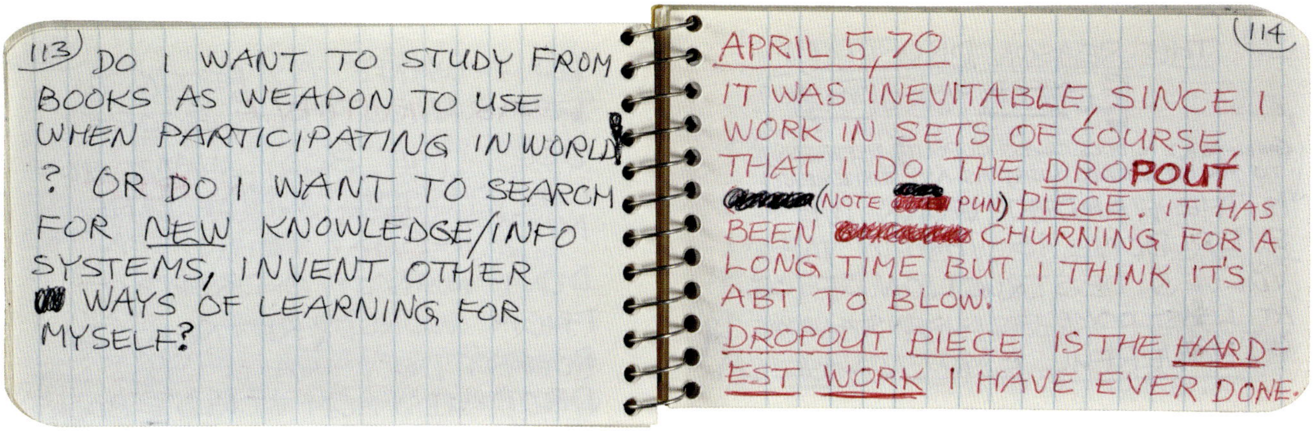

ABOVE: Lee Lozano, *Private Notebook 8*, pages 113–14, 5 April, 1970.

MANIFESTATION

On 3 January 1967, the French artist Daniel Buren, joined by three other artists – the Swiss Olivier Mosset, the French Michel Parmentier and the Swiss Niele Toroni – staged *Manifestation 1* at the Salon de la Jeune Peinture, Musée d'Art Moderne, Paris. The group, known collectively as Association Buren, Mosset, Parmentier, Toroni, spent several hours in the gallery producing works featuring a signature look upon which each had decided. Buren used alternating white and coloured vertical stripes; Parmentier, broad horizontal stripes alternating between white and a colour; Mosset painted single black circles centred on a white ground; and Toroni made marks with a 5-centimetre (2-inch) brush, each dab separated from the next by 30 centimetres (12 inches). To accompany the event, they issued a statement to journalists, which constituted a second manifestation:

> *Because painting is a game,*
> *Because painting is the application (consciously or otherwise) of the rules of composition,*
> *Because painting is the freezing of movement,*
> *Because painting is the representation (or interpretation or appropriation or disputation or presentation) of objects,*
> *Because painting is the springboard for the imagination,*
> *Because painting is spiritual illustration,*
> *Because painting is justification,*
> *Because painting serves an end,*
> *Because to paint is to give aesthetic value to flowers, women, eroticism, the daily environment, art, dadaism, psychoanalysis and the war in Vietnam,*
> *We are not painters.*[1]

At the conclusion of *Manifestation 1,* the artists removed all the work they had just made and hung a banner stating that Buren, Mosset, Parmentier and Toroni 'do not exhibit'. If you had attended in expectation of an event that would provide entertainment, you would have been disappointed.

The four artists were critical of the degree to which art had become just another part of the culture industry, pandering to people's desire for spectacle. 'What the bourgeoisie expects of art', wrote Buren in his 1971 essay 'Standpoints', 'is noise, "novelty", brio, and talent'.[2] Even though it professed opposition to conventional expectations and values, Buren considered avant-garde art to be equally guilty in this respect. He identified twentieth-century art as oscillating between two poles. The first, good, pole was symbolized by Paul Cézanne; the second, bad, one by Marcel Duchamp. Buren saw Cézanne's work as having posed two fundamental questions bearing upon the degree to which painting involves illusion: the illusion of a represented object rather than a real one, and the illusion of space created through perspective.

First of all, 'is it possible to manifest painting without making manifest that which is painted?' In other words, could one ever think 'this is a painting', or better still, 'this is painting', without always having to say 'this is a painting of … apples, trees, red rectangles, etc.'?[3] Second, 'can one abolish perspective, really remove the illusion of depth and make manifest the characteristic of the support on which one paints; i.e. a flat surface?',[4] Buren saw these same issues subsequently addressed in a positive way in the paintings of Piet Mondrian, Jackson Pollock, Barnett Newman and Frank Stella, although they remained unresolved. Duchamp's solution was to accept that any object represented within the frame of the canvas would inevitably be an illusion, so he concluded that the only way to avoid illusion was to display the object itself (see pages 84–5). But this apparently radical step, explained Buren, is actually regressive and fails to provide the solution it claims. In order to display the object – let us say the urinal that we acknowledge as Duchamp's *Fountain* – it has to be removed from its original context and brought into the museum. In this new location, it can be recognized as art, but only at the price of losing its originally designated function. It is therefore just as much a representation of what an actual urinal is in the world beyond the gallery as the painted apple is of a real apple:

> *The place where this urinal has just been put (the museum, the gallery, or any other defined artistic place) has the same function as the support or tableau for the 'apple'. The 'apple' is received inside the canvas, the urinal inside the museum. The framework of the representation has become enlarged. What has changed is the framework in which the object is seen, the container.*[5]

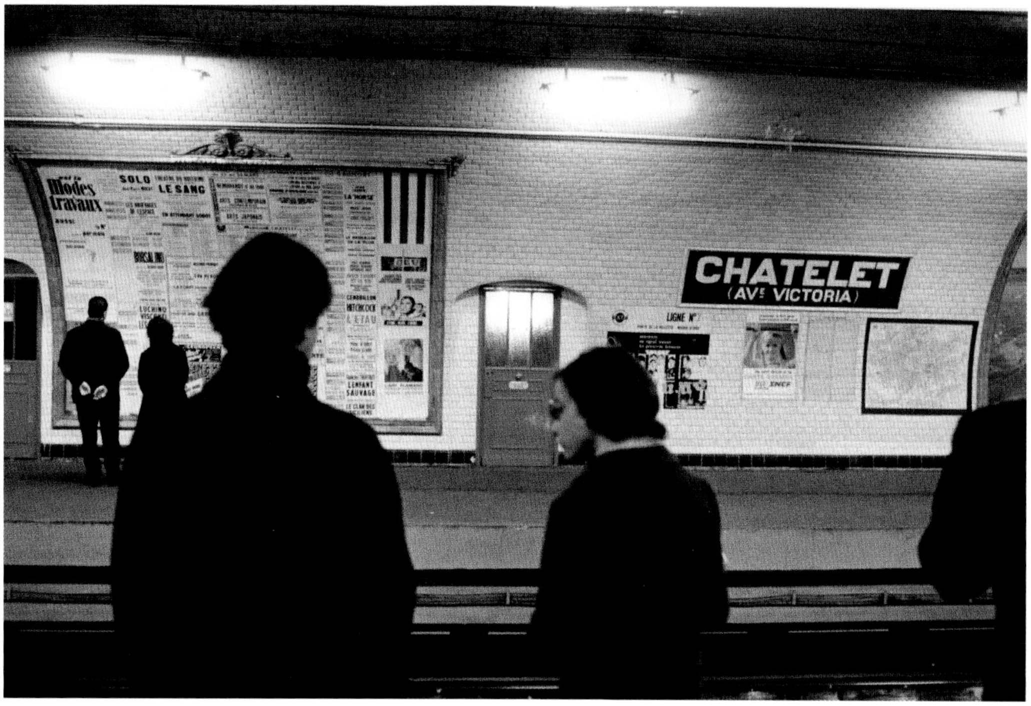

ABOVE: Daniel Buren, photo-souvenir from the series Cent Stations du métro parisien. Paper with white and blue stripes, alternating and vertical, 8.7 cm (3⅜ in) wide each, glue. Each sheet of paper *c.*99 × 56.4 cm (39 × 22⅛ in). Work in situ, Paris, 1970.

All that stemmed from Duchamp's example of the readymade – surrealism, pop art, much minimalism, conceptualism – was deemed by Buren to be a part of the negative pole. Buren's own work was 'neutral'. In its consistent use of the same format it avoided any idea that it is composed. A simple, brief description suffices for all instances, whether they appear on gallery walls, banners, sandwich boards, Métro announcement panels, advertising hoardings or elsewhere:

> *Vertical striped sheets of paper, the bands of which are 8.7 cms [3⅜ in] wide, alternate white and coloured, are stuck over internal and external surfaces: walls, fences, display windows, etc.; and/or cloth/canvas support, vertical stripes, white and coloured bands each 8.7 cms, the two ends covered with dull white paint.*[6]

The striped canvas he used was the kind you might expect to see on a shop awning. Painting the outer stripes white was a simple, non-intrusive way of denying such pieces of manufactured cloth the status of readymade. Duchamp's readymades rely on the museum to validate them as works of art, but in order for this to occur, the museum's own authority must be assumed. Buren's neutral stripes operate in quite a different way, allowing questions to be raised about how certain places might have the capability and licence to stipulate what is and what is not art. Their predictable regularity presents the fact that they are 'without composition', and because there is no internal detail to catch the viewer's eye, it is not so much the work as the location in which the work is encountered that commands attention.

'Every act is political', wrote Buren in his 1969–70 essay 'Beware', 'and whether one is conscious of it or not, the presentation of one's work is no exception'.[7] A corollary of this characteristic of Buren's work is that the place in which it is installed is the place in which it should be experienced. Other artists, such as South American-born Dutch conceptual artist Stanley Brouwn, in whose work the acts of walking and measuring the dimensions of the body predominate, and the Indo–German dancer/performer Tino Sehgal, have responded to this aspect of their work by refusing to have it reproduced. Buren has not prohibited his work being photographed, but he has stressed that any such image must be seen as a 'souvenir' of the work pictured, relating to it in much the same way as a postcard of the Eiffel Tower relates to the Eiffel Tower itself.[8]

CONCEPT

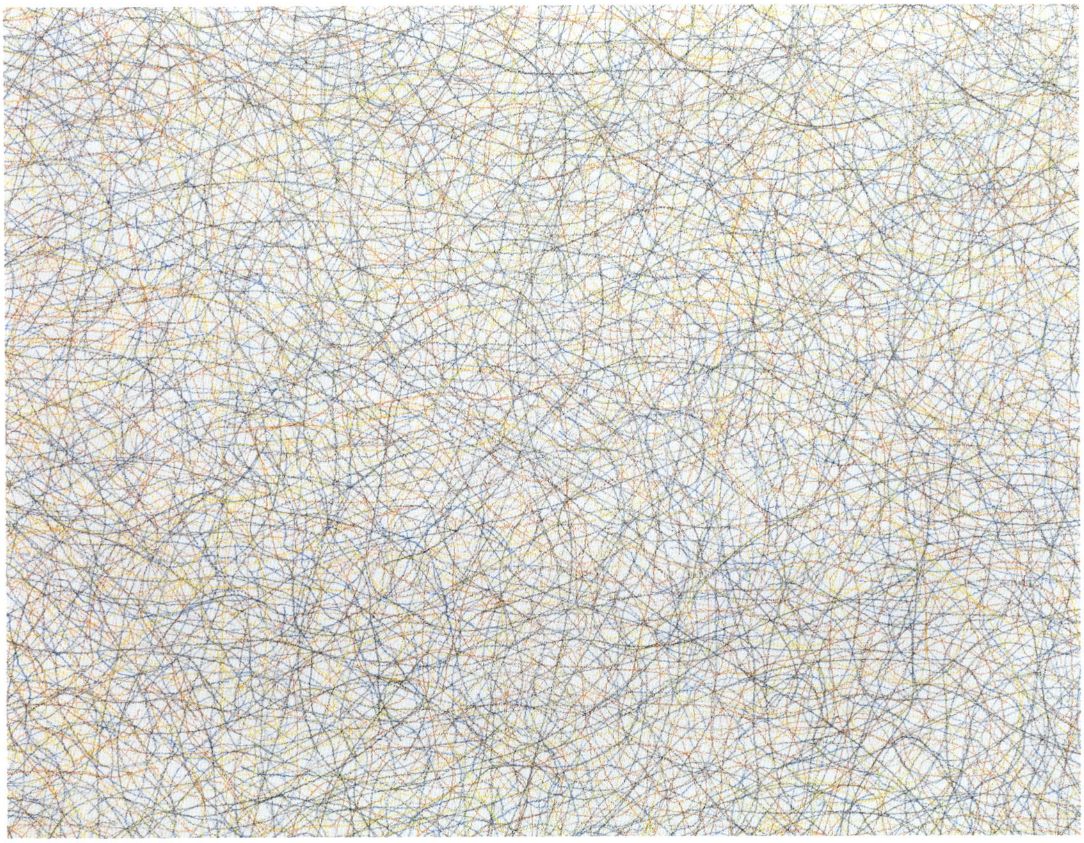

ABOVE: Sol LeWitt, *Wall Drawing #65: Lines not short, not straight, crossing and touching, drawn at random using four colors, uniformly dispersed with maximum density, covering the entire surface of the wall.* Red, yellow, blue, and black pencil. First drawn by David Schulman. First installation at Solomon R. Guggenheim Museum, New York, February 1971.

In his 1967 essay 'Paragraphs on Conceptual Art', the American artist Sol LeWitt made a distinction between what he termed conceptual and perceptual art. Perceptual art provides a sensation for the eye and, in reference to the art being made and discussed in the United States and Europe at that time, it would include op art, kinetic art, art using light (such as perhaps in the installations by American artist Dan Flavin), and 'colour art', which is to say abstract expressionism and post-painterly abstraction. In conceptual art, by contrast, it is the idea for the work that is of prime importance.

An idea requires planning and making decisions on how best to realize the finished work, but once this planning has been concluded, the actual execution is a straightforward process. 'The idea', LeWitt said, 'becomes a machine that makes the art'.[1] Once the making of the work has commenced, one should resist any temptation to adjust or reshape the idea since this would only compromise the piece and lead to repetition. What LeWitt is keen to stress is that the idea of a work is not the means to illustrate some theory or other, but is 'intuitive' and 'purposeless'.[2] He began another statement on his approach, 'Sentences on Conceptual Art', with the following:

Conceptual artists are mystics rather than rationalists. They leap to conclusions that logic cannot reach.[3]

It may seem to some that work made in this way appears lacking in emotional depth, but this is only because we have become accustomed to the expectation of expressive spectacle in the large gestures of abstract expressionism and the expansive sumptuousness of colour field painting. Curator and writer Bernice Rose has noted that the 1962 publication of Camilla Gray's book on constructivism and suprematism, *The Russian Experiment in Art*, sparked much debate in New York about the possibility of conceiving a new approach to art. It would be 'uncontaminated by the attitudes attached to traditional visual modes, whether representational or abstract'.[4] For LeWitt, however, the work of Aleksandr Rodchenko and Kazymyr Malevych was still 'too composed', but he shared their desire for a new art and his recourse to the use of system was one way of 'achieving an art as free from previous stylistic associations as could be conceived at that moment'.[5]

The titles of LeWitt's drawings are blankly and straightforwardly informational: for example, *Straight Lines, Shorter than 24 cm, Not Touching* or *Ten Thousand Lines, Five Inches Long, Within an Area of 6¾ × 5½ Inches*. The former is a wall drawing, the latter a work on paper. Drawing was something new in LeWitt's wall drawings because he was not the person who executed them. A new set of relationships is established between the mind of the artist, the eye, and the touch of the mark-making hand. Whether or not it was LeWitt's hand that carried out the work is of no importance. The draftsperson is not a cypher for the absent LeWitt, but an agent in the realization of the drawing. As the British art critic Lawrence Alloway put it:

Control is not a matter of manual participation but rather of setting up a system within which the execution of his system can only produce a LeWitt.[6]

The titles of LeWitt's works, therefore, act as both a set of instructions for the draftsperson and a description of the finished work.

David Shulman was employed by New York's Guggenheim Museum to execute *Lines, not short, not straight, crossing and touching, drawn at random, using four colours, uniformly dispersed with maximum density covering the entire surface of the wall*, and later recorded his experience. The instructions may seem simple, but they raised questions: where to start and how to proceed? How long is a 'not short' line? How do you cover the wall when the gallery has not provided you with a scaffold to aid access? Do you draw lines in alternate colours or finish all the lines in one colour before moving on to the next? And so on. Shulman talked of how physically demanding it was and he described his ultimate decision that the best way was to finish the yellow lines before moving on to black, then blue and finally red:

Once the individual difficulties of each colour were determined, any thought as to how the lines were going down in relation to lines previously drawn gradually diminished until there was no conscious thought given to the lines being drawn. The lines began to put themselves down. Doing the drawing I realized that totally relaxing my body was only one way of reaching a deep level of concentration. Another was in the mindless activity of doing the drawing.[7]

The inevitable consequence of using others to execute the work is that LeWitt did not know what the outcome would look like. He was equally interested in all results, whether or not he liked them. The mindlessness mentioned by Shulman was also acknowledged as an important aspect of the work's execution. LeWitt explained:

The draftsman and the wall enter a dialogue. The draftsman becomes bored but later through this meaningless activity finds peace or misery. The lines on the wall are the residue of this process. Each line is as important as each other line. All of the lines become one thing. The viewer of the lines can see only lines on the wall. They are meaningless. This is art.[8]

EMPLACEMENT / DISPLACEMENT

In 1993, Xu Bing took part in a conversation about art and cultural difference with another Chinese artist, Ai Weiwei, and the Taiwanese Tehching Hsieh. Hsieh is best known for a series of works of such severity and long time periods that it is impossible to categorize them as mere performances: 12 months attached to a partner by a 2-metre (6-foot 6-inch) rope, photographing himself punching a time clock each hour for 365 days, or living entirely outdoors – no lobbies, no shelters, no public transport – for the entire time. During the latter, he was living in New York but still officially an undocumented alien. In the course of the conversation, Ai observed:

> *Modern artists use a single point provided by the West to look at a landscape: what does the world look like? That which we see first is the philosophy, science, and culture of the West; inevitably there's something one-sided about that.*[1]

Ai's remark echoes German art historian Erwin Panofsky's argument in his 1927 study *Perspective as Symbolic Form*, in which perspective first creates distance between the observing human and the objects they observe, and then draws 'this world of things, an autonomous world confronting the individual, into the eye'.[2] Perspective thus accomplishes two things: the rational ordering of the world and its possession. While such possession is understood in Panofsky's essay primarily as a visual experience, it is, as Ai said, important to acknowledge the degree to which that experience endorses the implicit assumption in the Western mind that the proper relationship between viewer and land should be one of sovereignty. The land is at our disposal, to give us pleasure at its beauty, to manage or to colonize. This brings to mind one of the best known examples given by John Berger in his *Ways of Seeing* (1972), where he discussed Thomas Gainsborough's portrait of *Mr and Mrs Andrews*. The couple are situated on the left of the picture. Shotgun resting loosely in the crook of his right elbow, affectionate dog at his feet, Robert Andrews leans nonchalantly against the cast iron seat on which his wife, Frances, sits. The entire right half of the canvas is taken up with the landscape in which they are posing, a landscape that we can see is productive from the sheaves of corn stacked up in the field next to them. Berger said:

> *Among the pleasures their portrait gave to Mr and Mrs Andrews, was the pleasure of seeing themselves depicted as landowners and this pleasure was enhanced by the ability of oil paint to render their land in all its substantiality. And this is an observation which needs to be made, precisely because the cultural history we are normally taught pretends that it is an unworthy one.*[3]

The landscapes painted by the indigenous Australian artists associated with the Papunya Tula movement in the Western Desert of Australia's Northern Territory arise from and present a quite different relationship between human and land. Although these works began only in the early 1970s, when the Australian schoolteacher Geoffrey Bardon introduced acrylic paint and canvas to his pupils and others in the area, the visual style and vocabulary of the marks were not new. Clifford Possum Tjapaltjarri, one of the earliest and most widely known of the movement's artists, pointed out that spears, boomerangs, dancing boards and their bodies themselves have always been painted by the indigenous people.

Until the introduction of acrylics and canvas, a European importation, they had used ochres made from the rocks and earths of the area. As well as providing another medium through which to represent their stories of the Dreaming, the advent of paint and canvas inevitably also introduced their imagery to the art market. The paintings became commodities, a status that had the potential to cause friction with the

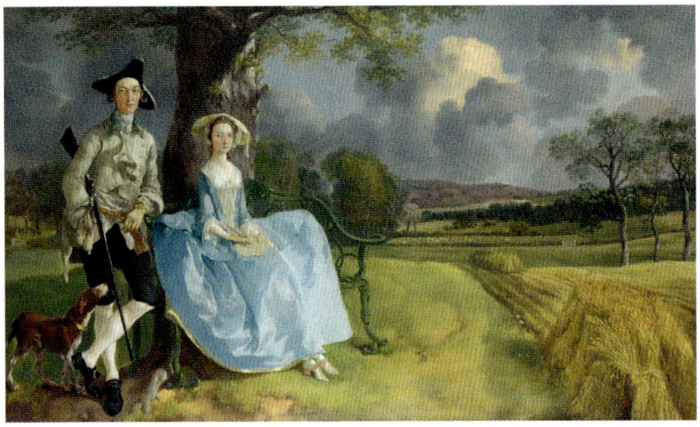

LEFT: Thomas Gainsborough, *Mr and Mrs Andrews*, *c.*1750. Oil on canvas, 69.8 × 119.4 cm (27½ × 47 in).

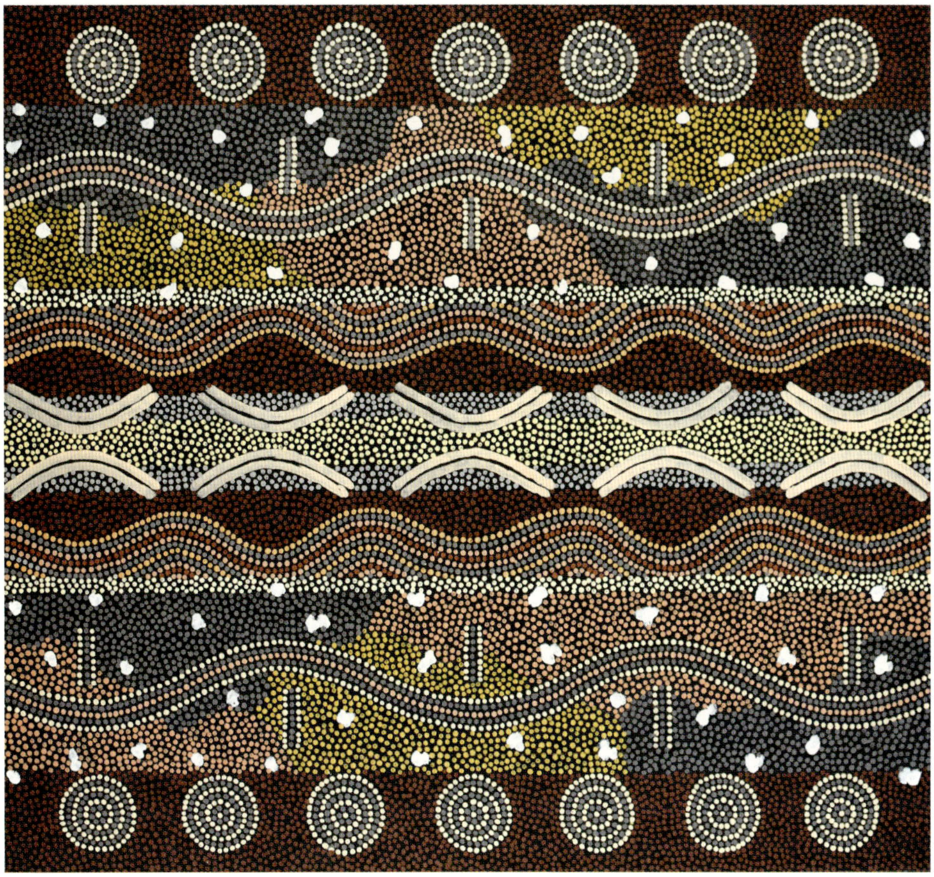

ABOVE: Clifford Possum Tjapaltjarri, *Napperby Dreaming*, 1998.
Synthetic polymer paint on Belgian linen, 122 × 134 cm (48 × 52¾ in).

cultural significance the imagery held within its own community. These paintings are complex: they can be understood both as images possessing status within the system of exchange and consumption that characterizes the contemporary art world of galleries, museums and exhibitions, and as gestures of belonging to and dwelling in a particular locale. New York-based anthropologist Fred Myers referred to this latter as 'emplacement', as distinct from the necessary 'displacement' that occurs in Western landscape painting – the landscape is 'over there' to be looked at, rather than here, where I am. This difference is reflected as much in the way they are made as in their compositional features, with the unstretched canvas laid out on the ground for the artist to work on.[4]

The paintings refer to events in the deep historical time of the ancestors known as the Dreaming. They depict passages through the landscape between sites of cultural and mythic significance as well as the rituals associated with the affirmation and sharing of that knowledge. A defining characteristic of such knowledge is that it is held by those to whom it has been vouchsafed and it is for them to pass on to those ready to receive it. It is not available for everyone to use and repeat, and it can be considered problematic for those who are uninitiated to learn and use it. Men and women have their own stories and rituals, and while what we see in these paintings is the depiction of a landscape, it is one into which they have been or are being appropriately introduced and guided by their elders and instructors. Caution about this has led to requests that some of the early paintings, in which their composition was more unguarded about the information they revealed, should no longer be displayed.

Certain features recur in the compositions, notably the use of repeated dots to describe the land and its various earths, and a lexicon of marks among which concentric circles might indicate water sources or places of encampment; arcs show dunes, escarpments, clouds or rainbows; and wavy lines map running water. Tjapaltjarri's *Napperby Dreaming*, for example, in its depiction of 'the ancestral origin of all the rain that falls in the Western Desert',[5] includes these symbols in addition to short vertical lines of lightning strikes and the larger white spots of hailstones.

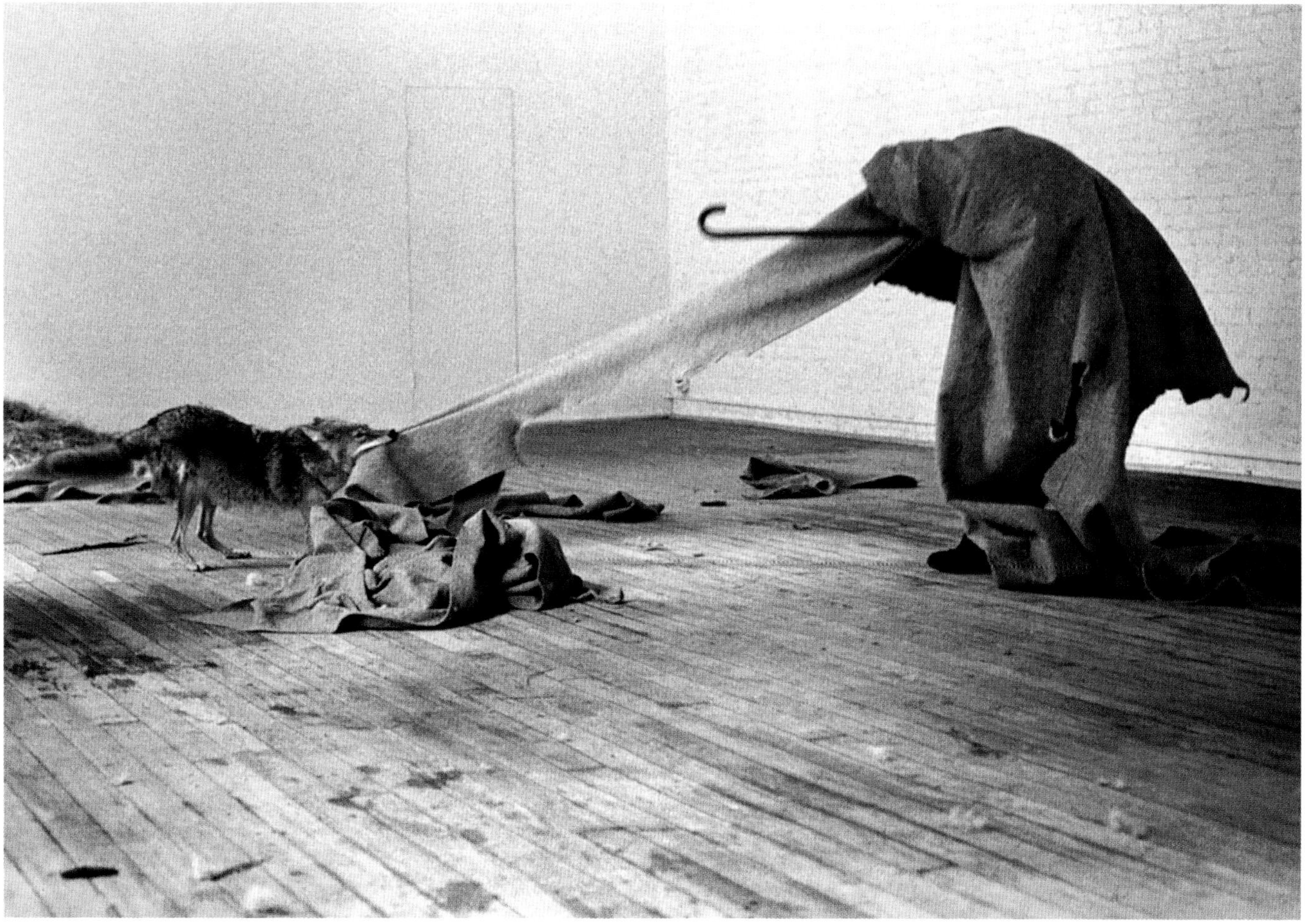

ABOVE: Joseph Beuys, *I Like America and America Likes Me*, 1974. Performance at Rene Block Gallery, New York.

(RE)INTERPRETATION

In 1974, the German artist Joseph Beuys made his first trip to the United States. He had declined to visit before on account of the country's involvement in the Vietnam war, and he only agreed on this occasion as they had signalled their withdrawal from the war. Even then, however, his aim was to be in the United States without quite fully entering the country. He was met at JFK airport in New York by gallery assistants, wrapped in felt and transported by ambulance to the Rene Block gallery, where he was ushered into a caged-off exhibition space that held a coyote. This was not the first time Beuys had worked with animals. Some years before he had sat in an enclosed gallery, his head covered in honey and gold leaf, one shoe with a felt sole, the other with a metal plate, talking softly to the dead hare he held in his lap. The performance, or action, *How to Explain Paintings to a Dead Hare* (1965) exemplified Beuys' belief that animals had a better understanding of art than humans.

Once installed in the New York gallery, and after a cautious period of getting to know each other, Beuys and the coyote spent eight hours a day for three days in each other's company. The felt in which Beuys wrapped himself was ripped by the coyote for bedding. In addition, a stack of copies of the *Wall Street Journal*, a voice of the rationalist United States, was placed in the enclosure each day, and these, too were urinated on and shredded for bedding litter. Vilified as a vicious predator and wherever possible eliminated by the continent's colonialist settlers, the coyote had a very different image as a trickster survivor in the stories of the country's indigenous population. The animal was, for Beuys, the true spirit of America, and he saw the performance, titled *I Like America and America Likes Me* and often simply referred to as *Coyote*, as a necessary reckoning with the living embodiment of that spirit in order to address the traumas of contemporary living. At the end of the performance, Beuys was again wrapped in felt and transported back to JFK by ambulance before immediately leaving the country.

Coyote or *I Like America and America Likes Me* was what Beuys called 'social sculpture', an action that prompts us to ask questions about 'how we mould and shape the world in which we live'.[1] For him, 'every living being is an artist' and this, of course, includes the coyote. Art is social sculpture, and in order to be able to recognize it as such, we must develop our sensitivity towards the varied forms it might now take. The felt used in the performance was among Beuys' signature materials, stemming from an incident in the artist's own mythologized life. Shot down in the Crimea during the Second World War, he had been rescued by Tatars who kept him alive by covering him in fat and wrapping him in felt. Fat, felt and the nourishing sweetness of honey consequently made repeated appearances in his work.

Art is social sculpture, and in order to be able to recognize it as such, we must develop our sensitivity towards the varied forms it might now take.

The overbearing, all-consuming nature of Western rationalism being pointed to by Ai Weiwei, Beuys and others is something against which non-Western artists have had to constantly struggle. Rasheed Araeen, born in Karachi in what was then pre-partition India, explained the situation like this:

> *The internationalism of modern art is false and phoney, since it offers no place for the participation of non-European people in its development and evolution. The projected 'internationalism' of modern art is in fact a reflection of international monopoly capital and its imperialist ethos. In the imperialist scheme of things the third world is placed on the periphery and therefore the third world artist should only play a secondary role within this context.*[2]

In entering into dialogue with Beuys' *Coyote*, Araeen's documented performance *I Love It, It Loves I* signals a thorough understanding of the Western artistic tradition it addresses, while at the same time revealing a quite different context within which to see it. *I Love It, It Loves I* comprises twelve landscape-format photographs arranged closely on the wall in a four by three grid. They show Araeen and members of his family slaughtering, preparing and eating a goat in the prescribed Islamic manner for Eid-al-Adha (the Festival of Sacrifice). The sequence runs from the first image, which, in a conscious echo of Beuys' performance, sees Araeen communicating gently with the goat, to the final one in which the whole family shares the feast. Underneath each image is a text in Urdu with an English translation that simply records the everyday conversation between family members while the activity was taking place. It is a special occasion because Eid-al-Adha is one of the two main annual holidays of Islam. However, in other respects, what we see documented is ordinary life.

Whenever we look at a work of art ,we are to an extent 'reading'.

BELOW: Rasheed Araeen, *I Love It, It Loves I*, 1978–83. Twelve colour photographs with text in both Urdu and English, 136.5 × 242 cm (53¾ in × 95¼ in).

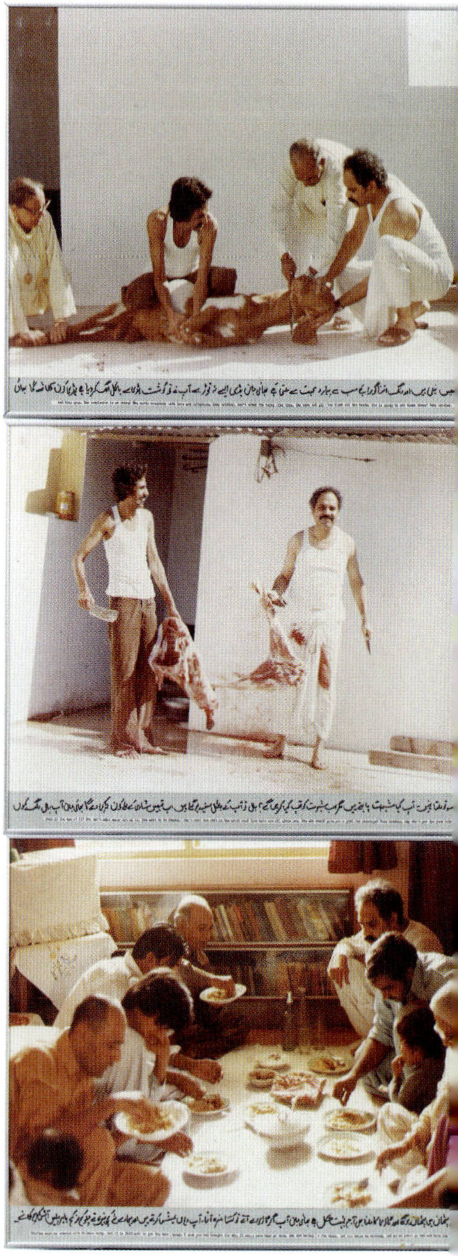

Araeen's composition presents a number of challenges to the viewer. The sequence is arranged so that it begins in the top right corner of the grid. This demands that it be read from right to left, a fact emphasized by the primacy of the handwritten Urdu text over the English translation that accompanies it. If we do not speak Urdu, we need assistance, and because so much of what happens in the art world is conducted in English, this can come as something of a shock. Indeed, however much we might otherwise like to think of it as a visual rather than a semantic exercise, we recognize that whenever we look at a work of art, we are to an extent 'reading'. In light of this, for example, how should we now evaluate Charles Henry's theory of line so prized by Georges Seurat – upward and to the right = gaiety; downward and to the left = sorrow (see pages 50–1)? The compositional structure of *I Love It, It Loves I* confounds any assumptions we might have been harbouring about how to make and how to look at and appraise a work of art. No approach is universally valid, and any that is promoted as such needs treating with profound scepticism.

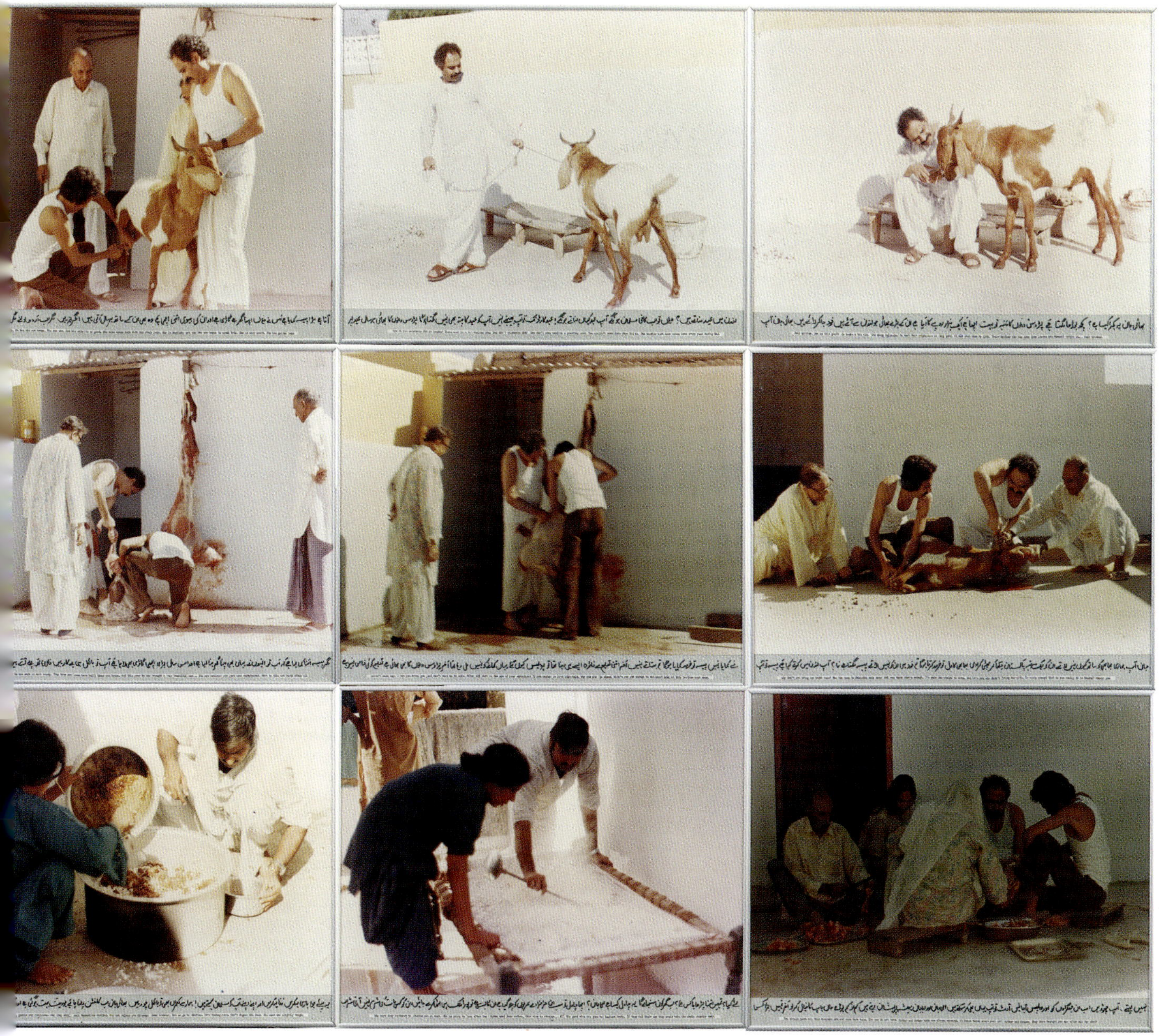

WORD

Among all the changes that have affected approaches and attitudes towards composition, one thing that has been accepted as constant is the distinction drawn between the different functions of images and words. Images represent, words signify. Words carry meaning that can be understood as directed and specific, whereas the compelling nature of a painting is that its possible significance is something that can only arise from the experience of viewing it. In the case of representational painting, it is not just what is depicted but the way in which it is depicted that counts. In instances where the meaning of the words is important, what they say can obscure all other aspects of their appearance.

One well-known painting in which the distinction between image and word is playfully highlighted is *The Treachery of Images*, a 1929 painting by the Belgian artist René Magritte. The canvas has two elements: a faithfully rendered representation of a pipe, under which are painted the words *Ceci n'est pas une pipe* (This is not a pipe). The assertion is true, whether we take it to be a caption to the image – because, of course, it isn't a pipe but only a picture of one – or a self-referential statement – 'This' is not a pipe. The words are rendered in cursive writing and consequently have the look of something handwritten rather than printed. In this case, since they are all equally elements of the painting, on what basis might we now distinguish between the hand-painted pipe and the hand-painted words? The words mean something and the words are inextricably part of the painting, and neither aspect can obscure or take precedence over the other.

Notwithstanding the visual and semantic ambiguities evident in Magritte's painting, it has largely remained the case that words as words are not appropriate material for composition. Indeed, as we saw, it is precisely this difference that contributed to the impact of Georges Braque's *Le Portugais*, where the letters were simply a part of the scene being depicted, either on a poster or in the price list written on the café window (see pages 62–5). In cubist collage, too, words are present as an integral part of the element being introduced: this is a newspaper, this is a piece of sheet music, this is an advertisement and so on. In each case, they are signs for objects present in the scene being depicted. Magritte's words do not introduce an object in amongst other objects in that way. They are unattached, free-floating forms. While they have potential to signify, they will be doing so as part of a composition in which any signification must be accepted as untrustworthy.

In instances where the meaning of the words is important, what they say can obscure all other aspects of their appearance.

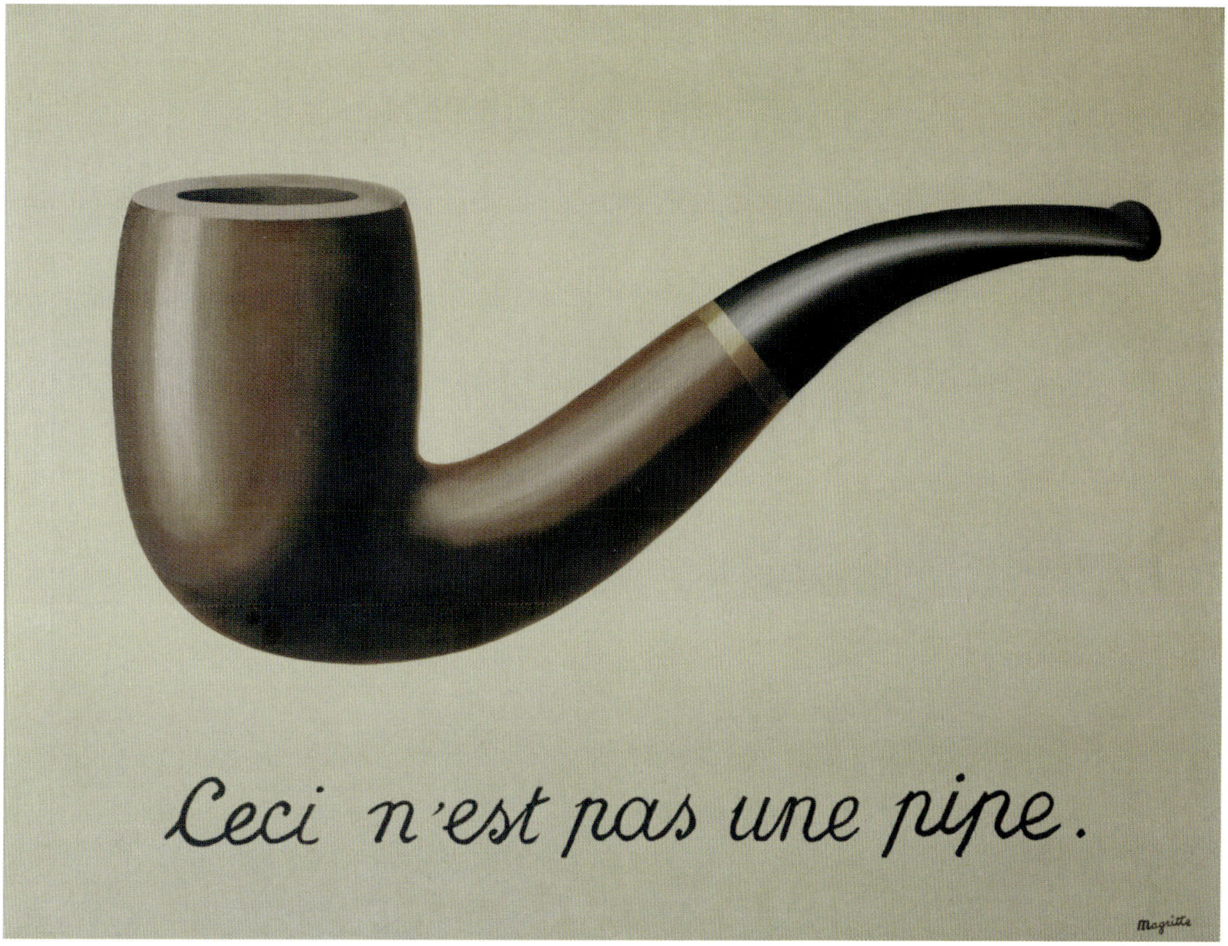

ABOVE: René Magritte, *The Treachery of Images: 'Ceci n'est pas une pipe'*, 1929.
Oil on canvas, 60.3 cm × 81.1 cm (23¾ × 32 in).

Xu Bing's *Landscript Drawings* are, as the somewhat oxymoronic title suggests, landscapes drawn using characters rather than line and shading. He explained, 'I sat on a mountain and, facing a real mountain, I wrote "mountain" … Where there was river water I wrote the character for "water".'[1]

There is perhaps an analogy here with the French writer Guillaume Apollinaire's *Calligrammes* (1918), a collection of poems with words that are distributed across the page to form an image, or with the *Words in Freedom* (1914) poems of the Italian writer Filippo Marinetti in which, for example, he conveys the feeling of driving fast through the countryside past lush fields full of grazing cattle with the diagonally positioned words '*vaaaaaches vert veeeeeeert vaaaaaches vaaaaches vaaaaches*'.[2] For Xu, though, word and image are not so much equivalent as congruent: 'You might also say I painted a mountain, as for Chinese people to write a mountain and to paint a mountain are the same thing.'[3]

Book from the Sky comprises books and scrolls presented on the walls, floor and across the ceiling of the space in which it is exhibited. All hand-printed, they were made using woodblocks of 4,000 different characters designed and carved by Xu. He settled on 4,000 as the generally accepted number of Chinese characters with which one needs to be familiar in order to be able to read. Xu devised the characters using the standard radicals for written Mandarin. They are, therefore, composed from recognizable elements, but they have been done so in such a way that the resulting compounds are not actual words in Chinese. They look like characters and suggest readability, but a closer inspection reveals a meaninglessness that is all the more potent for the fact that they appear on the very edge of legibility.

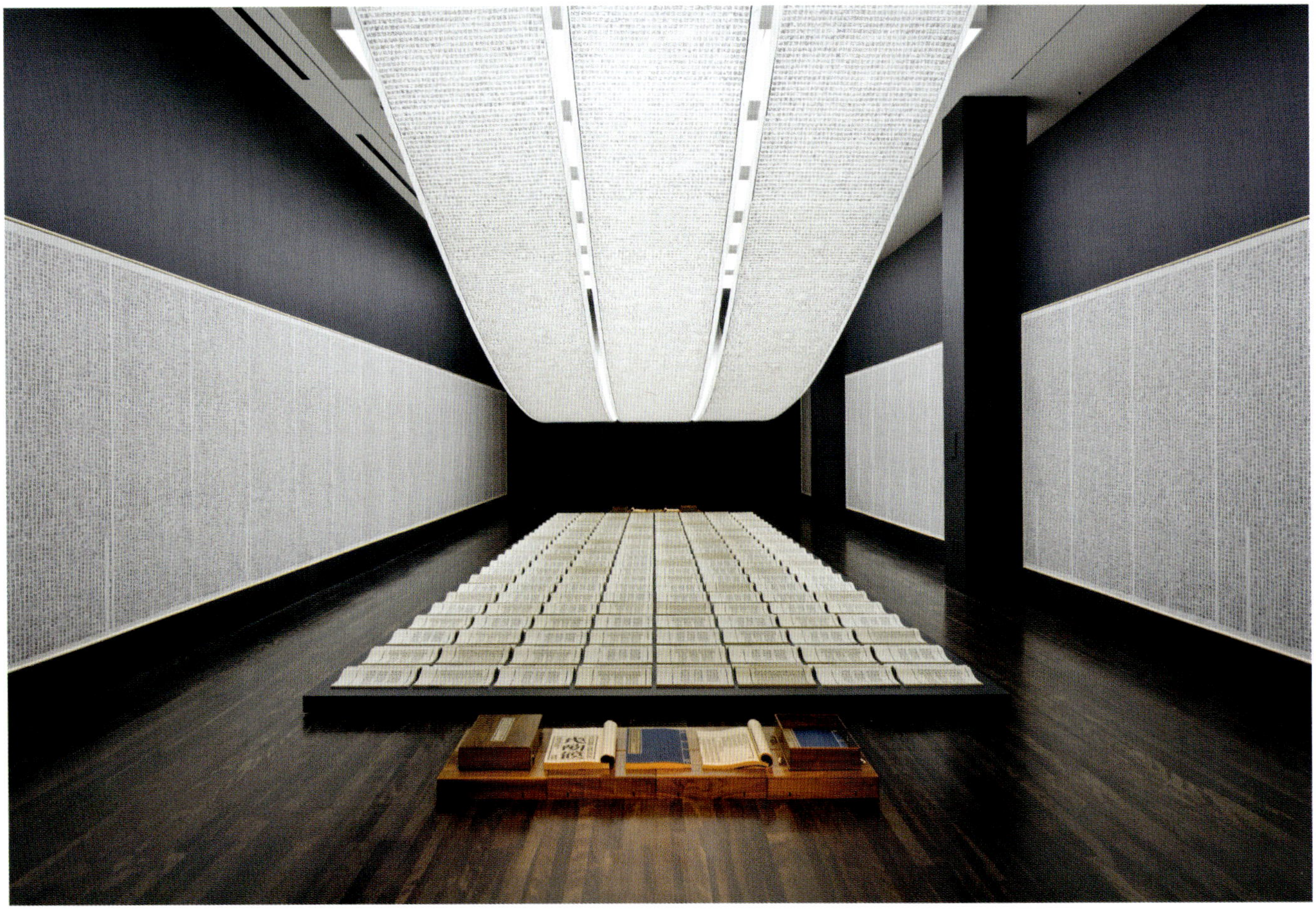

ABOVE: Xu Bing, *Book from the Sky*, 1987–91. Mixed media. Installation view, Blanton Museum of Art, Austin.

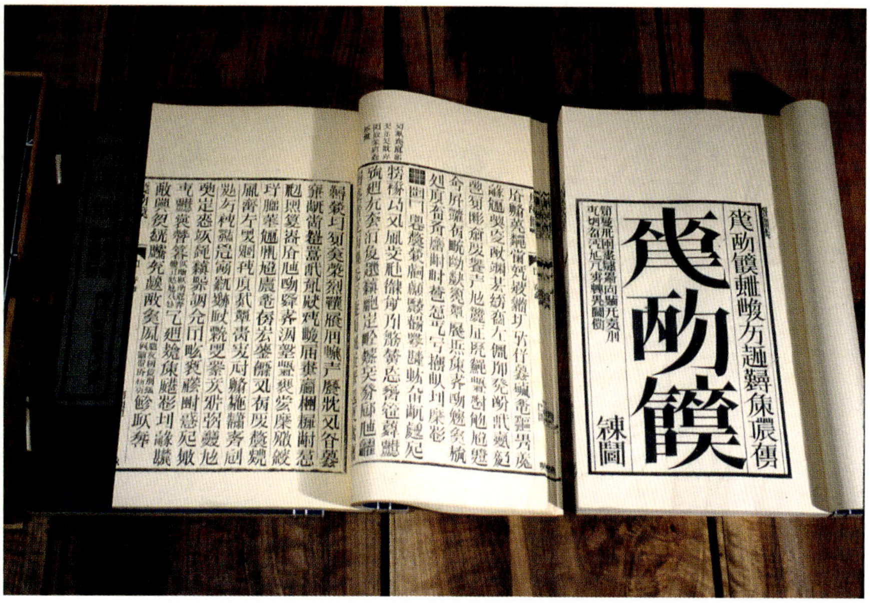

ABOVE: Xu Bing, *Book from the Sky* (detail), 1987–91. A wooden boxed set consisting of four volumes of woodblock hand-printed books.

Xu has described how, like everyone his age, his introduction to written language was both confused and confusing. After he had begun to learn traditional characters, Mao Zedong's government introduced guidelines to simplify their appearance. This meant that what had been taught had to be unlearned in order for further learning to progress. A short while later, however, there was an announcement that this experiment had proved unsatisfactory, so people were instructed to revert to learning and using the original script. Xu's path into language was thus a difficult one. The combination of accessibility and meaninglessness in *Book from the Sky* was Xu's aim:

> *The ambiguity that exists in the work allows people to interpret it from almost any angle or in relation to anything. … I like different people having different interpretations. It means that I have succeeded in denying the work a single emotive 'answer' and made it something everyone can connect with.*[4]

Such ambiguity has caused its own difficulties since, as Xu commented, officials could conclude that if *Book from the Sky* had no identifiable meaning, the absence must be intentional.[5] This made them feel uncomfortable because for them meaninglessness was modern art's biggest problem. Whether it is, in fact, a problem or a benefit, there is undoubtedly substance to the identification of that discomfort with Western art. Disinterestedness, or the acceptance that creative activity should not be directed towards the elucidation of any specific idea or end, has been a central tenet of Western aesthetics. It was a core belief, expressed most famously by the German philosopher Immanuel Kant in his 1790 *Critique of Judgement*: 'Beauty is the form of finality in an object, so far as perceived in it apart from the representation of an end.'[6] It has continued to hold sway as a key criterion of judgement until recently, transcending all differences of style even where work appeared in other respects to be far removed from the traditional forms of painting.

We could think, for example, of Sol LeWitt's description of conceptualism as the kind of art that is 'not theoretical or illustrative of theories; it is intuitive, it is involved with all types of mental processes and it is purposeless'.[7] A further aspect to Kant's notion of disinterestedness is the presumption of its universal applicability: 'The beautiful is that which, apart from a concept, is cognized as object of a necessary delight.'[8] In other words, the judgement that something is beautiful carries with it the conviction that others, whoever and wherever they are, ought to find it beautiful, too. Xu nevertheless saw *Book from the Sky*'s way of 'communicating by refusing to communicate' as the very thing that made the work 'distinctly Chinese'.[9]

DATE

The Japanese artist On Kawara made the first of his Date paintings, which are also known as the Today series, on 4 January 1966. Using white lettering on a monochrome background, he painted JAN. 4, 1966. This and all subsequent paintings in the series, which he continued for the greater part of his life, had a subtitle. For *JAN. 4, 1966* it is 'New York traffic strike'.

Like this first one, many of those painted up to October 1972 were subtitled with a headline taken from a local newspaper for that day (after October 1972 they were primarily given the day of the week on which that date fell). Reading through the subtitles of Kawara's works gives a brief history of major global events, including elections, assassinations, wars, the space race, riots, demonstrations, trade relations and much else.

There were some rules to the paintings. They had to be completed within the twenty-four hours of the day in question or they would be discarded, the date would always appear in white on a monochrome ground, and it would be styled according to the convention of the country in which Kawara was staying at the time. For example, at the beginning of March 1973, he was in Dakar, Senegal. By the middle of the month, he had moved down the West African coast to Freetown, Sierra Leone. These countries are living with the legacies of their French and British colonizers respectively, and the dates reflect this:

3 MARS 1973

MAR. 14, 1973

If his country of residence used anything other than the Latin alphabet, the date would be given in Esperanto, the artificial language constructed in the late-nineteenth century with the aim of providing a means of international communication.

When the paintings were finished they were stored in their own box together with newspaper cuttings from the day's press. As well as references to the day's events, some of the subtitles refer to Kawara's own daily life or to the process of making the Date paintings, and to the status of the finished work:

JAN. 13, 1966 'I thought about memory and sense'
JAN. 15, 1966 'This painting itself is January 15, 1966'
JAN. 16, 1966 'Janine came to my studio'
JAN. 18, 1966 'I am painting this painting'

No hierarchy can be constructed out of these subtitles. The personal and professional life of the individual, ideas about art and the wider world in which all this is situated are all embodied in the white date on the monochrome canvas. With the most stringent economy of means, Kawara's paintings mark the passage of time and, in doing so, they make space sufficient to accommodate all that happens within it. Like his communications with friends and colleagues – postcards giving the time at which he got up that day, or telegrams stating no more than the simple fact that, 'I AM STILL ALIVE' – Kawara's Date paintings offer us everything by specifying nothing but a brief twenty-four hour period. As he said on *JAN. 15, 1966*, the painting he was making at that moment is itself that day. All that is occurring outwith the painting, which is to say the entirety of the world's events on that date, can be found on the rectangle of the canvas.

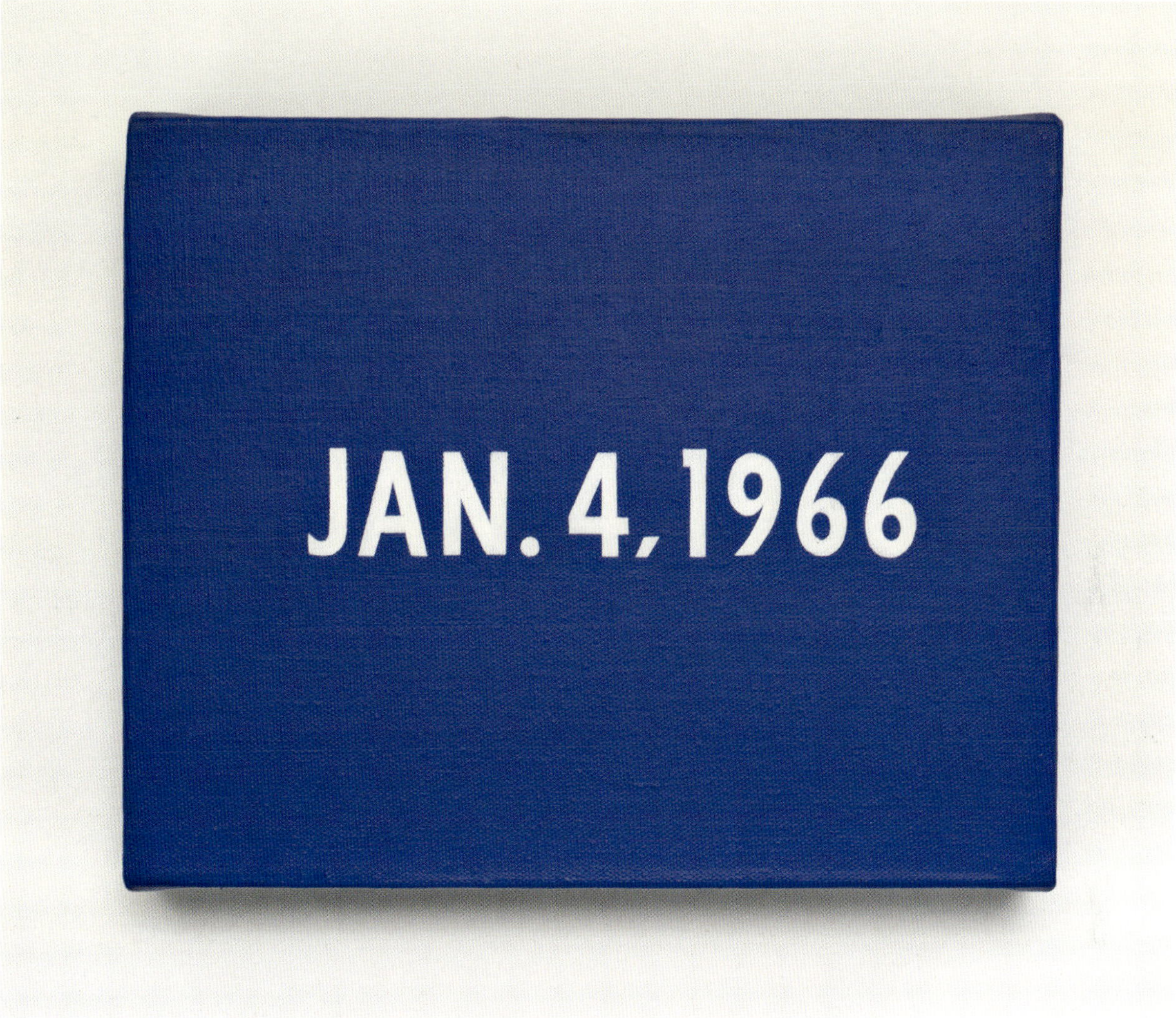

ABOVE: On Kawara, *Jan. 4, 1966*, from the Today series, 1966–2013. Acrylic on canvas, 20.3 × 25.4 cm (8 × 10 in).

With the most stringent economy of means, Kawara's paintings mark the passage of time and, in doing so, they make space sufficient to accommodate all that happens within it.

LANGUAGE

ABOVE: Cy Twombly, *Orpheus*, 1979. Oil-based house paint, oil paint [paint stick], wax crayon on canvas, 195.6 × 335 cm (77 × 131¾ in).

In 1951, Cy Twombly was invited by Robert Rauschenberg to spend the summer at Black Mountain College, the radical liberal arts institution in North Carolina. Students and faculty associated with Black Mountain during its brief period of existence include composers John Cage and David Tudor, poets Robert Creeley and Charles Olson, designer Buckminster Fuller, dancer Merce Cunningham, painters Willem and Elaine de Kooning, Kenneth Noland, Dorothea Rockburne, among many others. The year of its establishment, 1933, coincided with the closure of the Bauhaus by the Nazis, and several staff from there emigrated from Germany to join the college, notably Walter Gropius, Anni Albers and Josef Albers, who was Rector from 1941 to 1949.

Immediately after their stay at Black Mountain, Twombly and Rauschenberg travelled to Europe and North Africa, and in 1957 Twombly moved to Rome. Olson, who was Rector of the college at the time of his stay there, would write of Twombly the following year, 'There came a man who dealt with whiteness. And with space… What seems clear is, that two dimensions as surface for plastic attack is once more prime. And with perspective as aid gone, the whole Renaissance. Even line gone'.[1] In the writings of artists such as Barnett Newman and Donald Judd we find this refusal to rely on perspective cast in a positive light, since its absence marks a clear separation from the European tradition with which it is associated, and from which they desired to distance themselves. Twombly, as Olson's condensed description of abstract expressionism indicates, was fully engaged with the movement's precepts and practices. And it is through this approach that, once in Italy, he reconnects with Renaissance and Classical art. Marks, lines and squiggles start to emerge as legible letters and words in his painting in 1957 and from then on, in author Richard Leeman's words, 'entered inextricably into the weave of the artist's work'.[2] In his reinterpretation of *The Birth of Venus*, for example, it is his own signature – Cy Twombly / Roma / 1962 – large and prominent in the mid-right edge of the canvas that suggests the wooded shoreline of Botticelli's original.

Twombly painted *Orpheus* in 1979 and it was shown in the *Zeitgeist* exhibition, held in the Martin-Gropius-Bau close to the wall in a still-divided Berlin in 1982. Mounted the year after the Royal Academy, London's *A New Spirit in Painting*, the preponderance of painters in *Zeitgeist*'s line-up – forty out of a total of forty-six artists – reinforced the message of a resurgence in the importance of painting. In his review of the show, Wolfgang Max Faust analyzed the situation thus:

> *Just as art had to 'go through' language (conceptual art), nature (land art), technical media (photography, film, video), the artist's body (body art), and physical action (happenings, performances), presently much of its development seems to need to 'go through' images.*[3]

The canvas of *Orpheus* is white, the upper half covered with paint of a slightly creamier tone, the effect of which is to divide the painting into two largely distinct though not entirely separate zones. The oil-based house paint Twombly uses is fluid, and in the right-hand two thirds of the canvas it has been allowed to run down into the lower area, in several places reaching the bottom edge. The paint in the upper section has been applied over a number of crayon and paint stick marks of the kind enumerated by art critic Roberta Smith as 'scrawls, graffiti, letters, numerals, words, word fragments, diagrams and signs'.[4] Veiled and indistinct, their presence is ambiguous: are they emerging into clarity or retreating into obscurity? Across the width of the canvas Twombly has written the name Orpheus in Greek: Ορφεύς. The opening Omicron of the mythical poet's name is as much a large, enclosed field as it is a letter. Marked out in strong black it sits largely in the upper area, extending only a little across the loose divide between the two halves of the canvas. The remainder of the name is written on a slight downward slope so that the final sigma sits entirely in the lower half and reaches the right hand edge of the painting. In this double curve we see both the snake whose fatal bite sent Eurydice to the underworld, and the path up which she was returning towards the world of the living before Orpheus's look back condemned her to remain below.

In conversation with art dealer Heiner Bastian, Twombly explained that 'he understood scripture, text, quotations and words themselves both as forms, or as allusions to visual forms, and as emotional symbolic images'. Furthermore, the use of quotations or single words 'could instigate an interactive dialogue during the painting process'.[5] The six letters of Orpheus's name sit in a rhythmic visual flow across the canvas. There are two triplets: firstly, the loop of the opening omicron, the loop with appended line of rho and the loop of phi almost occluded by a heavy strike-through, whose several lines hint at the poet's lyre; secondly, the double curve that expands from the small, tight epsilon, through the bowl-like upsilon with its prominent diacritic, to the openness of the word-final sigma. Orpheus's presence spans and inhabits both halves of the composition. In a straightforward way we can see these as the upper space of life and natural phenomena, and the lower realm of souls, but as American writer Dean Rader argues, Orpheus's mythical existence has already been given prominence in the work of Rainer Maria Rilke: 'Poets are lenses for Twombly, and he tends to be moved by those figures who have been figured by another poet'.[6] Rilke's *Sonnets to Orpheus* are also grouped into two parts, and at their conclusion we see the two realms of the living and the dead bound together. Inspired by love and loss, 'Nature only lived, could only fully hear, when Orpheus sang'.[7]

The American artist Judy Chicago – at this point still known under her married name, Judy Gerowitz – had contributed to the 1966 *Primary Structures* exhibition at New York's Jewish Museum. The show was recognized both at the time and in the decades since as the key survey show of current trends in sculpture, particularly minimalism. In the following years, however, Chicago felt a personal sense of development in her practice but thought it was not matched by the kind of career advancement she saw among her male contemporaries. Talking of this with Lucy Lippard in a 1974 interview, she said:

> *When I was twenty-three, I was an up-and-coming young artist and so were a number of other women. As I went along, there were less and less women. As I started getting better and the careers of most of my male peers were going up, mine was sort of staying at the same place. I found I could get somebody to really respond to one work; they'd think that one was fantastic and I'd get a whole lot of feedback. But no comprehension of my work in terms of a whole series of ideas. I began to realize that a woman can do a single thing – that's sort of an accident; but if she makes a coherent body of work that means she has to be taken seriously in terms of ideas, and that moves into another place in the art world.*[8]

The Dinner Party (1974–9) stands up against and contests the male-centred history of art in which the attitudes Chicago spoke of are embedded. It provides the possibility of another lineage within which work might be conceived, realized and appraised. The central feature of the large installation is a triangular banqueting table laid with lavish place settings, each comprising an embroidered runner, a bespoke porcelain plate, a gold chalice and cutlery. There are thirty-nine named settings in all, thirteen arranged along each side. It is Leonardo da Vinci's *The Last Supper* three times over, at which women from myth, history, politics, the sciences and the arts are brought together. Their gathering brings the opportunity for conversation, a putative sharing, which Chicago saw as founding the possibility of a 'woman-formed' language. Such a language would be the means by which women could express themselves as women without the need for licence and approbation grudgingly bestowed by men.

In a journal entry on the design of the plates, Chicago wrote:

> *I want to make butterfly images that are hard, strong, soft, passive, opaque, transparent – all different states – and I want them all to have vaginas so they'll be female butterflies and at the same time be shells, flowers, flesh, forest – all kinds of things simultaneously.*[9]

Her emphasis on natural forms in this list resonates with the flowers, bleached skulls and landscape features that are so prominent in the work of Georgia O'Keeffe (see pages 98–9), and O'Keeffe does, indeed, have a special place at the gathering. The attendees at this feast run from sacred figures – Primordial Goddess, Fertile Goddess, Ishtar and Kali, through biblical and historical figures – Hapshetsut, Sappho, Boadaceia, Hildegard, up to what for Chicago are the final two exemplary twentieth-century artistic figures, Virginia Woolf and Georgia O'Keeffe. The table rests upon a Heritage Floor, a surface of 999 white triangular tiles, and on each one is written the name of another woman in gold. The floor is a major exercise in retrieval, bringing attention to hitherto largely ignored figures and placing them in the company of those who are more well-known. Thus, for example, the sixteenth-century Flemish painter Caterina van Hemessen sits among others including the singer Bessie Smith, the anthropologist, film maker and novelist Zora Neale Hurston, the traveller and archaeologist Lady Hester Stanhope, and the marine biologist and conservationist Rachel Carson. Collectively, the names indicate the existence of other contributions to culture that, once acknowledged, must change ideas about what is of value and relevance.

The production of *The Dinner Party* was a large-scale project. Researching, investigating techniques, developing methods of working, testing and fabricating the various elements involved well over a hundred people. In her study of *The Dinner Party*, the author and educator Jane Gerhard suggested that the runners, initially conceived essentially as backdrops to the plates, became important as 'the site where ideas about women's culture and women's history intertwined'.[10] Rather than having them held on rollers that allow only the section being worked on to be shown, as would have been usual, they were made on specially constructed frames so that the whole cloth was always visible. For Chicago this enabled an approach that was similar to the way of working on a painting. Instead of paint, however,

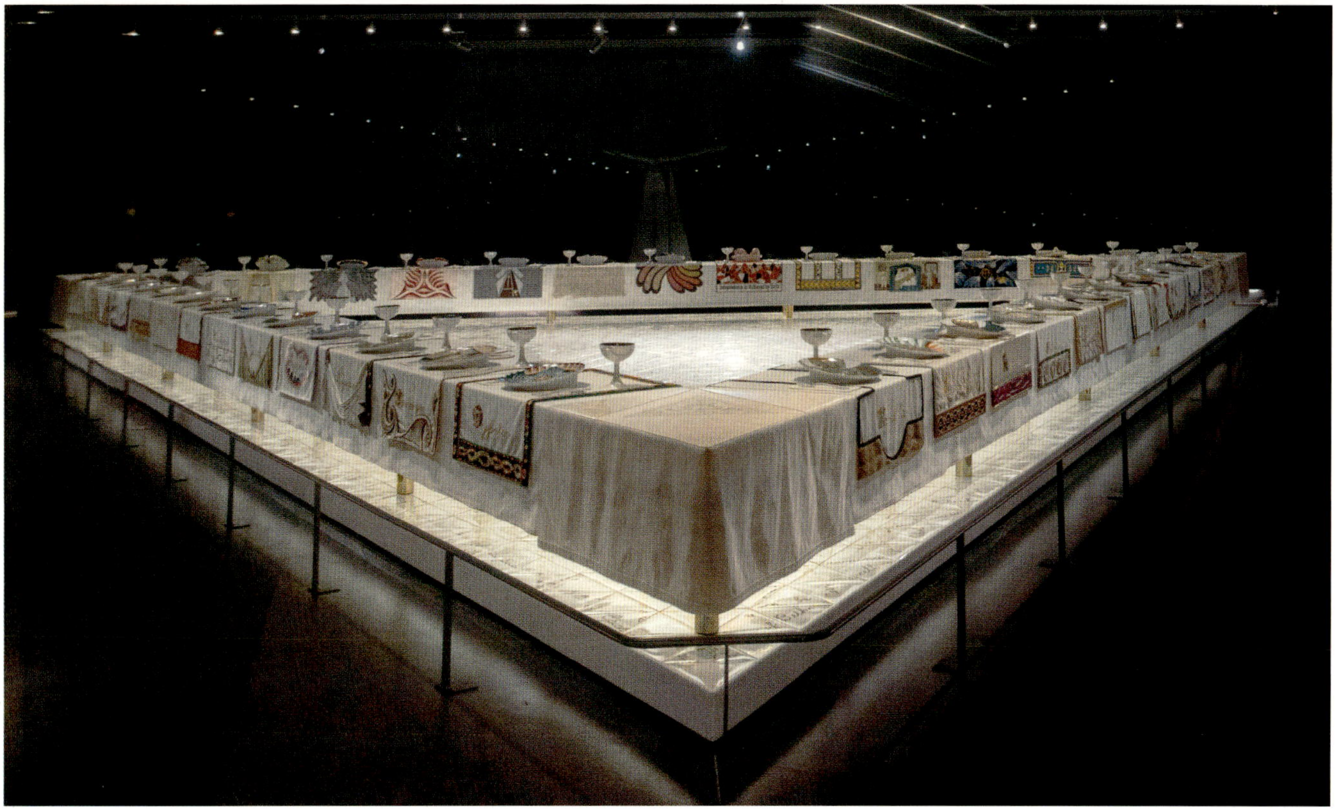

ABOVE: Judy Chicago, *The Dinner Party*, 1974–9. Ceramic, porcelain, textile, 14.6 × 14.6 m (48 × 48 ft). Installation view, Brooklyn Museum, New York.

it was stitching that was predominantly employed, a technique associated with women and women's work and traditionally considered distinct from 'serious' art. Research on the figures included in *The Dinner Party* was led by the American artist Ann Isolde who, like others working on the project, had gone through her entire art education without being shown the slide of a single work by a woman artist or having the opportunity to speak with a female tutor.

The Dinner Party constitutes an important expansion to our knowledge and understanding of the field of art, but it could not in any way be said to represent a completion. Even at its early showings, it was noted that the women at the banquet, as well as those on the heritage floor, are overwhelmingly white and drawn predominantly from Western culture. It was also remarked upon at the time that the organizational structure of the studio and the work patterns of those involved – no social conversation was allowed while working and no one could leave an allotted task to help another worker – replicated, rather than subverted, those prevalent in male-dominated society. Such criticisms notwithstanding, in the techniques and materials it uses, in its compositional arrangements, and in its explicit focus on the contributions of women in all areas of human endeavour, *The Dinner Party* provides some initial answers to the questions raised by British art historians Rozsika Parker and Griselda Pollock at the beginning of their book *Old Mistresses* (1981), published not long after *The Dinner Party*'s first showing:

> *Have there been female artists? If so, what have they created? Why did they produce what they did? What factors conditioned their lives and works? What difficulties have women encountered and how did they overcome discrimination, denigration, devaluation, dismissal, in attempting to be an artist in a society which since the Book of Genesis has associated the divine right of creativity with men alone?*[11]

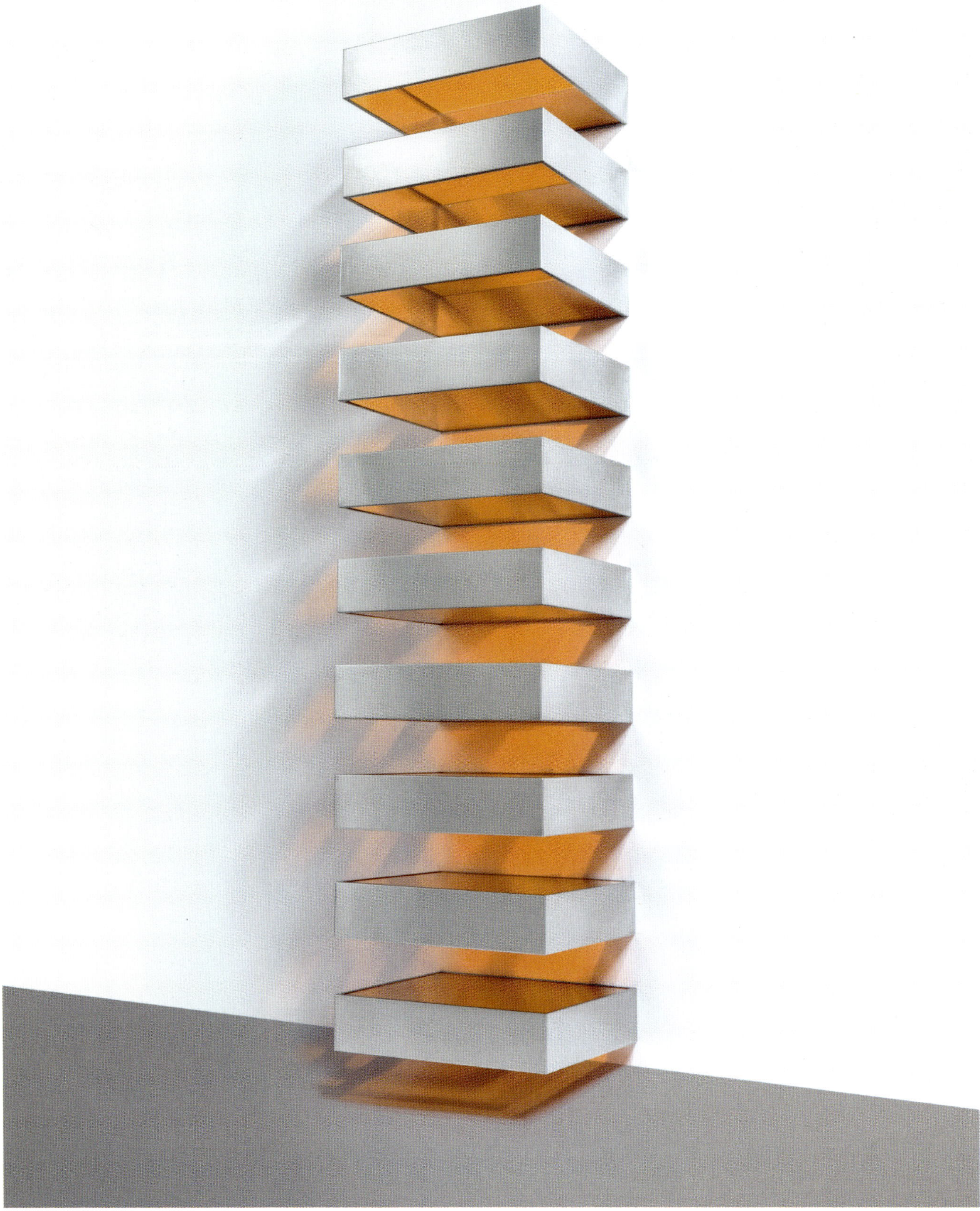

REPETITION

Different colours work differently on the eye. Some appear to project forward in relation to others that seem to recede. As is evident, for example, in Morris Louis's Unfurleds (see pages 150–1), the juxtaposition of different colours will always stimulate an optical modulation of the flat surface in this way. The inability of our eyes to avoid this effect is what led the American artist Donald Judd to begin working in three dimensions. 'I'm using actual space', he said, 'because when I was doing paintings I couldn't see any way out of having a certain amount of illusionism [in them].'[1] He called what he was doing 'three-dimensional work' – neither painting nor sculpture – and while he acknowledged that this work looked more like sculpture, for him it was actually closer to painting.[2]

Judd made the first of a number of works collectively referred to as 'Stacks' in 1965, a format he would return to over the next four decades. While each is made of a different material or combination of materials, they all have the same form and, almost invariably, the same dimensions. They comprise multiple identical units in the form of shallow rectangular boxes, with one of their long sides fixed to the wall, positioned vertically one above the other. They are separated by a distance equal to their height, and the instructions for installing them specify there must be at least the same distance between the top-most unit and the ceiling (if the ceiling is too low, you simply take one of the units away). The work is, therefore, entirely contained within the gallery space and there is no suggestion that one could imagine the line extending further up into the sky as there is, for example, in the case of the Romanian artist Constantin Brancusi's *Endless Column* (1934).

The repetition of units is an example of what Judd called 'a small, finite order'.[3] They are interchangeable and one does not relate to another beyond the fact that it is the next in the sequence – just as cars do as they come off an assembly line. Like the inescapable illusionism of two dimensions, Judd saw any attempt to relate the parts of a work as imbued with the spirit of European art:

> *When you start relating parts, in the first place, you're assuming you have a vague whole – the rectangle of the canvas – and definite parts, which is all screwed up, because you should have a definite whole and maybe no parts, or very few … The whole's it. The big problem is to maintain the sense of the whole thing.*[4]

On this issue, the American artist Mel Bochner considered it preferable not to think of work such as Judd's in terms of 'composition' at all:

> *The word 'arrangement' is preferable to 'composition'. 'Composition' usually means the adjustment of the parts, i.e., their size, shape, colour, or placement, to arrive at the finished work, whose exact nature is not known beforehand. 'Arrangement' implies the fixed nature of the parts and a preconceived notion of the whole.*[5]

OPPOSITE: Donald Judd, *Untitled*, 1968. Stainless steel and amber Plexiglas, 15.2 × 68.6 × 61cm (6 × 27 × 24 in).

The German–American artist Eva Hesse's *Accretion* (1968) consists of fifty fibreglass tubes leaning next to one another against a wall. The tubes are all of the same length, but we cannot say that they are identical since they have clearly been handmade. A parting paper tube (parting paper has a non-stick surface, so it is easy to release cast items during moulding) was wrapped in fibre and coated with resin. Once the resin was dry, the paper former was removed and a further coat of resin applied. There is no strict set of rules for arranging the tubes other than that they should be propped more or less upright in a line along a wall. The angle at which they lean does not need to be consistent, and the distance between the tubes can also vary according to the available space and the decisions of whoever is responsible for its installation at the time.

In an undated notebook entry, Hesse listed the dictionary definitions of several words that she would go on to use as titles for her works. Among them is Accretion: 'the growing of separate things into one, the whole resulting from this'.[6] This transition from separate things towards a resulting whole runs counter to Judd's insistence on the whole being the place from which you start.

A further notable contrast with Judd's approach is Hesse's reliance on making by hand rather than delegating the task of production to a firm of fabricators. Two years before *Accretion*, Hesse had made *Hang Up*. This is a large, thickly bandaged frame painted in a grey that is graded from light in the top left corner to dark in the bottom right. The frame is empty, so when hung it displays only a patch of blank gallery wall. A length of thick wire comes from the top edge of the frame, loops out and down almost to the floor and then back to the bottom edge. To quote Hesse, the work is both 'very, very finely done' and 'absurd'.[7] The extravagantly cared-for frame frames nothing, and furthermore the wire loop extends 2 metres (6 feet 6 inches) from the wall, so the usual spot from where a painting can be observed is denied to us. We can only look at it either from a distance or obliquely. And when we do, there is no revelation as there is, for example, when we look from the side to view the anamorphic skull in the sixteenth-century painting *The Ambassadors* by Hans Holbein the Younger.

'Art', as Hesse wrote in another notebook entry from 1967, 'is what it is'.[8] In the same entry, she also described art as 'detached but intimate, personal'.The tubes in *Accretion* are the same length as Hesse's height, but the work is not in the least representational or anthropomorphic. Judd talked of order as simple, 'like that of continuity, one thing after another'.[9] We can see that kind of order in his Stacks, with their evenly spaced, identical fabricated units that can be taken in all at once. But the irregular placement of individually handmade elements in *Accretion* rejects that possibility. It asks us to take our time and to travel along its length. That is to say, to take real time in real space to recognize how the gesture of making those elements, as much as the placing of the finished tubes, one after another, builds towards the whole.

Accretion ... asks us to take our time and to travel along its length ... to recognize how the gesture of making those elements, as much as the placing of the finished tubes, one after another, builds towards the whole.

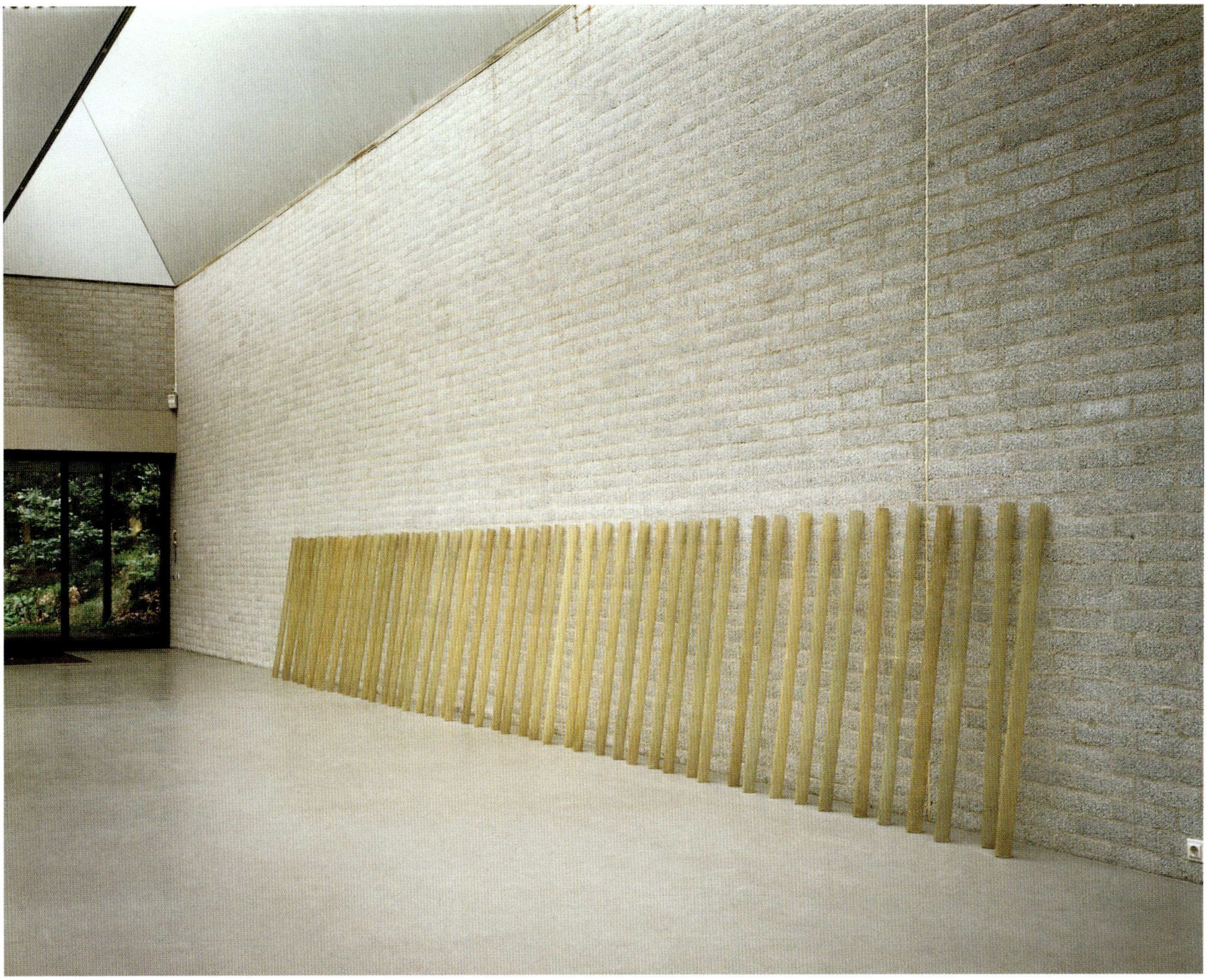

ABOVE: Eva Hesse, *Accretion*, 1968. Fibreglass, polyester resin; variable dimensions. Fifty units (each): 147.5 × 6.3 cm (58 × 2½ in). Installation view, Kröller-Müller Museum, Otterlo.

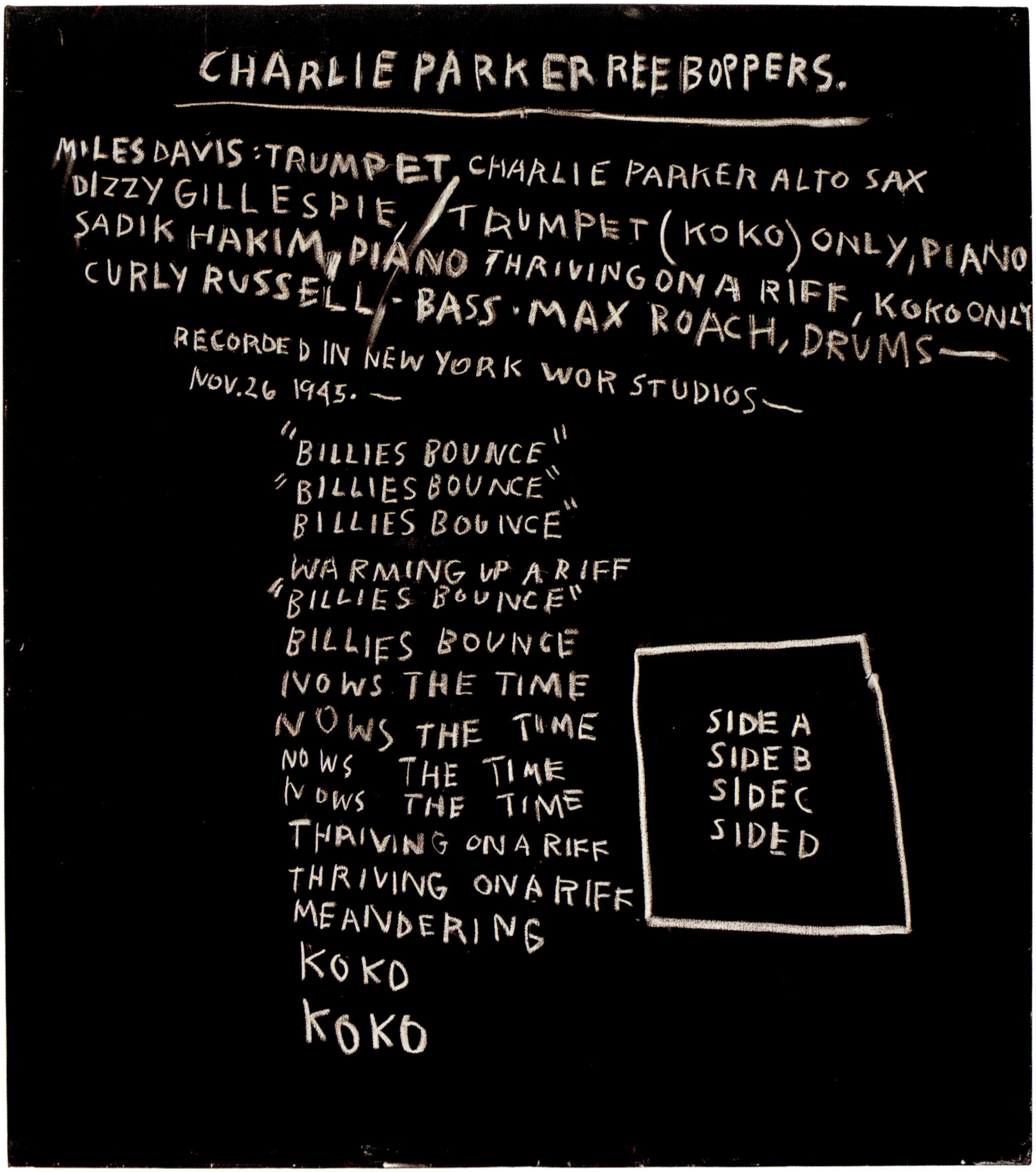

ABOVE: Jean-Michel Basquiat, *Discography One*, 1983.
Acrylic and oil pastel on canvas, 168 × 152 cm (66 × 59⅞ in).

The American artist Jean-Michel Basquiat made the observation that 'Black people are never really portrayed realistically ... they are not even portrayed in modern art.'[10] The work he made in a brief career, from the late 1970s to his untimely death in 1986, was as much as anything an attempt to rectify that situation. *Discography One* is one of a pair of black square canvases from 1983 on which, in the words of Canadian curator Marc Mayer, 'the half-remembered, daydreamy transcriptions of information on two favourite jazz album covers' are written in white paintstick.[11] *Discography One* carries the details of a 1945 recording session by the Charlie Parker's Reboppers. Under the band's name, which Basquiat deliberately spells REEBOPPERS, he gives the musicians and their instrumentation, then the studio and date, after which there is a list of every take – fifteen in all – recorded during the session. Only six tunes were covered, so names occur repeatedly, setting up a rhythm in the viewer's mind and body as they read.

Parker appears frequently in Basquiat's work, a major figure in his pantheon of Black cultural heroes, and Parker's music – his compositional technique of taking the chord structure of a well-known tune and layering it with a new melody over which he would then improvise – was something Basquiat carried over into his own work. 'Bebop's I guess my favorite music', said Basquiat, 'but I don't listen to it all the time; I listen to everything'.[12] The use of the black square in the composition of *Discography One* is not only the representation of an album cover containing Black music, jazz, played by Black musicians, it is also an iconic form in twentieth-century art that has been knowingly lifted out of its already established place in the museum in order to be put to work in this way. It is the black square of Kazymyr Malevych's first suprematist composition, it is the black square to which New York artist Ad Reinhardt devoted himself during the last decade of his life, and it is the kind of simple monochrome form associated with the minimalists for whom Reinhardt was an important precursor. We might also see the white writing on black ground of the final composition as constituting a 'mild satire'[13] on the blackboards filled with notes and diagrams by Joseph Beuys in his lecture-performances that are retained and lovingly preserved after the event. Next to the track list, Basquiat has drawn a square. It is the four sides of the double LP and also perhaps a further, somewhat ironic, critical nod towards minimalism, as it was when American artist Bruce Nauman taped out an area on his studio floor in order to make the short film, *Walking in an Exaggerated Manner Around the Perimeter of a Square*.

Judd's repetition is a 'small, finite order', one thing after another within a whole that is, anyway, more important than its individual parts. Hesse's repeated elements, to the contrary, enable an experience that builds through time towards a whole. And, differently again, for Basquiat, *Discography One* stresses that there is endless improvisational inventiveness to be found in repetition.

There is endless improvisational inventiveness to be found in repetition.

MULTIPLICITY

There are instances in which an artwork can be seen to resonate with a particular situation or event – the Spanish artist Pablo Picasso's *Guernica*, for example, painted as his immediate response to the German bombing of the Basque town. The Cuban artist Tania Bruguera has more explicitly approached art as something that can be useful. In talking of composition, we normally think in terms of the frame, of what exists and is arranged within it, and of how it sits within and relates to what surrounds it. For Bruguera, the frame is the art world. It is possible for people to enter it, but to do so they need to get past the 'gatekeepers'. It is neither possible nor productive to try to remove the gatekeepers. What she has done instead is to 'create several dimensions of the framework so you have so many gatekeepers that you actually create no gatekeepers'.[1]

As well as art, the 'dimensions' in which Bruguera works include politics, community action and education. There are three terms used by her to describe her approach to art. The first one is *arte de conducta*, which is usually translated as 'behaviour art', as distinct from performance, though she points out that this misses the sense of conduction, of the interpersonal communication, present in the Spanish word. Behaviour art involves other people, not just the artist herself. 'I don't want my work to represent something', she said, 'I want people not to look at it but to be in it, sometimes without even knowing it is art.'[2]

Immigrant Movement International was a long-term project conceived in 2006 and initially run in Queens, New York, as well as in other countries between 2010 and 2015. In the manner of the basic information given on a museum label, Bruguera stated that the medium of the work is 'Appropriation of Political Strategies, Arte Útil', and listed its materials as 'Immigration Policies and Laws, Immigrant Population, Elected Officials, Politicians, Community Organizations, Public Pressure, and Media'.[3] Roughly translated from Spanish as 'useful art', Arte Útil is Bruguera's term for art that does not merely comment on a situation, but actively engages with it with the aim of bringing about change. In the history of modern art, utility has habitually been the way to distinguish art from design, but this is not the case here. Helping to negotiate settlement status, running language classes, holding workshops on internet access, and so on, are both sociopolitical action and art.

Bruguera's project layers these frames, all with their own associated gatekeepers, over one another. A further term she has used to describe her working method is 'political timing specific art'. This variation on the much more familiar term 'site specific art' indicates that as well as the relevance of a given situation to the realization of a work, there is also an optimum moment in which to engage with that particular set of circumstances. The timing is crucial, since 'the piece will only be the way it is in that specific political moment; if it's done before or after it won't have the same consequences'.[4] One corollary of this is that once the situation alters, the character of the work will also change. Bruguera acknowledges that the meaning of her work cannot remain stable. As she has said:

> *A work that is political timing specific situates itself exactly between art and politics, between aesthetic criteria and political critique. The work can't be analyzed in only one of the two worlds it intervenes in; it can't be studied solely as artistic intention nor as a political intervention.*[5]

Importantly it is not that the work is neither one thing nor the other, but that it is both art and politics. Bruguera pays little attention to documenting her work, since it is the effects that occur within the lives of those who become involved with her projects that are of primary significance. 'I have always seen myself as an immaterial artist whose work lives in people's memory.'[6]

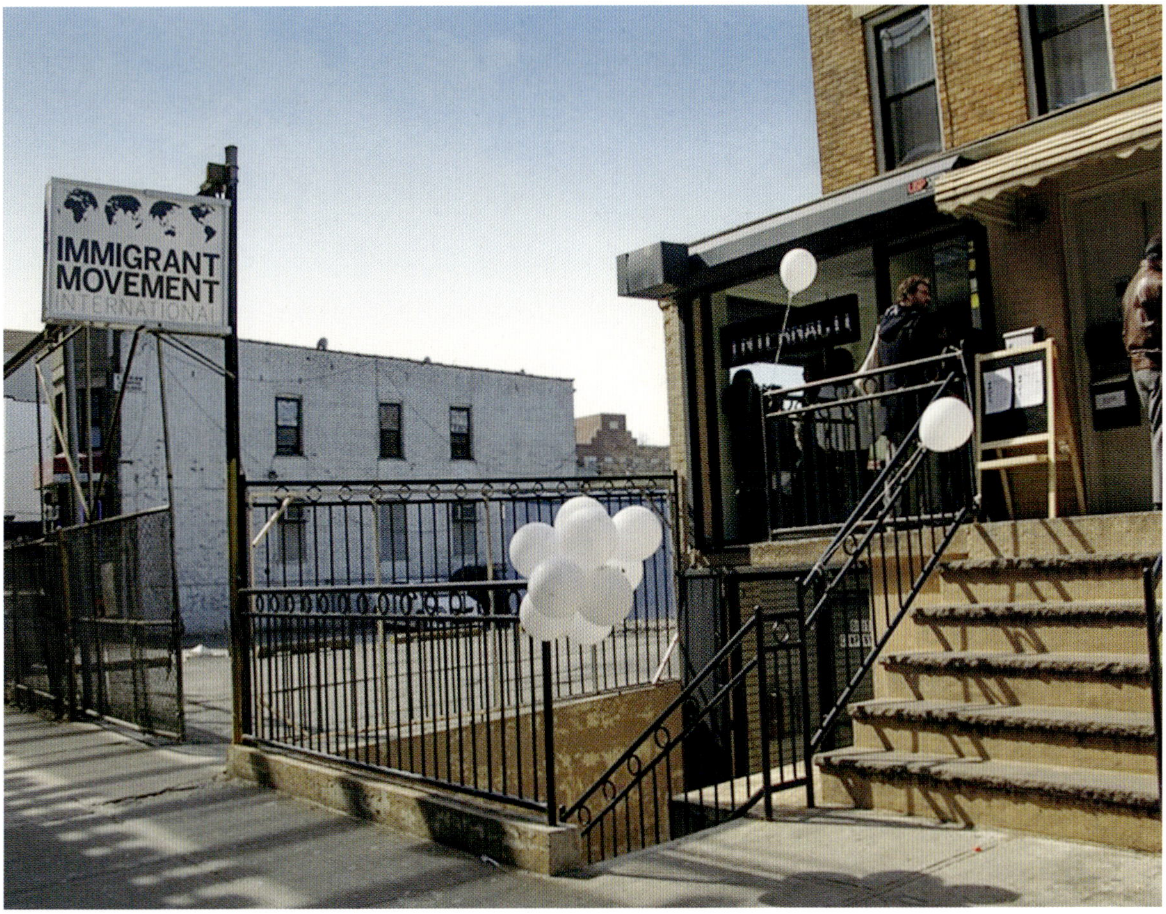

ABOVE: Immigrant Movement International headquarters in Corona, Queens, New York, 2012.

Arte Útil is Bruguera's term for art that does not merely comment on a situation, but actively engages with it with the aim of bringing about change.

CONTRIBUTION

The work of the Japanese artist Yoko Ono arose in the confluence of two creative strands: the performance events of the Japanese Gutai group, an avant-garde group that formed in the 1950s, and the approach to composition of the American composer John Cage and those around him. The Japanese composer Ichiyanagi Toshi had travelled to New York to study with Cage, who taught a class on experimental composition at the New School for Social Research between 1956 and 1960. Ono, who at that time was married to Ichiyanagi, also attended the sessions, and she recognized that Cage's approach – such as his involvement of chance in the compositional process – could have equal relevance for artistic activity beyond music.

For both Cage and the Gutai artists, such as Saburo Murakami, Kazuo Shiraga and Shozo Shimamoto, the composition of a work could be perceived as an event. In Ono's case, from the outset it is understood that an event is not a solo effort but something that necessarily involves other people. Her first exhibition of paintings in 1961 included several works in which visitors were invited to make a contribution towards their completion. The request came either through a written instruction, or verbally from gallery staff or Ono herself. *Painting to be Stepped On*, shown here in its first presentation, is a piece of canvas placed on the gallery floor along with a strip of card bearing the words that are both its title and invitation. The cumulative effect of the viewers'

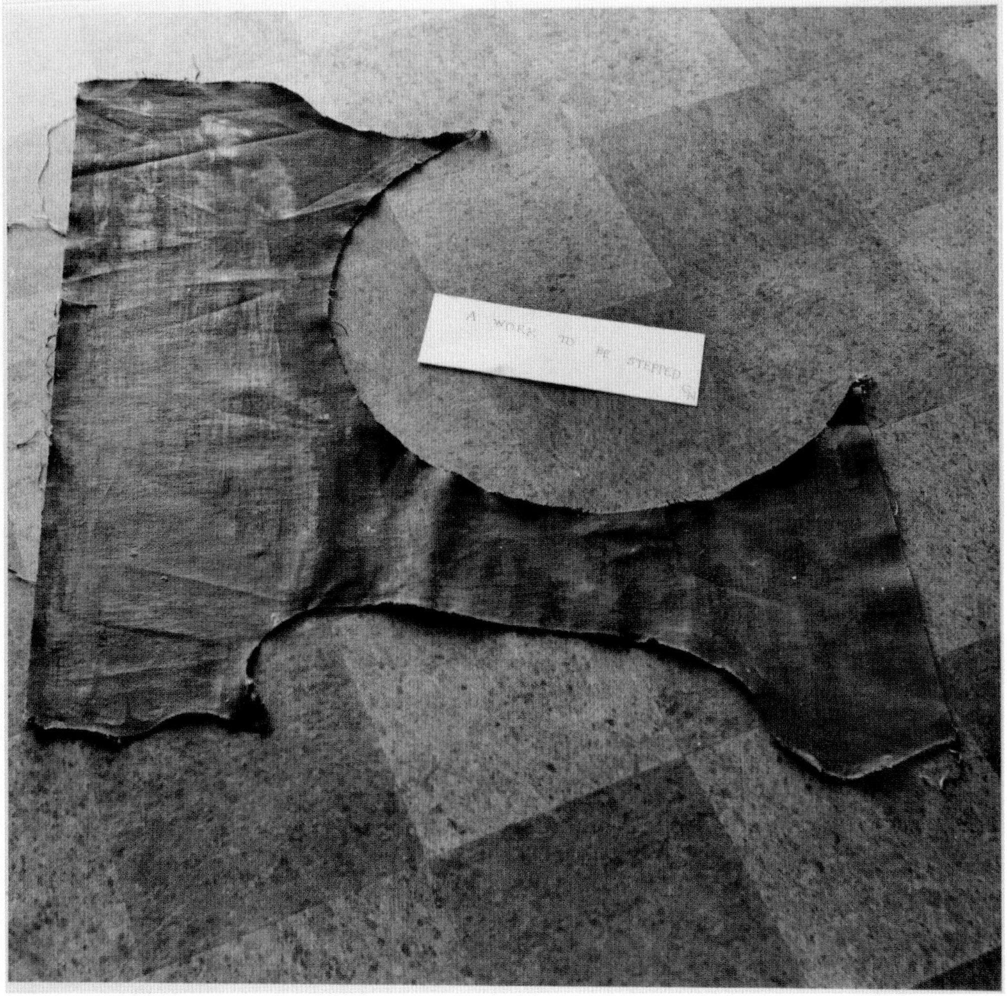

footprints on the fabric over time would make the painting. What is grasped immediately is that the process is open-ended and unforeseeable, and that it will look different on each occasion we see it. How often will it be exhibited? How many people will see it? Will they step on it or just stand to one side and look at it? What will they be wearing on their feet? Will it be raining outside so their shoes will be wet and muddy? It is not only that the fate of the painting must remain unknown but also that, because of this, we are ourselves free to imagine its completion. For example, it might be that so many feet pass over it that it is ultimately worn away to nothing.

The canvas of this first version of *Painting to be Stepped On* is irregularly shaped. One of its sides is a concave curve that seems to be a match for the disc of canvas that formed *Waterdrop Painting* (1961) in that exhibition. This again is placed on the floor so that, as its title suggests, visitors can drip water onto it. *Painting to be Stepped On*, then, is what appears to be an off-cut, a piece left over after the rest of the canvas has been taken for use in other works. It is a scrap that would likely simply be discarded, left to lie around on the studio floor to be walked over as you make your way over to work on something important. In bringing it into the gallery, making it the centre of attention, and designating an act that would otherwise be disregarded as the very thing that is constitutive of the work, Ono has upended every expectation. She ensured, in the most gentle, uncoercive manner, that we are all implicated in the making of the painting, because a decision not to step on the canvas would be as valid as choosing to walk on it.

The logical next step for Ono was to realize that a painting could come into existence through an instruction alone without the need for the artist to provide the initial material circumstances. An instruction could act like a musical score in which each person would be free to interpret and perform as they felt appropriate. Ono had an exhibition of such paintings in Tokyo in 1962. Under ideal circumstances, they would have been typed, but in the event they were written in neatly drawn characters by Ichiyanagi. The considered impersonality of the presentational style emphasizes that these are, indeed, scores. They are not to be mistaken for the paintings themselves; they are triggers for the paintings that each viewer can conjure in their own mind:

> *PAINTING TO BE CONSTRUCTED IN YOUR HEAD*
> *Go on transforming a square canvas in your head until it becomes a circle. Pick out any shape in the process and pin up or place on the canvas an object, a smell, a sound, or a colour that came to your mind in association with the shape.*[1]

She ensured, in the most gentle, uncoercive manner, that we are all implicated in the making of the painting.

OPPOSITE: Yoko Ono, *Painting to be Stepped On*, 1960/1. Installation view, AG Gallery, New York, 1961.

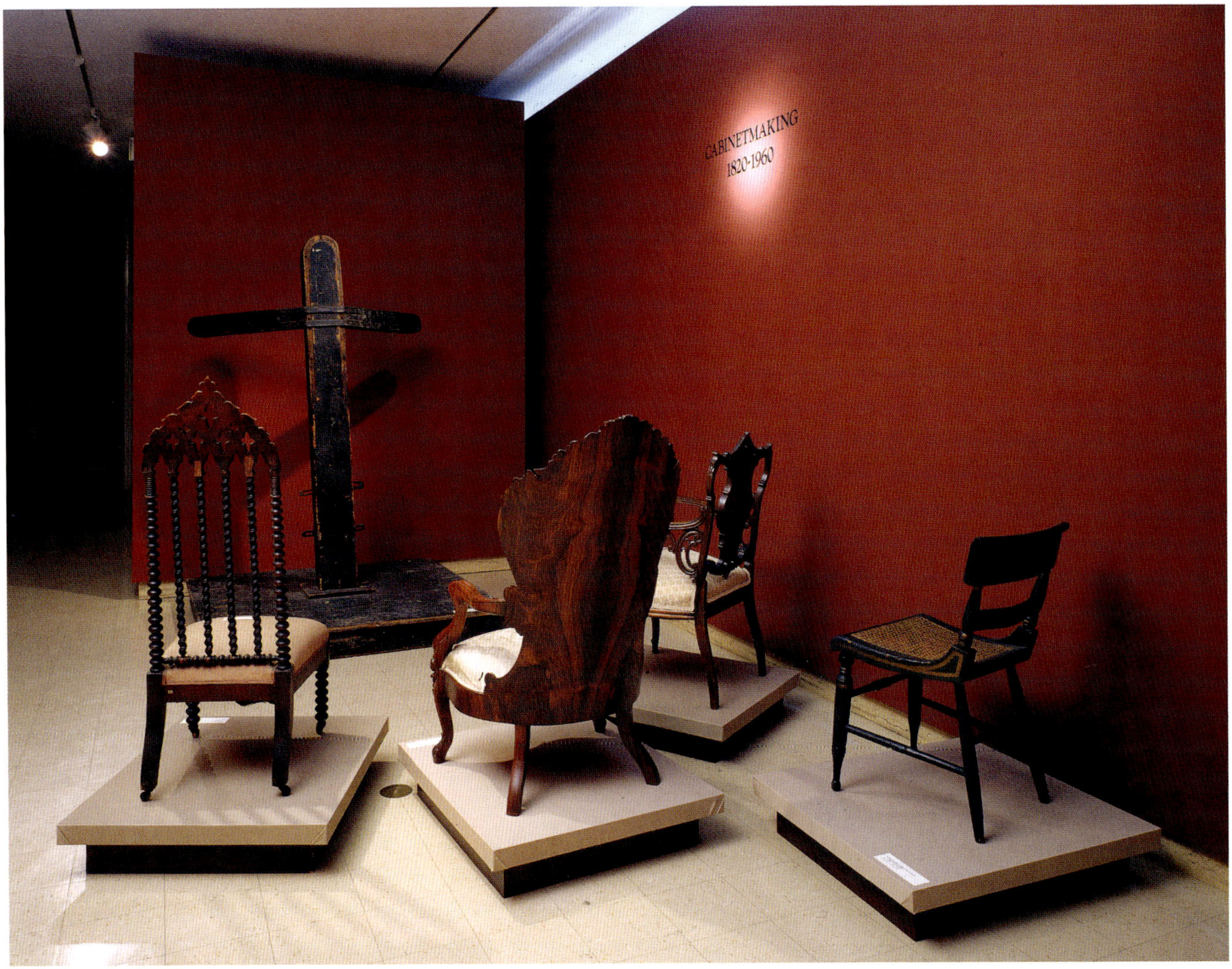

ABOVE: Fred Wilson, detail from *Mining the Museum: 'Cabinetmaking, 1820–1960'*, 1992–3. Installation view, Maryland Historical Society, Baltimore.

Composition here is a process of the selection of a set of objects and their arrangement in such a way as to reorder perception and invite new understanding.

THE SYSTEM OF ART

There are innumerable ways in which artists have revealed that it is not the artwork on its own, in isolation, that can be appraised and judged. It always requires a system: a market, a gallery, a dealer, an exhibition, critics and their associated press outlets, an opening, dinners and after parties, and so on. As Lee Lozano's *Dropout Piece* has shown us (see pages 161–3), this system provides a space within which the work can be recognized as a work, and it provides the evaluative framework through which it is judged. For the most part, all these supporting and contextual factors remain external to the artwork itself while they enable it to be displayed, but it can also be the case that they sit at the heart of an artwork's compositional structure.

For an exhibition in 1974, the American conceptual artist Michael Asher removed the wall between the showing space of the gallery and the gallery's office. No further objects were brought into the room since the work on display was simply the total, integrated space of the establishment. Thus, like Dorothy's dog Toto drawing back the curtain in the 1939 film *The Wizard of Oz*, Asher revealed the machinery that supports and maintains the aesthetic realm of art. A 1989 photograph by the American artist Louise Lawler, *How Many Pictures (Stella)* shows not a Frank Stella painting from the mid-1960s, but its reflection in the polished wood of the gallery's flooring. In other words, what we see is the museum itself as the institution that, as it functions, reproduces the ideological presumptions upon which the artworks it exhibits rely for their aesthetic valuation.

The Belgian artist Marcel Broodthaers traced this condition of art, its existence and its means of validation back to Marcel Duchamp's readymades (see pages 84–5):

> *[A]ny object can be elevated to the status of art. The artist defines this object in such a way that its future can lie only in the museum. Since Duchamp, the artist is author of a definition.*[1]

Broodthaers described the interdependence between artworks and the wider art world in a brief, circular text, first printed on the cover of the German art magazine *Interfunktionen* in 1974:

> *View*
> *according to which an artistic theory will function for the artistic product in the same way as the artistic product itself functions as advertising for the order under which it is produced. There will be no other space than this view, according to which, etc.*[2]

In response to this situation, Broodthaers decided to initiate his own 'Museé d'Art Moderne' in 1968. Its final appearance, in 1972, was the setting for his *Section des Figures: The Eagle from the Oligocene to the Present* exhibition. He gathered 266 items for this exhibition, including sculptures, paintings, prints, jewellery, posters, ceramics and photographs, each of which bore an image of an eagle. Ranging in age from the antique to the contemporary, some were loans from the world's major museums and others were cheap, mass-produced objects. Alongside each exhibit, Broodthaers placed a label stating alternately in German, French or English, 'This is not a work of art', a text combining Duchamp's demonstration that an artist could now designate a found object as a work of art with René Magritte's *The Treachery of Images* (see pages 174–5). However, regardless of what the label says, if we are looking at a work of art, it is not the individual items but the installation as a whole that is of significance. This includes not only all the objects, but also the fictional museum that had been realized by Broodthaers and, by implication, the sociopolitical system within which it can command attention as an artistic manifestation. In some respects, what Broodthaers was doing as an artist looks very much like what might otherwise be called curating. Australian art critic and historian Terry Smith observes:

> *Contemporary art and curatorial practice have been converging since the late 1960s, with consequences for the compositional modes of both. With installations in museums and alternative gallery spaces becoming the medium preferred by increasing numbers of contemporary artists, it was a matter of time before the staging of exhibitions of the work of other artists, and the radical reinstallation of museum collections, became a favoured activity.*[3]

Such reframing and reappraisal, often referred to as 'institutional critique', examined a wide variety of subjects, including censorship, feminism and female agency, and the brutal history of colonialsm. In 1990, the American artist Joseph Kosuth arranged a display at the Brooklyn Museum in New York in response to an attack by US Senator Jesse Helms on the National Endowment for the Arts for funding the American photographers Robert Mapplethorpe and Andres Serrano, whose work the senator deemed obscene. Serrano's photograph *Piss Christ* (1987) of a crucifix in a jar of urine, was arguably the most contentious image in this debate. Kosuth's *The Play of the Unmentionable* installation (1990) took works from the museum's permanent collection, all valued as significant examples from their respective times and cultures, but which would now be considered obscene if judged under this puritanical regime. Two years later, the American artist Zoe Leonard made an installation for the Baroque gallery in Kassel's Neue Galerie in Germany as part of that year's Documenta IX. She removed all paintings with exclusively male figures and hung in each vacated space a black-and-white photograph of a vagina.

One notable instance of 'radical reinstallation' was the outcome of research conducted by the American artist Fred Wilson into the holdings of the Maryland Historical Society in Baltimore. The resulting exhibition, *Mining the Museum*, juxtaposed objects that would hitherto have been displayed in quite distinct contexts, and in so doing made visible the irreducible connections between that which is celebrated as high culture, and the history of slavery and the oppression of the indigenous population upon which such cultural achievement rests. In a selection of wooden items, articles of furniture were placed next to a whipping post in *Cabinetmaking, 1820–1960* (see page 194), while one vitrine, labelled *Metalwork 1793–1880*, contained silver tableware together with a set of manacles. Composition here is a process of the selection of a set of objects and their arrangement in such a way as to reorder perception and invite new understanding. In her account of the project, co-curator Lisa G. Corrin wrote that in *Mining the Museum*, Wilson explored 'not what objects mean but how meaning is made when they are "framed" by the museum environment and museum practices'.[4]

EXPOSING THE SYSTEM

For her 2009 show, *Lux Interior*, the German artist Jutta Koether hung the exhibition's sole painting on a free-standing screen placed obliquely across the space, one foot on the lobby floor, the other on the slightly raised wooden platform establishing what would usually be recognized as the gallery's showing space. The painting was lit, not by the standard gallery spotlight, but by a larger light rescued from a New York gay night club that had closed down in the late 1980s in the wake of the AIDS epidemic. Koether's painting, *Hot Rod (after Poussin)*, was an interpretive reworking in near monochrome red of the seventeenth-century French painting *Landscape during a Thunderstorm with Pyramus and Thisbe* by Nicolas Poussin. Poussin's composition revolves around a diagonal line that begins in a distant lightning flash at the top and extends down through to Thisbe's angled body as she rushes towards her dead lover.

Drawing not only from Poussin's painting but also the British art historian T.J. Clark's study of it,[5] Koether's version emphasizes this diagonal, which establishes a strong axis around which brush marks cluster towards the top and bottom of the canvas. The exhibition of the work also involved a series of performance lectures given by Koether while moving around and underneath the painting. The use of strobe lighting created an atmosphere that suggested the artist and the painting might have been encountering one another in a club rather than a gallery. Taken together, the painting, its Poussin reference, its installation, and Koether's lectures exemplify, as the American art critic David Joselit has argued, that painting has become 'transitive'.[6] Like a transitive verb, which takes an object, transitive painting can no longer pretend to self-sufficiency, but must reckon with all those factors which, though external to it, are nonetheless necessary for its display as a painting. Russian artist Aleksandr Rodchenko's monochrome panels stood as a cipher for painting itself, as if to say all paintings are nothing more than objects for contemplation and commodities for exchange. In drawing the critique of the institutions of art into its frame of reference, Koether's *Hot Rod (after Poussin)* avoids any need for such compositional reductiveness.

RIGHT: Nicolas Poussin, *Landscape During a Thunderstorm with Pyramus and Thisbe*, 1651. Oil on canvas, 191 × 274 cm (75 × 108 in).

BELOW: Jutta Koether, *Hot Rod (after Poussin)*, 2009. Acrylic, pastel and mixed media on canvas, 203.2 × 264.2 cm (80 × 104 in). Installation view, Reena Spaulings, New York, 2009.

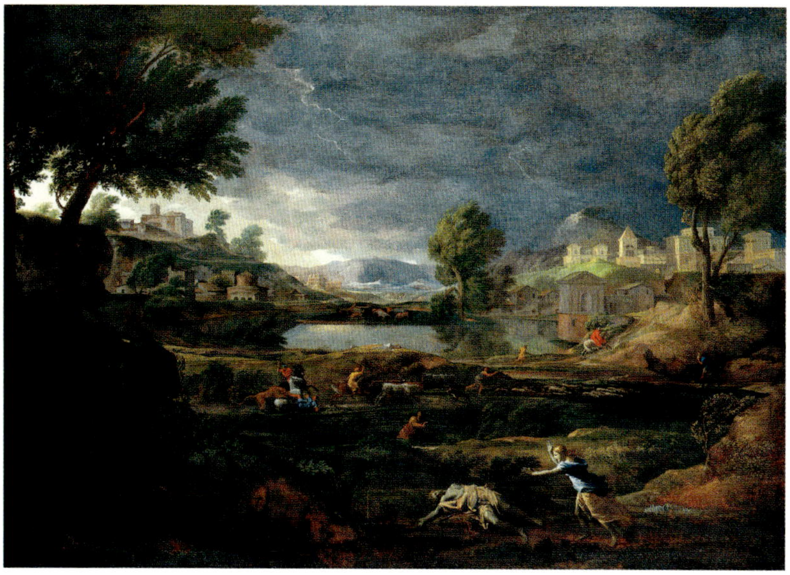

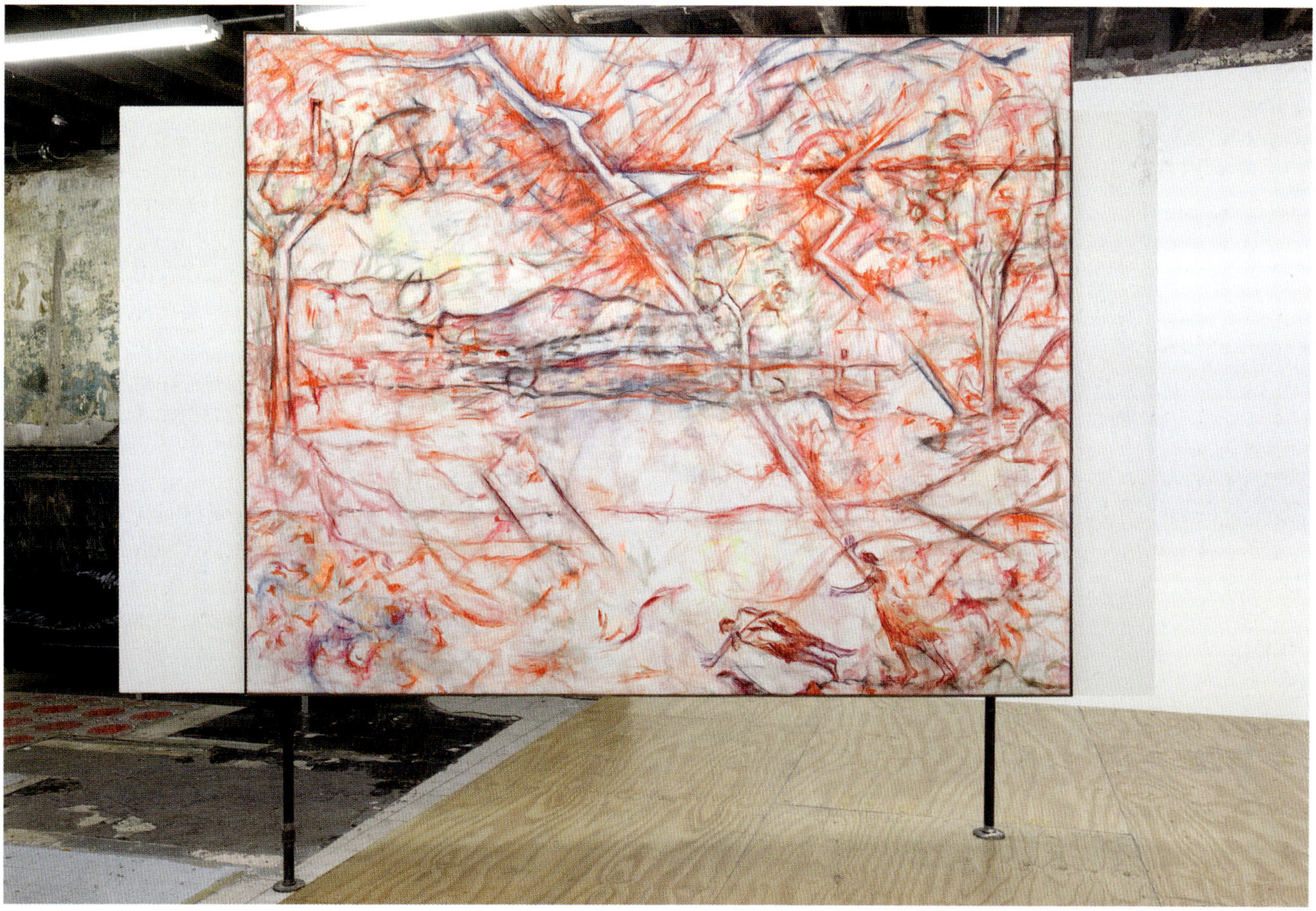

Algerian artist Lydia Ourahmane's sound installation *The Third Choir* appears to consist simply of twenty empty, used oil barrels arranged in a block of four by five. Ambient sound, broadcast via a radio transmitter, comes from a smartphone placed in the bottom of each barrel. The barrels themselves are painted in yellow and blue with a blue logo – the colours and insignia of Naftal, an Algerian national oil enterprise. Normally, these barrels would only be used in the country itself, and the oil they contained would be subsequently exported under their own auspices by various commercial oil companies.

Ourahmane's work, however, is much more than these twenty relocated and distinctively painted barrels: it encompasses all that was required to get them out of Algeria and into the gallery for exhibition. For this, the first artwork to be legally exported from Algeria since its independence in 1962, Ourahmane first needed to obtain permission for their export. This was a protracted process that involved negotiations with many agencies from the port authorities in Oran up to the Algerian Minister of Culture. She then had to arrange for them to be transported from Algeria, via Almeria in southern Spain, to the UK. The first leg from Oran to Spain is significant because it is one of the routes taken by refugees and asylum seekers trying to get from the Algerian coast to the European Union and from there to the United Kingdom. In another work, Ourahmane used a sound mix of conversations with some people who had tried unsuccessfully to make that journey.

The huge amount of documentation accumulated in the course of getting permission for the export of what is, under standard rules, unexportable; for making necessary transport arrangements; and for tracking the shipment on its route from Oran to Liverpool and then on to London is presented as part of the work. It records the manoeuvres by means of which what is not supposed to leave is given permission to do so, thereby exposing the plight of those whose movements are denied by the same processes that facilitate passage of natural resources and commodities – including artworks.

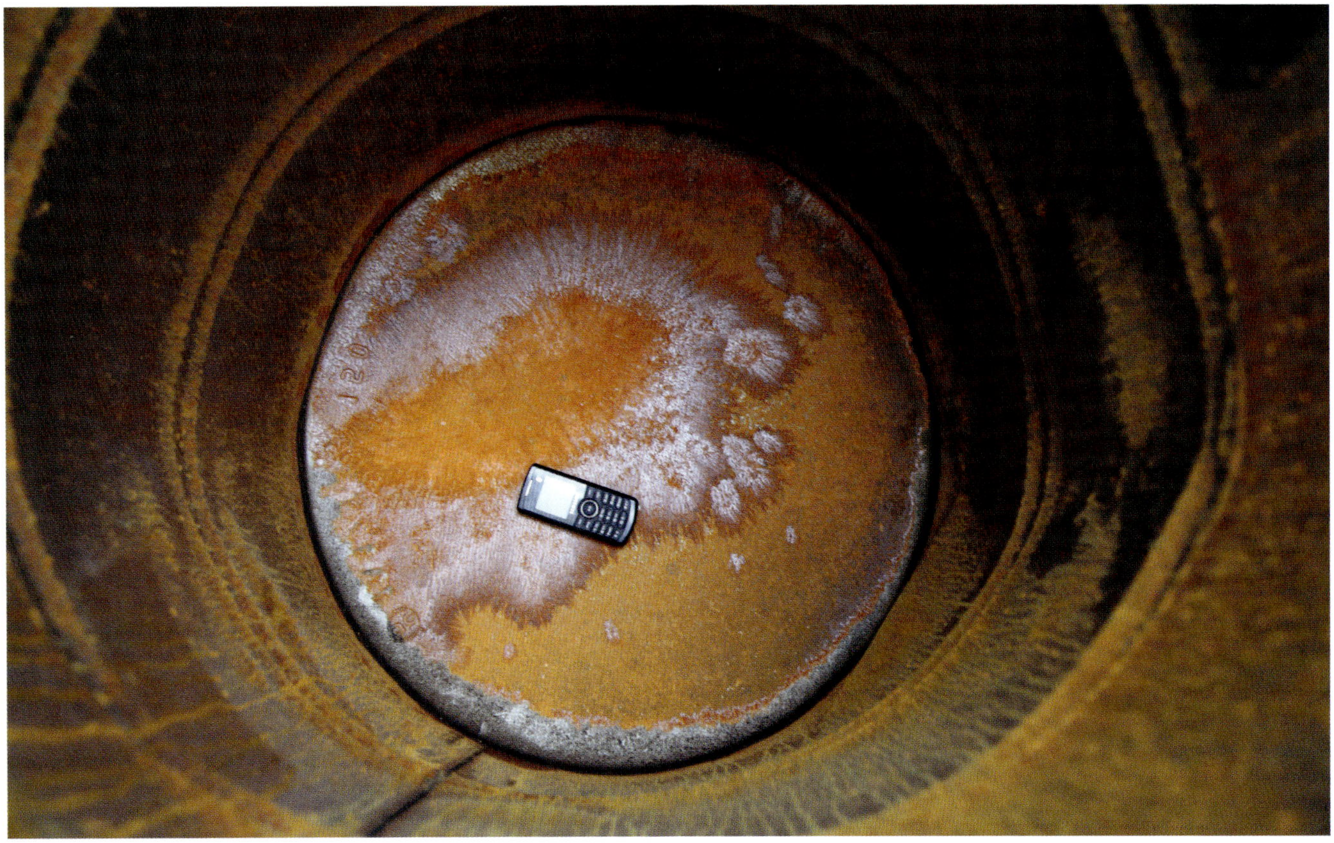

The Third Choir exposes the plight of those whose movements are denied by the same processes that facilitate passage of natural resources and commodities – including, now, artworks

OPPOSITE AND BELOW: Lydia Ourahmane, *The Third Choir*, 2014. Sound Installation: 20 units Naftal oil barrels exported from Algeria, CZ-5HE radio transmitter, 20 units Samsung E2121B phones; 300 × 500 cm (118 × 197 in). Installation view, Berlin Contemporary and Zachęta National Gallery of Art, Warsaw, 2015.

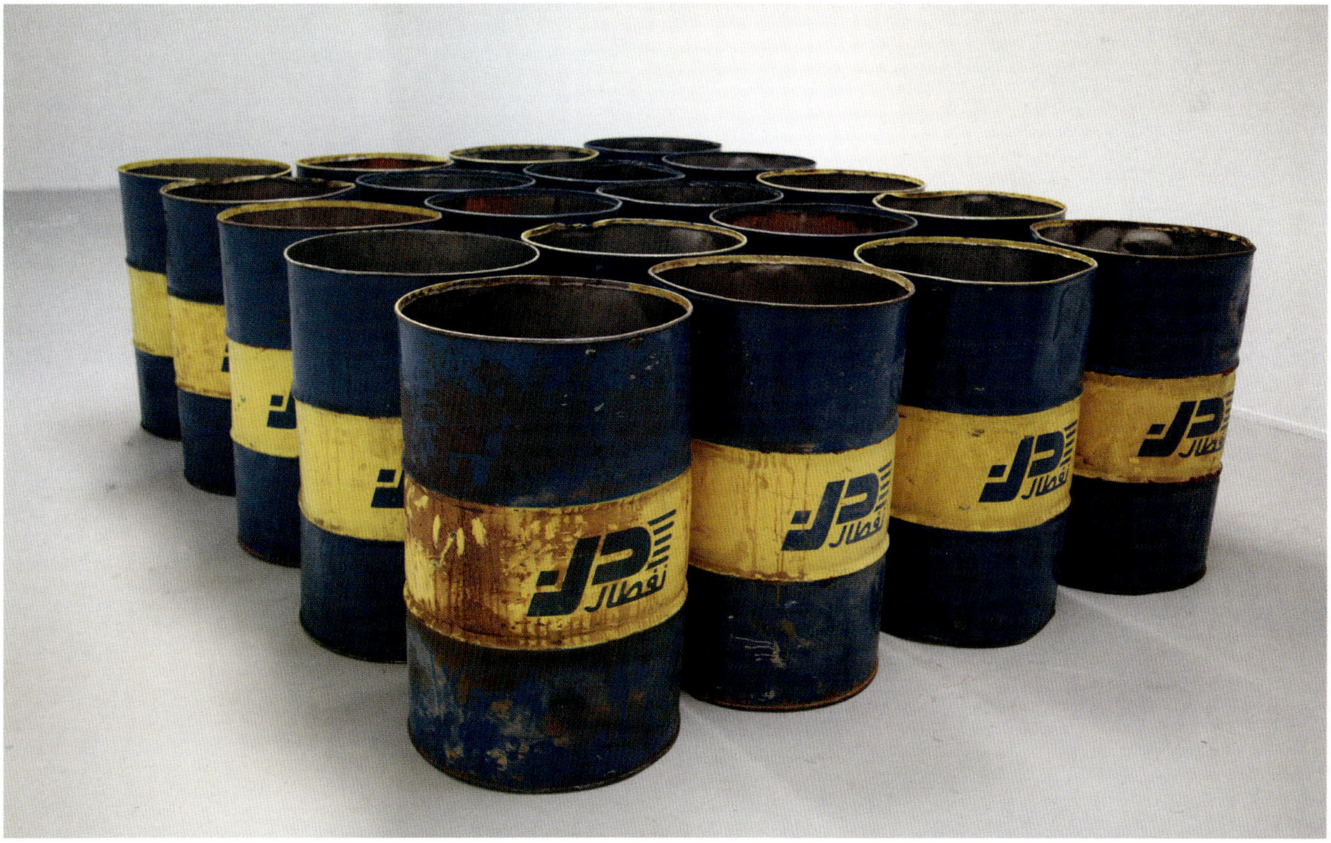

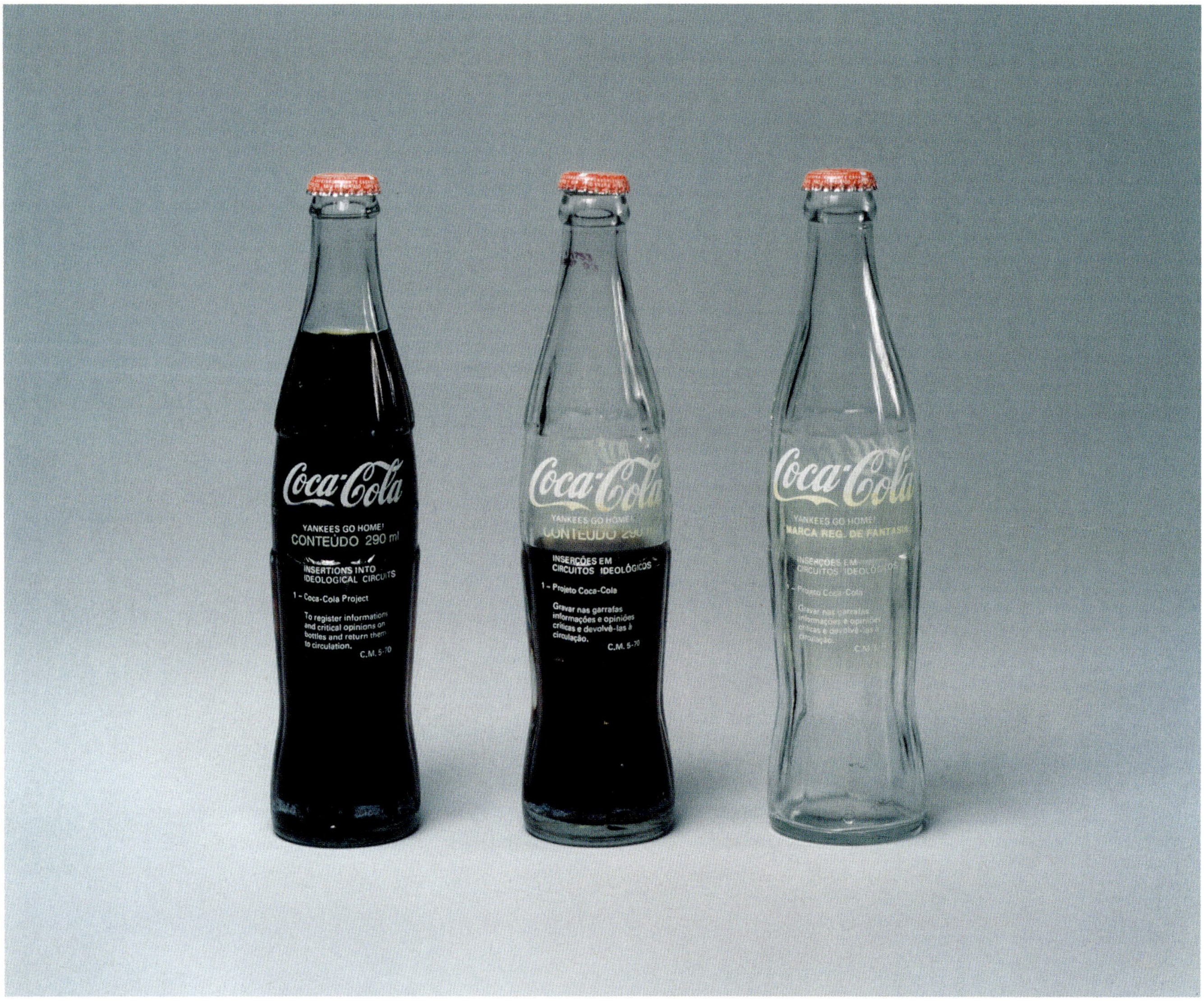

ABOVE: Cildo Meireles, *Insertions into Ideological Circuits: Coca-Cola Project*, 1970. Three glass bottles and adhesive labels with text, 15.5 × 5.5 cm (6⅛ × 2⅛ in).

DISTRIBUTION

One consideration that has haunted the making and appreciation of art throughout the period covered in this book is that of exclusivity. The hand of the artist fashions a work that is unique, which is irreplaceable, and for which there is no substitute. The advent of mass manufacturing and the need for art, as much as any other area of human activity, to accommodate itself to the new economic conditions it brought, were already beginning to undermine this presumption in the nineteenth century.

The multiple studies made by the French artist Claude Monet of haystacks (see pages 34–5), poplars on the Seine and the facade of Rouen cathedral are just one example. In Monet's case, it is still his hand that is responsible for the making of the work, but that direct attachment is soon broken. Marcel Duchamp purchased off-the-shelf items and signed them, the Hungarian painter László Moholy-Nagy directed fabricators to enamel an abstract composition onto metal panels of different sizes and mused that a painter could now work by simply picking up the telephone and issuing instructions. And perhaps the best-known twentieth-century example is the American artist Andy Warhol, who said in a 1963 interview, 'I think somebody should be able to do all my paintings for me',[1] and his studio, in which this did happen, was called the Factory.

Closely bound up with the incursion of mass-production techniques into the making of art is the question of its distribution and consumption. If the art object is unique, it is a straightforward task to ascertain where it can be found, viewed and appreciated. But now that we are all caught up within the impersonal operations of a society of mass-production, how is it possible to discover a unique personal experience?

Working in Brazil under a military dictatorship in which public displays of individual expression were severely curtailed, the conceptual artist Cildo Meireles initiated a project that had a maximum of public reach with the minimum degree of personal visibility. Before the widespread introduction of ring-pull cans, soft drinks were distributed in glass bottles, and once used they were collected and returned to the bottling plant for refilling and further redistribution. Meireles returned over 1,000 Coca-Cola bottles in this way, after having printed messages onto them. Because he used the same white ink as that used by the company for their logo, the messages were not especially noticeable when the bottle was empty. When refilled with dark fluid, however, they became instantly visible to the new customer. The messages were varied, ranging from the simple slogan 'Yankees Go Home' to basic instructions on how to assemble a Molotov cocktail and fundamental questions, such as 'Which is the place of the work of art?'

There are many aspects to a work that in some respects identifies both the repressive nature of the country's ruling military dictatorship and the controlling power of American capitalism. What it does not do, however, is attempt to inform its audience about a situation of which they were hitherto ignorant. It is not realistic to imagine that the people who bought the bottles that Meireles had returned to circulation were unaware of their own political and economic circumstances before reading its message. The art historian Jonah Westerman has stressed that 'the ideology at stake was never really in the bottle'. *Insertions into Ideological Circuits: Coca-Cola Project* 'was not about the message, it was about the circuit'.[2] The messages printed on the bottles would not change people's minds about the conditions under which they were living. What might happen, however, is that the encounter with one of Meireles's bottles might allow the person who came upon it a moment in which to reflect upon their understanding of those conditions.

To try and understand the work as an object is not the best approach. It is, rather, in our individual enjoyment of the sweet as a moment of sharing in the work that is of importance.

In a conversation with writer and curator Robert Nickas, the Cuban visual artist Felix Gonzalez-Torres* answered a question about how art can make this bridge between the public and private spheres by talking about On Kawara's Date paintings (see pages 178–9). In themselves, the dates are abstract, but what they provide is a marker identifying a moment of personal significance to whoever is viewing the painting:

> *When I say '1968' or '1967', I'm sure you have strong memories of those years. Meaning is created once something can be related to personal experience.*[3]

In the same interview, Gonzalez-Torres remarked on 'the radicality of certain forms of distribution' in his work.[4] On a number of occasions, his work comprised either a stack of identical sheets of paper or an arrangement of numerous individually wrapped candies. On encountering one of these works, viewers have the opportunity to take the top sheet from the stack or a sweet from the pile. If the number of visitors meant that the stack reduced or the pile dwindled, they would be replenished by the gallery staff, although how frequently and to what extent this is done is up to the exhibitor. In effect, these works are endless and are not unique. Gonzalez-Torres asked, 'What is this thing? A two- or three-dimensional object? Is the work the certificate of authenticity or the piece itself?'[5] If you and I take a sweet and eat it, knowing that the invigilator has two replacements to put on the pile once we've gone, we quickly recognize that, as with Meireles's circulation of altered Coke bottles, to try and understand the work as an object is not the best approach. It is our individual enjoyment of the sweet as a moment of sharing in the work that is of importance.

'Untitled' (Portrait of Ross in L.A.) is a pile of Fruit Flasher candies heaped into a corner. Gonzalez-Torres was influenced by the simple, clear forms of minimalism, and the arrangement here is reminiscent of several American artists: the 1964 untitled triangular corner piece by Robert Morris, Lynda Benglis's 1969 post-minimal polyurethane foam *Quartered Meteor*, and Robert Smithson's shells in a mirrored corner titled *Mirror with Crushed Shells (Sanibel Island)*, from the same year. The sweets/candies, with their multicoloured wrappers, are a portrait of Gonzalez-Torres's partner Ross Laycock, who had been diagnosed with HIV in 1988 and died in 1991, the same year the portrait was made. The ideal weight of the candies for the work is 79 kilograms (175 pounds), the average weight of a healthy individual and one which Gonzalez-Torres also used elsewhere. While in this instance we can recognize the importance of the artist's own circumstances in the conception and realization of the work, this should not lead us to attribute any fixed meaning to it. Formed in the loving relationship between Laycock and Gonzalez-Torres, *'Untitled' (Portrait of Ross in L.A.)*, with its inevitable religious overtones of consubstantiation, offers a starting point for innumerable other experiences of personal connection and interconnection. In doing so, it both dissolves and re-establishes our frame of reference. Of this and other candy works, Gonzalez-Torres has said:

> *It's a metaphor. I'm not pretending it to be anything other than this … I'm giving you this sugary thing; you put it in your mouth and you suck on someone else's body. And in this way, my work becomes part of so many other people's bodies. It's very hot. For just a few seconds, I have put something sweet in someone's mouth and that is very sexy.*[6]

* When appearing in an English text, Gonzalez-Torres wished his name to be written without the diacritics that would be used in his native Cuba and other Spanish-speaking contexts.

BELOW: Felix Gonzalez-Torres, *'Untitled' (Portrait of Ross in LA)*, 1991. Candies in variously coloured wrappers, endless supply; variable dimensions; ideal weight 800 kg (175 lb). Installation view, The Art Institute of Chicago, 2010

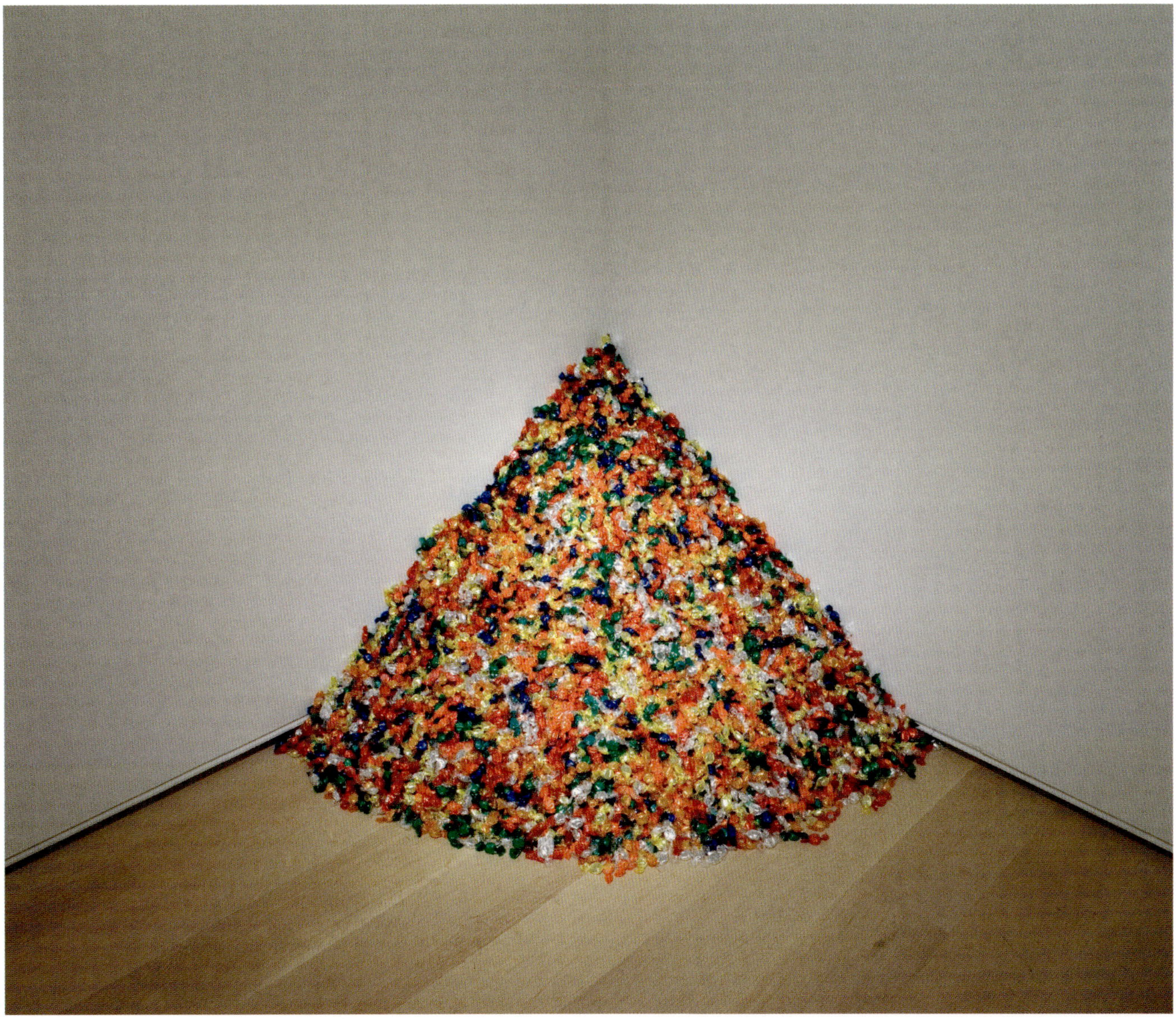

THE PEOPLE'S CHOICE

The American conceptual artist John Baldessari produced a number of canvases in the mid-1960s that contained only text, and one offered *Tips for Artists Who Want to Sell*. Rather than giving viewers what they want to see, it simply enumerates what it knows they would like. Among the things that sell are landscapes, marine pictures, flowers, animals and the Madonna and Child. In 1994, the Russian artists Vitaly Komar and Alexander Melamid undertook a more protracted investigation into what might please an audience, commissioning a marketing company to do a survey. Do people prefer outdoor or indoor scenes? Do they like animals and, if so, should they be wild or domesticated? What are their favourite colours? Do they want people in the scene? And so on.

Based upon the results of the survey, Komar and Melamid painted a scene titled *America's Most Wanted* containing all of the preferred elements in the appropriate proportions. It is a landscape with a meadow in the foreground, beyond which a lake stretches into the distance with hills descending towards the water from both sides. There are several trees, a stag and doe standing at the water's edge, a small group of people and, in the centre, the familiar figure of America's first president, George Washington. According to the survey, this composition contains just the right amount of everything that the majority of American people look for in a painting and can, therefore, be seen to constitute the country's most wanted work of art.

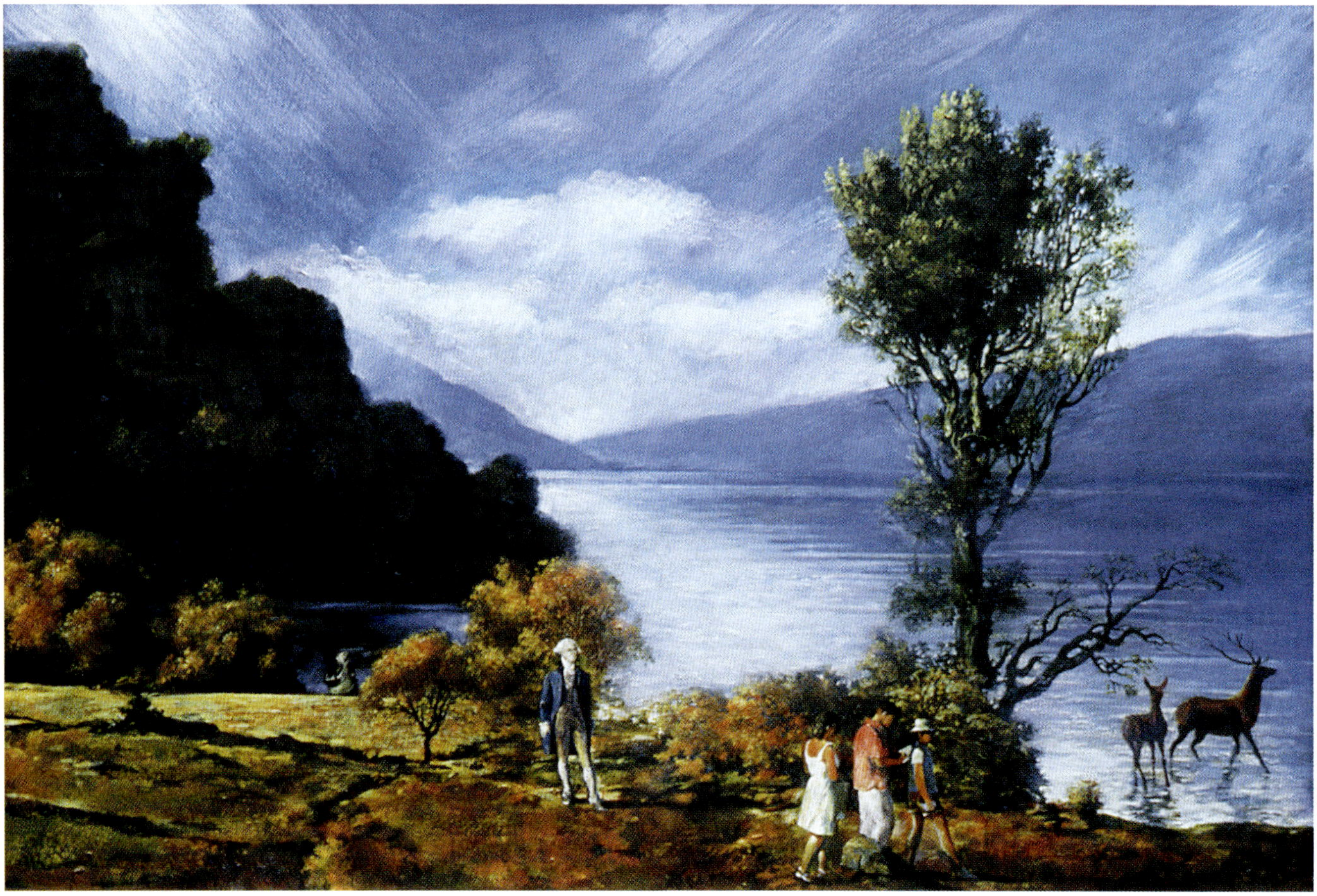

ABOVE: Komar and Melamid, *America's Most Wanted*, 1994. Oil and acrylic on canvas, 60.9 × 81.3 cm (24 × 32 in).

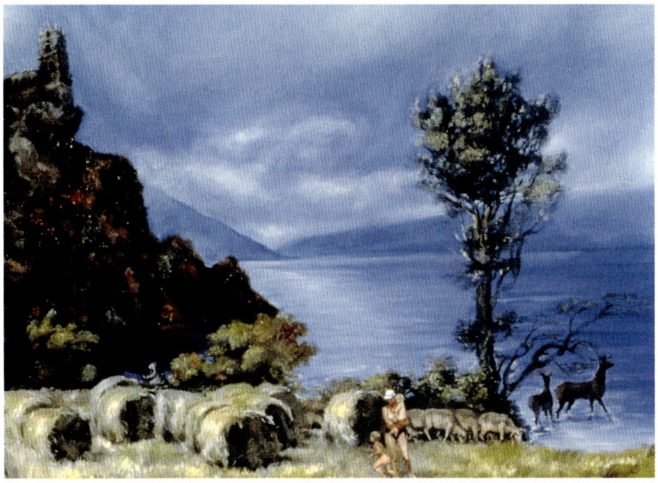

ABOVE: Komar and Melamid, *France's Most Wanted*, 1994. Oil and acrylic on canvas, 40.6 × 55. 9 cm (16 × 22 in).

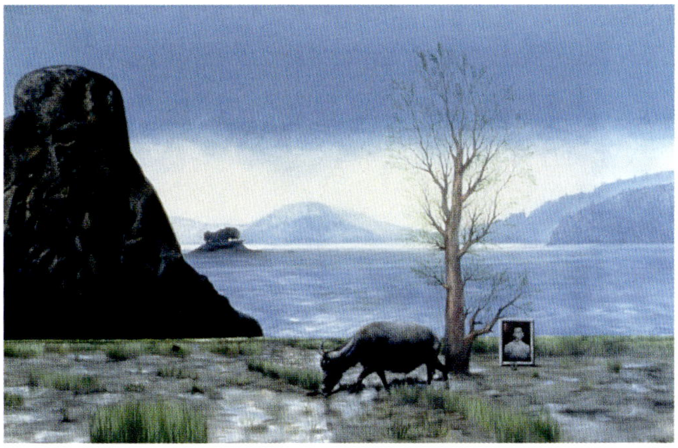

ABOVE: Komar and Melamid, *China's Most Wanted*, 1994. Oil and acrylic on canvas, 230 × 381 cm (90½ × 150 in).

The pair subsequently ran surveys in more than a dozen other countries and, regardless of the location, the results turned out to be surprisingly consistent. Several countries also favoured a national symbol, be it a flag or a founding political figure. With a few exceptions, the paintings are very much alike: a landscape with a roughly similar number of trees and the same ratio of land to water.

While the paintings in the series bear a strong similarity to second-hand shop pictures in a fake eighteenth-century style, the canvases only form part of the work. American art critic Arthur Danto wrote that Komar and Melamid's *America's Most Wanted* painting really must represent people who 'don't know much about art but know what they like'.[1] Despite the inclusion of all that people say they want, very few would actually choose to hang these paintings on the wall of their home. If you're looking for a landscape, you probably don't want, for example, George Washington stuck in the middle of it. Danto concluded his comments on the painting with the following:

> *As a painting it has no place in the art world at all. What does have a place in the art world is the performance piece by Komar and Melamid which consists in the opinion poll, the painting, the publicity, etc.*[2]

If we look for composition here, we must therefore find it in the overall performance, rather than the paintings themselves.

ARCHIVE

As we saw earlier, the new perspectives made possible as a result of the emerging technologies of the early twentieth century were quickly reflected in changes to compositional approach. Mass media, broadcasting and intercontinental communication make it seem as though it is possible to know all there is to know about what is happening in the world, and the arrival of digital media has exponentially increased this tendency towards feelings of omniscience.

The internet can bring everything to your fingertips, or at least it can appear to be that way. Artists have not been slow in using this vast store of information, or material, be it in visual, textual or auditory form. Something that was once obscure, or that would require a lot of time, energy and shoe leather to unearth, is now discoverable with comparatively little effort. Using the internet is now part of the air we breathe. It is not just a resource, an almost universal and infinite archive, but also part of the environment in which artists exist just as much as the art they make. Their work both draws upon and contributes to this archive. Questions of truth and accuracy are integral to this state of affairs. When men landed on the moon in 1969, no one questioned that they were there. It was only once the wherewithal to make more or less convincing mock-ups of the event arrived that we were given licence to doubt.

In 1999, the Lebanese artist Walid Raad instituted the Atlas Group, whose inception, membership and precise purpose he described slightly differently depending on the audience to whom he was speaking.[1] In reality, the group had no other member but himself and was a means to organize and frame the varied work he was making at that time. The majority of this material, notwithstanding its attribution to other, invented authors, was produced by Raad. It was all digitally rendered, so viewers would encounter the archive indirectly, or as slides in one of the lectures Raad gave as a representative of the group and its work. (In these lectures, incidentally, Raad was always honest about what was fabricated, and what was real.)

One fictional donor to the archive was the widow of historian Dr Fadl Fakhouri, who passed on 226 notebooks, 24 photographs and two 8mm films following her husband's death in 1993. The pages of *Notebook volume 72: Missing Lebanese Wars* each carry a newspaper cutting showing a photo-finish image taken at the Beirut racetrack. Around the clipping are notes, both in Arabic and English, giving information on the bets placed on that race by a group of Beirut historians along with some facts about the winner. The members of the betting circle, who were drawn from Lebanon's various political and religious groupings, were not betting on the race itself but on the distance between the horse's head and the finish line at the moment the photographer took his shot. Here, Eadweard Muybridge's galloping horses, triggering the camera shutter to reveal to us facts about the world that we cannot see (see pages 18–19), are reconfigured for changed circumstances and different times. In all of Fakhouri's photographs, the horse is never on the line but always just before or just past it.

As historians, those placing a wager know that history can never be written at the moment it occurs. Writing about events is always reflection or projection, but this is never to say that the historical account has no connection to truth. Think of the different versions of *The Execution of Emperor Maximilian* painted by the French artist Édouard Manet. As further news of the event in Mexico reached him in France, Manet adjusted his composition to take the new information into account. Nevertheless, the compositional structure common to all versions was borrowed from works by the Spanish painter Goya. Whichever version we look at, it is understood as a construction that, however fictional, aims at offering a truth about the real world. Neither Dr Fadl Fakhouri nor his widow existed, the group of friends with whom he visited the racetrack are imaginary, the bets were not placed, the notebook is a fabrication, the Atlas Group Archive is an invention, and yet it has a real, material existence as a meditation on truth and history.

OPPOSITE: Walid Raad / The Atlas Group, pages from *Notebook volume 72: Missing Lebanese Wars*, 2004. Archival inkjet print, each 111.8 × 127 cm (44 × 50 in).

1976–1983 / 2001
The Atlas Group

Description of the Winning Historian:

He could stand insults as long as they were couched in courteous terms

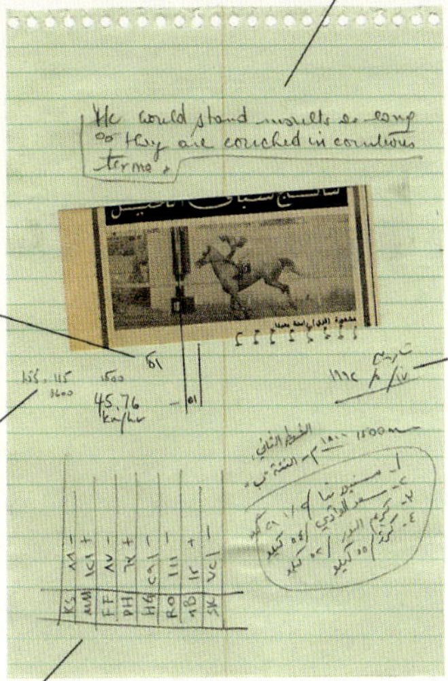

Distance Between Horse and Finish Line:

- 51

Date:

17 May 1992

Race Distance:

1500 m.

Winning Time:

1:55

Average Speed:

45.76 km/hr.

Historians' Initials and Bets:

1. KS -088
2. MM +121
3. FF +087
4. PH +063
5. HG -291
6. RO -111
7. AB +012
8. SK -721

1976–1983 / 2001
The Atlas Group

Description of the Winning Historian:

He is not merely miserable. He is brilliant at it. There seems no event, no matter how trivial that does not arouse him to a frenzy of self-mortification

Historians' Initials and Bets:

1. KS -717
2. MM +830
3. FF +729
4. PH -222
5. HG +311
6. RO +001
7. AB -921
8. SK -112

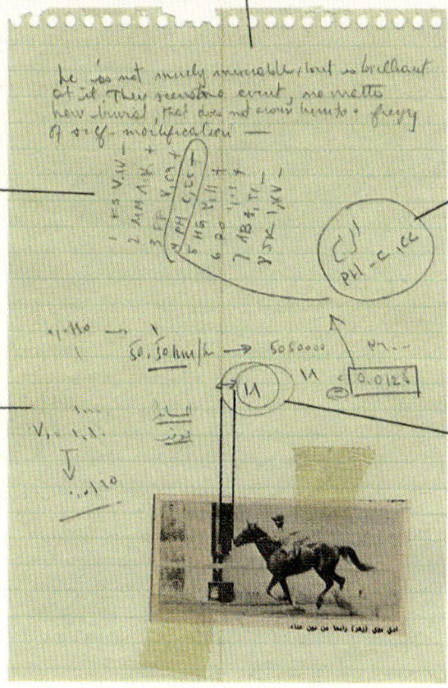

Winning Historian / Time:

PH - 222

Race Distance:

1000 m.

Winning Time:

1:10

Average Speed:

50.5 km/hr.

Distance Between Horse and Finish Line:

- 18

1976–1983 / 2001
The Atlas Group

Date:

7 June 1988

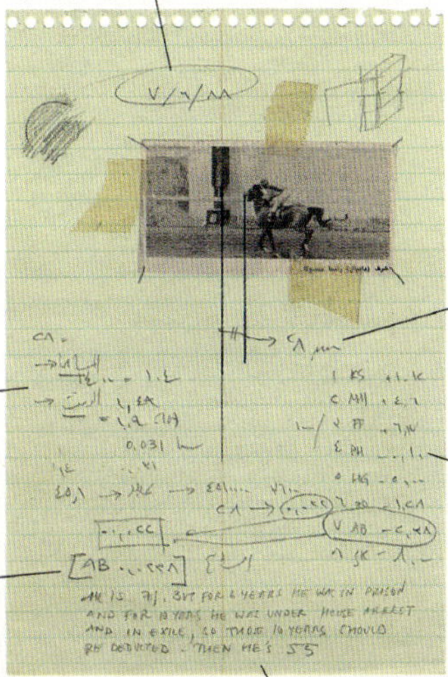

Distance Between Horse and Finish Line:

- 28

Race Distance:

1400 m.

Winning Time:

1:49

Average Speed:

45.1 km/hr.

Historians' Initials and Bets:

1. KS +112
2. MM +046
3. FF +618
4. PH -010
5. HG -500
6. RO -128
7. AB -238
8. SK -800

Winning Historian / Time:

AB - 23

Description of the Winning Historian:

He is 71. But for 6 years he was in prison and for 10 years he was under house arrest and in exile. So those 16 years should be deducted. Then he is 55

1976–1983 / 2001
The Atlas Group

Date:

25 November 1987

Historians' Initials and Bets:

1. KS +020
2. MM -310
3. FF +001
4. PH +023
5. HG -024
6. RO -117
7. AB -812
8. SK -091

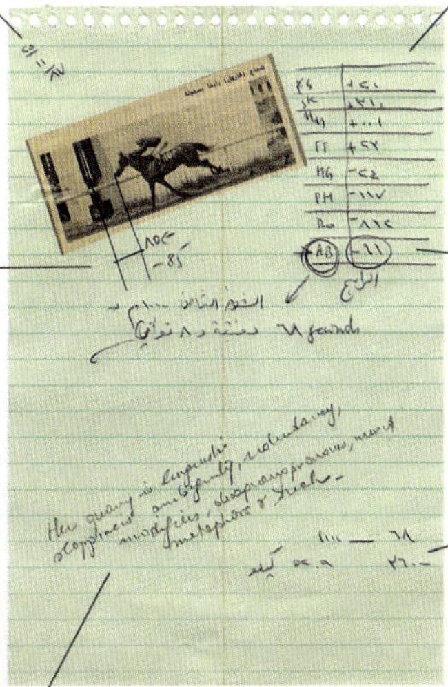

Distance Between Horse and Finish Line:

- 85

Winning Historian / Time:

AB - 91

Race Distance:

1000 m.

Winning Time:

1:08

Average Speed:

52.9 km/hr.

Description of the Winning Historian:

Her quarry is linguistic sloppiness, ambiguity, redundancy, modifiers, disagreeing pronouns, mixed metaphors and such

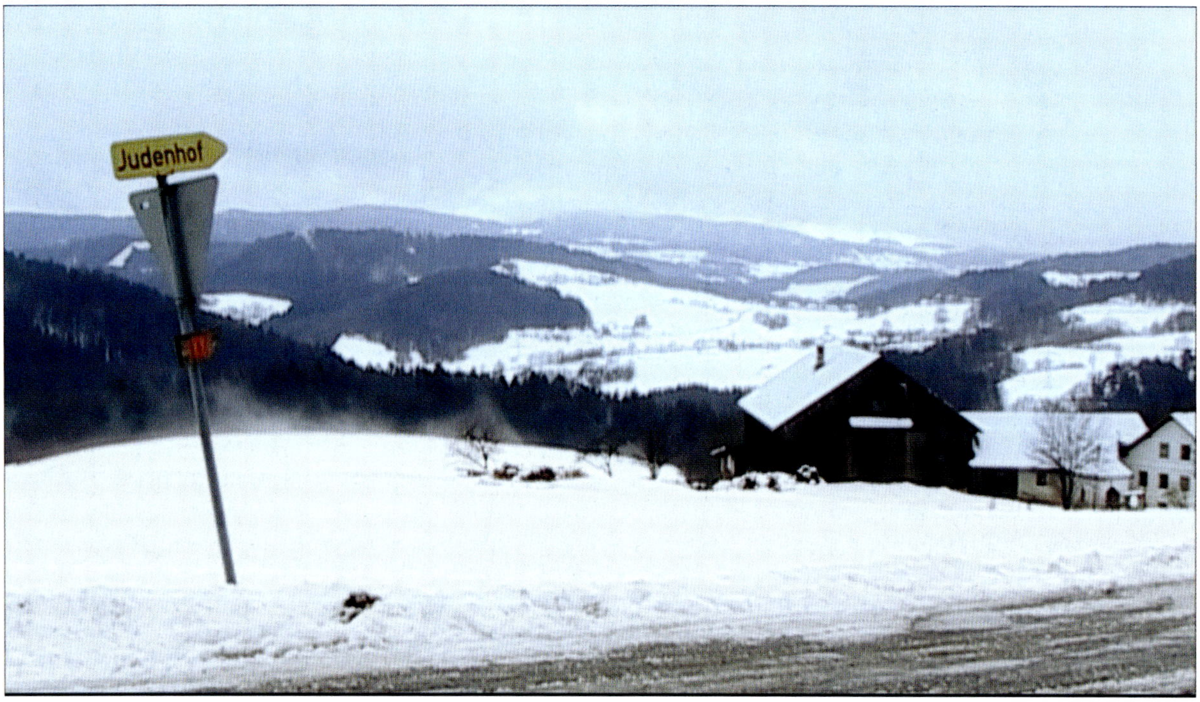

ABOVE: Susan Hiller, still from *The J. Street Project* (film), 2002–5. Single-channel film installation, colour, stereo sound, 67 min.

Exploring Berlin in 2002, at that time a city relatively unknown to her, the American artist Susan Hiller found herself on Judenstrasse. Her surprise at discovering a street still bearing the name of the community that the country had sought to systematically exterminate under the Nazi regime prompted the search for other examples across Germany. She found 303 streets, alleys, paths, and public areas beginning Juden-. These are not newly dedicated roads but ones that have either retained or reverted to their pre-war names. The group of works that came out of this research, *The J. Street Project*, is an archive of her findings, which constitutes, in Hiller's words, 'a commemoration of an absence'.[2] The material is presented in several ways: as 303 framed photographs, as a 67-minute video, as a wall display with a map of Germany marking each location and an alphabetical list of those locations, and, finally, as a book with a short text about the project along with the 303 photographs.

While the different works that constitute *The J. Street Project* could be understood as containing the same information, they each present it in a distinct way. The photographs are all portrait format and arranged alphabetically. As the format indicates, they are a roll-call of characters to be met with face to face. The video is shot in landscape format and has been edited according to the seasons in which the locations were filmed, and the lengths of clips varies depending on what was occurring when filming took place. On one occasion, we wait for the sun to fully set, on others for the hand on a clock above the street sign to click over to the next minute, for a chicken who begins crossing the road to reach the other side, and so on. Hiller described her research approach as 'cool',[3] and her ambition was simply to gather together a full list of German streets dedicated to Jews. There is no further investigation into the history of the places or of how they came to be named as they are. This coolness thus leaves it up to the viewer to construct their own emotional response. It might, of course, have been possible to include in the list those streets named after other related things, such as, for example, the synagogue. The important point for Hiller, however, was to see the work as 'a litany, a meditation',[4] and to invite the repetition of the word Juden over and over again. Such a litany can be experienced in the public space of the gallery or within the atmosphere of intimacy provided by the book.

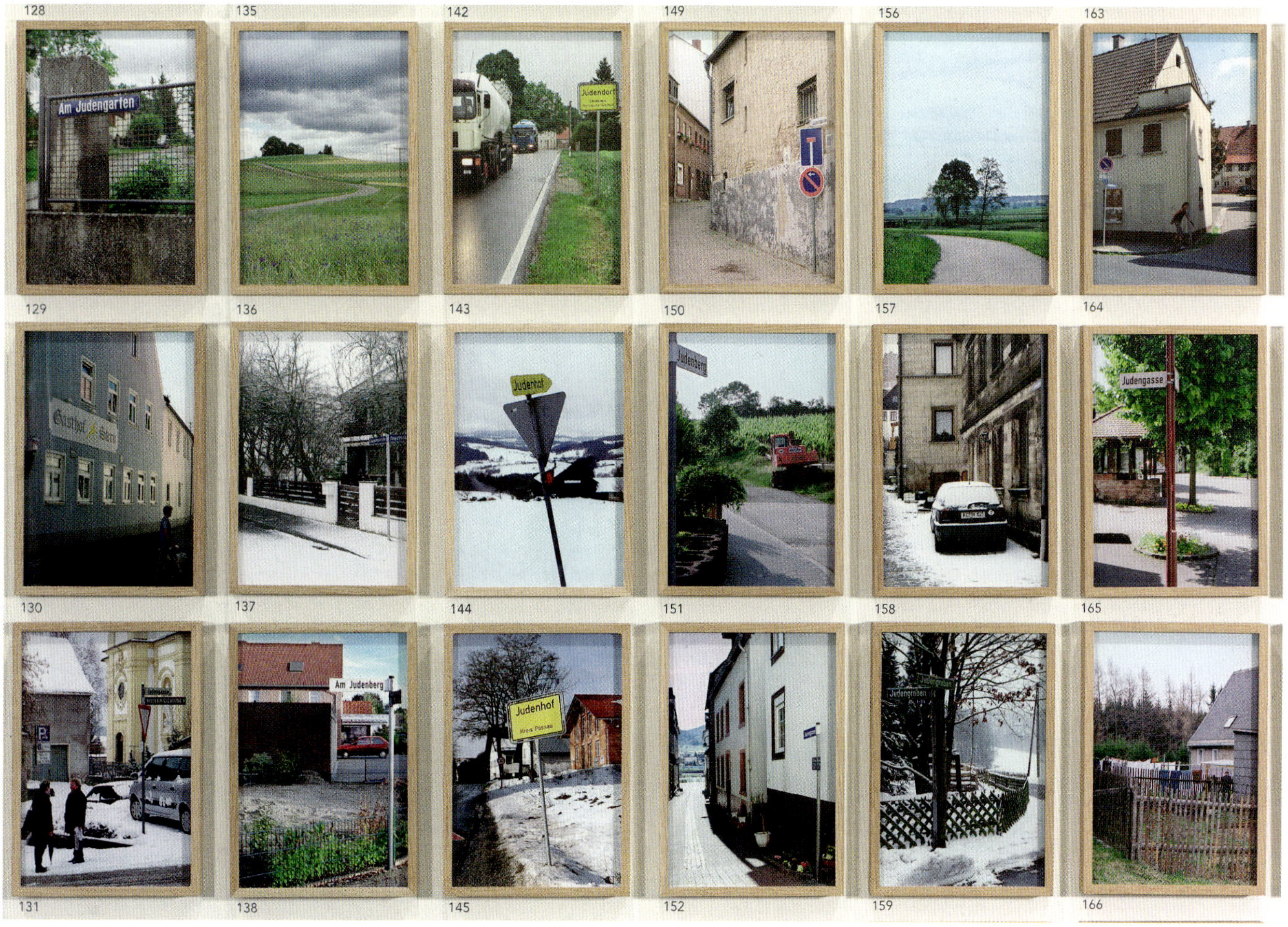

ABOVE: Susan Hiller, detail from *The J. Street Project* (index), 2002–5. Wall-based installation: 303 giclée prints mounted on Kapa Line foam board, oak frames, vinyl lettering for intrinsic list of locations and map, 197 × 1,000 cm (78 × 394 in).

HISTORY PAINTING

One significant point that all the works referred to in this book have in common is their collective rejection of the hierarchy of genres established by the French Academy of Painting and Sculpture and reinforced in its judgements throughout the seventeenth, eighteenth and early nineteenth centuries. The separation of paintings into distinct types, and the ranking of those types from still life – the least important – to landscape, genre (domestic scenes), and portraiture, to the most highly valued, history painting, was an expression not just of what was thought to matter in art but more broadly of social practices and ideas. The two most important types of painting – portraiture and history painting, the latter including religious and mythological themes – required an ability to render the human figure. This expertise could only be acquired by drawing the live model, and since women were essentially barred from attending such classes their output was forcibly restricted to the lesser categories.

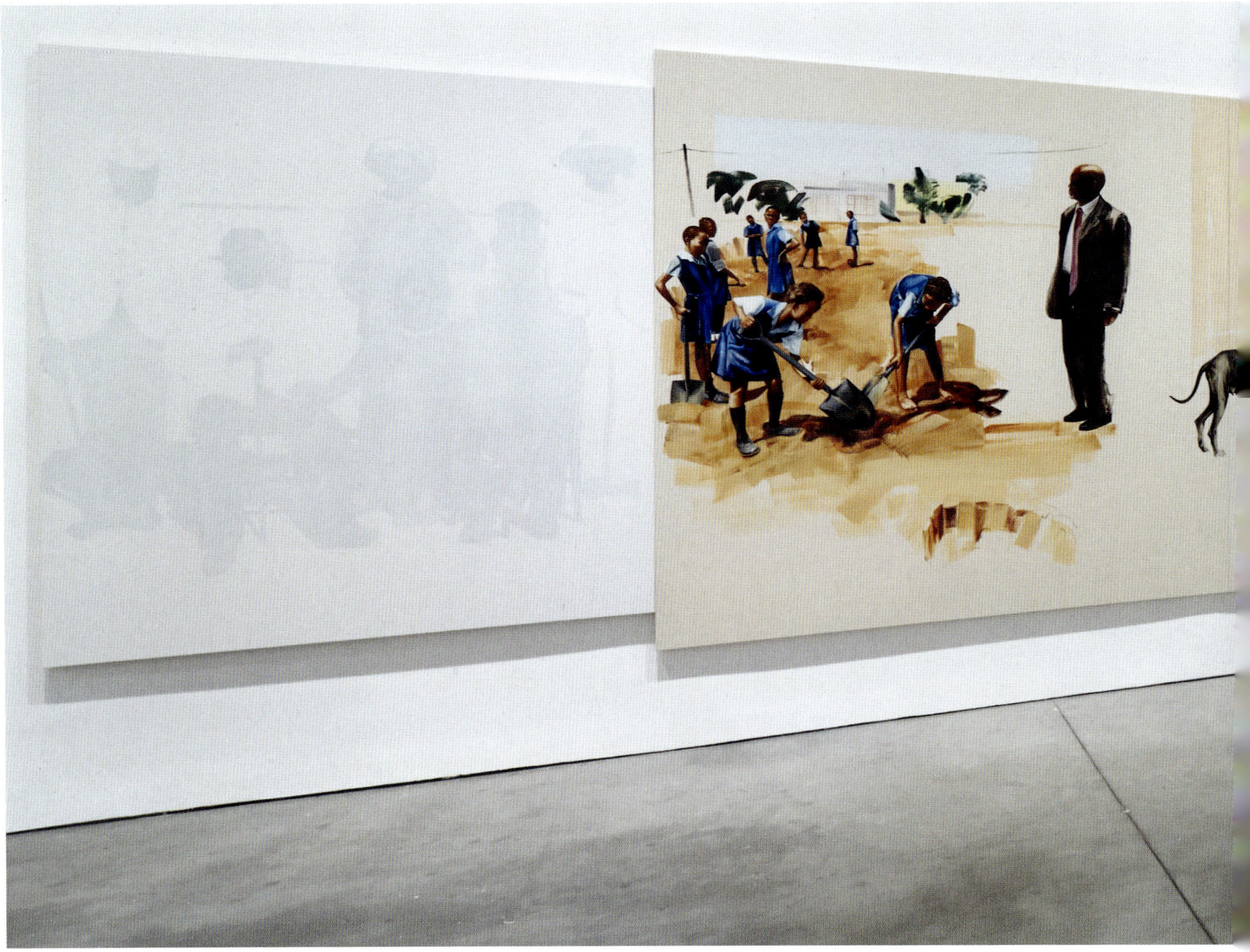

Despite the loosened grip of academic control, these categories have not disappeared but instead, as boundaries between the genres and their relative values have been eroded, they have become available for exploration. The Motswana painter Meleko Mokgosi, for example, made a conscious use of the traditional hierarchy in a multi-part project, *Democratic Intuition*, produced between 2013 and 2019. He has always considered himself to be a history painter, but at the same time he has asserted that, 'deviating from academic painting formulae was one of my primary goals'.[1] *Democratic Intuition* is composed in chapters, each of which is itself made up of several panels. His use of the term 'chapter' for each group of works refers less to literature than to the narrative structure of film; various images and texts, using differing scales, formats and techniques – painting, print, image transfer, etching – are brought together as a montage. The overall title is taken from the writing of the Indian critical theorist Gayatri Chakravorty Spivak on aesthetics and education in a world that promotes the universally desirable benefits of democracy. Spivak is perhaps best known for a 1988 essay that questions the extent to which those who are socially and politically marginalized are able to speak as and for themselves, to represent and be represented.[2] In speaking of *Democratic Intuition*, Mokgosi has drawn a simple equivalence between the political and artistic realms: democracy is about representation, and painting is about representation.[3]

BELOW: Meleko Mokgosi, *Democratic Intuition, Exordium*, 2013–present. Oil and charcoal on canvas, seven panels. Installation view, Jack Shaiman, New York.

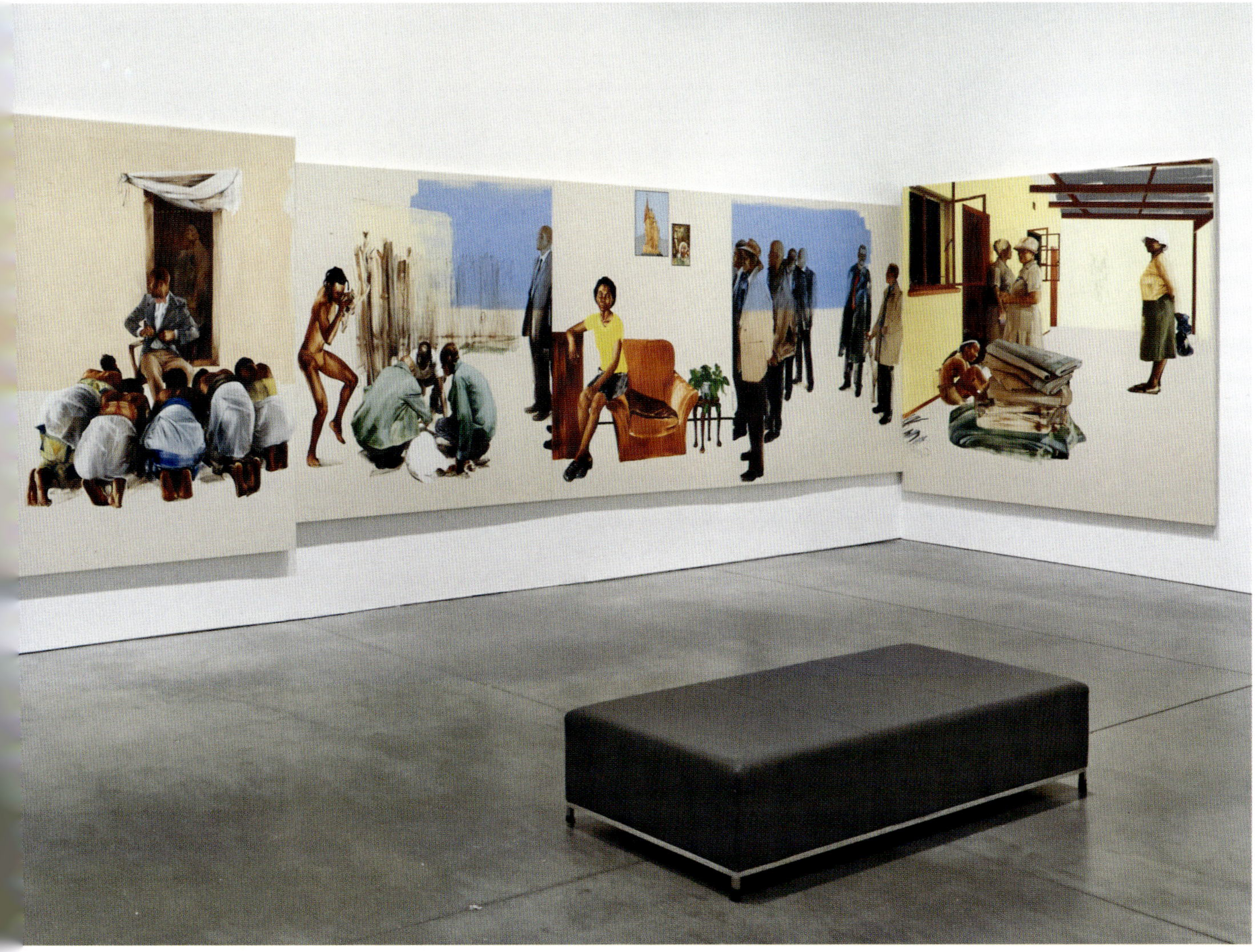

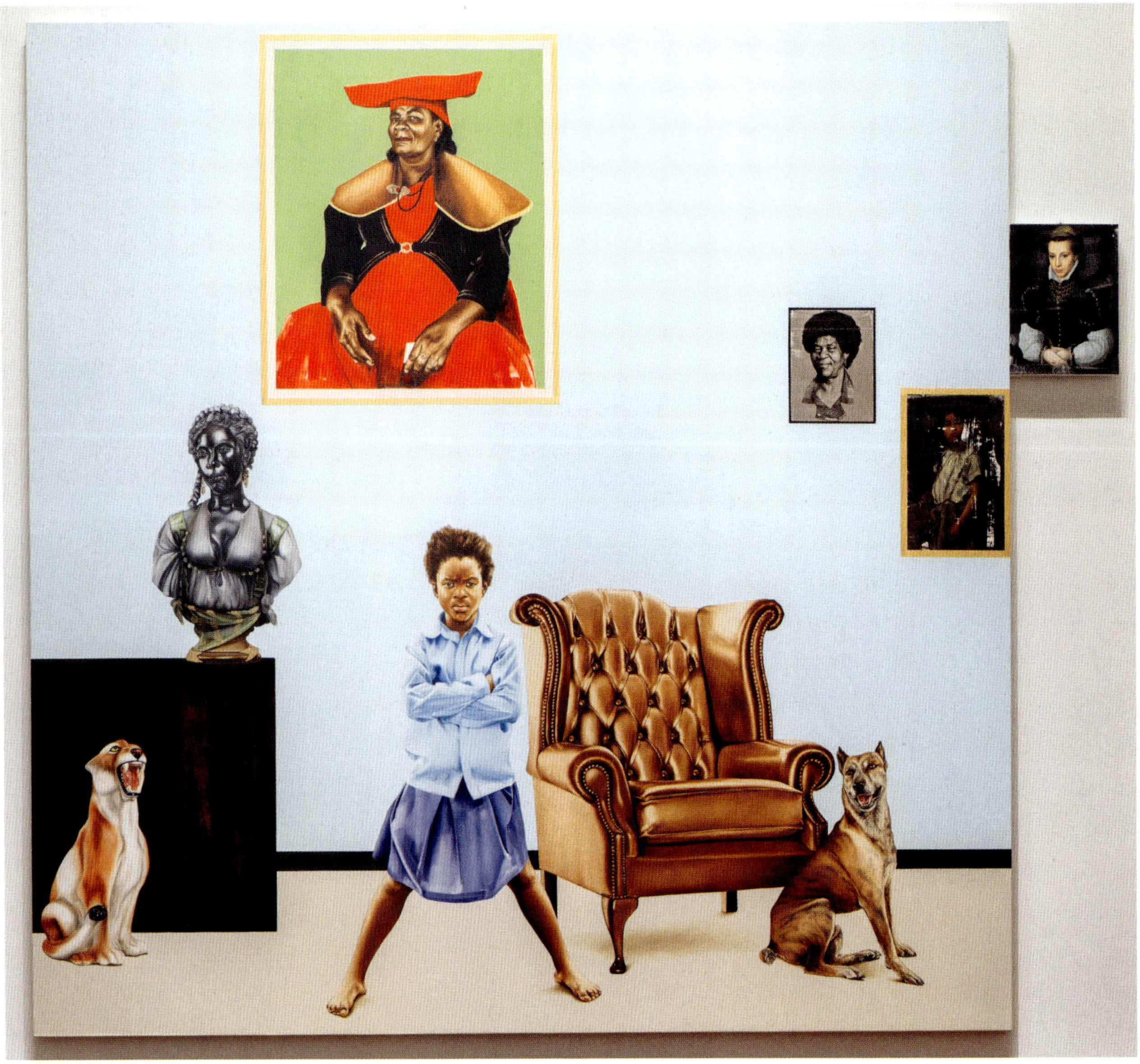

ABOVE: Meleko Mokgosi, *Acts of Resistance I*, 2018.
Oil on canvas, 274.3 × 274.3 × 5 cm (108 × 108 × 2 in).

What might such a gesture of defiance by one who is powerless signify?

The chapter titled *Acts of Resistance* was realized through working with the collections of the Baltimore Museum of Art. *Acts of Resistance I* incorporates explicit reference to two of the collection's paintings in particular. The first is *Little Gypsy*, the figure of a defiant gypsy girl painted by the nineteenth-century French artist Alfred Dehodencq. What might such a gesture of defiance by one who is powerless signify in a representation created by someone with considerably more power than the painting's subject? Second is the portrait of a young woman by the sixteenth-century Flemish artist Caterina van Hemessen. The portrait's subject is richly dressed, with decorative gold chains around her neck and waist. The museum's wall label described the chains with reference to fashion, but for Mokgosi, the chains stood more than anything as symbols of gendered social restrictions. Such restriction is reflected in van Hemessen's own life. She ceased making work upon marriage, but before that, echoing the innovation of Iaia of Cyzicus as recounted by Pliny, she had in 1548 painted what is recognized as the first self-portrait by an artist of either sex at work – a compositional approach hitherto unknown in the Renaissance.

The people featured in Mokgosi's paintings are Black, including among them recognizable figures from the political and cultural life of southern Africa. History painting constructs a narrative, an allegory that resonates with actions, events and attitudes at work in the world. One question Mokgosi has confronted in his compositions is how it might be possible to make such works when the overwhelming tendency among viewers is to see a person's colour – if they are not white – as the primary subject of the painting:

> *Representations of white subjects are seldom affected by the politics of whiteness because it is these very politics that have rendered the white subject universal and therefore not immediately subject to race discourse. What then can one make of representations that take the Black subject and render it within an allegorical context? Is it possible to overcome the baggage of Blackness when viewing and analyzing representation of a Black subject?*[4]

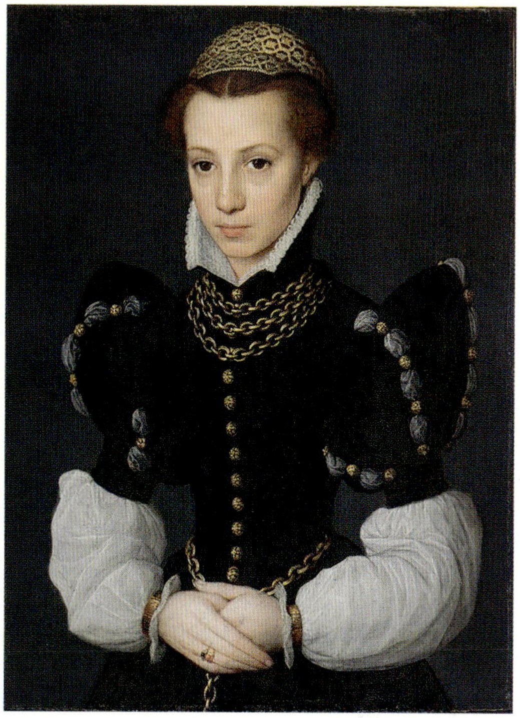

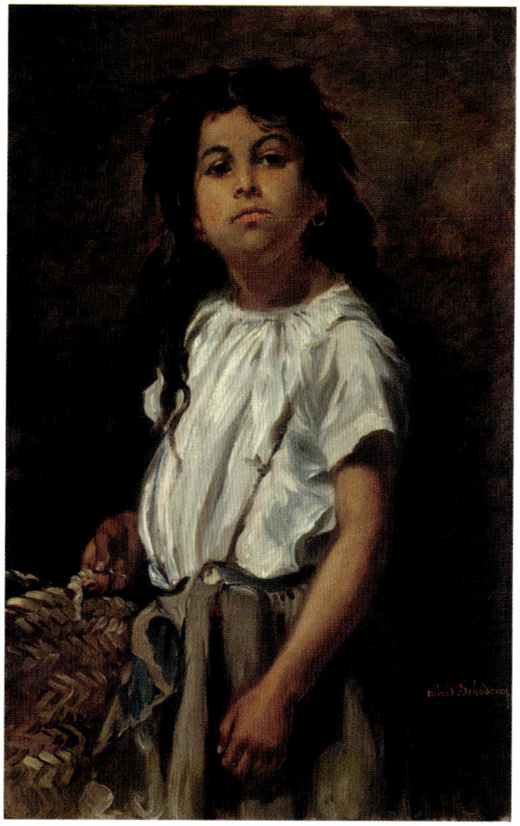

TOP RIGHT: Attributed to Catarina van Hemessen, *Portrait of a Young Lady*, 1560. Oil on panel, 30.4 × 22.9 cm (12 × 9 in).

BOTTOM RIGHT: Alfred Dehodencq, *Little Gypsy*, *c.*1850. Oil on canvas, 75.1 × 49.5 cm (29⅝ × 19½ in).

The usual way to model the volume of arms, legs and face would be through layers of paint, the lightest of which is uppermost in order to indicate how light is falling on the body and to define its contours. By contrast, Mokgosi has prepared his surfaces with a clear size and uses thin washes that allow the ground colour of the cotton duck canvas to show through. It is this ground, therefore, that provides the lightest tone to flesh built largely using raw sienna, burnt sienna, raw umber and burnt umber. Adding white paint would be a literal imposition of whiteness upon a Black body, and Mokgosi uses none in depicting his figures:

> *Defined loosely, highlights are the points at which light touches the surface of an object, therefore illuminating it and giving it visibility and form, rendering it legible to others. Here one can interpret 'light' as a metaphor connected to a specific politics; just as darkness is connected to the politics of blackness and the creation of the African savage in the race discourse.*[5]

Acts of Resistance IV is an elongated oval in which the central figure of a young girl in a shift dress relaxes on a settle. The dress is blue, the colour traditionally used for the Madonna's garments in paintings of religious subject matter. The girl's left hand hangs loosely from the arm resting on the settle arm, while in her right, although we cannot see it clearly because it is obscured by her fingers, she evidently holds a smartphone in the contents of whose screen she is thoroughly absorbed. A narrow chest of drawers standing against the wall to her left supports a television set. In contrast to the girl's smartphone, the television is old CRT technology. It is bulky and extends over the edges of the piece of furniture on which it sits. Another work in the museum's collection is a fifteenth-century tondo by the Italian painter Sandro Botticelli, *Madonna Adoring the Child with Five Angels*. In the Botticelli painting, all seven figures are white, epitomizing the accepted manner in which this and other biblical scenes have been depicted in Western art. The painting both exemplifies and reinforces a narrative structure and compositional approach that has, in Mokgosi's words, 'taught viewers to read spirituality and adoration in the specifics of a subject's gender and race'.[6] In *Acts of Resistance IV*, a small oval panel on the wall above the girl shows a mother and child. Her head is covered, as the Madonna's traditionally is, but also as one would habitually see on women in tropical and equatorial countries around the world. The woman and child in the panel are Black, but the shape of the panel, the format of the composition on it, and its position on the wall must leave us in no doubt that this is a Madonna and Child. This, too, is an image of spirituality and adoration.

Botticelli's composition is deconstructed and reconstituted in Mokgosi's painting. The black-and-white image on the television screen is a familiar photograph of Winnie Madikizela-Mandela, fist raised in defiant Black power salute, surrounded by African National Congress (ANC) supporters making the same gesture. Madikizela-Mandela is not captured head-on but from a vantage point slightly to her left, so that in Mokgosi's composition she appears to be looking out from the television screen directly towards the girl. There is thus a zig-zag line, a visual and temporal journey from the Madonna in the small oval looking lovingly at her child, down to Madikizela-Mandela looking out from Apartheid-era South Africa with passion and concern towards the girl who, in turn, is concentrating on the messages of today on her phone.

OPPOSITE: Meleko Mokgosi, *Acts of Resistance IV*, 2018. Oil on canvas, 209.5 × 122 × 3.8 cm (82½ × 48 × 1½ in).

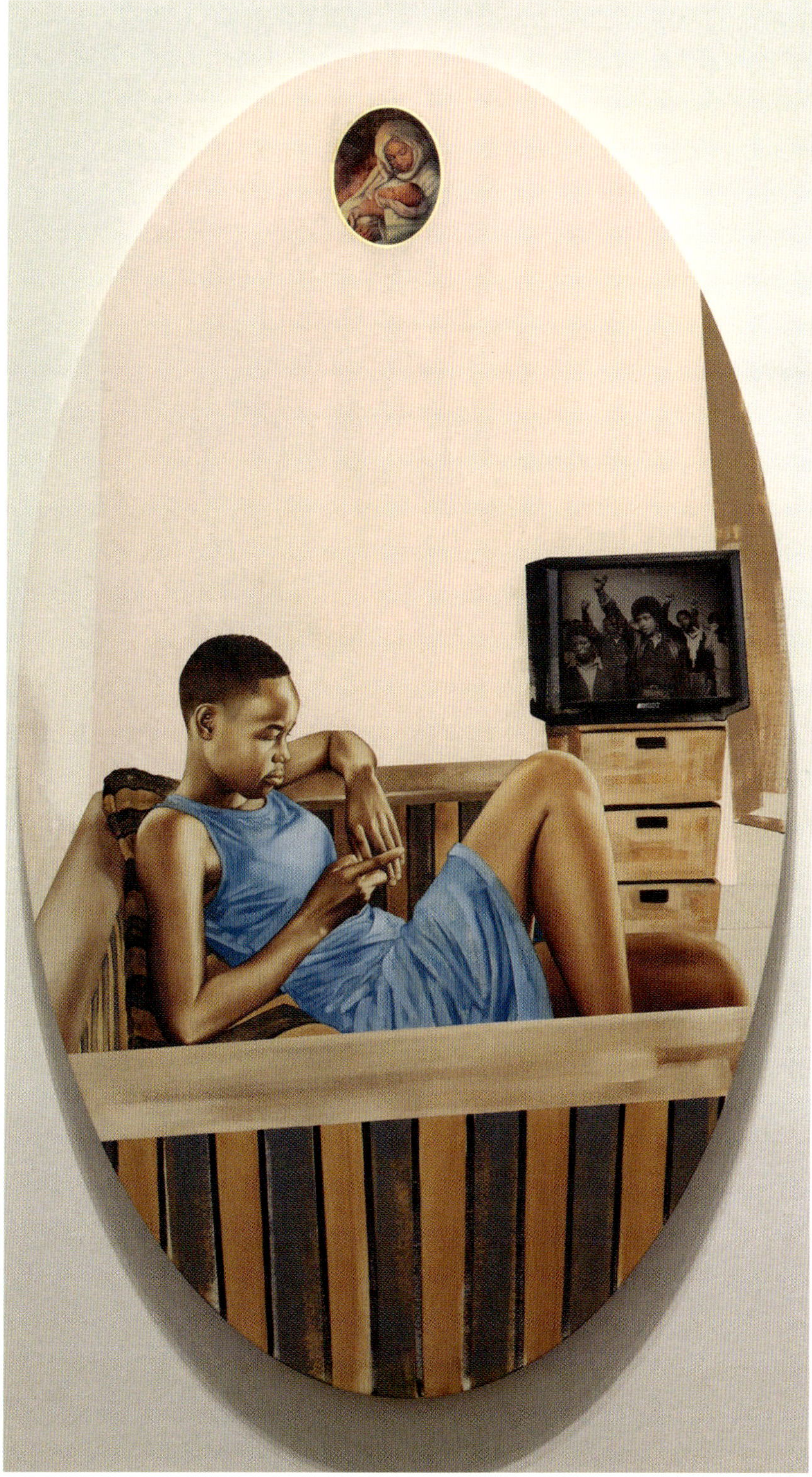

KEY MOVEMENTS

The movements mentioned in the course of this book are briefly summarized below, arranged in roughly chronological order. The list makes no pretence to being a comprehensive survey of the whole period – there are, of course, many other aspects of the art of the past century and a half that fall outside the theme under discussion here.

The sequence of styles reflects the persistent ambition to accommodate and express the experience of modernity. It does not continue beyond them into what we might think of now as the contemporary period – a period in which the rendering of material reality, everyday experience, knowledge, imagery and information into the zeroes and ones of the digital landscape constitutes a new kind of abstraction and dematerialization.

Realism

A movement in the mid-nineteenth century, especially in France, in which the traditional preference for historical, religious and mythological themes was rejected in favour of the natural treatment of scenes from ordinary life. Artists associated with the movement include Gustave Courbet, Jean-François Millet and Rosa Bonheur.

Impressionism

Impressionism continues the preference for the realistic treatment of contemporary experience. Artists focused on capturing the visual impression of a scene at a particular moment rather than on an analysis of its permanent features. The style takes its name from Claude Monet's painting of Le Havre, *Impression, Sunrise*, shown at the first impressionist exhibition in 1874. It was initially applied pejoratively – that is, the works of the impressionists, who included Monet, Pierre-Auguste Renoir, Alfred Sisley and Camille Pissarro – were criticized as providing only the impression of a painting rather than the real thing.

Symbolism

As much a tendency in the literary as the visual arts from the mid-1880s to 1910, symbolism used symbols as a means to suggest ideas and feelings. Odilon Redon saw 'suggestive art' as 'a method … which the imagination has liberated from those bothersome worries presented by the details of the exterior world in order to represent only imaginary objects'.[1] Themes of religious mysticism, decadence and eroticism featured in an approach that emphasized subjective over objective truth. Artists associated with the tendency included Edvard Munch, James Ensor, Ferdinand Hodler.

Synthetism

A style of painting closely related to symbolism and characterized by flat areas of colour, which are sometimes delineated by black lines. Synthetism is notably associated with the artists Paul Gauguin and Émile Bernard, in Pont Aven, Brittany, in the 1890s. Maurice Denis explained that 'to synthesize is not necessarily to simplify in the sense of suppressing certain parts of the object: it is to simplify in the sense of rendering intelligible'.[2]

Divisionism and Pointillism

A late nineteenth-century style of painting in which the paint is applied in adjacent areas of pure colour rather than being mixed on the palette, as in the work of Vincent van Gogh. Juxtaposed colours of differing hues create an optical vibration of greater intensity than if they had been mixed on the palette before application. Georges Seurat's approach, in which the colours were applied in small dots, is referred to as pointillism.

Fauvism

A style of painting developing from divisionism in which bold colour, freely handled, is of primary importance. Its name comes from a review of the 1905 Salon d'Automne in which a classically styled sculpture placed in a gallery of paintings by artists including Henri Matisse and André Derain was described by the critic Louis Vauxcelles as '*Donatello parmi les fauves*' (Donatello among the beasts).[3]

Cubism

Dispensing with any reliance on the spatial illusion created by perspective, cubism built the solidity of the three-dimensional world on the insistently two-dimensional surface of the canvas. Prizing Courbet's realism and Cézanne's modelling of form, Pablo Picasso and Georges Braque treated landscapes, figures and objects as a series of juxtaposed planes and surfaces aimed at giving a full sense of their material presence in space rather than a mere depiction of how they appear when seen from a single point of view. Cubism is usually divided into two phases: analytic, from 1907 to 1911, during which period it was sometimes difficult to distinguish between the work of the two artists, and synthetic, from 1912 to the outbreak of the Second World War. The second phase saw the introduction of lettering, collage and *papiers collés* (pasted paper). Despite the fractured nature of its imagery, the cubists considered themselves realists and did not see their innovations as a move towards abstraction. Besides the two main protagonists, Picasso and Braque, others included Juan Gris, Fernand Léger, Albert Gleizes and Jean Metzinger.

Simultanism

Associated with the cubists, though never fully in tune with their approach, Robert Delaunay developed his own style, to which he gave the name simultanism. The term is taken from the nineteenth-century work on the simultaneous contrast of colours in painting by Michel Eugène Chevreul.

Futurism

A movement concerned with the dynamism of the modern world, its motion, not least mechanical, and its swift pace. 'The Founding and Manifesto of Futurism', written by the poet F.T. Marinetti and published in the French newspaper *Le Figaro* in 1909, declares: 'We intend to exalt aggressive action … We affirm that the world's beauty has been enriched by a new beauty: the beauty of speed … Except in struggle there is no more beauty'.[4] Artists include Giacomo Balla, Umberto Boccioni, Gino Severini, Carlo Carrà, Luigi Russolo and Valentine de Saint-Point.

Expressionism

A movement primarily in German art in which form and colour are exaggerated or otherwise distorted to express an inner emotional state. Expressionism is associated with two distinct groups: the Dresden-based Brücke, formed in 1905 and including Ernst Ludwig Kirchner, Karl Schmidt-Rottluff, Erich Heckel and Fritz Bleyl, and based in Munich in 1912, the Blaue Reiter, including Wassily Kandinsky, Franz Marc, Gabriele Münter, and August Macke. Other closely associated figures include Edvard Munch, Oskar Kokoschka and Emil Nolde.

Dada

Dada was a deliberately meaningless word chosen to name a movement thoroughly opposed to the oppressive, murderous logic that led to the slaughter of the First World War. Techniques of chance, illogic and deliberate incoherence were used in the creation of work. Insofar as it rejected bourgeois norms and expectations, it could be understood as anti-art. The movement began in Zurich in 1916 at the Cabaret Voltaire, run by Hugo Ball and Emmy Hennings. Further centres of Dada activity, some more in alignment with revolutionary politics, others more freely anarchic, appeared in Berlin, Hamburg and elsewhere. Figures include Jean (Hans) Arp, Kurt Schwitters, Raoul Hausmann and Hannah Höch. Though not a part of any group, Marcel Duchamp and Man Ray are closely associated with the spirit of the dada movement.

Surrealism

A word originally coined by Guillaume Apollinaire in 1917, in his programme note to the Diaghilev ballet *Parade*, with music by Erik Satie and costumes by Picasso, and which he saw as moving beyond the 'realism' of cubism. The term was adopted by André Breton to name the literary and artistic movement that succeeded dada, carrying on the earlier movement's use of chance and irrationality. In his 1924 'Manifesto of Surrealism', Breton wrote that experience 'has found itself increasingly circumscribed. It paces back and forth in a cage from which it is more and more difficult to make it emerge.'[5] He placed great weight on psychoanalyst Sigmund Freud's analysis of dreams as offering the best means of escape from the cage, since 'the mind of the man who dreams is fully satisfied by what happens to him'.[6] Surrealism is defined in the manifesto as 'psychic automatism in its pure state',[7] which is to say, action free from guidance by conscious thought. Artists include Max Ernst, André Masson and Salvador Dalí.

De Stijl

A group of Dutch artists, designers and architects who aimed to discover 'a perfect equilibrium of artistic relationships' in which all could participate,[8] and who initially adhered to the principles of neo-plasticism as outlined by Piet Mondrian in his writings.

Mondrian wrote: 'Art makes us realize that there are fixed laws which govern and point to the use of the constructive elements, of the composition and of the inherent interrelationships between them. These laws may be regarded as subsidiary laws to the fundamental law of equivalence which creates dynamic equilibrium and reveals the true content of reality.'[9] A journal of the same name was founded in 1917 by Theo van Doesburg and Mondrian. Mondrian distanced himself as Van Doesburg broadened the scope, both of the group's principles – for example, he introduced diagonal lines into his designs – and the journal's content, which included contributions from dadaists such as Arp, Schwitters and Tristan Tzara.

Suprematism

The term used by Kazymyr Malevych for his style of non-objective painting from 1915 onwards, in which he avoided representation in favour of composition using basic geometrical forms and a narrow range of unmodulated colour. 'To the suprematist', according to Malevych, 'the visual phenomena of the objective world are, in themselves, meaningless; the significant thing is feeling, as such, quite apart from the environment in which it is called forth.'[10]

Constructivism

A movement in Russia which, unlike Malevych's more detached stance, saw possibility in the application of the principles of abstract composition to the task of design and production in the post-revolutionary society. Brothers Antoine Pevsner and Naum Gabo wrote in their 'Realistic Manifesto' (1920):

> *The blossoming of a new culture and a new civilization with their unprecedented-in-history surge of the masses towards the possession of the riches of Nature, a surge which binds the people into one union, and last, not least, the war and the revolution (those purifying torrents of the coming epoch), have made us face the fact of new forms of life, already born and active ... The distracted world of the cubists, broken in shreds by their logical anarchy, cannot satisfy us who have already accomplished the Revolution or who are already constructing and building up anew.*[11]

Abstract expressionism

Term applied to the usually large-scale gestural painting in the United States, especially New York, in the 1940s and 1950s. Used in particular with reference to Jackson Pollock, Willem de Kooning and those associated with them. It was further characterized by art critics Harold Rosenberg, who used the term 'action painting',[12] and Clement Greenberg, who wrote of 'American-type painting'.[13] A related term, colour field painting, was more commonly applied to the work of Barnett Newman, Mark Rothko and Clyfford Still. Rosenberg described the abstract expressionist painting as an event rather than an object. This conception of the artwork would become increasingly prevalent in the subsequent decades.

Post-painterly abstraction

A term coined in 1964 by Clement Greenberg in reference to the large, flat areas of unmodulated colour, notably in the works of Ellsworth Kelly, Kenneth Noland, Jules Olitski and Morris Louis. As the term suggests, it signalled a turning away from the gestural marks of abstract expressionism that were coming to be seen, in themselves, as tokens of emotional engagement.

Pop art

A term coined by art critic Lawrence Alloway who, along with Richard Hamilton and Eduardo Paolozzi, was part of the Independent Group in Britain in the mid-1950s exploring the impact of mass cultural forms on the arts. Other key British figures were Peter Blake and Pauline Boty. Subsequently, and perhaps more recognizably, it was applied to work in the United States in the early 1960s by Andy Warhol, James Rosenquist, Roy Lichtenstein, Tom Wesselmann and others who similarly used mass-cultural imagery in their paintings. A parallel phenomenon in Germany, involving painters Gerhard Richter and Sigmar Polke, together with dealer Konrad Fischer, was called capitalist realism.

Minimalism

Work using one or few basic forms so that attention can be focused on the unity of the overall work and its relation to its surrounding space and to the viewer. Traditional notions of composition, which prioritize the arrangements of parts within an overall frame, are inadequate for such work. Its invitation to the viewer is to consider factors outside the 'frame' of the art object, which led to it being termed 'theatrical'. Also called primary structures, and ABC art, the term minimal, generally disliked by those artists associated with the style, was a disparaging one used by the philosopher Richard Wollheim to indicate his belief that such work had minimal art-content.[14] The three key texts on minimalism – Donald Judd's 'Specific Objects', Robert Morris's 'Notes on Sculpture', and Michael Fried's 'Art and Objecthood' – were published in 1965, 1966 and 1967, respectively.

Op art

An abbreviation of optical art, a type of abstraction, so called in respect of its use of line, shape and colour to engender optical effects such as flickering, pulsating and the illusion of movement. The style, which was given its name on the occasion of the 1965 *The Responsive Eye* exhibition at the Museum of Modern Art, New York, is most closely identified with Victor Vasarely and the early work of Bridget Riley.

Conceptualism

A tendency first defined by American philospher and artist Henry Flynt in 1961 as that art 'of which the material is "concepts"'.[15] Rejecting the presumption that art can be identified with certain kinds of object – paintings and sculptures – conceptualism was concerned with questioning what art is or could be. There is no signature style, though art critic Tony Godfrey identified four common forms:

> *A readymade, a term invented by Marcel Duchamp for an object from the outside world which is claimed or proposed as art, thus denying both the uniqueness of the art object and the necessity for the artist's hand; an intervention, in which some image, text or thing is placed in an unexpected context, thus drawing attention to that context: e.g. the museum or the street; documentation, where the actual work, concept or action, can only be presented by the evidence of notes, maps, charts or, most frequently, photographs; or words, where the concept, proposition or investigation is presented in the form of language.*[16]

Conceptualism's ephemeral, easily distributable nature encouraged the notion that the work of art was becoming dematerialized. Key figures include Sol LeWitt, Joseph Kosuth, Christine Kozlov, Adrian Piper and Robert Barry in the United States, and Art & Language in Britain. It has since become widely used to describe any work that does not conform to the traditional ideas of painting and sculpture.

Postmodernism

A term first used of the work of Robert Rauschenberg by the American art critic Leo Steinberg in 1961,[17] but which enjoyed widespread use from the mid-1970s through the 1980s, not least as a means to acknowledge that the succession of styles, tendencies and movements from realism through to post-painterly abstraction had run its course. Part of what held all those previous moments together was an underlying sense of progress rooted in Western colonial thought and practice, with each style being understood as drawing on and building upon its predecessor in the creation of something new and original. Constant circulation of images within an increasingly sophisticated and all-encompassing media landscape led French philosopher Jean Baudrillard to speak of the 'simulacrum', an image for which no original could be identified.[18] Originality ceased to be a prized quality, and all visual and material forms were considered available to be appropriated and recontextualized without needing to make reference to any earlier appearance or to any significance it may have had at that time. Neo-expressionism in Germany is one instance of such reappropriation and recontextualization.

NOTES

Two helpful sourcebooks gather together many writings by artists, critics and theorists from throughout the period under discussion here: *Theories of Modern Art: A Source Book by Artists and Critics*, Herschel B. Chipp with Contributions by Peter Selz and Joshua C. Taylor, University of California Press; and *Art in Theory: An Anthology of Changing Ideas 1900–2000*, edited by Charles Harrison and Paul Wood, Blackwell. In the notes that follow, references to documents reprinted in these sourcebooks will be given as Chipp, and Harrison and Wood, respectively, together with the relevant page number.

6 Introduction

1. Ad Reinhardt, 'How to Look at Space', *Arts and Architecture*, January 1947, p 23.
2. Virgil, *The Aeneid*, Book 1, ll. 455–61; trans. C Day Lewis, Oxford University Press, Oxford, 1986, p 20.
3. Charles Bouleau, *The Painter's Secret Geometry: A Study of Composition in Art, with a Preface by Jacques Villon*, Dover Publications, Mineola, NY, 2014, p 6.
4. Alois Riegl, 'The Main Characteristics of the Late Roman *Kunstwollen*', *The Vienna School Reader: Politics and Art Historical Method in the 1930s*, ed. Christopher S Wood, Zone Books, New York, 2000, pp 87–9.
5. Bouleau, op. cit., p 40.
6. Erwin Panofsky, *Perspective as Symbolic Form*, trans. Christopher S Wood, Zone Books, New York, 1991, p 28.
7. Giorgio Vasari, *Lives of the Artists*, trans. George Bull, Penguin, Harmondsworth, 1987, vol. I, p 191.
8. Bouleau, op. cit., p 31.
9. Leon Battista Alberti, *On Painting*, trans. with an Introduction and Notes by John R Spencer, Yale University Press, New Haven, CT, and London, 1966, p 68.
10. Ibid. p 72.
11. Ibid.
12. Pliny the Elder, *The Natural History*, Book 35, Chapter 36: Artists Who Painted with the Pencil. Available at: https://www.perseus.tufts.edu/hopper/text?doc=Perseus%3Atext%3A1999.02.0137%3Abook%3D35%3Achapter%3D36
13. Pliny the Elder, *The Natural History*, Book 35, Chapter 40. Available at: https://www.perseus.tufts.edu/hopper/text?doc=Perseus%3Atext%3A1999.02.0137%3Abook%3D35%3Achapter%3D40
14. Gertrude Stein, 'Composition as Explanation', *Look at Me Now and Here I Am: Writings and Lectures 1911–45*, ed. Patricia Meyerowitz, Penguin, Harmondsworth, 1971, p 24.
15. Charles Baudelaire, 'Le Peintre de la vie moderne', *Le Figaro*, 26 November, 29 November and 3 December 1863. 'The Painter of Modern Life', in Baudelaire, *The Painter of Modern Life and Other Essays*, trans. and ed. Jonathan Mayne, Phaidon, London, 1995, pp 1–40.
16. Clement Greenberg, 'Abstract, Representational and So Forth', *Art and Culture: Critical Essays*, Beacon Press, Boston, 1989, p 136.
17. Leo Steinberg, 'Other Criteria', *Other Criteria: Confrontations with Twentieth-Century Art*, Oxford University Press, London, Oxford and New York, 1972, pp 73–4.
18. Ibid. p 88.
19. Lawrence Alloway, 'The Arts and the Mass Media', *Architectural Design*, February 1958, in Charles Harrison and Paul Wood, eds, *Art in Theory 1900–1990: An Anthology of Changing Ideas*, Blackwell, Oxford and Cambridge, MA, 1992, p 701. Alloway also quotes himself in 'The Development of British Pop', in Lucy R Lippard et al., *Pop Art*, Thames & Hudson, London, 1970, p 36.
20. Joseph Kosuth, 'Art after Philosophy, Part I', *Studio International*, vol. 178 no. 915, October 1969; reprinted in Kosuth, *Art after Philosophy and After: Collected Writings, 1966–1990*, MIT Press, Cambridge, MA, and London, 1991, p 18. Kosuth is here quoting himself from an auto-interview conducted as 'Arthur R Rose', in 'Four Interviews', *Arts Magazine*, vol. 43 no. 4, February 1969, p 23.
21. Jean-François Lyotard, 'Section 2 – The Problem: Legitimation', *The Postmodern Condition: A Report on Knowledge*, trans. Geoff Bennington and Brian Massumi, Manchester University Press, Manchester, 1984, p 6.
22. Terry Smith, *The Contemporary Condition: The Contemporary Composition*, Sternberg Press, Berlin, 2016, p 22.

18 CHAPTER I: A NEW VISION

1. Said by a character in *Le Petit Soldat*, dir. Jean-Luc Godard, 1960.

20 The Burial of Romanticism

1. Quoted by Georges Riat, *Gustave Courbet, Peintre*, Paris, 1906, cited by Alan Bowness in *Gustave Courbet*, Bowness et al., exh. cat., Royal Academy of Arts, London, 1978, p 15.
2. Quoted by Alan Bowness in his introductory essay to *Courbet*, exh. cat., Arts Council of Great Britain, London, 1978, p 15, citing Georges Riat, *Gustave Courbet: Peintre, Floury*, 1906, vol. 2, pp 86–7.
3. Quoted Bowness, op. cit., p. 15, citing Riat, op. cit., vol. 3, p 191.

24 The Impact of the Camera

1. Karl Marx and Friedrich Engels, 'Manifesto of the Communist Party', in Karl Marx, *The Revolutions of 1848: Political Writings Vol. 1*, ed. David Fernbach, Penguin/New Left Review, Harmondsworth, 1973, p 70.
2. Baudelaire, 'The Painter of Modern Life', p 13.
3. Ibid. p 9.
4. Ibid.
5. Walter Benjamin, 'The Work of Art in the Age of Its Technological Reproducibility', in *Selected Writings Volume 4: 1938–1940*, trans. Edmund

Jephcott et al., and ed. Howard Eland and Michael Jennings, Belknap Press of Harvard University Press, Cambridge, MA, and London, 2003, p 263.

6. Richard Kostelanetz and John Cage, 'The Aesthetics of John Cage: A Composite Interview', *The Kenyon Review*, vol. 9 no. 4 (Fall 1987), p 106.

28 Attention

1. Jules-Antoine Castagnary's review of the 1879 Salon in Siècle, quoted in Jonathan Crary, *Suspensions of Perception: Attention, Spectacle, and Modern Culture*, MIT Press, Cambridge, MA, 2001, p 90.
2. Ibid. p 126.

32 The Third Dimension

1. From John Ruskin, *The Cestus of Aglaia*, ch. 1, excerpted under the title, 'The Tenth Muse', in Humphrey Jennings, *Pandaemonium 1660–1886: The Coming of the Machine as Seen by Contemporary Observers*, Picador, London, 1987, p 305.
2. Linda Nochlin, *The Body in Pieces: The Fragment as a Metaphor of Modernity*, the Walter Neurath Memorial Lecture 1994, Thames & Hudson, London and New York, 1994, p 25.
3. Ibid. p 26.
4. Quoted in Charles Stuckey, 'The Predications and Implications of Monet's Series', *The Repeating Image: Multiples in French Painting from David to Matisse*, ed. Erik Khang, exh. cat., Walters Art Museum, Baltimore, MD, 2007, p 92.
5. Ibid. p 83.

36 *Ukiyo-e*: The Influence of Japan

1. Quoted in Lionel Lambourne, *Japonisme*, Phaidon, New York, 2005, p 34.
2. Quoted in ibid.
3. Hugh Honour and John Fleming, with additional material by Michael Archer, *A World History of Art*, Laurence King, London, 2009, p 712.
4. Vincent van Gogh, letter to Theo van Gogh, October 1888, in Herschel B. Chipp, *Theories of Modern Art: A Sourcebook by Artists and Critics*, University of California Press, Berkeley, Los Angeles and London, 1973, p 39.
5. Quoted in Honour and Fleming, loc. cit., p 712.
6. Vincent van Gogh, letter to Theo van Gogh, October 1888, in Chipp, p 41.
7. Ibid. p 40: 'This time it's just simply my bedroom, only here colour is to do everything …'
8. Frank Getlein, *Mary Cassatt*, Abbeville Press, New York, 1980, p 100.
9. Griselda Pollock, *Mary Cassatt*, Jupiter Books, London, 1980, p 71.

42 Dream and Symbol

1. Paul Gauguin, Letter to Émile Bernard, November 1888, in Chipp, p 60.
2. Paul Gauguin, Letter to Émile Schuffenecker, August 1888, in Chipp, p 60.
3. Paul Gauguin, 'Diverses choses 1896–1897', unpublished notebook excerpted in Chipp, p 65.
4. André Fontainas, review of Gauguin's exhibition and his painting *Whence do we come? What are we? Where are we going?* in *Mercure de France*, XXIX (January–March 1899), English translation from Paul Gauguin, *Letters to Ambroise Vollard and André Fontainas*, ed. John Rewald, Grabhorn, San Francisco, 1943, reprinted in Chipp, p 73.
5. Jean Moréas, 'Manifeste du symbolisme', *Le Figaro*, 18 September 1886. Translation available at https://www.poetryintranslation.com/PITBR/French/MoreasManifesto.php.
6. Paul Gauguin, letter to André Fontainas in response to his review in *Mercure de France*, in Harrison and Wood, p 25.
7. Charles Baudelaire, 'Correspondances', in *Charles Baudelaire: Selected Poems*, Penguin, Harmondsworth, p 41.

44 Expression

1. Anna McNay, 'Paula Modersohn-Becker: An Intensely Artistic Eye', a review of the exhibition at the Musée d'Art moderne de la Ville de Paris, 8 April–21 August 2016, *Studio International*, August 2016.
2. Modersohn-Becker quoted in ibid.
3. Rainer Maria Rilke, 'For a Friend', in *Selected Works, Volume II: Poetry*, trans. J B Leishman, The Hogarth Press, London, 1976, p 200.
4. Frank Whitford, *Expressionist Portraits*, Thames & Hudson, London, 1987, p 36.
5. Friedrich Nietzsche, *Thus Spoke Zarathustra*, trans. with an introduction by R J Hollingdale, Penguin, Harmondsworth, 1969, pp 43–4.
6. Ibid.
7. *'Primitivism' and Modern Art: Affinities of the Tribal and the Modern*, ed. William Rubin. exh. cat., New York, Museum of Modern Art.
8. Ernst Ludwig Kirchner, 'Programme of Die Brücke', in Harrison and Wood, pp 67–8.

50 Optical Colour

1. Guillaume Apollinaire, *Les Peintres cubistes*, Paris, 1913, in Chipp, pp 235–6. This is in the section on Jean Metzinger, whose opening paragraphs were adapted from Apollinaire's review of Paul Signac's *D'Eugène Delacroix au néoimpressionisme* in *L'Intransigéant*, 7 August 1911. It is also in Guillaume Apollinaire, *Apollinaire on Art: Essays and Reviews, 1902–1918*, Thames & Hudson, London, 1972.
2. Michel Eugène Chevreul, *The Principles of Harmony and Contrast of Colours*, Garland Publishing Inc., New York and London, 1980, p 87.
3. Ibid. p 88.

54 After Nature

1. Maurice Denis, 'Cézanne', *L'Occident*, Paris, September 1907, in Harrison and Wood, p 46.
2. Cézanne quoted in Denis, 'Cézanne', in Harrison and Wood, pp 42–3.
3. Paul Cézanne, Letter to Émile Bernard, 12 May 1904, in Harrison and Wood, p 38.
4. Cézanne, Letter to Émile Bernard, 23 October 1905, in Harrison and Wood, p 39.
5. Cézanne quoted in Denis, 'Cézanne', in Harrison and Wood, p 46.
6. Maurice Merleau-Ponty, 'Cézanne's Doubt' in *Sense and Non-Sense*, Northwestern University Press, Evanston, IL, 1964, p 15.

58 CHAPTER II: A NEW REALITY

1. Perry Anderson, 'Modernity and Revolution', *New Left Review*, 144, March/April 1984, p 104.
2. Ibid.
3. Filippo Tomaso Marinetti, 'The Founding and Manifesto of Futurism', *Futurist Manifestos*, ed. Umbro Apollonio, Thames & Hudson, London, 1973, p 22.

60 The Layered Frame

1. Henri Matisse, 'Notes of a Painter', in Chipp, p 132.
2. Ibid. p 133.

62 Building a New Reality

1. Paul Gauguin, Letter to Émile Bernard, November 1888, in Chipp, p 60.
2. Daniel-Henry Kahnweiler, *Der Weg zum Kubismus* (*The Rise of Cubism*), in Chipp, p 252.
3. Ibid.
4. Maurice Denis, 'Definition of Neotraditionism', 1890, in Chipp, p 94.
5. Guillaume Apollinaire, 'On the Subject in Modern Painting', in *Apollinaire on Art: Essays and Reviews 1902–1918*, Thames & Hudson, London, 1972, p 197.
6. Ibid.
7. Juan Gris quoted in John Golding, *Cubism: A History and an Analysis 1907–1914*, Faber & Faber, London, 1971, p 115.
8. Georges Braque, 'La Peinture et nous', *Cahiers d'art*, 1954, quoted in Golding, p 92.
9. Daniel-Henry Kahnweiler, *Juan Gris, His Life and Work*, trans. Douglas Cooper, Curt Valentin, New York, 1947, p 68. Quoted in Christine Poggi, *In Defiance of Painting: Cubism, Futurism and the*

Invention of Collage, Yale University Press, New Haven and London, 1992, p 86.

66 The Death of Time and Space

1. Umberto Boccioni, Carlo Carrà, Luigi Russolo, Giacomo Balla and Gino Severini, 'Futurist Painting: Technical Manifesto 1910', in Apollonio, pp 27–31.
2. Ibid. p 29.
3. Ibid. p 28.
4. Filippo Tommaso Marinetti, 'Founding and Manifesto of Futurism', in Apollonio, p 22.
5. Boccioni et al., in Apollonio, p 28.
6. Marinetti, in Apollonio, p 22.
7. Quoted in Gordon Hughes, 'Envisioning Abstraction: The Simultaneity of Robert Delaunay's *First Disk*', *The Art Bulletin*, vol. 89 no. 2, June 2007, p 306.
8. Marcel Proust, *À la recherche du temps perdu*, trans. C K Scott-Moncreiff and Terence Kilmartin, Penguin, Harmondsworth, 1983, 3 vols, vol. 2, p 1062.
9. Robert Delaunay, 'On the Construction of Reality in Pure Painting', in Harrison and Wood, p 153.
10. Robert Delaunay, *Du cubisme à l'art abstrait: les cahiers inédits de Robert Delaunay*, S.E.V.P.E.N., Paris, 1957, p 81; quoted in Hughes, 'Envisioning Abstraction', p 307.
11. 'simulacrum': a 1912 note in the Bibliothèque nationale de France Delaunay archive quoted in Tara Ward, '"The World is Round": Robert Delaunay and Representation', *Oxford Art Journal*, vol 41 no 2, 2018, p 216; 'Effects' and 'objects': Robert Delaunay, 'On the Construction of Reality in Pure Painting', [1912], in Harrison and Wood, p 154 ['We are no longer dealing here either with effects (neo-impressionism within impressionism), or with objects (cubism within impressionism) …'].
12. See Bridget Riley, *Learning from Seurat*, Courtauld Gallery and Ridinghouse, London, 2015.
13. 'About Curves: Bridget Riley in Conversation with Paul Moorhouse', in Robert Kudielka, ed., *Bridget Riley: The Curve Paintings 1961–2014*, De La Warr Pavilion, Bexhill-on-Sea, and Ridinghouse, London, 2015, p 47.
14. 'Practising Abstraction' – Talking to Michael Craig-Martin, in Robert Kudielka, ed., *Bridget Riley: Dialogues on Art*, Philip Wilson Publishers, London, 1995, p 56.
15. Ibid.
16. 'About Curves', p 47.
17. Ibid. p 51.
18. Ibid.
19. Ibid.
20. Conversational remark made at a dinner hosted by Monet in November 1894, reported by Octave Mirbeau. See Richard Schiff, 'Risible Cézanne', in *The Repeating Image: Multiples in French Painting from David to Matisse*, op. cit., p.21.
21. 'About Curves', p 48.

72 Collage

1. Richard Huelsenbeck, *En Avant Dada: A History of Dadaism*, in Robert Motherwell, ed., *The Dada Painters and Poets*, The Belknap Press of Harvard University Press, Cambridge, MA, and London, 1951, p 41.
2. Dawn Adès, *Dada and Surrealism Reviewed*, Hayward Gallery, London, 1978, p 99.
3. Hausmann quoted in Hans Richter, *DADA: Art and Anti-Art*, Thames & Hudson, London, 1978, p 118.
4. Hannah Höch, 'A Few Words on Photomontage', in Maud Lavin, *Cut with the Kitchen Knife: The Weimar Photomontages of Hannah Höch*, Yale University Press, New Haven, NJ, and London, 1993, p 220.
5. Denise Toussaint, 'Dismantling Colonial Representation: The Photomontages of Hannah Höch', *de arte*, vol. 51 no. 1, 2016, p 40.
6. See Romare Bearden and Carl Holty, with an introduction by Ralph Ellison, *The Painter's Mind: A Study of the Relations of Structure and Space in Painting*, Garland Publishing, New York and London, 1981.
7. 'Uses of the Past', Bearden and Holty, p 74.
8. Romare Bearden, 'Encounters with African Art', in *The Romare Bearden Reader*, ed. Robert G. O'Meally, Duke University Press, Durham, NC, p 166.
9. Ibid.
10. Romare Bearden, 'Rectangular Structure in My Montage Paintings', *Bearden Reader*, p 130.
11. Faith Ringgold in interview with Hans Ulrich Obrist, in *Faith Ringgold*, Serpentine Gallery and Koenig Books, London, 2019, p 38.
12. Michael Fried, 'Art and Objecthood', *Artforum*, June 1967, reprinted Gregory Battcock, ed., *Minimal Art: A Critical Anthology*, E P Dutton & Co., Inc., New York, 1968, p 147.
13. Martha Rosler in interview with Benjamin Buchloh, in *Martha Rosler: Positions in the Life World*, ed. Catherine de Zegher, Ikon Gallery, Birmingham, Generali Foundation, Vienna, and MIT, Cambridge, MA, and London, 1999, p 27.
14. Martha Rosler, *Decoys and Disruptions: Selected Writings 1975–2001*, MIT, Cambridge, MA, 2004, p 353. Quoted in Stephanie Schwartz, 'Martha Rosler's Protest', *Arts*, vol. 9, no. 92, 2020. Available at: https://www.mdpi.com/2076-0752/9/3/92
15. Ibid.
16. Rosler, *Decoys and Disruptions*, p 355. Quoted in Stephanie Schwartz, op. cit.
17. Ibid.
18. Said to Michael Rush in an interview for the *New York Times*, quoted in Alison Rowley, 'Exhibiting "Martha Rosler"? A Feminist Response to Martha Rosler: Positions in the Life World', *n.paradoxa*, online, issue 14, February 2001, p 37. Available at: https://www.ktpress.co.uk/pdf/nparadoxaissue14_Alison-Rowley_35-42.pdf?
19. 'Resonant Surgeries: The Collaged World of Wangechi Mutu', interview, Border Crossings, February 2008, no pag. Available at: https://bordercrossingsmag.com/article/resonant-surgeries-the-collaged-world-of-wangechi-mutu.

20–4. Ibid.

84 The Readymade

1. Pierre Cabanne, *Dialogues with Marcel Duchamp*, Thames & Hudson, London, 1971, p 47.
2. Ibid. p 48

86 Chance

1. Georges Hugnet, 'The Dada Spirit in Painting', in Motherwell, p 134.
2. Quoted in Dawn Adès, *Dada and Surrealism Reviewed*, p 67.
3. Tristan Tzara, 'Seven Dada Manifestos', in Motherwell, op. cit., p 81.
4. Quoted in Motherwell, op. cit., p 294.
5. Ibid.
6. Adès, op. cit., p 67.
7. Quoted in Motherwell, op. cit., p 294.
8. Ibid. p 293.
9. Quoted in Motherwell, op. cit., p 78.

88 Accessing the Unconscious

1. André Breton in *Le Cadavre exquis: son exaltation*, exh. cat., Galerie Nina Dausset, Paris, 1948.
2. Ibid.
3. André Breton, 'Manifesto of Surrealism', in *Manifestoes of Surrealism*, Ann Arbor, MI, University of Michigan, 1999, p 26.
4. Man Ray, *Self Portrait*, Little, Brown & Co., Boston, MA, and Toronto, 1963, p 129.
5. Ibid.
6. Walter Benjamin, 'Little History of Photography', *Selected Writings, Volume 2: 1927–1934*, The Belknap Press of Harvard University Press, Cambridge, MA, and London, 1999, p 523.
7. Ibid.

8. Louise Bourgeois, 'On Early Paintings', *Louise Bourgeois: Destruction of the Father, Reconstruction of the Father – Writings and Interviews 1923–1997*, ed. and with texts by Marie-Laure Bernadac and Hans-Ulrich Obrist, MIT Press, Cambridge, MA, in association with Violette Editions, London, 1998, p 45.
9. Bourgeois quoted in Deborah Wye and Carol Smith, The Prints of Louise Bourgeois, Museum of Modern Art, New York, 1994, p 148.
10. Mignon Nixon, 'Losing Louise', *October*, 134, Fall, 2010, p 126.
11. Quoted in Wye and Smith, loc. cit., p 148.
12. Bourgeois, op. cit., p 114.
13. Jerry Gorovoy and Pandora Tabatabai Asbaghi, *Louise Bourgeois: Blue Days and Pink Days*, Fondazione Prada, Milan, 1997, p 98.

94 The New Total Realism

1. Guillaume Apollinaire, *Apollinaire on Art: Essays and Reviews 1902–1918*, p 45.
2. Wassily Kandinsky, 'On the Question of Form', *The Blaue Reiter Almanac*, ed. Wassily Kandinsky and Franz Marc, Thames & Hudson, London, 1974, p 178.
3. Henri Rousseau, letter to the Mayor of Laval, 10 July 1898, quoted in Roger Shattuck, *The Banquet Years: The Origins of the Avant Garde in France 1885 to World War 1*, Vintage Books, New York, 1968, p 60.
4. Kandinsky, op. cit., p 165.
5. Ibid.
6. Quoted in Jill Carrick, 'Phallic Victories? Niki de Saint Phalle's *Tirs*, *Art History*, vol. 26 no. 5, November 2003, p 717.
7. Quoted in Johanna Fateman, 'Self Made', *Artforum*, vol. 59 no. 7, May 2021 (article accessed digitally, so no pagination).
8. Donald Judd, 'In the Galleries', *Arts Magazine*, December 1962, in Donald Judd, *Complete Writings 1959–1975*, Nova Scotia College of Art and Design and New York Press, 1975, p 61.
9. Poster for McLellan Galleries, 1993, quoted in Carrick, op. cit., p 716.
10. Quoted in Lisa Mintz Messinger, 'Georgia O'Keeffe', *Metropolitan Museum of Art Bulletin*, Fall 1984, p 23.
11. Kathleen Pyne, 'Georgia O'Keeffe: Black Iris', *Making Modernism: O'Keeffe, Preston, Cossington-Smith*, ed. Lesley Harding and Denise Mimmocchi, Art Gallery of New South Wales, 2017, p 36.
12. Quoted in Julia Markoe, 'Rejecting the Feminine Mystique: Re-interepreting Georgia O'Keeffe', *Bowdoin Journal of Art*, 2016, p 3.
13. Jack Cowart, Juan Hamilton and Sarah Greenough, *Georgia O'Keeffe: Art and Letters*, National Gallery of Art, Washington, 1987, p 180.
14. Apollinaire quoted in Poggi, op. cit., p 61.
15. Richard Calvocoressi, 'Georg Baselitz', Georg *Baselitz: Paintings 1960–83*, Whitechapel Art Gallery, London, 1983, p 12.

102 CHAPTER III: A NEW MEANING

1. Georg (György) Lukács, 'The Metaphysics of Tragedy', *Soul and Form*, trans. Anna Bostock, Merlin Press, London, 1974, p 167.
2. Clement Greenberg, 'Abstract, Representational, and So Forth', *Art and Culture: Critical Essays*, op. cit., p 133.

104 Automatic Composition

1. Quoted in Sanford Schwartz, 'Hilma af Klint at the Guggenheim', *Ruritan*, vol. 38 no. 4, 2019, p 88.
2. Ibid.
3. Rudolf Steiner, *Theosophy*, trans. Catherine E Creeger, with an introduction by Michael Holdrege, Anthroposophic Press, Hudson, NY, 1994, p 159.
4. Annie Besant and C W Leadbeater, Introduction to *Thought Forms*, The Theosophical Publishing House, London, 1901. Available at: https://www.gutenberg.org/files/16269/16269-h/16269-h.htm

108 The Spiritual in Art

1. Wassily Kandinsky, *Concerning the Spiritual in Art*, trans. Michael T H Sadler, Part I, Section II: 'The Movement of the Triangle' [1910], Dover Publications, Mineola, NY, 2000. Available at: https://www.gutenberg.org/ebooks/5321
2. Ibid., Part II, Section VI: 'The Language of Form and Colour'.
3. Wassily Kandinsky, 'On the Question of Form', *The Blaue Reiter Almanac*, op. cit., p 149.
4. Franz Marc, *Aphorisms*, in Chipp, p 180.
5. Franz Marc, 'How Does a Horse See the World?', in Chipp, p 178.
6. Ibid.
7. Ibid.
8. Franz Marc, Letter to August Macke, 12 December 1910, in Franz Marc and August Macke, *Briefwechsel 1910–1914*, DuMont, Cologne, 1964, p. 28; trans. Annika Grotjohann and Daniel Oberfeld in their essay 'Evaluation of Franz Marc's Color Theory Using Implicit Testing Procedures', *Art & Perception* 6, 2018, p 42.
9. Franz Marc, 'Two Pictures', in *The Blaue Reiter Almanac*, p 67.

112 Line and Colour

1. Mondrian quoted in Frank Elgar, *Mondrian*, Thames & Hudson, London, 1968, p 138.
2. Mondrian quoted in ibid.
3. Piet Mondrian, 'Dialogue on the New Plastic', in Harrison and Wood, p 284.
4. Theo van Doesberg, 'De Stijl: Manifesto I', in Harrison and Wood, p 279.
5. Newman quoted in Thomas B. Hess, *Barnett Newman*, Tate Gallery, London, 1972, p 14.
6. Barnett Newman, 'The Plasmic Image: Part I', in Hess, op. cit., p 22.
7. Hess, op. cit., p. 34.
8. Newman quoted in Hess, op. cit., p 77.
9. Newman quoted in Hess, op. cit., p 77.
10. Hess, op. cit., p 77.
11. Bowling quoted in Dorothy C Rowe, 'Nonsynchronous Cartographies: Frank Bowling's Map Paintings', *Small Axe*, vol 17 no 2 (41), July 2013, p 267.
12. Bowling quoted in Mel Gooding, *Frank Bowling*, Royal Academy of Arts, London, 2011, p 67.
13. Frank Bowling and Frank Thomson, 'A Conversation between Two Painters', *Art International*, October–November 1976, p 65; also quoted in Kobena Mercer, 'Black Atlantic Abstraction: Aubrey Williams and Frank Bowling', *Discrepant Abstraction*, ed. Mercer, InIVA, London, and MIT Press, Cambridge, MA, and London, 2006, p 203.
14. Ibid.
15. 'A Conversation, with Okwui Enwezor and Olu Oguibe', *NKA Journal of Contemporary African Art*, Spring, 1996, p 23.
16. John Holt, 'Anwar Jalal Shemza: A Search for the "Significant"', *Third Text*, vol. 12 no. 42, 1998, p 105.
17. Ibid. p 106.
18. Notebook comment quoted in Holt, op. cit., p 106.
19. Kobena Mercer, 'The Longest Journey: Black Diaspora Artists in Britain', *Art History*, June 2021, p 489.
20. Ibid.
21. Paul Klee, 'Creative Credo', in Chipp, p 184.

120 Supremacy

1. Wassily Kandinsky, *Concerning the Spiritual in Art*, Section VI: 'The Language of Form and Colour' [1910], Dover Publications, Mineola, NY, 2000. Available at: https://www.gutenberg.org/cache/epub/5321/pg5321.html
2. Ibid.
3. Kazymyr Malevych, 'Suprematism', in Chipp, p 346.
4. Ibid. p 342.

5. Ibid. pp 344.
6. Ibid. p 343.
7. Kazymyr Malevych, 'Introduction to the Theory of the Additional Element in Painting', in Chipp, p 338.

122 Put to Work

1. Malevych, 'Suprematism', in Chipp, p 346.
2. Naum Gabo, 'The Realistic Manifesto' [1920], in Chipp, p 328.
3. Stepanova quoted in Camilla Grey, *The Russian Experiment in Art 1863–1922*, Thames & Hudson, London, 1971, pp 250–1.
4. Alexander Lavrentiev, *Varvara Stepanova: A Constructivist Life*, ed. and intro. John E Bowlt, Thames & Hudson, London, 1988, p. 83.
5. Alexander Rodchenko and Varvara Stepanova, 'Programme of the First Working Group of Constructivists' [1921], in Harrison and Wood, p 317.
6. Alexander Rodchenko and Varvara Stepanova, 'Productivist Manifesto', [1921], in David Elliott, ed., *Alexander Rodchenko*, Museum of Modern Art, Oxford, 1979, p 130.
7. El Lissitzky, 'A and Pangeometry', in Harrison and Wood, p 304. Throughout the essay, El Lissitzky uses the abbreviations 'A' and 'F' for Art and Form respectively.
8. Ibid. p 304.
9. Ibid. p 305.
10. Ibid.
11. See, for example, Lynn Gumpert, 'El Lissitzky's *Proun I. Kestnermappe*', *Bulletin 2*, University of Michigan Museums of Art and Archaeology, 1979, p 57.
12. Lissitzky quoted in Christina Lodder, 'El Lissitzky and the Export of Constructivism', in *Situating El Lissitzky: Vitebsk, Berlin, Moscow*, ed. N Perloff and B Reed, Getty Publications, Los Angeles, 2003, p 38.
13. Lissitzky quoted in Gumpert, op. cit., p. 63. Lissitzky's statement on the first showing of the Proun Room at the 1923 Great Berlin Art Exhibition is collected in Sophie Lissitzky-Küppers, *El Lissitzky: Maler, Architekt, Typograf, Fotograf, Errinerungen, Briefe, Schriften*, VEB Verlag der Kunst, Dresden, 1967 (quotation translated here at p 361).
14. Lissitzky quoted in Gumpert, op. cit., p. 63.
15. Lissitzky quoted in ibid.

126 Into the Surface

1. Tristan Tzara, 'Seven Dada Manifestos', in Motherwell, op. cit., p 81.
2. Lucio Fontana, 'The White Manifesto', in Edward A Shanken, ed., *Art and Electronic Media*, Phaidon Press, London and New York, 2009, pp 194–5.
3. Ibid.
4. Jaleh Mansoor, *Marshall Plan Modernism: Italian Postwar Abstraction and the Beginnings of Autonomia*, Duke University Press, Durham, NC, 2016, p 70.
5. Ibid.
6. Gustav Metzger, 'Manifesto Auto-Destructive Art', in *gustav metzger: 'damaged nature, auto-destructive art'*, Metzger et al., Coracle Press, London, 1996, p 59.

128 Beyond the Canvas

1. Imi Knoebel in conversation with Johannes Stüttgen, *Imi Knoebel: Works 1966–2014*, Kunstmuseum, Wolfsburg, 2015, p 18.
2. Ibid. p 63.

130 Total Environment

1. Robert Irwin, 'Notes toward a Model', in Hugh M Davies and Robert Irwin, *Robert Irwin: Primaries and Secondaries*, ed. Sherri Schottlaender, exh. cat., Museum of Contemporary Art, San Diego, 2008, p 149.
2. Ibid.
3. Ibid.
4. Robert Irwin, 'Being and Circumstance: Notes toward a Conditional Art', in Davies and Irwin, op. cit., p 181.
5. Hugh M Davies, 'Robert Irwin: 'One Perspective', in Davies and Irwin, op. cit., p 31.
6. Germano Celant, 'Urban Nature: The Work of Maria Nordman', *Artforum*, March 1980, p 64.
7. Maria Nordman and Ian Wilson, 'In Flight Interview', in Maria Nordman, *Geo-Aesthetics Presencing: De Tempo Real*, Walther König, Cologne, 2013, p 139.
8. Michel de Certeau, *The Practice of Everyday Life*, University of California Press, Berkeley, CA, 1988, p 117.
9. Quoted in James Merle Thomas, 'Close-Up: On an Untitled 1979 Work by Maria Nordman', *Artforum*, October 2011.
10. Ibid.
11. Maria Nordman in conversation with the author, 29 July 2022.
12. Poster announcing *Alameda + Temple*, 1995.

136 The Digital Context

1. Delaroche quoted in Stephen Bann, *Paul Delaroche: History Painted*, Reaktion Books, London and Princeton University Press, Princeton, 1997, p 17.
2. From the manuscript 'Working with Maiakovsky' [1940], published in excerpts in *From Painting to Design*, exh. cat., Cologne, Gallery Gmurzynska, 1981, pp 190–1, quoted in Magdalena Dabrowski, 'Aleksandr Rodchenko: Innovation and Experiment', in *Aleksandr Rodchenko*, ed. M Dabrowski, L Dickerman and P Galassi, exh. cat., New York, The Museum of Modern Art, 1998, p 43.
3. Nam June Paik, 'Cybernated Art' [1966]. Available at: https://monoskop.org/images/6/6f/Paik_Nam_June_1966_2003_Cybernated_Art.pdf
4. Quoted in David A Ross, 'Nam June Paik's Videotapes', in *Nam June Paik*, ed. John G Hanhardt et al., exh. cat., Whitney Museum of American Art, New York, 1982, p 104.
5. Walter Benjamin, 'The Work of Art in the Age of its Technological Reproducibility', op. cit., p 268.
6. Shoshana Zuboff, 'Dilemmas of Transformation in the Age of the Smart Machine', in David Trend, ed., *Reading Digital Culture*, Blackwell, Oxford, 2001, p 127.
7. See Michael Archer, 'This is the Procedure', in Keith Tyson et al., *Keith Tyson*, Thames & Hudson, London, 2022.
8. Brian W Kernighan and Dennis M Ritchie, *The C Programming Language*, Prentice Hall, Upper Saddle River, NJ, 1978.
9. Hannah Fry, *Hello World: How to Be Human in the Age of the Machine*, Penguin, London, 2018, p. xiii.
10. Shraddha Nair, 'Gamescapes: Cao Fei Recalls "RMB City", the Virtual World and Its Future', *Stir World*, 25 August 2020, no pag., available at https://www.stirworld.com/think-opinions-gamescapes-cao-fei-recalls-rmb-city-the-virtual-world-and-its-future
11. Ibid.
12.. China Tracy [online avatar of Cao Fei], 'RMB City Manifesto (RMB – to be ReMember)', in Cao Fei, *I Watch That Worlds Pass By*, ed. R Wiehager, C Ganzenberg and W Xiaoyu, Daimler Art Collection and Snoeck Verlagsgesellschaft mbH, Berlin and Cologne, 2015, p 199. Quoted in Jori Snels, 'The Politics of Aesthetics, Space and Community: An Analysis of *Same Old, Brand New* by Cao Fei', *Art & the Public Sphere*, vol. 7 no. 1, 2018, p 67.
13. Rosemary Heather, 'Residency in RMB City', *Border Crossings*, vol. 30 no. 2, June–August 2011, p 103.
14. Gilles Deleuze, *Bergsonism* [1966], trans. Hugh Tomlinson and Barbara Habberjam, Zone Books, London, 1991.
15. Nair, op. cit.

144 CHAPTER IV: A NEW FRAMEWORK

1. 'What is Pop Art?', Roy Lichtenstein interviewed by Gene Swenson, *ARTnews*, November 1963. Lichtenstein is here answering the question 'Antagonistic critics say that Pop Art does

not transform its model. Does it?' Available at: https://www.artnews.com/artnews/news/top-ten-artnews-stories-the-first-word-on-pop-183/
2. Ibid. (In answering Swenson's previous question.)
3. *Roy Lichtenstein*, ed. Robert Rosenblum and Sarat Maharaj, exh. cat., Tate Liverpool, 1993, p 10.

146 Freeing the Line

1. Wilhelm Worringer, *Abstraction and Empathy: A Contribution to the Psychology of Style*, trans. Michael Bullock, Elephant Paperbacks, Chicago, 1997, p 75.
2. Bernice Rose, *Jackson Pollock: Drawing into Painting*, exh. cat., Museum of Modern Art, Oxford, 1979, p 19.
3. Jackson Pollock, 'My Painting', *Possibilities I*, Winter 1947/48, p 79; reprinted in Chipp, p 546.
4. Harold Rosenberg, 'The American Action Painters', *Art News*, December 1952; reprinted in Rosenberg, *The Tradition of the New*, University of Chicago Press, Chicago and London, 1982, p 25.
5. That this double level was understood at the time is evidenced by the fact that, when the series was exhibited as part of a British Council tour of Eastern Europe, they had to be retitled as *Portrait of a Man in the Style of Jackson Pollock*, *Portrait of a Man in Winter 1920…* and *Portrait of a Man in Disguise …*
6. Gordon Bennett, artist journal, 1992.

150 Not Composing?

1. Helen Frankenthaler in Emile De Antonio, *Painters Painting: A Candid History of the Modern Art Scene, 1940–1970*, Abbeville Press, New York, 1984, p 82.
2. Louis quoted in John Elderfield, *Morris Louis*, exh. cat., Hayward Gallery, 1974, p 9. Elderfield's note says: 'This familiar quotation seems to have its origin in James McC. Truitt's "Art-Arid D.C. Harbours Touted 'New' Painters", *The Washington Post*, Thursday, December 21, 1961, p 20'.
3. Walter Darby Bannard, 'Morris Louis and the Restructured Picture', *Studio International*, vol. 188 no. 968, July–August 1974; available at: http://wdbannard.org/1974-Morris-Louis-Restructured-Picture-31.htm
4. Clement Greenberg, letter to the Editor, *Art International*, May 1965, p 66.
5. Ibid.
6. 'Questions to Stella and Judd', interview by Bruce Glaser, ed. Lucy Lippard, *Art News*, September 1966, reprinted in Battcock, op. cit., p 158.
7. Ibid.
8. Brian O'Doherty, *Inside the White Cube: The Ideology of the Gallery Space*, The Lapis Press, Santa Monica and San Francisco, 1986, p 29.
9. Pat Steir interviewed by Anne Waldman, *BOMB*, Spring, 2003, p 33.
10. Pat Steir in Conversation with Mickalene Thomas, video available at: https://www.youtube.com/watch?v=r7YI7J6txns
11. Pat Steir, 'The Paint Makes Its Own Image', *Apollo*, vol. 189 no. 671, January 2019, p 32.
12. Steir interviewed by Waldman, op. cit., p 36.
13. Ibid.
14. Ibid.

156 Borrowing

1. Elaine Sturtevant, interview with Peter Halley, *Index Magazine*, 2005, available at: http://www.indexmagazine.com/interviews/sturtevant.shtml
2. Elaine Sturtevant, website announcement for her exhibition, Image Over Image, Moderna Museet, Stockholm, 2012. Available at: https://www.modernamuseet.se/stockholm/en/exhibitions/sturtevant/

160 Dematerialization

1. Lucy Lippard, ed., *Six Years: The Dematerialization of the Art Object 1966–1972*, University of California Press, Berkeley, CA, 1997, p xii.
2. Ibid. p 101.
3. Lee Lozano, 'Open Hearing', *Art Workers Coalition Handbook*, New York, 1969, p 38. Quoted by Helen Molesworth, 'Tune In, Turn On, Drop Out: The Rejection of Lee Lozano', *Art Journal*, vol. 61 no. 4, Winter 2002, p 68.
4. Notebook page reproduced in Jo Applin, 'Hard Work: Lee Lozano's Dropouts', *October*, 156, Spring 2016, p 88.
5. Keith Arnatt, 'Is It Possible for Me to Do Nothing as My Contribution to This Exhibition?', in Lippard, op. cit., p 172.
6. Applin, op. cit., p 94.
7. Robert Smithson, 'A Sedimentation of the Mind: Earth Projects', *Artforum*, vol. 7 no. 1, September 1968; reprinted in *Robert Smithson: The Collected Writings*, ed. Jack Flam, University of California Press, Berkeley, CA, 1996, p 111.
8. Ibid.

164 Manifestation

1. Daniel Buren, Olivier Mosset, Michel Parmentier and Niele Toroni, 'Statement', Harrison and Wood, p 850.
2. Daniel Buren, 'Standpoints', in *Five Texts*, Jack Wendler Gallery, London and John Weber Gallery, New York, 1973, p 40.
3. Ibid. p 32.
4. Ibid.
5. Ibid. p 37.
6. Daniel Buren, 'Beware', in *Five Texts*, op. cit., p 12.
7. Ibid.
8. Daniel Buren, *Legend*, 2 vols, Warehouse Publications, London, 1973, cover text to both volumes.

166 Concept

1. Sol LeWitt, 'Paragraphs on Conceptual Art', *Artforum*, vol. 5 no. 10, Summer 1967, p 79; reprinted in Harrison and Wood, p 834.
2. Ibid.
3. Sol LeWitt, 'Sentences on Conceptual Art', *Art-Language*, vol. 1 no. 1, 1969; reprinted in Harrison and Wood, p 837.
4. Bernice Rose, 'Sol LeWitt and Drawing', *Sol LeWitt: The Museum of Modern Art*, ed. Alicia Legg, exh. cat., Museum of Modern Art, New York, 1978, p 36.
5. Ibid. p 35.
6. Alloway, quoted in ibid. p 40.
7. Shulman quoted in ibid. p 42.
8. LeWitt quoted in ibid. p 40.

168 Empacement/Displacement

1. 'A Conversation with Hsieh Tehching from *The Black Cover Book*', *ARTMargins*, MIT Press, Cambridge, MA, 2015, p 112.
2. Erwin Panofsky, *Perspective as Symbolic Form*, op. cit., p 6.
3. John Berger, *Ways of Seeing*, BBC and Penguin Books, London, 1972, p 108.
4. Fred Myers, 'Emplacement and Displacement: Perceiving the Landscape through Aboriginal Australian Acrylic Painting, *Ethnos Journal of Anthropology*, vol. 78 no. 4, 2013, pp 435–63.
5. https://www.cooeeart.com.au/gallery/paintings/18161/

170 (Re)Interpretation

1. Caroline Tisdall, *Joseph Beuys*, exh. cat., Solomon R Guggenheim Museum, New York and Thames & Hudson, London, 1979, p 6.
2. Rasheed Araeen, catalogue statement for the exhibition CONTACT: From Contemplation to Agitation, Krakow, Poland, 1980, in *Making Myself Visible*, Third Text Publications, London, 1984, p 5.

174 Word

1. Maya Kóvskaya, 'A Lexicon for Seeing the World: Xu Bing, Language, and Nature', *Yishu: Journal of Contemporary Chinese Art*, vol. 17 no. 6, November/December 2018, p 15.
2. Filippo Tommaso Marinetti, *Words-in-Freedom (Chaudronneries)* [c1912]. Exhibited in *Futuris-*

mo e Futurismi, Palazzo Grassi, Venice, 1986. Reproduced in the catalogue, Pontus Hulten et al., *Futurismo e Futurismi*, Bompiani, Milan, 1986, p 188.
3. Kóvskaya, op. cit., p 15.
4. Karen Smith, *Nine Lives: The Birth of Avant-Garde Art in New China*, Timezone 8, Hong Kong, 2006, p 347.
5. Ibid. p 336.
6. Immanuel Kant, *The Critique of Judgement*, trans. James Creed Meredith, Oxford University Press, Oxford, 1980, p 80.
7. Sol LeWitt, 'Paragraphs on Conceptual Art', loc. cit., p 834.
8. Kant, op. cit., p 85.
9. 'Playing with Words, Interview', in Jerome Sans, ed., *China Talks*, Timezone 8, Hong Kong, 2009, p 12.

180 Language

1. Charles Olson, 'Cy Twombly', in *Collected Prose*, ed. Donald Allen and Benjamin Friedlander, University of California Press, Berkeley, Los Angeles and London, 1997, p 175.
2. Richard Leeman, *Cy Twombly*, Thames & Hudson, London, 2005, p 87.
3. Wolfgang Max Faust, 'The Appearance of the Zeitgeist', *Artforum*, January, 1983, p 87.
4. Roberta Smith, 'The Great Mediator', in Demosthenes Davvetas et al., *Cy Twombly*, ed. Harald Szeeman, exh. cat., Whitechapel Art Gallery, London and Prestel Verlag, Munich, 1987, p 15.
5. *Cy Twombly*, cat. rai., ed. Heiner Bastian, 4 vols, Schirmer/Mosel, Munich, vol. IV, 1995, p 36.
6. Dean Rader, 'Poetry / painting / history / hermeneutics', *Jacket2*, available at: https://jacket2.org/reviews/poetrypaintinghistory-hermeneutics
7. Rainer Maria Rilke, Sonnet II 28, *The Sonnets to Orpheus*, trans. Leslie Norris and Alan Keele, Skoob Books, London, 1991, p 55.
8. Judy Chicago talking with Lucy Lippard, *Artforum*, September 1974, p 60.
9. Quoted in Jane F Gerhard, *The Dinner Party: Judy Chicago and the Power of Popular Feminism, 1970–2007,* University of Georgia Press, Athens, GA, 2013, p 130.
10. Ibid. p 111.
11. Rozsika Parker and Griselda Pollock, *Old Mistresses: Women, Art and Ideology*, Routledge & Kegan Paul, London, 1981, p 1.

184 Repetition

1. 'Questions to Stella and Judd', interview by Bruce Glaser in Battcock, op. cit., p 155.
2. Judd's work and his writings about the ideas behind it were hugely influential at the time and have remained so since. He was articulate in pointing out the complexity in work that was often pejoratively described and dismissed as 'minimal'.
3. Donald Judd, 'Some Aspects of Colour in General and Red and Black in Particular [1993], in *Donald Judd Writings*, ed. Flavin Judd and Caitlin Murray, Judd Foundation and David Zwirner Books, New York, 2016, p 853.
4. Battcock, op. cit., pp 151–4.
5. Mel Bochner, 'Serial Art, Systems, Solipsism', in Battcock, op. cit., p 94.
6. Eva Hesse, Notebooks / c.1967, in *Eva Hesse: Sculpture*, ed. Nicholas Serota, exh. cat. Whitechapel Art Gallery, London, 1979, no pag.
7. Cindy Nemser, An Interview with Eva Hesse, Artforum, vol 8 no 9, May 1970, p 62, quoted in James Meyer, 'Non, Nothing, Everything: Hesse's "Abstraction"', *Eva Hesse*, San Francisco Museum of Modern Art, CA, 2002, p 59.
8. Eva Hesse, Notebooks / 1967, in *Eva Hesse*, op. cit., no pag.
9. Donald Judd, 'Specific Objects', *Arts Yearbook*, 1965. Reprinted in Donald Judd, *Complete Writings 1959–1975*, op. cit., p 184.
10. Jean-Michel Basquiat speaking in *State of the Art: Ideas & Images in the 1980s*, Channel 4 TV series, 1985, Episode 6: 'Identity'. Printed in Sandy Nairne in collaboration with Geoff Dunlop and John Wyver, *State of the Art: Ideas & Images in the 1980s*, Chatto & Windus, London in collaboration with Channel Four Television Company Ltd, 1987, p 242.
11. Marc Mayer, 'Basquiat in History', in *Basquiat*, ed. Mayer et al., exh. cat., Brooklyn Museum, New York, and Merrell, London and New York, 2005, p 53.
12. Collected in Jean-Michel Basquiat, *Basquiat-isms*, ed. Larry Warsh, Princeton University Press, NJ, 2019, p 37. From Jean-Michel Basquiat, 'I Have to Have Some Source Material around Me', interview by Becky Johnston and Tamra Davis, Beverley Hills, CA, 1985 and reprinted in Dieter Buchhart and Sam Kelle, eds, *Basquiat*, Hatje Kantz, Ostfildern, 2010, p xxi.
13. Mayer, op. cit., p 53.

190 Multiplicity

1. 'Picking Up the Power, Tania Bruguera and Gregory Sholette in Conversation', *World Records Journal*, vol. 4, p 87.
2. Tania Bruguera interviewed by RoseLee Goldberg, quoted in David Joselit, *After Art*, Princeton University Press, Princeton, NJ, 2013, p 63.
3. Ashram Osman and Daniela N Fuentes, 'An Interview with Tania Bruguera', *On Curating*, Issue 19, 2012. Available at: https://www.on-curating.org/issue-19-reader/tania-bruguera-interviewed.html#.Y15Csi2l23U
4. *Tania Bruguera in Conversation with Claire Bishop*, Fundación Cisneros, New York, 2020, p 46.
5. Ibid. p 50.
6. Ibid. p 51.

192 Contribution

1. *Painting to Be Constructed in Your Head,* 1962. Ink on paper, handwritten in Japanese by Ichiyanagi Toshi, exhibited at Sogetsu Art Center, Tokyo, 24 May 1962. Published in English in Yoko Ono, *Grapefruit*, Wunternaum Press, Tokyo, 1964. See Alexandra Munroe with Jon Hendricks, eds, *YES YOKO ONO*, Japan Society, New York and Harry N Abrams, Inc, New York, 2000, p 81.

194 The System of Art

1. Marcel Broodthaers, 'Methode', in *Der Adler vom Oligozän bis heute*, Kunsthalle, Dusseldorf, 1972, vol. 1, p 13. Quoted in Rainer Bürgermeister, 'Section des Figures: *The Eagle from the Oligocene to the Present', Broodthaers: Writings, Interviews, Photographs*, ed. Benjamin H D Buchloh, MIT Press, Cambridge, MA, 1988, pp 141–2.
2. Marcel Broodthaers, Cover text for *Interfunktionen*, issue 11, Fall 1974.
3. Terry Smith, *The Contemporary Condition: The Contemporary Composition*, op. cit., pp 67–8.
4. Lisa G Corrin, 'Mining the Museum: An Installation Confronting History', *Curator*, vol. 36, no. 4, 1993, p 306. Corrin's emphases and punctuation.
5. T J Clark, *The Sight of Death: An Experiment in Art Writing*, Yale University Press, New Haven, CT, 2008.
6. David Joselit, 'Painting Beside Itself', *October*, 130, Fall 2009, pp 125–34.

200 Distribution

1. Andy Warhol interviewed by Gene Swenson, *ARTnews*, November 1963; reprinted in Harrison and Wood, p 731.
2. Jonah Westerman, 'Cildo Meireles: Insertions into Ideological Circuits: Coca-Cola Project 1970'. Available at: https://www.tate.org.uk/research/publications/performance-at-tate/perspectives/cildo-meireles
3. 'Felix Gonzalez-Torres: All the Time in the World', interview with Robert Nickas, *Flash Art*, January/February 2006, p 91.
4. Ibid., p 90.

5. Ibid.
6. Quoted in Nancy Spector, *Felix Gonzalez-Torres*, Solomon R Guggenheim Museum, New York, 1995, pp 147–50.

204 The People's Choice

1. Arthur C Danto, *After the End of Art: Contemporary Art and the Pale of History*, Princeton University Press, Princeton, NJ, 2014, p 213.
2. Ibid. p 216.

206 Archive

1. Interview with Walid Ra'ad by Alan Gilbert, *BOMB*, 1 October 2002. Available at: https://bombmagazine.org/articles/walid-raad/
2. Susan Hiller talking about *J Street Project* at the Contemporary Jewish Museum. Available at: https://www.youtube.com/watch?v=594aC-cLjHgs
3. Ibid.
4. Ibid.

210 History Painting

1. 'Painting Historiography: Meleko Mokgosi's Democratic Intuition', interview with Ashleigh Barice, *Soundings*, issue 79, Winter 2021/22, p 159.
2. Gayatri Chakravorty Spivak, 'Can the Subaltern Speak?', in Cary Nelson and Lawrence Grossberg, eds, *Marxism and the Interpretation of Culture*, Macmillan, London, 1988.
3. Meleko Mokgosi, 'Democratic Intuition', *Gagosian Quarterly*, Winter 2020, no pag. Available at: https://gagosian.com/quarterly/2020/11/02/essay-meleko-mokgosi-democratic-intuition/
4. Ibid.
5. 'Painting Historiography', op. cit., p 159.
6. 'Meleko Mokgosi's Acts of Resistance', an interview with Meleko Mokgosi by Michael Anthony Farley, *BmoreArt*, November 2018, no pag. Available at: https://bmoreart.com/2018/11/meleko-mokgosis-acts-of-resistance.html

216 KEY MOVEMENTS

1. Odilon Redon, 'Suggestive Art', excerpt from *À soi-même: Journal (1867–1915)*, Floury, Paris, 1922; in Chipp, p 118.
2. Maurice Denis, 'Synthetism', excerpt from Cézanne, *L'Occident*, Paris, 1907, in Chipp, p 105.
3. Louis Vauxcelles, Le Salon d'Automne, *Gil Blas*, 17 October 1905.
4. Filippo Tommaso Marinetti, 'The Founding and Manifesto of Futurism', in Apollonio, op. cit., p 21.
5. André Breton, 'Manifesto of Surrealism', in Breton, *Manifestoes of Surrealism*, op. cit., p 10.
6. Ibid. p 13.
7. Ibid. p 26 [Breton's precise line is: 'psychic automatism in its pure state'].
8. Theo Van Doesburg, *Principles of Neo-Plastic Art*, translated by Janet Seligman, New York Graphic Society, 1968, p 40.
9. Piet Mondrian, 'Plastic Art and Pure Plastic Art', *Circle*, J L Martin, Ben Nicholson and Naum Gabo, eds, Faber & Faber, London, 1971, p 45.
10. Kazymyr Malevych, 'Suprematism', in Chipp, p 341.
11. Naum Gabo, 'The Realistic Manifesto, Moscow, 5 August 1920', in Chipp, p 326.
12. Harold Rosenberg, 'The American Action Painters', originally published in *ARTnews*, January 1952' reprinted in Rosenberg, *The Tradition of the New*, op. cit., pp 23–39.
13. Clement Greenberg, '"American-Type" Painting', *Art and Culture: Critical Essays*, op. cit., p 208.
14. Richard Wollheim, 'Minimal Art', *Arts Magazine*, January 1965; reprinted in Battcock, op. cit., p 387.
15. Henry Flynt, Concept Art, 1961. Available at: http://www.henryflynt.org/aesthetics/conart.html
16. Tony Godfrey, *Conceptual Art*, Phaidon, London, 1998, p 7.
17. Leo Steinberg, 'Other Criteria', *Other Criteria: Confrontations with Twentieth-Century Art*, op. cit., p 91.
18. Jean Baudrillard, *Simulacra and Simulation*, trans. Sheila Faria Glaser, University of Michigan Press, Ann Arbor, MI, 1994.

INDEX

Page numbers in **bold** indicate illustration captions.

PICTURE CREDITS

7 Schuppi/Wikipedia, CC by-SA 4.0; 8 The Picture Art Collection/Alamy Stock Photo; 10 Fine Art Images/Heritage Images via Getty Images; 11 incamerastock/Alamy Stock Photo; 14 Wikipedia CC0; 15 Courtesy of the artist, Vitamin Creative Space and Sprüth Magers; 18 Public domain via Wellcome Collection; 20–1 Universal Art Archive/Alamy Stock Photo; 22 incamerastock/Alamy Stock Photo; 24 Christophel Fine Art/Universal Images Group via Getty Images; 27a & b Courtesy of the artist; 28, 31 Vidimages/Alamy Stock Photo; 29 The Walters Art Museum; 33 Wikipedia CC0; 34 Gift of Arthur M Wood, Sr in memory of Pauline Palmer Wood/Art Institute of Chicago; 35 Mr and Mrs Lewis Larned Coburn Memorial Collection/Art Institute of Chicago; 36l Van Gogh Museum, Amsterdam (Vincent van Gogh Foundation); 36r Granger Historical Archive/Alamy Stock Photo; 37 Rijksmuseum, Amsterdam; 38 Helen Birch Bartlett Memorial Collection, Art Institute of Chicago; 40 H O Havemeyer Collection, Bequest of Mrs H O Havemeyer, 1929/The Metropolitan Museum of Art, New York; 41 Robert A Waller Fund/The Art Institute of Chicago; 42 The Picture Art Collection/Alamy Stock Photo; 44a TimeTravelRome/Wikipedia, CC by 2.0; 442b Carole Raddato/Wikipedia, CC by-SA 2.0; 45, 46 Paula Modersohn-Becker Museum. Public domain via Wikimedia Commons; 47 Kunstsammlungen Böttcherstraße, Bremen. Public domain via Wikimedia Commons; 49 Asar Studios/Alamy Stock Photo; 51 The Kröller-Müller Museum, Otterlo. Public domain, Wikimedia Commons; 52–3 Science History Images/Alamy Stock Photo; 54 Bridgeman Images; 56–7 Helen Birch Bartlett Memorial Collection/The Art Institute of Chicago; 58 © DACS 2023. Photo Rheinisches Bildarchiv Cologne (rba_c005051); 60 © Succession H Matisse/DACS 2023. Photo Collection of Mr and Mrs John Hay Whitney, The National Gallery of Art, Washington; 63–5 © ADAGP, Paris and DACS, London 2023. Photo akg-images; 67 IanDagnall/Alamy Stock Photo; 68 Granger/Shutterstock; 71 © Bridget Riley 2023. All rights reserved; 72a © Succession Picasso/DACS, London 2023. Photo Album/Alamy Stock Photo; 72b © Succession Picasso/DACS, London 2023. Photo RMN-Grand Palais/Scala, Florence; 75, 76 © DACS 2023. Photo akg-images; 78 © Romare Bearden Foundation/VAGA at ARS, NY and DACS, London 2023. Photo akg-images; 79 Artefact/Alamy; 81 Courtesy of the artist and Mitchell-Innes & Nash, New York; 82l & r © Wangechi Mutu. Courtesy the artist and Victoria Miro; 83 © Wangechi Mutu. Courtesy Sikkema Jenkins & Co. Photo Erma Estwick; 84 © Association Marcel Duchamp/ADAGP, Paris and DACS, London 2023. Photo Sidney and Harriet Janis Collection, The Museum of Modern Art, New York/Scala, Florence; 86 © DACS 2023. Photo © Tate; 89 © ADAGP, Paris and DACS, London 2023. Digital image The Museum of Modern Art, NewYork/Scala, Florence; 90 © Man Ray 2015 Trust/DACS, London 2023. Photo Telimage, Paris; 93 © The Easton Foundation/VAGA at ARS, NY and DACS, London 2023. Photo Christopher Burke; 94 Henri Rousseau, Public domain, via Wikimedia Commons; 96 © Niki de Saint Phalle Charitable Art Foundation/ADAGP, Paris and DACS, London 2023. Courtesy Niki De Saint Phalle Charitable Art Foundation. Photo © Roger Cohen; 97 © Niki de Saint Phalle Charitable Art Foundation/ADAGP, Paris and DACS, London 2023. Courtesy Niki Charitable Art Foundation and Galerie GP & N Vallois, Paris © André Morin; 98 © Georgia O'Keeffe Museum/DACS 2023. Photo Christie's Images/Bridgeman Images; 101 © Georg Baselitz 2023. Bavarian State paintings collections, on loan from the Wittelsbacher Ausgleichsfonds, Munich; 102 Zentrum Paul Klee, Bern, Bildarchiv; 105 Rhododendrites/Wikipedia, CC by-SA 4.0; 106, 108 The Picture Art Collection/Alamy Stock Photo; 109 Peter Horree/Alamy Stock Photo; 110 Album/Alamy Stock Photo; 113 akg-images; 114–15 © The Barnett Newman Foundation, New York/DACS, London 2023. Photo World History Archive/Alamy Stock Photo; 117 © Frank Bowling. All rights reserved, DACS/Artimage, 2023; 119 © The Estate of Anwar Jalal Shemza. All rights reserved, DACS 2023. Photo Photo12/Ann Ronan Picture Library/Alamy Stock Photo; 120 incamerastock/Alamy Stock Photo; 122 © UPRAVIS, Moscow. Digital image, The Museum of Modern Art, New York/Scala, Florence; 123 © UPRAVIS, Moscow. Photo Album/Alamy Stock Photo; 124 Digital image, The Museum of Modern Art, New York/Scala, Florence. Photo Jonathan Muzikar; 125 Album/Alamy Stock Photo; 126 © Lucio Fontana/SIAE/DACS, London 2023. Photo Photo 12/Alamy; 129 © Imi Knoebel/Artists Rights Society (ARS), NY and DACS, London 2023. Courtesy Dia Art Foundation, New York. Photo Bill Jacobson Studio, New York; 130 ARS, NY and DACS, London 2023. Photo Hugh Davies; 133–35 © Maria Nordman. Courtesy of the artist; 137 © Nam June Paik Estate. Photo The Solomon R Guggenheim Foundation/Art Resource, NY/ Scala, Florence. Photo Erika Ede; 139–39 © Dara Birnbaum and Electronic Arts

Birnbaum and Electronic Arts Intermix. Courtesy of the artist, Electronic Arts Intermix, New York and Marian Goodman Gallery; 140 © Keith Tyson. Courtesy the artist and Hauser & Wirth. Photo Peter Mallet; 141 © Keith Tyson. Courtesy the artist and Hauser & Wirth. Photo Prudence Cuming; 142 Courtesy of the artist, Vitamin Creative Space and Sprüth Magers; 144, 145 © Estate of Roy Lichtenstein/DACS, London 2023. Photo © Tate; 146 © The Pollock-Krasner Foundatiion, ARS, NY and DACS, London 2023. Digital image, The Museum of Modern Art, New York/Scala, Florence; 148 © ART & LANGUAGE; Courtesy Lisson Gallery. Photo Ken Adlard; 149 © The Estate of Gordon Bennett. Photo Art Gallery of New South Wales/Brideman Images; 150 © Helen Frankenthaler Foundation, Inc/Artists Rights Society (ARS), NY and DACS, London 2023; 151 © Maryland College Institute of Art (MICA), Rights Administered by ARS, NY and DACS, London. All Rights Reserved 2023. Photo NPL/DeA Picture Library/ Bridgeman Images; 152 © Estate of Hollis Frampton. Photo Addison Gallery of American Art, Phillips Academy, Andover/Art Resource, NY/Scala, Florence; 155 © Pat Steir; 156 © Sturtevant Estate, Paris. Courtesy Thaddaeus Ropac Gallery, London ·Paris ·Salzburg ·Seoul. Photo Arpad Dobriban; 157 © DACS 2023. Courtesy Ronald Feldman Gallery, New York; 158r © Walker Evans Archive, The Metropolitan Museum of Art. The Metropolitan Museum of Art, Gift of the artist, 1995 (1995.266.4) Image The Metropolitan Museum of Art/Art Resource/Scala, Florence; 158l Artokoloro/Alamy Stock Photo; 163 © The Estate of Lee Lozano. Courtesy Hauser & Wirth; 165 © DB-ADAGP, Paris and DACS, London 2023. Photo Michel Cenet; 166 © ARS, NY and DACS, London 2023. Photo © Lieven Herreman, courtesy M – Museum Leuven; 168 Heritage Image Partnership Ltd/Alamy Stock Photo; 169 © The Estate of Clifford Possum Tjapaltjarri. Licensed by DACS, 2023; 170 Courtesy Ronald Feldman Gallery, New York. Photo Carolina Tisdall; 172–3 © Rasheed Araeen. All Rights Reserved, DACS 2023. Courtesy Rossi & Rossi; 175 © ADAGP, Paris and DACS, London 2023. Photo Bridgeman Images; 176, 177 © Xu Bing Studio; 179 © One Million Years Foundation. Courtesy One Million Years Foundation and David Zwirner; 180 © Cy Twombly Foundation; 183 © Judy Chicago. ARS, NY and DACS, London 2023. Photo Randy Duchaine/Alamy Stock Photo; 184 © Judd Foundation/ARS, NY and DACS, London 2023. Photo Christie's Images/Bridgeman Images; 187 © The Estate of Eva Hesse. Courtesy Hauser & Wirth. Collection Kröller-Müller Museum, Otterlo, the Netherlands. Photo Victor Nieuwenhuijs; 188 © The Estate of Jean-Michel Basquiat/ADAGP, Paris and DACS, London 2023. Photo akg-images; 191 © ARS, NY and DACS, London 2023. Courtesy of Queens Museum; 192 Courtesy Yoko Ono. Photo George Maciunas; 194 Courtesy of the Maryland Center for History and Culture. Item # MTM 037b; 197a Nicolas Poussin, Public domain, via Wikimedia Commons; 197b Courtesy of the artist and Reena Spaulings Fine Art, NY/LA. Photo Farzad Owrang; 198, 199 Courtesy of the artist and Chisenhale Gallery, London; 200 © Cildo Meireles. Courtesy Galerie Lelong & Co, New York; 203 © Estate of Felix Gonzalez-Torres. Courtesy of The Felix Gonzalez-Torres Foundation; 204–5 Courtesy of the artists and Ronald Feldman Gallery, New York; 207 © Walid Raad. Courtesy Paula Cooper Gallery, New York; 209 © The Estate of Susan Hiller. All rights reserved, DACS 2023. Photo by Todd-White Art Photography; 208 © The Estate of Susan Hiller. All rights reserved, DACS 2023; 210–12, 215 © Meleko Mokgosi. Courtesy of the artist and Jack Shainman Gallery, New York; 213a Attributed to Catharina van Hemessen, Public domain, via Wikimedia Commons; 213b The Baltimore Museum of Art: The George A Lucas Collection, purchased with funds from the State of Maryland, Laurence and Stella Bendann Fund, and contributions from individuals, foundations, and corporations throughout the Baltimore community, BMA 1996.45.80. Photo Mitro Hood.

ACKNOWLEDGEMENTS

I would like to thank my editor, Rachel Silverlight, to whom I am grateful both for the invitation to consider working on this book, and for her perfect combination of critical feedback and encouragement throughout its writing. Thanks also to Ellie Corbett and others at Ilex, in particular Giulia Hetherington and Jennifer Veall for their dedicated work in assembling such a strong set of images. Thank you to the artists, and to those responsible for the oversight of estates, for their generous engagement and for the constructive and helpful comments they have offered on the texts. I have been fortunate to speak over several decades with many students at Ealing, Havering, Wimbledon, Chelsea, Oxford and Goldsmiths, and I thank all of them for their guidance in helping me appreciate that what is there is what needs to be looked at. Lastly, I could only do this with the support of my wife, Petonelle, and our family.

AUTHOR BIOGRAPHY

Michael Archer is an art critic, writer and Professor Emeritus at Goldsmiths, University of London. He holds a BA in History of Art from the University of Cambridge and an MA in Aesthetic Education from Manchester University. Formerly Editor at *Artscribe* and Assistant Editor at *Art Monthly*, his work has appeared in newspapers and journals including *Artforum*, *Art Monthly*, *Frieze*, *Parkett* and the *Guardian* and in numerous monographs and catalogues. He is the author of *Art Since 1960* (Thames & Hudson), and contributed chapters on modern and contemporary art to Hugh Honour and John Fleming's *A World History of Art* (Laurence King).